IMPROVING BANKING SUPERVISION

Also by David G. Mayes

PUBLIC INTEREST AND MARKET PRESSURES (*with W. Hager, A. Knight and W. Streeck*)

MODERN PORTFOLIO THEORY AND FINANCIAL INSTITUTIONS (*with D. C. Corner*)

THE EVOLUTION OF THE SINGLE EUROPEAN MARKET

SOURCES OF PRODUCTIVITY GROWTH

THE SINGLE MARKET PROGRAMME AS A STIMULUS TO CHANGE (*with P. E. Hart*)

INEFFICIENCY IN INDUSTRY (*with C. Harris and M. Lansbury*)

THE EVOLUTION OF RULES FOR A SINGLE EUROPEAN MARKET (*editor*)
   1   Industry and Finance
   2   Rules, Democracy and the Environment
   3   Social and International Issues

FOREIGN DIRECT INVESTMENT AND TRANSITION (*editor with G. Csaki and G. Foti*)

THE EXTERNAL IMPLICATIONS OF EUROPEAN INTEGRATION (*with others*)

ACHIEVING MONETARY UNION (*with A. Britton*)

A NEW STRATEGY FOR SOCIAL AND ECONOMIC COHESION AFTER 1992
   (*with I. Begg*)

THE EUROPEAN CHALLENGE

A STRATEGY FOR THE ECU (*with A. Britton and Ernst & Young*)

SHARPBENDERS (*with P. Grinyer and P. McKierman*)

INTEGRATION AND EUROPEAN INDUSTRY (*with M. Macmillen and P. van Veen*)

THE EXCHANGE RATE ENVIRONMENT (*with S. Brooks and K. Cuthbertson*)

APPLICATIONS OF ECONOMETRICS

THE PROPERTY BOOM

INTRODUCTORY ECONOMIC STATISTICS (*with A. C. Mayes*)

Improving Banking Supervision

David G. Mayes
Liisa Halme
and
Aarno Liuksila

The views expressed in this publication are those of the authors and are not necessarily shared by the Bank of Finland

palgrave

First published 2001 by
PALGRAVE
Houndmills, Basingstoke, Hampshire RG21 6XS and
175 Fifth Avenue, New York, N.Y. 10010
Companies and representatives throughout the world

PALGRAVE is the new global academic imprint of
St. Martin's Press LLC Scholarly and Reference Division and
Palgrave Publishers Ltd (formerly Macmillan Press Ltd).

ISBN 0–333–94896–3

This book is printed on paper suitable for recycling and
made from fully managed and sustained forest sources.

A catalogue record for this book is available
from the British Library.

Library of Congress Cataloging-in-Publication Data

Mayes, David G.
    Improving banking supervision / David G. Mayes, Liisa Halme, and Aarno Liuksila.
        p. cm.
    Includes bibliographical references and index.
    ISBN 0–333–94896–3
        1. Banks and banking–State supervision–Scandinavia. 2. Banking law–
Scandinavia. 3. Banks and banking–State supervision. 4. Banking law. I. Halme,
Liisa. II. Liuksila, Aarno. III. Title.

HG3140.A6 M39 2001
332.1′0948–dc21   2001021891

10   9   8   7   6   5   4   3   2   1
10   09   08   07   06   05   04   03   02   01

Printed and bound in Great Britain by
Antony Rowe Ltd, Chippenham, Wiltshire

Contents

List of Tables

List of Figures

Preface

At the time one always tries to take the best decisions in the light of the expected future and the practicalities of the present circumstances. With the benefit of hindsight it is possible to see that different decisions might have been better and hence one always poses the question 'Could we have done this better even with what we knew at the time?' When mistakes have been made, there is always a post-mortem and a set of changes implemented to try to make sure that history does not repeat itself. The Finnish banking crisis at the beginning of the 1990s was one of the most difficult economic challenges policy-makers have had to face since the postwar recovery. While it was clear at the time that action was needed, most of the parties involved found themselves relatively powerless to act. Where action was possible there was always the fear that it would precipitate the very crisis everybody hoped to avoid and that subsequently those who took it might be blamed for imposing unnecessary costs on society.

It is easy to list what might have happened that would have made the crisis much milder. There was a general expectation that the changes in the former Soviet Union would be quite rapid and would not involve anything like as deep a downturn as has actually been experienced. Although the authorities were convinced that adherence to the exchange rate peg with the ECU was the only viable route to price stability, they had hoped that the exchange rate tensions within the European Monetary System's Exchange Rate Mechanism would be resolved much earlier and with little drama. These and other factors would have meant that fewer of the exposures of the Finnish banking system would have resulted in non-performing loans and the rapid upward valuation of liabilities. However, these ifs and maybes are not the way to look at the problem. It would be equally inappropriate to take no action if one had taken a large risk but been lucky enough to get away with it – if you drive round a corner too fast but don't hit anything, you still don't drive round too fast next time.

Finland had the misfortune to endure the crisis – an experience from which it has not yet fully recovered. The sensible thing to do is to reflect on it and then implement a series of changes that will make the chances of repetition small. Of course, the new precautions must not themselves impose disproportionate costs on society. An efficient and effective financial system helps the economy grow faster and invest in the process of structural change. Such investment inevitably involves risks. Good management of both financial and commercial companies means managing those risks, not failing to take them. The authorities have to try to design a system that is likely to deliver the appropriate balance.

But Finland is not special in these regards. It may have endured a worse crisis than other western industrialised countries, but the ingredients of the problem and its solution are generally applicable. Unfortunately the learning process is slow. Some of the same mistakes have been made again in the run-up to the Asian crises at the end of the 1990s. It is therefore important for the authorities in Finland not just to do their best to learn themselves from the experience and implement measures in response but to help others avoid getting into similar difficulties. This book forms part of that response. The Bank of Finland has already published articles on the crisis and how it was tackled. Outsiders have, of course, done the same, drawing on different parts of the inside experience.

However, the Bank of Finland has a particular responsibility not just because of its role in trying to maintain the stability and efficiency of the financial system but also because one of the responses to the crisis has been to transfer administrative responsibility for the supervision of banks and securities markets from the Ministry of Finance to the Bank of Finland – an operation that is kept separate from the Bank and run by the Financial Supervision Authority. The Bank has therefore been responsible for ensuring the return of the both the banking system as a whole and all the individual banks within it to adequate capitalisation and to implementing a regime whereby good management in the future will make any repetition of the experience of the early 1990s unlikely.

The early stages of this process involved detailed negotiations with the banks and very tight controls. It also involved very large injections of public money, a substantial portion of which has now been repaid. With a return to healthy banks and strong growth in the economy over a number of years expected to continue into the future we are now in a position to step back and consider a more fundamental change to the system. That is the intention of this book.

The book blends law and economics to suggest how a regulatory system that provides a network of incentives for all those involved in financial markets can be put together to try to ensure that banks manage their risks prudently. Many of the ideas employed here have already been adopted in practice – some in the United States, most notably in New Zealand – but Europe on the whole has been slow to adopt them.

There are three key messages. First of all, banks must have good corporate governance structures, proper capitalisation and be run by people of repute if they are to stand a proper chance of success. Secondly, the banks need to disclose, in public and using clear and comparable information, enough detail on their financial state and risk management practices that market participants as well as the regulators can hold an informed view of their state and prospects. Lastly we need to have a credible means of persuading banks that next time we will act early and ensure bank resolutions without public money if they become undercapitalised. Banks must come to expect that they will not be allowed to continue trading unchanged if they fail to meet the minimum levels for prudent operation.

People are always surprised that regulators would prefer not to have the opportunity to exercise discretion in favour of individual banks. If the opportunity for discretion exists everyone will tend to act in the expectation that it will be exercised in their favour. This will tend to result in people running just the sort of risks we want to avoid. In New Zealand intervention by the authorities is not only compulsory but progressive as banks become undercapitalised. If the banks involved do not act voluntarily the authorities will compel them, ultimately taking them into statutory management and out of the hands of the existing shareholders. In the United States intervention becomes mandatory if capital falls too far and the bank is then closed. The proposals in the book do not seek to attain a hypothetical world outside previous experience but to implement the best of current practice. They are deliberately a practical proposition.

All of the changes advocated will involve quite substantial alterations in behaviour and indeed legislation, but these will be swimming with the tide of the modern age of transparency, and encouragement of the process of change. We can never be in a position where we can provide legislation that will cover every detailed development that can happen to financial markets in advance. However, moving towards widespread public disclosure does not mean that we will cease to pay attention to banks either individually or as a group. On the contrary, disclosure means that the process of supervision is widened. All the stakeholders in banks need to take a view and not just the regulator. Furthermore, the regulator can turn its focus more towards problems that affect the financial system as a whole and concentrate on the increasing problems of cross-border supervision. International co-ordination among authorities is becoming increasingly important as our main banks themselves become more international. The ECB Banking Supervisory Committee is focusing on what it describes as 'macro-prudential' supervision while the European supervisors continue to develop their bilateral exchanges of information. It is likely that there will be increased pressure for wider international institutional changes as well.

However, it is no good getting the microstructures right if macro-policy creates instability. Here Finland has done a lot to get away from the shocks that can destabilise a small country. Finland joined EMU in the first wave so that it now has the stability of the euro area as a whole. This entails not just a single monetary policy but prudent constraints on fiscal management as well. It is not that prudence would not have been possible in the previous independent regime but, rather, that having the peer pressure of ten fellow members and the Commission (not to mention the ECB) makes good performance seem much more likely to financial markets, price setters and hopefully to wage bargainers. Credibility may seem an overused word but it is the credibility of macroeconomic policy and financial supervision in international eyes that matters. It is no good simply believing in ourselves – others have to believe us. That belief depends upon the regulatory framework, the institutional set up and the visible incentives for all those concerned to make it work.

Emerging markets may find it will take some time to adopt these principles but the less the reputation of current systems the greater the benefits from making credible improvements. The international organisations are joining the chorus for prudent behaviour in both macroeconomic policy and financial sector management. It is to be hoped that this book offers food for thought on how to speed up achieving those goals. The 1990s have been a decade of hard lessons. Learning them will provide a benefit in the decades to come. Finland does not want to experience the costs of the financial crisis again and naturally would want others to avoid them as well.

Helsinki   DAVID G. MAYES

Acknowledgements

We are grateful to current and former colleagues in the Bank of Finland and the Finnish Financial Supervisory Authority who have written material on financial supervision over the last ten years that we have been able to draw on in writing this book. Although, where possible, their contribution has been cited in the text, more informal influence will have been ignored. We thank in particular, Heikki Koskenkylä, for his contributions to Chapters 2 and 3, Jukka Vesala for his contributions to Chapters 3, 4 and 10, and Juha Tarkka, who suggested we write the book and provided insights into the handling of the Finnish crisis. Other colleagues have provided comments, particularly on Chapter 2. Mikko Niskanen and Markku Malkamäki were especially helpful. The Board of the Bank of Finland have been very supportive – Matti Louekoski in formally releasing all the material we use and Esko Ollila, Deputy Governor, in encouraging our work. However, we must make it clear that the views we express are our own.

The book draws heavily on the experience in New Zealand and Geoff Mortlock, Denys Bruce, Peter Ledingham and Bruce White of the Reserve Bank of New Zealand were helpful, both in articulating many of the original ideas and in correcting misperceptions. Senior executives in New Zealand banks willingly participated in interviews and provided helpful material for us to understand the impact of the system. Deutsche Bank, formerly through Bankers Trust, have continued to provide us with disclosure material some of which is reproduced in Chapter 7 – our use of their material rather than that from other registered banks does not imply any favourable or unfavourable judgement on status and performance of any bank.

We have benefited from the comments of others in a range of seminars given on parts of the book in Finland, Sweden, the United Kingdom, Estonia, New Zealand and Germany among others over the three years the work has been in the making. The Bank of England provided specific help for Liisa Halme through the Centre for Central Banking Studies and the UK Financial Services Authority for David Mayes. Jeremy Richardson was particularly helpful in his detailed scrutiny of part of the material we draw on. We thank Bill Allen, Richard Brealey, Charles Goodhart, Juliette Healey and David Swanney for their comments on Chapters 4 and 5. Kevin Dowd offered some constructive referee's comments as did David Llewellyn and Karel Lannoo. We hope they are not too disappointed by the result. Some of the work was undertaken while David Mayes was at South Bank University and has been an important contribution to the founding of its new Centre for Monetary and Financial Economics.

D. G. M.
L. H.
A. L.

Acknowledgements

1 Introduction

In many countries bank failures are largely unheard of and the idea of a threat to the financial system seems remote. Even in the United Kingdom, where names like Barings and BCCI spring readily to mind, there is no expectation of any serious threat to the main banks. While most retail deposits are insured, depositors do not rely on the insurance in order to feel their deposits are safe. Although banking inherently involves taking risks, those risks have been thought relatively minor, especially across large institutions. In other countries, such as the United States, bank failures are more common and depositors do have an eye to insurance, especially since the Savings and Loan difficulties in the 1980s. Even large problems with individual banks can appear manageable,[1] as with Credit Lyonnais, for example. Banking crises are associated with the developing world. In this environment it is easy for complacency to set in. Both supervisors and the supervised can convince themselves that existing safeguards are adequate, rather than accepting that they have been lucky not to face more exacting shocks.

The major banking crises in the Nordic countries (Denmark, Finland, Iceland, Norway and Sweden) in the last decade therefore came as a rude awakening. The international community was already aware of the weakness in the regulation of banking and the increasing risks that were arising from deregulation and globalisation (Hunn *et al.*, 1989, for example). The development of the Basel Accord on Capital Adequacy in the years up to its adoption in 1988 was perhaps the most obvious response.[2] However, the rate of introduction was measured, partly because adaptation needs to be reasonably slow if it does not have a harsh effect on banks' business and actually cause difficulties itself. But the measured pace was also partly because the risk was not seen as immediate.

The sheer size of the crises in the Nordic countries is daunting. The direct costs to the taxpayer of the bailout of the banks was 3–4 per cent of GDP in Norway (1987–89), 4–6 per cent in Sweden (1990–93) and 8 per cent in Finland (1991–93). However, this does not take into account the consequential decline in economic activity. Swedish GDP fell by 5 per cent between 1990 and 1993 and Finnish GDP by a massive 12 per cent (14 per cent between peak and trough quarters).[3] Only part of these declines can be attributed to the banking crisis. The collapse of the Exchange Rate Mechanism of the European Monetary System in 1992/3 and, particularly for Finland, the fall of the former Soviet Union also had a direct impact. However, these declines need to be compared not with a static level of GDP but with the growth that would otherwise have taken place over these years (after subtracting any previous growth on the back of the excessively risky lending). Nevertheless it seems reasonable to attribute a cost of over

10 per cent of GDP to the Finnish banking crisis. This is larger than the impact of any other single concentrated shock over the last fifty years.[4] While GDP has now returned to its previous trend as a result of very rapid growth in the second half of the 1990s, the scars of the crisis still remain, with unemployment around 10 per cent and unlikely to fall back to pre-crisis levels for some time yet.

The reaction to the crises has been substantial with a strong determination to avoid any repetition and to create prudent and well-capitalised yet efficient banks. This has involved both institutional change and substantial banking regulation. These changes apply not just to the Nordic countries but to the world as a whole. For example, in 1998 the United Kingdom created a new embracing financial services regulator (the Financial Services Authority) and, after a thorough review by the Wallis Commission, Australia also transformed its regulatory structure.

International agreement on minimum standards for financial regulation has also continued to develop. Indeed while this book was in preparation the Basel Committee on Banking Supervision has produced a new consultative document proposing an updating of current standards. This suggests that in future capital adequacy for banks should be based on three 'pillars': 'minimum capital requirements, which seek to develop and expand on the standardised rules set forth in the 1988 Accord; supervisory review of an institution's capital adequacy and internal assessment process; and effective use of market discipline as a lever to strengthen disclosure and encourage safe and sound banking practices'. While it is difficult to disagree with these principles as they have widespread acceptance, the main theme of this book is that more can be done. We focus on the third of these pillars and argue that considerably more can be obtained from market discipline in encouraging prudent behaviour by banks without imposing exacting burdens on them.

Although there are still some areas relating to international agreements and rules to be completed, the overall generalised picture of what can be expected in the area of financial supervision is now fairly clear. However, there are some gaps. The European Union, for example, has not completed the full range of measures for the operation of the single European financial market and some problems of jurisdiction under the operation of the principle of 'home country control' remain to be sorted out. We address the question of these gaps throughout the book but particularly deal with home country control in Chapters 4 and 10.

More recently, the European banking crises of the early 1990s have become supplanted in people's minds by the Asian crises of 1997 and the subsequent crises in Russia, Brazil and elsewhere in 1998. To some extent this has altered the focus both to the global level, with worries about the contagion of financial problems from weak to stronger countries, and to problems outside the OECD. There is a danger therefore of reducing attention on the problems at home before the lessons of recent years have been fully learnt and the consequent changes in the framework of financial regulation implemented.

However, these wider crises and the nature of the international response also offer suitable cautions. As part of their reaction, international organisations, including the IMF and the OECD, have been stressing that although sound macroeconomic management may be a key to avoiding such crises in the future, along with a substantial range of structural reforms to create transparent and undistorted economies, a strong banking system is also an essential ingredient.[5] These proposals share a number of common elements. The first is that it ought to be easier to identify emerging problems. In part this is a request for the quality of information from both lenders and borrowers to be improved. It is particularly a request for transparency (see IMF, 1999) for example. Transparency means not just that data are available but that they should be of such a form and content that they allow one to get a good idea of what is actually going on. Additionally, there is a role for the authorities in ensuring that these data are put together in a coherent manner so as to provide indications of emerging risks.

National and international authorities have an important role to play in trying to prevent crises emerging in the first place, rather than in just trying to limit the damage and allocate the losses in a fair manner after the event. Not only is it impossible to prevent all crises but crisis prevention comes at a cost. Restrictions on lending and the taking of risks can slow the growth of the economy and blunt the incentives to faster progress. The authorities therefore have to strike a balance between the costs of holding back the financial system and the costs of crises. While this is acknowledged in the current debate, there is little agreement on how one should decide exactly where the dividing line can be drawn. Furthermore, the sheer existence of mechanisms to handle crises effectively may make their occurrence more likely – the well-known problem of moral hazard.

Information on emerging risks is only part of the picture – much of the remainder is the encouragement of prudent behaviour. The emphasis here is on the encouragement of proper practice as it is difficult to penalise imprudent behaviour because those that have actually encountered the excess risks will already have accumulated losses. Furthermore, those who are facing likely difficulty will need all the resources they can find to avoid converting risk into failure.[6] As the proposed new Basel Accord illustrates, there are two facets to this form of encouragement. The first is to insist that banks have enough capital to cover most of their normal risks – including those that are off the balance sheet or more readily hidden. The second is to ensure that the procedures for assessing and monitoring risks are adequate.

However, there is only so much that these approaches can hope to achieve. The information and prudential constraints then provide an input to the next step in the argument, namely that both borrowers and lenders have responsibilities.

Financial markets themselves should be pricing risk appropriately and the private sector needs to take a share in 'resolving its own mistakes' or in 'coping with wide fluctuations' depending upon how you view the issue.

The last lesson of recent years comes from Japan. Here we have seen a rapidly growing economy turned into a stagnant one in the 1990s. Even now, despite virtually zero interest rates and unsustainably expansionary fiscal policy, it has not proved possible to turn the economy round. As we discuss in the next chapter on the Nordic crises, the Japanese experience has a number of common features with other crises, including the pursuance of unsustainable policies (Cowling and Tomlinson, 2000) and the pricking of an asset prices bubble (Edison *et al.*, 2000). However, it also contains lessons about the behaviour of banks. Opaque structures and reporting conventions have made it difficult to establish the extent of losses or exactly where the liability for them is to fall. In part, therefore, the failure of the Japanese economy to recover is because there has been widespread insurance against these risks in the form of increased saving. However, the balance of this book is about the avoidance of financial crises in the first place rather than their resolution.

1.1   A NEW DIRECTION

The changes in banking regulations over the last 15 years and many of those still in train represent an attempt to define minimum prudential standards for the operation of banks. In many countries the measures introduced go well beyond this and banks have to produce a wealth of detailed statistics for financial supervisors. This trend towards more intrusive regulation may reduce the risk of bank distress, but it also imposes some costs. Firstly, there is the cost of compliance in providing the extra information. There is a cost in meeting conditions designed to apply to all businesses, which may not be appropriate to a particular instance. Thus banks may be less profitable and more inefficient than they need be for a given level of risk. The flexibility of banks is thus reduced, to some extent reversing some of the gains that were intended by the process of financial deregulation during the 1980s.

In any case intrusive regulation is in danger of implying that regulators may be more effective at running banks than those employed to do so in the banks themselves. Not only must this be a fallacy, since regulators will always have less information than the respective bank managements, but it opens up the danger that the regulator may be thought to be responsible for the continued wellbeing of each individual bank. This is clearly not possible as risk can only be managed, not removed, if banks are to perform a useful role in society. It also suggests that there is an implicit guarantee of health offered by the regulator to a compliant bank. This in turn implies the expectation that there is an obligation to bail out banks that get into difficulty. This raises its own irony. If the management of banks think that they are subject to guarantee in the event that the bank gets into difficulty they will be inclined to take greater risks – an archetypal case of 'moral hazard'.

This therefore raises the question of whether there are other means of getting the improved prudential operation of banks generally thought desirable in the light of the costly crises of the early part of the 1990s, but without excess costs of supervision. In the pages to come we develop a set of suggestions that explore the ways in which incentives can be developed for banks to run themselves more prudentially. These incentives come not so much from the rules, penalties and advice of the supervisors but from the pressures of all the other groups involved in financial markets as well: owners, shareholders, depositors, borrowers, creditors, competitors, analysts, journalists and rating agencies.

This more market-based approach is just one of the three pillars proposed by the Basel Committee. In the draft proposals issued in 1999 this was by far the shortest pillar. The bulk of the document was devoted to development of the measures of capital adequacy. We hope to encourage the development of a pillar of more equal stature.

1.2 GETTING IT WRONG NEXT TIME

Unfortunately, it is not readily possible to know how successful any policy of financial supervision is in heading off crises. We know when it fails but we cannot know what crises were successfully avoided. The best we can do is to point to combinations of circumstances that, although potentially dangerous, did not result in substantial problems. We do this in part in the next chapter by contrasting the case of Denmark, which got through the last two decades without a financial crisis, with that of its Nordic neighbours, who were not so fortunate. In this process, the relative strength of the Danish banks was an important contributory factor but by no means the only one.

One can look at the problem of financial supervision from the 'half-empty' and 'half-full' points of view. Here we have stressed that efficient but effective supervision cannot hope to insulate the economy from all financial shocks. The issue is to take supervisory methods to their efficient limits by using the range of methods available without imposing any undue burden. It is equally possible to point out that the vast majority of banks, far from failing over the last few decades, have been highly profitable. Not only that but in most years most members of the OECD have been mercifully free of not just banking crises but of significant problems with individual institutions.

We all try to learn from our mistakes. Supervisors and market participants alike have put in place safeguards against the repetition of earlier problems. Hence we expect that the next financial crisis will have rather different causes from the last. The key ingredients seem to be an incipient problem that is either not detected or not appreciated by the current surveillance methods and a severe shock that causes a big change in asset prices (as suggested in Feldstein (1991) regrettably too close to the unravelling of the Nordic crises at the beginning of the decade for preventative action to be taken). What is surprising is how easy it is to point to the problem with the benefit of hindsight. Figure 1.1, drawn from Bäckström (1997), must surely have rung strong warning bells in Sweden in the late 1980s. It must have been very difficult to point to events that could justify such a large increase in asset prices. Similarly, it must have been very difficult to believe that such an increase in lending could take place without a substantial deterioration in quality.

Bäckström (1997) points to a combination of an unsustainable macroeconomic policy and an unwillingness to act by the Swedish Supervisory Authority as being the principal reasons why such a financial bubble could emerge. This combination meant that a sharp cycle became increasing likely while at the same time the ability of banks to withstand it was reduced. Undoubtedly financial deregulation led to a change in the environment, which was difficult to assimilate.

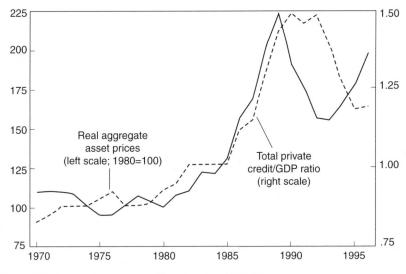

Figure 1.1   Asset prices* and credit in Sweden, 1970–97

Note: *Weighted average of equity and residential and commercial real estate price indices deflated by CPI. The weights are based on the composition of private sector wealth.

Source: BIS, Bäckström (1997).

Deregulation offers new market opportunities to some financial institutions and serious threats to the established and previously protected position of others. When such new opportunities arise, most institutions will rush to take advantage of them (Hunn *et al.*, 1989). The moral hazard is obvious. If you do not take up the opportunity then you are likely to lose market share, probably for a long period. If the gains turn out to be small then your competitors will be in the same position and not much will be lost. (And in the extreme, if it is a disaster you expect that the financial system will be bailed out.) The Savings and Loan crisis in the United States had similar characteristics.

A similar moral hazard applies to those under threat. If they act quickly and forcefully they may be able to salvage at least some of their position. At the same time that they have to compete aggressively for business, in a way they are not used to, they will have to implement major efficiency drives, thereby placing the institution under stress from two directions. The worst that can happen to them is that their new risky strategy fails but failure, in the sense of takeover or substantial decline, would have been the outcome from doing nothing as the protection from their previously regulated position disappeared.

We can easily recreate that sort of scenario for the future. The creation of the euro area is a major step into the unknown. It could lead to a substantial internationalisation of banking (as we outline in Chapter 3). This in itself could lead to three problems: (i) the banking system could become more leveraged because assets can be used more efficiently internationally; (ii) increased competition could push banks into being more aggressive (taking greater risks); (iii) and finally supervisors may be less alert to the problem because it is revealed by the operations of banks outside the borders of the supervisor's country. This would provide the weakening of the banking system.

The macroeconomic misperception could occur because the euro area does well. Starting from a relatively depressed economy and a high level of unemployment it is only to be expected that above-average growth will occur for a number of years. At some stage people will argue that there has been a permanent increase in growth prospects in Europe, just as they did with the Thatcher regime in the United Kingdom in the mid-1980s (Thatcher, 1995) and New Zealand after the reforms of the second half of the 1980s (Prebble, 1994). In developments similar to those experienced in the United States of the late 1990s the existence of the European Central Bank and the change in regime may lead to a perceived ability to hold inflation lower compared to previous pressures.

In these circumstances asset prices will rise. Any such rise tends to overshoot (Dornbusch, 1976; Feldstein, 1991). All we require is that people believe that future prospects are substantially improved. This is quite likely given the degree of international pessimism that has surrounded the first months of the euro area's existence. A decline in the favour that surrounds the United States at the time of writing would also help to swing the pattern of investment. We have to anticipate the trigger, which suggests that this new view is mistaken and causes a rapid downward realignment after the period of substantial improvement and optimism. There are many possibilities – a political difficulty that suggests that fiscal rectitude will not be pursued because the Stability and Growth Pact is too onerous, for example. A serious setback to the European Union's expansion prospects could be another source of sharp reversal.

There is no reason why we should look to Europe for the crisis. We could easily set out a problem for the United States, based on the concerns expressed by the Federal Reserve over the last few years. Their worry has been that the take-off in stock market prices may be based on an optimistic view of the potential for the 'new economy' that appears to be emerging. If expectations are rapidly revised downwards, because some of the high-flying companies get into difficulty or real constraints in the US economy suggest that the decline in inflation compared with unemployment is only temporary, then it would be possible to envisage a credit crunch, if borrowing turns out to be too highly geared. The fact that the Fed is so alert to the problem may reduce its likelihood but ...

1.3   STRUCTURE OF THE BOOK

In the chapters that follow we begin by exploring the Nordic banking crises of a decade ago as a pointer to the origin of financial crises and their development (Chapter 2). We use these experiences to suggest where financial supervision has been inadequate and what pitfalls we have to watch out for in future occasions. This is followed, in Chapter 3, by a brief assessment of the challenges that lie ahead for supervisors in a world of increasing globalisation, size and complexity of banks and other financial institutions, rapid technical change, particularly IT, and rapid innovation. We are especially concerned in these circumstances that current national-based supervision regimes – in the EEA in particular – will find themselves both underinformed and underpowered to head off incipient crises.

Having set out the context from backward and forward-looking points of view we go on in Chapter 4 to explain what we consider to be the principal ingredients of a good regime for financial supervision. We explore what supervision is for, what it covers and how it can be implemented. Particular attention is paid to the incentives for prudent behaviour. We conclude that such a regime has three main ingredients:

- careful control of the right of establishment as a bank;
- a system of supervision substantially complemented by market discipline stemming from public disclosure;
- an efficient system for handling banking problems and crisis management.

We elaborate this in the context of international co-ordination in the EEA.

The next six chapters form the heart of the book. The first of these (Chapter 5) sets out how it would be possible to ensure a framework for corporate governance in banks that encourages incentives to operate prudently on directors, shareholders and the other stakeholders in financial institutions (including supervisors and government). We are particularly concerned to establish responsibility. Chapter 6 goes on to explain how more market discipline can provide the incentives for more prudent management, given that the corporate governance structure allows them to operate. We suggest that these incentives not only encourage the stakeholders to focus where they can have most effect but that this regime also lowers the costs of supervision to all parties, including the taxpayer.

The key ingredient for effective market discipline is public disclosure by banks of their structures, accounts and balance sheets, risk exposures and strategies for managing risks. This is the subject of Chapter 7. This information, released quarterly, to international financial reporting standards, does no more than present in public the sorts of information that managers have to provide to their boards and to supervisors to convince them that the bank is being well run. However, while supervisors may set minimum standards they do not need to prescribe what is appropriate for each individual bank. It is for the banks themselves to convince the markets, particularly analysts, counterparties and the rating agencies that their provisions and procedures are adequate.

These ideas are not fanciful because they have already been implemented in a number of countries. The most comprehensive adoption is in New Zealand, so we make substantial reference to the experience there since 1996, when the regime was introduced. We show how disclosure documents work in practice and how directors can be made liable for their content. However, New Zealand is in many respects unusual, having foreign-owned banks and no deposit guarantee scheme. We therefore consider in some detail how this regime can be transposed elsewhere and set out the necessary conditions, which we consider to be feasible for a wide range of countries, should they choose to adopt this approach. We explore, in particular, cases where the operation of the market may be rather weak, either because banks are not publicly quoted or do not have much in the way of subordinated debt that is actively traded.

However, one essential element in encouraging prudent behaviour is the system that is expected to operate should something go wrong. Chapters 8, 9 and 10 are devoted to this issue. Our principal concern here is with the issue of how to ensure orderly exit by banks that are in difficulty or that have failed. The typical experience in many countries in the past has been that problem banks are bailed out. This encourages moral hazard – the taking of greater risks because the downside is limited – particularly where there is also deposit insurance. In practice both the need to act quickly and legal restraints serve to make bailing out both likely and expected. We therefore explain (in Chapter 8) how a system can be set up that not only tends to reduce the costs of banking crises by making the penalties for worsening capital adequacy progressive but discourages banks from getting into such a position in the first place. Ideally market solutions can be found for recapitalisation either from existing shareholders or new owners. In those cases the role of the authorities is limited to orchestration and authorisation. If this fails the authorities will have step in. After explaining the difficulties with the existing legal systems in the United States and Europe we go on (in Chapter 9) to explore how the legal framework can be changed to allow intervention by the authorities when banks become insufficiently capitalised. Our proposal not only allows the authorities to act swiftly but enables them to have a choice on predetermined criteria of the feasible route that will minimise the potential costs to society as a whole.

Chapter 10 concludes this discussion by considering the problems of cross-border banking and multinational financial groupings. We consider how the authorities should react and who among them should take the lead in the current European environment. We make recommendations for improving the flow of information among the authorities and for resolving conflicts of interest among the different countries involved. Given our proposals for improved powers of action for the authorities in crises we do not come out in favour of major institution-building.

The final chapter considers implementation and draws our conclusions.

2 The Financial Crisis of the Early 1990s and its Lessons

The accepted analysis of the Nordic banking crises concludes that they were primarily generated by a poorly managed process of financial liberalisation and pushed over the top by a strong economic cycle, only some of whose profile was outside the control of the domestic authorities (for example, see Drees and Pazarbasioglu (1998)). Thus the implication is that the crises were largely avoidable. One of the ways to consider the problem is to examine other countries, such as the United Kingdom, which also had an asset price boom in the 1990s but did not have the financial crisis, and look for the features that distinguished the Nordic experience.

All crises are different and indeed the Nordic crises differ from each other. However, the Nordic crises are in some sense typical and therefore worthy of study as lesson for others. For example, of the range of 16 crisis indicators considered by Kaminsky and Reinhart (1999) in their study of 26 banking crises in the last two decades, Denmark showed 71 per cent of the available indicators, Finland 81 per cent, Norway 87 per cent and Sweden 93 per cent. Honkapohja and Koskela (1999) describe Finland's case as a 'classical financial crisis'. The Finnish crisis is also memorable simply because of its size. It is the biggest setback to GDP experienced by any of the members during the life of the OECD[1] and by several measures it was more acute than the Great Depression of the 1930s (Honkapohja and Koskela, 1999), which was relatively mild in Finland by comparison with most industrialised countries. In their comparison of the two recessions, Kiander and Vartia (1996) show a long list of similarities in both causes and path of development. However, size of the recession and the extent of suffering it causes should not be equated (Kiander and Vartia, 1996). In the Great Depression there was little insurance for those losing their jobs, while in the 1990s the system of support in the Nordic countries was among the most comprehensive available.

2.1 SEVEN COMMON FEATURES IN THE NORDIC CRISES

In discussing the Nordic crises we have put their experience into a framework that can be generalised to other countries. Some of the seven factors we list in Table 2.1 and develop in the rest of this section are specific to the Nordic circumstances but events of a similar nature have characterised other crises (Kaminsky

Table 2.1 Characteristics of the Nordic financial crises

1. A major regulatory change that opens both buyers and sellers to new opportunities and risks of which theyhave little experience.
2. A period of rapid economic growth.
3. A rapid rise in asset prices.
4. A weak framework for supervision.
5. A tax regime that encourages borrowing.
6. Unsustainable macroeconomic policies.
7. A substantial adverse shock.
(8. Relatively undiversified economies).

and Reinhart, 1999; Lindgren *et al.*, 2000; Mishkin, 2000). Since we are discussing a collapse the generalised picture is obviously going to be one of a cycle with financial exposure increasing too rapidly, the bubble being pricked and then a disorderly decline before sustainable growth can be restored. While cycles seem to be an inevitable feature of economies, disorderly ones, particularly on the scale we describe are avoidable. Even a shock of the size of the collapse of the former Soviet Union on Finland could have been weathered much more successfully had the country not already been well on the way to financial disaster.

We therefore structure the discussion in terms of three phases:

- Is it possible to avoid generating some of the shocks that drive the financial economy into unsustainably risky expansion?
- Is it possible to avoid structuring the financial and macroeconomic system so that imprudent responses to the shock develop?
- Is it possible to avoid the perpetuation of the errors to the point that they become extreme?

We do not consider the question of whether it is possible to get an orderly exit from an unsustainable position. In part this is because this is by definition impossible, as we would not have a crisis if an orderly exit were possible. However, the main reason is simply because crisis avoidance rather than resolution is the point of this book.

The Nordic banking crises emerged in the late 1980s and reached their most serious proportions in 1992, although it was not until the mid-1990s that the situation was clearly resolved and firm growth resumed (see Figures 2.2 to 2.10). The timing was not identical in the four countries (Iceland is excluded from this discussion), with Denmark encountering the problems rather earlier than the others, followed by Norway and Finland having the last, and worst, crisis largely in phase with Sweden. We can look for the causes earlier in the 1980s and require about a ten-year period to build up the full picture. Although Denmark is sufficiently different that we might argue that it should be treated differently, the fact that the difficulties were more drawn out, starting at the beginning of the 1980s, but that even at their peak in 1992 they did not threaten the financial system so seriously acts as an informative pointer to the others. Earlier action by the authorities, less compounding factors and a measure of better luck enabled them to survive at rather lower cost, even though the extent of the bank losses over the decade from 1982 were the largest in proportionate terms of all the four countries.

In the light of this it is surprising, with the benefit of hindsight, that the Danish experience did not worry their neighbours. If that were not enough, the Norwegian crisis ran one or two years ahead of Sweden and Finland. Clearly, on the one hand people try to rationalise their own difficulties as being somewhat different and resolvable, while on the other the pressures of the problem themselves lead people to avoid implementing the unpleasant solutions in the hope that the need will not actually arise. In what follows we seek to show how that rationalisation took place and how the policy mix was effective in postponing change.

While it is simplistic to point to any single cause it is generally accepted[2] that the Nordic crises had a common trigger in the deregulation of the financial sector that characterised the 1970s, 1980s and 1990s in the OECD countries.[3] Clearly this does not constitute a necessary cause as most countries avoided such crises and none experienced problems on the scale of the Nordic experience. However, it is our starting point for the process.

2.1.1   A Major Regulatory Change that Opens both Buyers and Sellers to New Opportunities and Risks in which they have Limited Experience

It is not necessary for the origin of a financial crisis itself to be a financial stimulus, although this helps. If the stimulus lies elsewhere then the first question will be why the financial sector over-responded. This question has been extensively analysed in the literature, particularly in the case of exchange rates, with the Dornbusch (1976) overshooting model. What is required is something that moves expectations of future gains substantially so that financial markets are prepared to advance funds much more liberally than before and to raise and secure them in ways they would not previously have thought prudent. If the change in expectations is proved right and there is no counter-shock before they are realised, then no crisis is likely. It is the counter-shock or the sudden realisation that the expected gains may be ephemeral that brings the whole edifice down.

However, in the case of the Nordic crises of the 1980s/90s the origin was more straightforwardly financial in its own right, namely financial liberalisation. In Figure 2.1 we have illustrated the pattern of relaxation of controls in the case

14

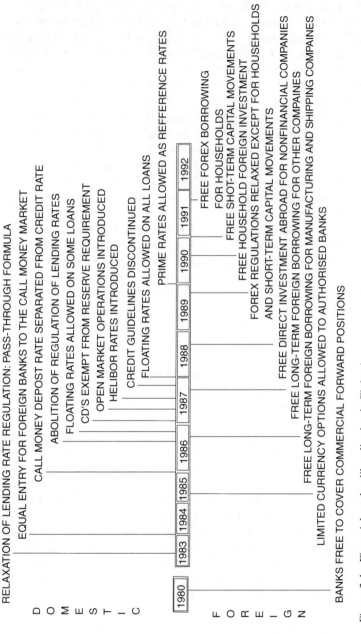

Figure 2.1 Financial market liberalisation in Finland

Source: Nyberg and Vihriälä (1994).

of Finland. Although the measures are not equal in importance, the main period for the removal of domestic restrictions was between the second half of 1986 and the end of 1987. Foreign exchange restrictions were eased rather more slowly but foreign borrowing was also permitted for the company sector during this same period.

When financial markets are liberalised there is considerable pent-up demand from borrowers, whose credit has been previously rationed. At the same time financial institutions gain more ready access to funds and are able to move into new markets. They therefore both have the perceived opportunity for growth in size and profits and the means of seeking it. This sets the scene for a lending boom. In the previous regime banks are normally protected from the full pressure of competition both through restriction on entry and controlled prices (interest rates and margins).[4] This means that they will tend to lack experience in risk management and in marginal lending and will not have the information systems to cope with such developments. Such a combination is a recipe for trouble. Entering new markets involves investment in both physical and human capital before the hoped for returns appear, hence further weakening the structure of the capital base of the banks in the short run.

What the Nordic countries faced, therefore, was a substantial structural adjustment in their financial markets. The consequences of this depended upon whether this could be a smooth shift to a new more liberalised state. Obviously the answer will be affected by the extent and speed of the changes. As is described in the sections on the individual countries, the changes were not identical and were neither the largest nor the fastest in the OECD. The consequences must therefore depend on other factors, such as the pre-existing strength of the banks, the reaction of the supervision authorities and the state of the general economic cycle. We deal with these in turn.

Nevertheless, it is clear that, in the absence of any other actions, financial deregulation will tend to have an expansionary effect on the economy. As with other supply-side shocks to the economy, the normal response by the authorities would be to accommodate the initial impact, even if any subsequent feedback effects would be neutralised if they upset the general balance in the economy. It will depend upon the nature of the operation of the new financial system as to whether deregulation is a step gain or a continuing gain that is reflected in a sustainably more rapid rate of growth. In the short run, therefore, the improvement in expectations will appear to have been fulfilled and hence to some extent may be self-sustaining.

In the Nordic case it is not clear how much discretion they had over the timing and extent of financial deregulation, although it could have occurred earlier had the authorities wished to take a lead in this trend. As it was, to quite a large extent the timing of the deregulation was driven by competition among the OECD countries, particularly in the EEA. As this is a government-inspired change it could in principle have been timed to help the economy recover from a period of difficulty, if that were predictable sufficiently far in advance. In practice the phase of impact on the economic cycle was much more unplanned and, as we note later, this contributed to the differences in impact across the four countries.

These observations about financial liberalisation are general and apply to countries outside the Nordic area (Cottarelli *et al.*, 1995; Davis, 1995; Hunn *et al.*, 1989). What is rather more surprising is that the Nordic countries were not the first to liberalise and the dangers were already known in the mid-1980s. New Zealand, for example, liberalised around the same period, 1984–87, and there the Treasury (finance ministry) not only offered cautions but commissioned three academic studies (of which Hunn *et al.* (1989) was one) to draw attention to the experience in other countries. Cautionary tales may not be enough to sway markets and New Zealand was 'lucky' to have its surge in lending cut back summarily by the October 1987 stock market crash before reaching Nordic proportions.

As we noted in Chapter 1, although countries that have not yet liberalised will face the same potential problems as their predecessors, financial liberalisation is not the only source of financial crises. Even so the countries that faced problems from deregulation in the 1980s and 1990s can face further problems in the future, as financial changes from new sources of competition and the breaking down of barriers between markets, particularly within Europe, open up a scramble to expand or protect market share. In other words there will be a continuing potential for financial markets themselves to generate conditions that could lead to financial crises.

Such circumstances are always difficult for financial institutions because they are faced by the typical dilemma of do they fail to follow the market trend and hence run the risk of being left behind or do they follow and run the risk of financial disaster. It requires very considerable strength of mind to follow the first strategy, as there will be a period when the bank appears to be underperforming in comparison with its competitors. In that period it will become vulnerable both to takeover by more aggressive institutions and to enforced management change by the shareholders who see their value rising relatively slowly.

To some extent, therefore, the problem is that actions which make sense to each individual bank in isolation add up a serious threat to the system when taken together because all have exposed themselves not just to similar risks simultaneously but to a risk that is likely to realise. In a competitive market it is impossible for all companies to succeed in gaining market share and increased profit. Some are bound to be losers. If these losses spread directly from the weaker to the stronger institutions they can cascade through the system – more rapidly if there is contagion, in the sense that people come to believe that the stronger may also have problems. In some circumstances this can reflect the sorts of traditional debt deflation (King, 1994) that we discuss below.

2.1.2 A Period of Rapid Economic Growth

A financial bubble, caused by regulatory or other changes, independent of changes in the real economy is, of course, possible, but a change in the real environment helps change expectations. If an economy expands rapidly and initially without obvious difficulty there is a natural tendency for people to think that this change can be sustained and that perhaps to some extent it represents a change in trend rather than just the upturn in another business cycle. By the very nature of such a discussion there is little empirical basis on which a decision can be made. As output rises above trend or faster than trend, the longer it lasts, particularly compared to previous cycles, the greater the believability of the argument that there has been a fundamental change in how the economy works. This is exacerbated if, as in the case of the United Kingdom in the mid-1980s or New Zealand in the mid-1990s, there has been a major regime change to which one can point as a possible cause. Governments responsible for the regime change will be particularly keen to find evidence that the pattern has changed for the better (Thatcher, 1995, p. 500, for example). They may even go rather further and deliberately try to create the atmosphere of optimism and enthusiasm (Lawson, 1992, p. 639). (This is, of course, a symmetric problem. Orphanides (2000) documents how in the 1970s the Federal Reserve was slow to recognise that the underlying rate of sustainable growth in the economy had fallen. As a result an over-expansionary policy was run for several years, making a substantial contribution to the inflation that lasted more than a decade before the Volcker and Greenspan contractions had their full effect.)

The degree of rationalisation in these circumstances can be very considerable. As growth in New Zealand took off in 1994–95, it was argued that the decade-long reform process provided the means of faster growth and that the large gap between GDP per capita in New Zealand and that in the better-off parts of the OECD demonstrated the scope for such an improvement.[5] Quah (1997), inter alia, argues that there are growth (or convergence) 'clubs' to which countries may belong. A divergent member can expect to converge towards the mean of that club if it removes the reasons for divergence. Indeed by changing its characteristics a country can change the club to which it belongs.

There is less justification for this 'catch-up' interpretation in the case of Finland, as to some extent the cause of the extra growth was explicable in terms of the fall in energy prices and a rise in the price of forest products (Honkapohja and Koskela, 1999). In either event, while one might not expect an offsetting fall in GDP at a later date, there seems little reason to expect that these would permit a sustained increase in the growth *rate* once the initial impact had passed. The fall in unemployment to historically low levels and the pick up in inflation (Figure 2.2) should have acted as a clear warning that growth was not merely unsustainable but 'too fast'.

In the case of Finland and Sweden the stimulus from deregulation coincided with a recovery in the economy, which together lead to an extended period of growth – in retrospect this extended the degree of overshooting and helped

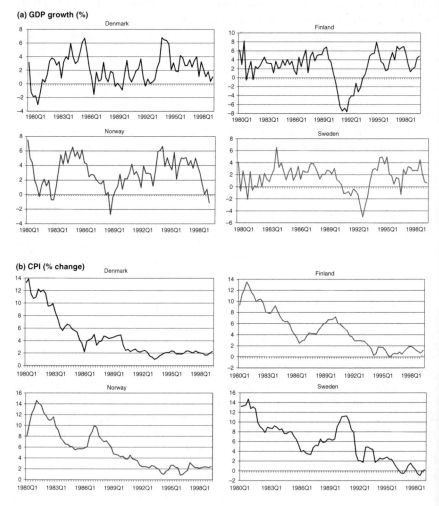

Figure 2.2   The macroeconomic picture in the Nordic countries, 1980–98

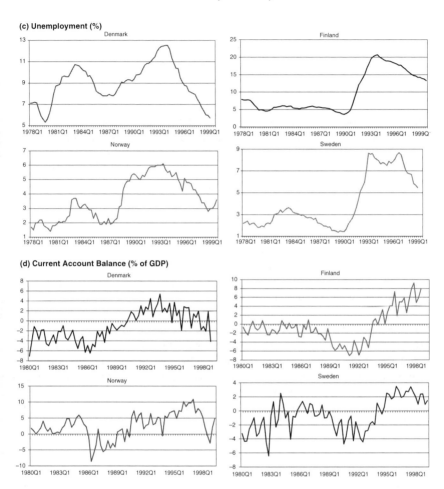

Figure 2.2 Continued

accentuate the cycle, particularly for Finland. In the Norwegian case, however, the downturn came rather earlier (1986), before such a substantial growth had been able to emerge. Nevertheless the crisis was still severe. Ironically, continuing growth can help the banks resolve their own difficulties by providing new sources of funds to offset the bad loans that have accumulated from the initial excess expansion of lending. The growth itself will, of course, reduce the number of loans that turn out to be bad. Thus in some senses the early slowdown in the Norwegian economy meant that the bad loans were exposed rather more rapidly. They were therefore not so readily disguised by growth nor allowed to build up so far. It is difficult to judge which of these two effects will have the greater impact – the opportunity to recover from the initial over-expansion or the opportunity to make the problem even worse.

2.1.3   A Rapid Rise in Asset Prices

The lending boom and the associated expansion of the economy in the Nordic countries led to rapid increases in asset prices that were in turn used to collateralise further lending. This was particularly obvious in the case of house prices (see Figure 2.3). It is always difficult to establish the role of house and other asset prices in the economy, as they will adjust rapidly in response to any change in the expected rate of return from the assets. In so far as the expansion of the economy leads people to think that the long-run rate of growth may be rather higher than they previously expected, or indeed that financial deregulation will lead to lower real interest rates, all that possible future gain will be capitalised in current asset prices. If this change in expectations turns out to be correct then there will be only a transitional problem as the change in wealth leads people to bring forward their spending plans.

The problem this bringing forward generates is straightforward. If consumption rises there will be relatively little new saving in the short run (in a national accounting sense as the asset price rises will not be directly translated into incomes). At the same time the increase in growth prospects is being reflected in a surge in investment. Hence some of the new borrowing will have to be financed from external sources. If the improvement in prospects is not a worldwide phenomenon then residents of other countries will be anxious to get a share of the

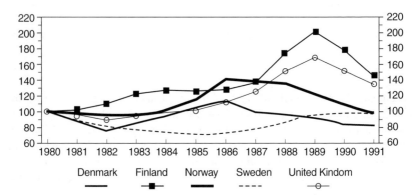

Figure 2.3   House prices in relation to consumer prices, (1980 = 100)
Source: Munthe *et al.* (1992).

benefits and there will be an inflow of funds and a rise in the exchange rate. While banks may cut interest rate margins, as the result of the increased competition, the level of domestic interest rates will tend to rise.[6] This may encourage foreign currency borrowing at lower foreign rates (a particular feature of the Finnish experience). If, as in the case of all but Denmark, the crisis includes a sharp fall in the value of the exchange rate, any unhedged borrowing will turn out to be very expensive just at the moment when the banks are at their most exposed.

If on the other hand the rise in asset prices is too great then there will tend to be excess lending on the basis of collateral whose value subsequently falls. This will contribute directly to the crisis phase of the cycle. There will also be concern that the rapid increase in consumption is not consistent with price stability, so this will tend to encourage a tightening of monetary policy. Such a tightening may initially help to drive up the exchange rate further and hence enable the cycle to develop. In the case of Finland there was only limited movement in the real exchange rate during the period 1987–89 until a step up on trying to maintain parity under the terms of the ERM with the ECU. Hence the expansion was able to continue for longer.

2.1.4 A Weak Framework for Supervision

The first set of three characteristics we have considered related to the cause of the financial boost and the immediate factors that help to either sustain or mute it. In the case of the Nordic crises financial liberalisation, increased growth and the rapid rise in asset prices helped to increase the chance of their being a bubble rather than a smooth adjustment to the positive supply shock. The second set of characteristics that we now consider relate primarily to public sector actions or inaction that helped create the conditions that allowed the problems to develop and worsen.

It is a well-known irony that deregulation is usually a paranym and what it actually denotes is reregulation – the replacement of one set of rules by a new set, which may indeed be more extensive but different in character. In many countries, including the Nordic region (and New Zealand), financial liberalisation involved a substantial measure of removing one set of rules before ensuring that those to regulate the new behaviour were in place. The new rules need to focus on prudential management, corporate governance and the framework for effective operation of market discipline to counteract the forces of more open competition. It is this framework of new rules that is the focus of this book.

It has been a long-standing concern in the literature that fierce competition among banks may reduce prudential standards to an unacceptable level (see Dewatripont and Tirole (1993) for a discussion of this point and of the literature on what can be done to offset any such threat effectively). It should therefore have been clear that pre-emptive action to head off the chance of such a decline was required.[7] According to Drees and Pazarbasioglu (1998) regulators in the Nordic countries also did not have strong regard to the scheduling of the measures so that the boom characteristics could be relatively controlled. (In New Zealand the authors of deregulation have made no secret of the fact that they introduced reforms on a pragmatic basis, trying to get the momentum of change rolling and make it difficult to return to the previous regime (see Massey, 1995, for example).)

Some of the fault that can be laid at supervisors' doors is that they did not act even when they saw the signals. Bäckström (1997) in his response to questions helps explain this in the case of Sweden. He suggests that for those involved, whether regulators or bankers, the last time there had been a serious financial crisis was in the 1920s. This was outside their professional experience and hence they were not really considering the possibility. Pre-emptive action would therefore have been inconceivable. Substantial evidence was needed before supervisors felt confident enough to contemplate major action.

In part this may be related to the specific circumstances of the crisis and the fact that the supervisors themselves were on unfamiliar ground and hence exposed to greater risks than had been normal. However, the major characteristics of the weak supervision regime were common to many countries and it was the realisation of this that had led to the development of the Basel Committee. It is characteristics such as this that differentiate the Nordic experience from that of the United Kingdom, for example. The United Kingdom also experienced an asset bubble in the second half of the 1980s (Figure 2.3). However, this was not the first such bubble – house prices doubled in the period 1971–73 (Mayes, 1979) – nor was it the first experience with financial deregulation and consequent difficulties for financial institutions. There was a secondary banking crisis in 1973/5 (Reid, 1982).

The authorities in the form of the Bank of England were not only alert to the problems of financial fragility but had been a leading force behind the Basel process and the Cooke Committee of 1974/5. The Herstatt collapse and its ramifications for international transmission of risks also helped sharpen supervisors' awareness of the widening range of risks to the system. In the period from 1989 to 1991 the United Kingdom experienced considerable problems with the banking sector. By the end of 1991 losses from bad loans had amounted to 3 to 3.5 per cent of total lending. Although some of this was associated with the tightening of monetary policy and the downturn in the domestic economy a substantial proportion came from exposure to emerging markets. On top of this the BCCI scandal emerged in 1991 and the bank was closed down, leading to pressure on some other banks, which, while of similar origin, were sound. Unlike the Nordic case, however, the banks were strong enough to survive without assistance,

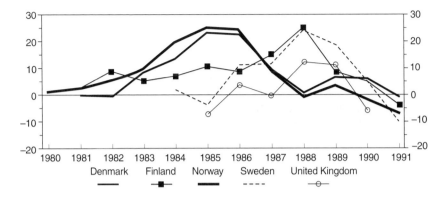

Figure 2.4 Real increase in lending, per cent p.a.
Source: Munthe *et al.* (1992).

despite big losses for the major institutions. In part this came from a much more limited lending surge in the previous period (see Figure 2.4). The UK authorities were worried by a lending surge half that of Nordic proportions

A tradition of regulation cannot be equated with tight supervision. As Berg (1993, p. 442) puts it: 'Each of the countries have histories of strict banking regulations, not for prudential reasons, but as important components of their monetary policies .... To the banking industry this meant safe and stable environments, with an implicit government guarantee [of] average industry profitability ... Supervisors had been lulled into the belief that is an inherently stable industry.'

Although the Basel accords on capital adequacy had been agreed in 1988 and of course their general tenor had been known for some time, many signatories, including the Nordic countries other than Denmark, did not phase them in rapidly or pre-emptively (see Arestis *et al.*, 1999). As a result they were not in place for the onset of the crisis. It is not so much that stronger banks would have been able to weather the crisis, but that had much more stringent capital requirements been in force earlier then it less likely that the banks would have become so exposed. It is unfortunate that international agreements of this complexity and coverage take so long to negotiate. A completed accord even three years earlier would have meant that the authorities in Sweden and Finland were acting before the liberalisation boom got underway and that those in Norway would have been compelled to take more restrictive action earlier thereby reducing the scope of the crisis (although advancing the date of its onset).

Now, of course, one would expect the Basel Accords to have been implemented and the discussion to be about how much of the proposals set out in the 1999 Consultation document from the Basel Committee (Basel Committee on

Banking Supervision, 1999a) should be anticipated. Indeed the main purpose of this book is to encourage authorities not merely to anticipate the Basel Committee's new proposals for a third 'pillar', labelled *market discipline*, for improved prudential behaviour but to take it substantially further. In any event we can expect the banks' in the more advanced countries at least, to be stronger than they were a decade ago and hence more able to withstand an adverse financial shock. Whether they have learnt and applied all the lessons from the earlier crises is much more debatable.

2.1.5   A Tax Regime that Encourages Borrowing

There are some specific characteristics of the Nordic situation that appear to have exacerbated the position compared to other countries, such as the combination of high income-tax rates and allowances against interest costs on borrowing. As is clear from Figure 2.5 real after-tax interest rates were either zero or slightly negative in Norway, Sweden and Finland during the main liberalisation period. It is not surprising therefore that this helped encourage dissaving, quite substantially in Sweden and, particularly, Norway.

The more general interest is therefore whether there are characteristics in the structure of countries that lead them to build up incipient financial problems either faster or further than others. Tax incentives are not the only regulatory candidate. The importance of debt versus equity can also matter for the responsiveness of the economy. Countries with high proportions of equity will be more vulnerable to the wealth effects we have described through swings in stock market valuations and hence more at risk from declines in the value of collateral. Where the emphasis is on debt then the problem of bad loans will tend to come through rather more extensively for the banking system. The Nordic countries were more to the debt than the equity end of the spectrum.[8]

2.1.6   Relatively Undiversified Economies

There is one aspect that can affect susceptibility to crises, which only applies to the Nordic countries to a limited extent but might well affect other small open economies much more substantially – namely a lack of diversification. In a less diversified economy, shocks that affect the major activities of the economy will have a much greater impact on the whole economy. Cycles therefore tend to be of greater amplitude. The same concentration may make it more difficult to restructure activities away from an adversely affected sector. Hence, other things being equal, the chance of financial crises will be increased.

However, economies for which such vulnerability is well known will seek to structure their financial sector so that this greater volatility can be absorbed

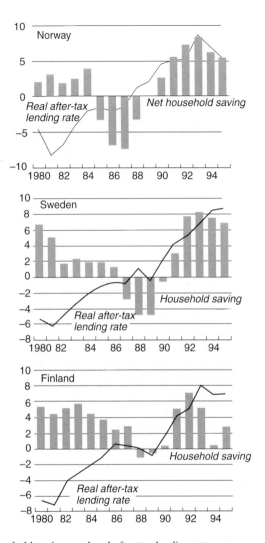

Figure 2.5 Household savings and real after-tax lending rates

Note: Household saving as a percentage of disposable household income.

Source: Drees and Pazarbasioglu (1998).

without causing a crisis. Agricultural finance is, for example, well adjusted to the experience that revenues are highly dependent on annual crops. Not only will the revenues vary markedly but once the yield is established for a particular harvest there will be little chance of the borrowers altering their circumstances for another year.[9] Neither borrowers nor lenders therefore push themselves to the limit such that even a number of consecutive bad years cannot be sustained. The larger problem comes when economies are new to such vulnerability and only appreciate its possible extent when the first serious shock occurs.

Norway was a little unusual in the possession of a substantial resource in North Sea oil and gas, which exposed it to fluctuations in these commodity prices. Open and relatively undiversified economies tend to be most at risk to external shocks. We have therefore added this as a parenthetical eighth characteristic of the Nordic crises (in Table 2.1) because it does not apply to all of the countries. Industrialised countries are normally not so exposed to the primary sector, which is a notorious source of shocks. However, both Sweden and Finland had exposure to the forest industry. Open economies also tend to try to have structures that allow them to absorb much of the external shock through the exchange rate or other external sector means, so that the cyclical (and structural) effects are reduced. In the case of Norway this has meant reinvesting North Sea oil and gas proceeds in foreign financial assets. In this way fluctuations in income flows are to some extent neutralised by transforming them into changes in foreign-currency-denominated wealth that only the public sector can access. Norway has also been able to avoid some of the worse aspects of the 'Dutch disease' with asset prices and unemployment rising as a result of natural resource discoveries. However, in the case of these specific Nordic financial crises, it is probably only the effect of the collapse of the Soviet Union on Finland, which could be described as the sort of shock that is sufficiently large and unpredictable that it could be expected to cause problems even for a country in good shape. This then takes us directly to the next step in the cycle of events which is the immediate cause of the crisis or the pricking of the bubble that leads the pent up problem to emerge in a sharp and costly manner rather than an orderly reversal.

2.1.7   A Substantial Adverse Shock

In the case of Denmark there was no explicit shock leading to the downturn of the second half of the 1980s (mirroring to some extent the lack of an explicit trigger for the financial difficulties in the first place). This contributed to the orderly reversal despite the substantial cost of the banking losses. In Norway the principal trigger appears to have been the fall of oil prices in 1986 (Munthe *et al.*, 1992). In the Finnish and Swedish cases the sharp jolt is more complex. There is a clear discontinuity from the speculative attacks that led to the collapse in the ERM in September 1992 and the major devaluations of their currencies. However, these events occurred well after the financial problems had emerged in 1990 and reflect problems in the process of resolving the crisis that may have affected its depth rather than a trigger as such. Even in the case of Sweden it was rather more the ending of the upswing of the cycle and restrictive monetary policy in the face of inflationary and exchange rate pressure that precipitated the crisis than some extra external event. Only in the case of Finland is there good reason to point to an unrelated external shock as a trigger. Nevertheless some authors point to policy as the immediate cause. Ahtiala (2000) blames the tightening in monetary policy in late 1989, when interest rates were raised by 4 percentage points (a total of 6 percentage points for the year as a whole). He argues that this move precipitated a crisis, replicating the error of the Federal Reserve at the time of the 1929 Crash when it should have expanded liquidity. Had the Bank of Finland instead sought to shield firms and households from the collapse in asset prices then the cost to the economy could have been smaller.[10]

There is some controversy over the relative importance of the shock from the collapse of Soviet trade (Figure 2.6). Clearly Finland, with the Soviet Union accounting for 15 per cent of its trade, was in a completely different position even from Sweden, where the share of trade was less than 1 per cent. If we compare

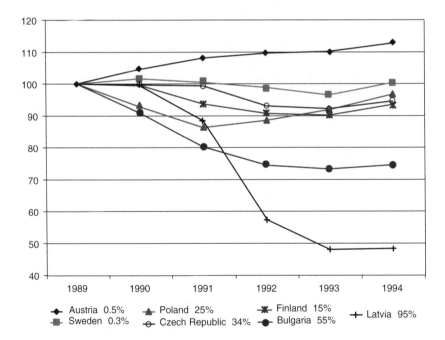

Figure 2.6 Fall in GDP compared with trade share % with the Soviet Union
Source: Tarkka (1993), Bank of Finland.

the size of the GDP downturns following the collapse of the Soviet Union, as shown in Figure 2.6, there is quite a close correlation between the share of the previous trade with the Soviet Union and the downturn in GDP. There is thus prima facie evidence that a substantial proportion of the extra difficulties in Finland compared with the other Nordic countries was due to the collapse of the Soviet Union. Indeed the extent of that difference is sufficiently big that straight extrapolation suggests a sizeable recession for Finland at the beginning of the 1990s from that cause alone.

There was a further generalised asymmetric shock that applied to any countries that tried to limit exchange rate fluctuations with the euro – namely, the impact of the unification of Germany. German interest rates had to rise to finance the rapid increase in social security liabilities and the need to invest in public sector infrastructure and restructuring of state firms on a massive scale. This placed exchange rate pressure on other countries that did not need such high rates. Attempts to sustain exchange rate regimes usually result in fairly dramatic adjustment processes (see Eichengreen, 1999, for example) when the authorities have to give up defending a particular parity.

2.1.8   Unsustainable Macroeconomic Policies

Macroeconomic policy can be a key ingredient of financial crises by allowing or indeed driving the economy away from longer-term equilibrium. Berg (1993) argues that policy makers did not merely do little to prevent the crises from developing 'they in some cases contributed to make things worse.' When the adjustment back towards equilibrium comes it may be both substantial and rapid. The dilemma in the case of Finland in the early 1990s was obvious. Finland was using exchange rate targeting as a means of ensuring price stability and also as a precursor of entry into the European Union and the Exchange Rate Mechanism of the European Monetary System in particular. As borrowing began to rise rapidly in 1987 and 1988 (Figure 2.7) the appropriate course of action from the point of view of financial stability would have been to raise interest rates to choke off the demand. However, doing so would probably also have raised the exchange rate.

However, the restraint of demand and hence borrowing would have been appropriate for reasons of price stability in any case (Figure 2.2). The Finnish government chose not to tighten fiscal policy in 1988 or 1989 in any substantial way and aimed instead at reducing direct taxes. Corsetti and Roubini (1996) argue that Finland ran fiscal deficits far in excess of those expected purely from the severity of the economic downturn at the beginning of the 1990s. As a consequence external and public sector debt were run up to unsustainable levels. They argued that 'a substantial fiscal retrenchment [would] be required' if the public

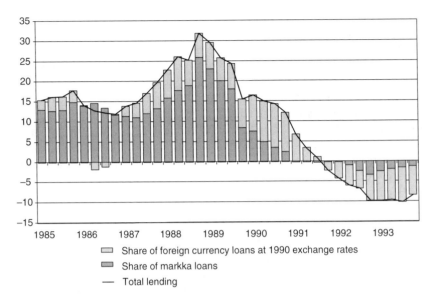

Figure 2.7 Bank lending to the corporate and household sectors in Finland
Source: Koskenkylä (1998).

sector were not to become insolvent. Such moves have occurred, assisted by the requirements of the Maastricht Treaty for membership of Stage 3 of EMU. However, Corsetti and Roubini do admit that in the first couple of years there could have been some doubt about whether the shock to the Finnish economy was transitory or permanent. During that period allowing the deficit to rise to the extent it did might have been appropriate but in their opinion the permanent nature and hence the need for action must have been clear before the end of 1992. Their comments therefore might appear to relate rather more to unsustainable macroeconomic policy in counteracting the crisis rather than contributing to causing it in the first place. However, they also show that during the 1980s fiscal policy was becoming increasingly unsustainable, with systematic slippage in targets for spending cuts and hence fiscal balances. Without this trend, the financial crisis could have been weathered with considerably less impact on external and government debt, despite the perceived need to recapitalise the banks from taxpayer funds.

The exchange rate constraint meant that monetary policy could not be used to offset the lack of downward fiscal pressure. Allowing the expansion to develop too rapidly increased the likelihood of having to make a harsh downward adjustment rather than a smoother introduction of restraint. The Bank of Finland was aware of the problem (Lehmussaari, 1990, for example[11]) but only published strongly worded statements, since it felt unable to act.

The exchange rate regime is one of the most commonly cited causes of financial crises (Mishkin, 2000). In the case of 'fixed' exchange rates, the problem is that increasing effort is spent on defending a peg that has become unrealistic compared with the sustainable long-run value (in real terms). Defending the rate itself exacerbates the problem, as high rates of interest have to be offered. These attract short-run capital that can rapidly exit when the peg becomes unsustainable. Insofar as this capital has been used for domestic lending this can place a severe strain on the banks. The problem is particularly acute if the borrowing is in foreign currency because in this case although banks may have technically matched assets and liabilities if they on-lend to the private sector in foreign currency they merely convert the currency risk into a credit risk for themselves. The short-run nature of the debt means that the banks (and the borrowers) rapidly run into cashflow problems, exacerbated by the banks' need to recapitalise at a time of weakness.

While most commentators have restricted their analysis of the problems of the Nordic economies to the 1980s and 1990s, Jonung *et al.* (1996) suggest that the problems are much longer lasting. Both Finland and Sweden had had an enviable record of low unemployment since the Second World War. However, the methods of achieving this may themselves have been unsustainable in the long run. That unsustainability became more marked as time went on and the financial crises can be seen in part as the realisation of that unsustainability. The authors characterise Sweden, in particular, as having experienced continuing lack of competitiveness in the tradeables industries as the result of increases in labour and other costs. The resulting loss of demand was made up by tax-financed public expenditure. In effect 'the public sector acted as employer of last resort' (p. 58). Finland, on the other hand, had tried to resolve the same problem by a sequence of devaluations 'no less than nine times between the end of World War II and 1973'. With the first oil crisis in 1973 Sweden also adopted the Finnish route to adjustment. However, the Finnish problem remained more acute than the Swedish, particularly because the Finnish 'solution' had led to higher investment and faster growth and hence a greater shortfall of domestic saving. The problem is cumulative and the continuing saving deficiency resulted in an accumulation of debt.

Jonung *et al.* can therefore argue that 'These problems had been on the agenda long enough to deserve being called "traditional". By the late 1980s, it became increasingly clear that these macroeconomic balances were unsustainable.' This helps provide a rationale for inaction. It was not that the problem was not recognised but that its solution required a major shift in long-standing economic policies. Such shifts are difficult to push through in the absence of a crisis. Indeed there are some that have argued that in a sense one should manufacture a 'crisis' in order to get the political support for the fundamental change. (See Deane

(1996) for example for a description of the New Zealand foreign exchange 'crisis' of 1984 and how it was argued that previous policies just could not be pursued any longer.) In the case of Finland and Sweden no such 'manufacturing' took place and hence the push to change came from a very real crisis itself.

There is a clear difference here between the experience of Denmark and that of the other Nordic countries. By the end of the 1980s Denmark had already reached a stable and sustainable position within the ERM of the European Monetary System. It had adjusted its exchange rate downwards by over 20 per cent during the decade and had also adjusted its budgetary position to much more sustainable levels. This helps explain why Danish problems, although large, were resolvable without a crisis

The Finnish and Swedish examples fit well into the pattern analysed by Kaminsky and Reinhart (1999) of twin (banking and currency) crises:

> We find that: problems in the banking sector typically precede a currency crisis – the currency crisis deepens the banking crisis, activating a vicious spiral; financial liberalisation often precedes banking crises. The anatomy of theses episodes suggests that crises occur as the economy enters a recession, following a prolonged boom in economic activity that was fuelled by credit capital inflows, and accompanied by an overvalued currency. (p. 473)

Norway has much of the characteristics but Denmark does not. '[T]he incidence of crises where the economic fundamentals were sound was rare.' (ibid, p. 474).

In one sense following unsustainable macroeconomic policies is almost inevitable as the authorities are faced by an unpleasant choice. Because there has been a credit surge, particularly if it involves foreign currency borrowing, borrowers are very vulnerable. If the exchange rate were to fall then this would increase the domestic currency liabilities of borrowers. If domestic interest rates are raised in order to stop the exchange rate falling then this increases the costs to borrowers in domestic currency. Either action will make the debt position worse and slow the economy, which will itself spread the problem to others on the brink of difficulty and so on in a downward spiral.

The credit surge takes the economy into the typical problems of 'debt-deflation' once the limits to the process of growth are encountered (King, 1994). On the way up, increases in asset prices encourage increases in borrowing (if only to maintain something like the previous relationship between debt and wealth). Although some of that may go into the driving up of asset prices even further, one consequence is the fall in the savings ratio (Figure 2.5). On the way down, real interest rates rise rapidly, asset prices fall, borrowers are forced into massive saving to reduce their indebtedness and interest payments rise rapidly. This is exacerbated when some of the debts are denominated in foreign currency and hence are increased in size in domestic currency terms while the corresponding assets held against them fall in value. The greater the 'bubble' on the way up the more difficult it is to avoid a 'hard-landing' on the way down.

The interesting distinction between the United Kingdom and the Nordic countries in the early 1990s is that while the United Kingdom also underwent a strong economic downturn, following a major surge in lending it did not experience a banking crisis. (While the BCCI crisis broke in 1991, this was for reasons of fraud unrelated to the business cycle, Dale (1993).) However, the UK lending surge was only of the order of 10 per cent in both 1988 and 1989 – notably less than that experienced in any of the four Nordic countries we have considered. Furthermore the provision for losses (as a percentage of loans) was higher than in any of those countries in 1986, 1987 and 1989 (and higher than Sweden and Finland in all years until 1991). UK banks thus tackled the problems head-on at an earlier stage. However, according to Munthe *et al.* (1992) the United Kingdom banks were under less legal obligation to identify poorly performing loans than their Norwegian counterparts were at that time.

There was also little unhedged foreign-currency-denominated borrowing to compound the problem. The United Kingdom experienced a house price boom between 1986 and 1989 well in excess of any of the Nordic countries except Finland (Figure 2.3) and banks exposed to the unwinding of this were most affected. Even at the end of 1991 all the eight largest banks in the United Kingdom made a profit and had capital adequacy clearly in excess of the 8 per cent minimum.

Even so the consequences for the real economy were considerable. Consumption fell by 3.5 per cent between the peak and trough in the downturn, although real disposable income actually rose slightly (1.1 per cent) (King, 1994). This was an 8 per cent fall compared to trend growth. King (1994) suggests that the role of housing debt can be appreciated by the fact that expenditure (other than on housing) by those households without mortgages rose slightly between 1989 and 1991 while it fell by 4 per cent for those with mortgages. The problem seems to be that the economy cannot handle such a sharp and substantial transfer of wealth from borrowers to lenders without some measure of deflation, even if it only goes as far as a slowdown in the rate of economic growth.

The cause of the rise in lending cannot realistically be laid at the door of financial deregulation, as that had occurred rather earlier in the United Kingdom than in the Nordic countries. It was rather more due to the continuing rise in growth expectations as the economy continued to grow faster than expected following the sharp recession of the earlier 1980s.

It might appear at first blush that the difficulty with macroeconomic policy in the run-up to the crisis did not bode well for Finland inside the Eurosystem. Monetary policy is now determined by the needs of the euro area as a whole.

If borrowing from the banks were to expand rapidly just in Finland the authorities again would have little ability to act except through exhortation and controls over individual banks to ensure capital adequacy and due prudence. Three factors render this a much more limited risk. The first is simply that borrowers, lenders and the authorities have the experience of the crisis firmly in mind. Secondly, the supervision system has been substantially improved so that the prudential controls within banks make it much less likely that they would make poor quality loans.[12] The exposure to risks from property-based collateral and to borrowing in foreign (non-euro) currencies is now not only much better understood but explicitly incorporated in measurements of Value at Risk and capital adequacy. Membership of the euro area itself makes it much less likely that there would be interest rate incentives for foreign borrowing as the 'country' risk premium has been greatly reduced.

Lastly the operation of the macroeconomic system under the euro area is itself changed. Fiscal authorities are acutely aware of the limitations placed on them, not just by the terms of the Stability and Growth Pact but by competitive pressures in a system of lower barriers. This awareness also extends to those setting prices and wages. There is no exchange rate mechanism to accommodate any adverse cost movements as in the past (Mayes and Vilmunen, 1999).[13] Those agreeing the cost increases know that it will be more difficult to pass them on, as other suppliers within the euro area will not be faced by the same difficulties. The loss of income or jobs will therefore fall directly on those covered by the particular bargain not by the economy at large. Fiscal policy is perceived as not being an effective means for responding to nominal shocks (Flemming, 1987).

In this way the Finnish economy is likely to be more flexible in response not only to (asymmetric) shocks that affect it alone but also to (symmetric) shocks that affect the whole euro area. With Finland having only been in the EU for five years it is also likely that the Finnish economy will converge towards the rest of the euro area, making asymmetric shocks less likely and less severe in their size. However, the problem is not removed.

It is noticeable that none of the other Nordic countries have chosen to enter the euro area. Norway and Iceland remain in the EEA and have not joined the EU while Denmark and Sweden are in the EU but not in the euro area. One is tempted to ask whether their experience from the banking crisis of the beginning of this decade has influenced their decisions. By remaining outside the area they have maintained the ability to run a more flexible macroeconomic policy. But if they seek to maintain exchange rate targets this still exposes them to the threat of rapid adjustments in the future if they move away from long-run equilibrium and substantial realignment appears necessary. If they shadow the euro through ERM2, whether or not explicitly, they run the risk of returning to an unsustainable combination of policies, as set out in Padoa-Schioppa (1987) for example.

The commitment to maintain the exchange rate regime will tend to look rather more convincing for those countries that enter the euro area – even if monetary policy may upon occasion no longer be so appropriate to their individual needs.

The macroeconomic cycle and the financial expansion tend to become intertwined. If the financial innovation comes at a time when the economy is sluggish or when monetary policy is tight then the lending expansion itself will at a lower level and the chance of crisis much more muted. Indeed financial liberalisation can form an important part of a cyclical recovery. This finding is common to other structural changes. Where these are generated by regulatory change the authorities have some discretion over timing. The extent of the discretion is, however, relatively limited. In rapidly changing industries such as the financial sector, delay can effectively kill the market opportunity. Organisations such as the London Stock Exchange and Lloyds, which have a strong element of mutuality in their organisational structure, find it more difficult and time consuming to take decisions and hence can lose market share while they seek agreement on change. Bringing forward change may also be difficult as ill-thought-out legislation can be more damaging than late legislation. A substantial measure of agreement with the private sector is usually necessary to ensure that legislation is workable and that the spirit of the new regime is actually implemented.

However, it is always possible to think of reasons for delay and some of the role of political decision-making is to overcome this inertia. Some substantial moves have been made quickly, such as the creation of the new Financial Services Authority in the United Kingdom in 1998.

2.2 DENMARK

The Nordic banking crises differ in character and timing, as is clear from Figures 2.8 and 2.9. The problems appeared earliest in Denmark, but they were also the least acute – two small banks were closed and a third ceased trading temporarily. While others got into difficulties there was only a limited systemic threat, even from the problems of the seventh largest bank, Kronebanken, in 1984–85, so it is not really appropriate to describe this as a crisis in the normal sense of the word. Although the main surge in lending covered the years 1983–87 in a pattern very similar to that of Norway, the highest loss provisioning actually occurred in 1982 and in 1990–92 the losses were only around 2 per cent of the loan portfolio – less than half the peak in the other three countries. Indeed, using the figures in Møller and Nielsen (1995, Table 2.2), Danish banks actually had to make rather larger provisioning for losses (compared to lending) for the period 1982–93 as a whole. Since their losses were spread out over a rather longer period, this increases the chance that banks may be able to cope with them without recourse to help from the public sector.

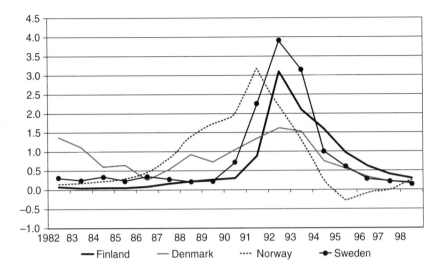

Figure 2.8 Ratio of loan losses to average total assets of Nordic banks
Source: Koskenkylä (1998).

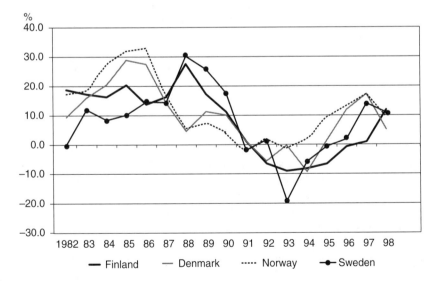

Figure 2.9 Rates of growth in bank lending in the Nordic countries
Source: Koskenkylä (1998).

Table 2.2 Losses and provisions made by
Nordic banks 1982–93 (% of lending)

	Denmark	Finland	Norway	Sweden
1982	3.1	0.6	0.2	0.5
1983	2.5	0.5	0.3	0.5
1984	1.5	0.5	0.3	0.7
1985	1.5	0.6	0.4	0.5
1986	0.6	0.6	0.5	0.6
1987	1.1	0.7	1.3	0.5
1988	2.0	0.7	2.0	0.3
1989	1.6	0.7	2.6	0.4
1990	2.3	0.6	2.3	1.2
1991	2.7	1.7	4.3	4.0
1992	3.3	5.8	2.5	7.6
1993	3.2	5.6	1.6	6.3
Ave. 1982–93	2.1	1.5	1.5	1.9
Ave. 1990–3	2.9	3.4	2.7	4.8

Source: Møller and Nielsen (1995).

On the whole capitalisation of the Danish banks was sufficient for them to get through the difficulties, either on their own or by merger. There were only three instances where an injection of public funds was required. The rather milder pattern in Denmark appears to stem from a number of causes. First of all, according to Munthe *et al.* (1992), the impact of financial deregulation in Denmark was much more limited. Not only were the changes rather smaller in extent than in the other countries but behaviour had to quite some extent anticipated the changes, so there was no great alteration in a short period of time. Similarly the economic cycle was less marked, with strong growth over the period 1983–86, but decline to standstill or slow growth rather than a substantial recession in the downturn (Figure 2.2). However, with a growth of real lending around 60 per cent greater than the increase in GDP over the period 1984–86 the potential for a crisis existed had Denmark been subjected to a substantial shock on the scale of the other three countries. Even so Danish banks had not tapped sources of funding that would prove very expensive in a crisis – such as short-term foreign currency borrowing – to the extent of its neighbours.

The losses in Denmark were spread rather more evenly over the banks than in the other Nordic countries. Hence for any given level of losses it would have been easier for the Danish banks to resolve the problem without state assistance. If the losses are concentrated in just a few banks then it is more likely that they will face insolvency. However, Møller and Nielsen (1995) also argue that the Danish banks may have been able to survive more readily because they were under less competitive pressure. Not only were there more banks proportionately in Denmark but many of them were small, with a strong preference for remaining independent. This had two consequences. First of all margins were not eroded so much in the face of the competition that followed liberalisation. Secondly, the relatively high cost structure in Danish banks offered scope both for increased efficiency and for absorbing shocks.

One key factor assisting the more favourable outcome in Denmark may have been accounting principles based on 'mark to market' (Møller and Nielsen, 1995). This has twin benefits. First of all, it tends to make problems more obvious. Detection may therefore be easier (and hence earlier) by the bank itself. Secondly, the accounting basis also means that provisions therefore have to be made and made public when the accounts are published. There is thus less opportunity to hide the problem and hope that difficulties can be resolved before they are revealed. The system thus not only encourages early action but also encourages more prudential behaviour because banks know that any difficulties they do encounter are more likely to be made public. This will make them somewhat more risk-averse. The information will also come available to the supervisor, who can apply pressure. These threats between them may have encouraged the Danish banks to be rather better capitalised in the first place and hence more able to face the difficulties.

Early provisioning in itself may tend to help spread the impact and indeed reduce the overall size of the problem. Once action is started and provisioning begins to be made, banks will have to cut back their activities and might avoid making more poor quality loans. The benefits of good financial reporting standards and the incentives to greater prudence if a bank knows its position will be disclosed and become public knowledge are key themes that we develop in this book.

Møller and Nielsen (1995) also argue that the corporate governance of Danish banks tends to make them more prudent, as major lending decisions are normally taken at board level, where non-executive directors are present. Such directors are likely to take a different attitude towards risk, which might reduce shareholder value, than do managers, whose performance may in part be assessed on the ability to bring in new business.

Denmark was also early in introducing deposit insurance in 1988. While implicit guarantees may have existed elsewhere, a key part of maintaining confidence in the other Nordic countries once the crisis had broken was to issue a public guarantee to all depositors and creditors – but not to shareholders. It is therefore possible that Denmark faced a different level of moral hazard from the other countries. Møller and Nielsen reject the idea that bankers themselves might have run greater risk because they knew that smaller deposits were insured. They feel that a more plausible argument was that the depositors themselves may have taken less care in considering the security of their deposits after insurance was introduced. In any case insurance was only introduced during the period of difficulty, not beforehand. Therefore only behaviour in the second half of the period could be blamed on greater moral hazard (if at all).

2.3   NORWAY

The contrast of the Norwegian case with that of Denmark illustrates neatly which ingredients turn a source of potential difficulty into an actual crisis. Although the growth of lending was very similar, in Norway it followed a period of rapid financial deregulation. Norwegian banks were not so well capitalised and non-traditional sources of funding were used extensively. Whereas, at end-1983 loans amounted to only 88 per cent (79 per cent) of customer deposits for the commercial (savings) banks, they had risen to 147 per cent (118 per cent) by end-1987. One third of the increase in commercial banks' assets came from foreign borrowing. It is interesting that most of the losses related to loans outstanding to existing customers (3/4 in 1990 and 2/3 in 1991 according to CREBA (1992)). The problem was not primarily loans to new higher risk customers.

Unlike Denmark, Norway had a shock – in this case a fall in oil prices during the winter of 1985/6, which not only triggered a downturn in its own right but a fiscal retrenchment by the government as well. This was followed by a large number of liquidations in the commercial sector and the contagion from the US stock market crash in 1987.

Over the period September 1988 to December 1991 22 banks in Norway needed a capital injection or guarantee. Only one bank, Norion, closed. Thirteen savings banks among these problem banks were all merged with other savings banks in a progressive consolidation of the sector, although some of the successor banks also got into difficulties. With the exception of Sunnmørsbanken, the initial need for recapitalisation was restricted to the savings bank sector and substantial progress was made in 1989 towards bringing the Norwegian banking sector up to the capital requirements of the Basel Accord. However, there was a further deterioration in 1990 and by the end of 1991 all of the three largest commercial banks in Norway – Den norske bank, Christiana bank and Fokus bank – had required substantial capital injections. In the case of both Christiana bank and Fokus bank their existing capital base was wiped out. In both cases general meetings of the banks failed to agree to write-down the existing share values to zero before the government's injection and this had to be done by Royal Decree. (This issue of the ability to wipe out existing shareholder funds is an important one, as it strengthens the incentives to shareholders to ensure prudent management. We return to this issue in Chapter 8.) By 1992 the three largest Norwegian commercial banks were in public ownership. The holding in Den norske bank only rose to 55 per cent while the holding in Christiania bank was total and that in Fokus bank similar save for a small offering to the private sector in 1992.

The problems of 1991 were exacerbated by a decline in banks' asset values, particularly through the decline of the property market. As is clear from Figure 2.3 house prices have played an important role in changing asset values in only some of the Nordic countries – Norway and particularly Finland.

2.4   FINLAND

In the banking crisis, Finland was the hardest hit of the Nordic countries. It was also hit last (Figure 2.8), although the pattern is similar to that of Sweden. Comparisons are difficult because until 1991 banks in Finland reported actual losses, whereas in Norway and Denmark provisioning would have been more obvious as estimated values were used. Lending was growing rapidly throughout the period but the rate doubled during 1987–88, reaching over 30 per cent by the end of 1988. What is interesting for Finland is the growth in foreign currency borrowing, which continued to increase in the second half of 1989 and through 1990, when the growth rates in overall lending were falling rapidly (Figure 2.7). Household debt rose from 25 per cent of GDP in 1980 to 45 per cent in 1992, with nearly half of that rise occurring in 1987–88. Corporate debt on the other hand did not take off until 1989 when it rose from 70 per cent of GDP to near 90 per cent in a couple of years.

Finland had all seven of the characteristics of the crises that we have mentioned:[14]

(i)   The tax system encouraged lending by banks and borrowing from them. Debt was taxed substantially less than equity for firms. Households could deduct interest on borrowings against income tax (a major concession for a country where the marginal income tax rates were among the highest in the OECD), while tax exemption on low-yielding bank deposits enabled banks to obtain funds at low rates.

(ii)   There was a substantial programme of deregulation in the financial sector during the period 1983 to 1991 (Nyberg and Vihriälä, 1994), whose impact was concentrated around 1986–87.

(iii)   A relatively weak framework of financial supervision.

(iv)   A period of rapid growth in the real economy at above the long-run sustainable level. If deregulation were introduced in a period when the economy is depressed then its stimulative impact might be considerably reduced. In Norway, Sweden and Finland deregulation occurred when the economy was already growing rapidly.

(v) An asset price boom. House prices doubled between 1986 and 1989 while stock market prices increased more than threefold between 1985 and 1988. The world stock market decline in October 1987 was completely reversed by the end of the first quarter of 1988 on the Helsinki exchange.

(vi) Unsustainable macroeconomic policies. During the 1980s Finland had tried to achieve price stability by targeting the exchange rate but had had to adjust the peg on a number of occasions. In June 1991 with the negotiations to become a member of the EU, Finland started to shadow being a member of the Exchange Rate Mechanism of the European Monetary System.

(vii) A shock that reversed fortunes rapidly. The obvious shock for Finland was the collapse of the former Soviet Union. The loss of Soviet export markets represented about 2.5 per cent of GDP in its own right (Nyberg and Vihriälä, 1994), although allowing for ancillary services in the parts of Finland most affected would increase that figure. (Exports to the Soviet Union formed 15 per cent of the total in 1986–89, although they had been as high as 25 per cent in 1981–83.) As much of the production for these markets was not suitable for domestic consumption or export to the Western world production had to be shut down rather than prices lowered.

To some extent Finland was the victim of bad luck. It received favourable shocks in the mid-1980s. The terms of trade improved by over 15 per cent between the beginning of 1986 and mid-1988. Bilateral trade with the Soviet Union meant that Finland was somewhat isolated from the detrimental effects of oil price rises. The coincidence with financial deregulation was also something that would have been difficult to avoid. The regulatory changes were years in the making and holding them off purely for macroeconomic reasons would have been difficult. Similarly the severity of the downturn was due primarily to external factors. The combination was particularly unfortunate. The timing of German unification meant that European interest rates were high at a time when Finland was in recession to add to the other problems. Nevertheless it appears unlikely that without the external factors that Finland might have been able to have as soft a ride as Denmark and get through without the need for an injection of public funds.

However, other aspects of the problem were clearly the result of bad judgement rather than bad luck. It seems incredible with the example of Norway so close to hand that the rapid rise in lending did not ring alarm bells sufficiently for considerably earlier and stronger action. It was only in early 1989 that the Bank of Finland raised interest rates and imposed a special reserve requirement to try to reduce the rate of growth of lending. By late 1987, with lending growing at 20 per cent a year, it must have been clear that corrective action was required. Ironically the nature of the tightening exacerbated the problem, not simply because increased borrowing costs provoked servicing difficulties for borrowers[15] but because higher interest rates in Finland encouraged banks, in particular, to borrow in foreign currencies at substantially lower rates. Somehow there seemed to be little fear that the exchange rate might fall at some stage, even though the rise in interest rates caused it to appreciate. Fiscal policy showed only a small tightening as an increase in indirect taxation and a decrease in government expenditure were offset by a cut in direct taxes.

Nevertheless the turnround in the economy was swift. In the second half of the year the trade balance became negative and exports slowed. Growth of GDP also fell rapidly, passing through zero during 1990 and recording 0.0 per cent for 1990 as a whole, compared with 5.4 per cent for 1989. Unemployment, which had fallen from 5 to 4 per cent during 1987–89, began a steep rise. The banking crisis also began to emerge in 1990. The central bank for the savings banks, Skopbank, became a cause of concern for the authorities during 1989 and by October 1989 the savings banks were required to inject 1.8bn FIM and a programme for reducing the risks on its loan portfolio was agreed with the authorities. This did not work and by September 1991 the Bank of Finland had to takeover Skopbank at a cost of some 14bn FIM in total. Approximately half of the overall bank losses were concentrated in the savings bank sector, which had taken the opportunity of deregulation to expand its lending aggressively into new areas.

The collapse of the real economy began in earnest in 1991, with a decline of 7.6 per cent followed by a further fall of 3.8 per cent in 1992. The recession continued into 1993 (a fall of 1.2 per cent) but exports had already started to recover at the end of 1991. This is all the more surprising because the exchange rate peg with the ecu held until September 1992. Thereafter the exchange rate fell by some 20 per cent before starting to recover in the second half of 1993.

The extent of state support thought necessary in Finland was massive by comparison with the other Nordic countries (Table 2.3) and by 1995 some 17.2 per cent of GDP had been injected into the banking system (more than half of which was later repaid, giving an estimated net cost of around 7 per cent of GDP (Koskenkylä, 1998)).

Table 2.3 Public sector support for the banking system in the Nordic countries 1989–95 (% of GDP, gross figures)

Norway	Sweden	Finland	Denmark
2.6	6.1	17.2	0.5

The strengths and weaknesses of the Finnish banking system are difficult to disentangle. Even at the end of 1991 the average capital ratio according to the Basel criteria was 9.7 per cent. Up until the crisis profitability was good. However, the fact that it was possible to reduce both the number of personnel in the industry and the number of branches by a factor of two between 1990 and 1997 suggests that there was very considerable over-capacity (Figure 2.10). Some of the problem can be traced to the rapid development of short-run money markets following the exemption of bank CDs from the cash reserve requirement in January 1987 (Malkamäki and Solttila, 1991) and their development into the main instrument of open market operations by the Bank of Finland during the year (Kontulainen, 1991).

The Finnish crisis combines at least four themes : (i) the mistakes in financial system oversight and regulatory responses; (ii) the real shock from the collapse of Soviet trade; (iii) the existence of a latent fundamental disequilibrium in the structure of economy and; finally, (iv) the role of aligning macroeconomic policy to EU and EMU membership. It is difficult to get agreement as to the importance of each of these. However, views about what should have been done to avoid or at least reduce the severity of the crisis depend upon the analysis of where the problem lay. In the same way the appropriate route to tackling the crisis was dependent on the analysis of its causes. There was extensive debate at the time about what to do (Ahtiala, 1993; Kiander, 1993; Koskela and Paunio, 1993; Kukkonen, 1993; Valkonen and Vartia, 1992) and the debate about the causes and the appropriate actions is by no means dead even now (Tarkka, 1993; Honkapohja and Koskela, 1999; Ahtiala, 2000).

We do not need to assign weights, as our task here is merely to identify causes in order to draw lessons. However, it is necessary to go as far as the sorts of measures that were used in the initial stages of the resolution of the crisis and the *expectation* of what those measures might be as they affected the depth of the crisis itself. The simplest of these is the expectation by banks, their shareholders, depositors and creditors of what would happen in the case of difficulty. The expectation was that all banks would survive in some form or other, even if they had to be merged. Hence less was at risk and banks could themselves go nearer the brink with some confidence that they would be rescued. This expectation was fuelled by two main factors: the extent of the bailouts occurring in Sweden and the early indication from the assistance by the Bank of Finland to Skopbank in 1991.

Finland had had compulsory deposit insurance since 1969, although the insurance schemes for the savings and co-operative banks had already been in place for forty years (Nyberg and Vihriälä, 1994). The main steps undertaken in 1992 were designed to avoid the difficulties turning into a credit crunch. In March the government provided an 8bn FIM facility that the banks could draw on to augment their Tier 1 capital. There was only a small penalty in the interest rate,

(a) *Employees*

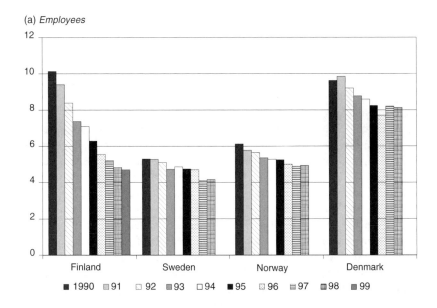

(b) *Branches*

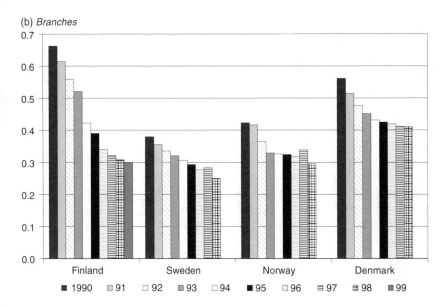

Figure 2.10 Bank branches and employees per 1000 inhabitants in the Nordic countries
Source: Koskenkylä (1998).

designed to be enough to encourage early repayment, but there was an interesting incentive in the tail in that these certificates could be converted into voting stock if interest was not paid for three successive years or solvency fell below the legal minimum. In April Finland established a 20bn FIM Government Guarantee Fund to protect depositors and in August it issued an unconditional guarantee that the stability of the banking system would be secured under all circumstances.[16]

Clearly, the shape of a crisis can be affected by the usual moral hazards that arise from the expected safety nets that exist to alleviate it. The authorities face a dilemma in that they want to make sure that there is confidence in the integrity of the banking system on the one hand and yet as little incentive as possible for the banks themselves to take undue risks on the other. In the Finnish case the explicit guarantees were limited and the insurance funds would not have coped with a serious general crisis. The rescue measures had to be developed rapidly at the time. Even the role of the Bank of Finland as 'lender' of last resort was not explicit beforehand. They had followed the precepts of 'constructive ambiguity' in this regard. The question therefore is what people thought the implicit guarantees were at the time. There is little doubt that bank deposits were thought to be completely safe. The subsequent political reaction also suggests that the expected set of safeguards was very considerable. One might perhaps link that sort of expectation to the public attitude that had supported the development of the very extensive social safety net in Finland during the preceding decades.

Of course, the existence of expected satisfactory exit strategies is not normally taken into account explicitly in making either specific or generalised lending (or borrowing) decisions in the period of growth into the crisis. It has a much more subtle effect on behaviour. Here we have merely attempted to suggest that one might be able to assess what was implicitly expected in Finland from the nature of the reaction of the authorities when the crisis broke and the extent of support for those actions. Seeing the reactions in one crisis will of course itself help form expectations of what the authorities might do in future crises and trying to change those expectations provides a difficult task for the authorities, which we tackle in succeeding chapters.

The expected actions of the authorities, should anything go wrong, help affect the risk decisions that people take beforehand. It is clear, for example, from the ensuing controversy that the Norwegian authorities' action in extinguishing existing shareholder value before taking over some of the banks came as a surprise.

2.5 SWEDEN

Of all the Nordic countries, the losses in the Swedish banking system were greatest (Figure 2.11). Provisioning was 12 per cent of GDP in 1990–93. However,

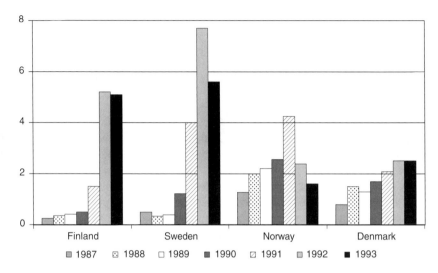

Figure 2.11 Credit losses of deposit banks (parent companies)
(% of lending outstanding)
Source: Koskenkylä (1998).

the situation was also resolved rather more quickly than in Finland and with much more limited use of public funds. The two largest banks, Skandinaviska Enskilda Banken and Svenska Handelsbanken, were able to get through the crisis without the need for public funds, although they had to make very heavy provisioning. However, the third largest, Nordbanken, in which the state held a controlling interest, did need recapitalisation along with the remainder of the seven largest banks as did the largest savings bank Första Sparbanken (in 1991).

Bank lending in Sweden also accelerated rapidly – by some 63 per cent in real terms between 1987 and 1989 – slightly more than in Finland. This surge in lending was financed by borrowing in foreign currency so that by 1990 the large banks had foreign currency denominated assets as half of their portfolio (Munthe *et al.*, 1992). A substantial proportion of this new lending was backed by real estate. Asset prices doubled in real terms between 1985 and 1989 (Bäckström, 1997). Like Finland the financial deregulation coincided with a rapid pick-up in the rate of growth of demand, although the timing was around a year earlier. Sweden also pursued a monetary policy aimed at maintaining the exchange rate until it was driven from shadowing the ERM at the same time as Finland, in September 1992. The exchange rate peg was abandoned in November 1992 and replaced by an inflation target.

The downswing in Sweden was generated rather more by the internal dynamics of the cycle than by external factors, since neither oil prices nor the collapse of the Soviet Union had the importance for the Swedish economy that they did for Norway and Finland respectively. The initial recovery was equally rapid and the economy appeared to have stabilised as early as 1993. Only 'appeared to', as there was a further loss of confidence and slip in the exchange rate in 1994.

Bäckström (1997) from his position at the head of the central bank (Sveriges Riksbank) argues that there are three main ingredients to preventing (his word) financial crises:

- A monetary policy aimed at price stability.
- Attention to the common indicators, which would allow the detection of the problem early on.
- A focused supervisory authority alert to the problems of the credit market in a deregulated environment. The Swedish authority not only permitted poor loans without intervening; it also failed to insist on adequate documentation of loans so that their quality could be revealed.

2.6 SOME OTHER LESSONS FROM THE NORDIC CRISES

The official report on the crisis in Norway (Munthe *et al.*, 1992) provides one insight (p. 93) that rings very true. When new regimes are being implemented much of the effort of the supervisory organisation goes into the implementation process rather than the monitoring of the health of individual institutions or systemic risk. Because so much work is involved in the sheer process of financial liberalisation or indeed regulation, there is a danger of taking one's eye off the ball. While financial crises are by their very nature unpredictable, this particular lesson does seem to have a continuing applicability. When the authorities are heavily involved in the implementation of a new system, such as the euro area, then they will have more concerns than when they are operating a mature and continuing system. One of the implications from this observation may help explain the recent trend for trying to separate responsibility for systemic issues from supervision of the individual financial institutions. This separation already exists in both Finland and Sweden, with the central bank having responsibility for the system-wide issues and the supervisory authority for the institutions.[17] One institution can then worry about implementation and the other about continuing operation.

In any case a second conclusion of Munthe *et al.* (1992, p. 92) will also apply more acutely in these circumstances. They point to the irony that despite the fact that everybody is aware that there are cycles in activity and in asset prices there is a tendency to base business decisions on a continuation of current trends. Thus, for example, both public and private sectors increased their rate of construction at a time when it should have been clear that costs were well above their long-run trend and postponing rather than following normal patterns (let alone bringing it forward) would have made sense. In periods of substantial regime change it becomes more difficult to decide whether faster rates of growth are the result of the regime change and will be permanent, or if they are transient and will be offset, or if they are a single step gain in levels. This is particularly true in the United States at present with the discussion over the existence and extent of the 'new economy' (Federal Reserve Bank of San Francisco, 2000). Decisions have to be taken before the answers are known. If they are over-optimistic then there will be a much more acute cycle when the problem is realised.[18]

Thus the supervisor will tend to be more preoccupied at exactly the time that uncertainties are increased and the risks of inappropriate actions rise. Even though New Zealand was well prepared for the results of financial deregulation in the mid-1980s, it is notable that its stock market crash in 1987 exceeded that in the United States. One of the reasons was that private individuals had got drawn into direct participation in the stock market through 'share clubs' and other new investment vehicles. Some of this participation came through loans supported by property so liquidation was necessary when income streams fell, exacerbating the problem. Innovations can lead to new (and hence inexperienced) people being exposed to existing risks as well as existing institutions being exposed to new risks. Both will lead to mistakes.

Since our prime concern in this book is the avoidance of crises not how to resolve them if they do occur, the lessons that concern us from crisis resolution are those that relate to improving the chance of avoiding the crisis in the first place. For example, one of the contributing factors to getting into a crisis state is that early action is not forthcoming. If there is a strong expectation that the state will bail out those in difficulty then there may be less incentive either to avoid the problems or to resolve with private rather than public funds.

If we want some reassurance about the generality of the applicability of the findings from the Nordic crises we need look no further than the conclusion of Lindgren *et al.* (2000) on the Asian crises later in the 1990s:

Financial and corporate weakness combined with macroeconomic vulnerabilities to spark the crisis. Formal and informal currency pegs, which discouraged lenders and borrowers from hedging, also contributed to the outbreak. Capital flows had helped fuel rapid credit expansion, which lowered the quality of credit and led to asset price inflation. The inflated asset prices encouraged further capital inflows and lending ... Highly leveraged corporate sectors ... and large unhedged short-term debt made the crisis countries vulnerable to changes in market sentiment in general and exchange and interest rate changes in particular. Weaknesses in bank and corporate governance and lack of market discipline allowed excessive risk taking as prudential regulations were weak or poorly enforced. Close relationships between governments, financial institutions, and borrowers worsened the problems. More generally, weak accounting standards, especially for loan valuation, and disclosure practices helped hide the growing weakness from policymakers, supervisors, market participants, and international financial institutions – while those indicators of trouble that were available seem to have been largely ignored. (pp. 1, 4)

Not only are similar features observed but the problems are compounded. Clearly these countries, even if they had learned the lessons from the Nordic countries, had not acted upon them.

There is clearly a balance to be drawn in assigning responsibility but Lawson (1992, p. 630) offers some helpful insights in a political reflection on the excess boom in the United Kingdom in the 1980s, which took place roughly at the same time as the Nordic experience but without quite such an unfortunate outcome.

We are left with some key questions: was the government responsible for the banks taking leave of their senses? Were the banks, by contrast, largely responsible for the excesses of the credit binge? The point here is not that the banks should put the public interest above profit. The point is that by acting in the imprudent way they did, they inflicted terrible damage on their own profit-and-loss accounts and balance sheets. The authorities cannot 'fine-tune' bank lending. This is one of the reasons why the economic cycle cannot be avoided. Had I been able to foresee how excessive the lending would become, my only useful weapon ... would have been to raise interest rates sooner and even more sharply than I did ... a financially deregulated economy, while more efficient and dynamic, is also probably less stable, by virtue of an amplified credit cycle ... recognizing this, borrowers need to exercise prudent self discipline and lenders to develop a far more sophisticated risk analysis ... It is clearly not good enough for a bank to look at a potential corporate borrower in isolation. The industry risk also needs to be assessed ... Above all, its vulnerability to changes in economic conditions has to be taken fully into account.

Thus in his view all the parties made mistakes including himself. He is particularly concerned that the forecasting profession as a whole underestimated what was going on in the boom and emphasises the ability that people have to explain away rises in the money supply. However, the main conclusion is that the authorities and the banks share the blame – banks cannot look merely at their own affairs and ignore how changes in the market as a whole might cause problems. They have to realise that they live in a relatively volatile environment; one in which macroeconomic shocks do happen. The problem is to get that message across without the bitter personal experience that a crisis involves.

3 Coming Challenges to Financial Supervision

3.1 THE CHANGING STRUCTURE OF BANKS AND BANKING

During the 1990s the complexion of world banking has changed. At the beginning of the decade Japanese banks dominated the league table of the largest banks (Table 3.1), while as the decade progressed American banks grew rapidly in size. This pattern of relative decline and growth is in part explicable by the differing performance of the two economies. Between 1990 and 1999 US GDP

Table 3.1   Banking league table (ranked by tier 1 capital)

Rank	1990		1998	
	Name	*Country*	*Name*	*Country*
1	Sumitomo	Japan	HSBC	UK
2	Dai-Ichi Kangyo	Japan	Chase Manahattan	US
3	Fuji	Japan	Credit Agricole	France
4	Credit Agricole	France	Citicorp	US
5	Sanwa	Japan	Tokyo-Mitsubishi	Japan
6	Mitsubishi	Japan	Deutsche	Germany
7	Barclays	UK	BankAmerica	US
8	National Westminster	UK	ABN AMRO	Netherlands
9	Deutsche	Germany	Sumitomo	Japan
10	Industrial Bank of Japan	Japan	Dai-Ichi Kangyo	Japan
11	UBS	Switzerland	Fuji	Japan
12	Citicorp	US	Sanwa	Japan
13	Paribas	France	NationsBank	US
14	Tokai	Japan	UBS	Switzerland
15	HongKong	HongKong	Barclays	UK
16	Bank of China	China	Credit Suisse	Switzerland
17	L-Term Credit Bank of Japan	Japan	Sakura	Japan
18	BNP	France	Rabobank	Netherlands
19	SBC	Switzerland	National Westminster	UK
20	Tokyo	Japan	Halifax	UK

Source: *The Banker*, July issues.

grew by 27 per cent in real terms while that of Japan grew by only 12 per cent. The Japanese difficulties impacted particularly strongly on the financial sector, with the decline in asset prices and profitability of major companies resulting in substantial retrenchment, similar to the problems of debt-deflation (King, 1994). Substantial attempts to reflate the economy both through monetary policy with interest rates of virtually zero in nominal terms and through fiscal policy had not had a strong effect by the end of the decade. On the other hand, the recovery in the United States had been aided by regulatory change with the opening of cross-state banking permitting the formation of even larger conglomerates.

Europe has not been without its own pressures and the creation of the euro area in 1999 has assisted a further surge in amalgamations (Table 3.2). On the whole these amalgamations have been within existing national boundaries, although there are some well-known cross-border deals – Merita–Noordbanken–Christiana–Unibank, for example, linking major banks in Finland, Sweden, Norway and Denmark. Koskenkylä (2000) lists over 30 major restructurings in the Nordic countries alone in the second half of the 1990s and about 100 for the 1990s as a whole.[1]

The combination of these forces means that the authorities have been prepared to accept considerable concentration within the European countries, while banks and their shareholders have exercised considerable caution with respect to international deals. The amalgamations, particularly in the United States, have involved the acquisition of a lot of the smaller banks (Berger *et al.*, 1998). The introduction of the euro may help reduce the barriers that would lead European banks to look rather more like their US counterparts and, as domestic opportunities for acquisition are used up, this may be the only way forward.

However, the US banking sector has strikingly different characteristics from its European counterpart. Not only has the process of consolidation been rather more dramatic, with the number of banks being virtually halved over the last twenty years, but entry and exit have also been vigorous, with aggregate new entrants amounting to over 40 per cent of the current number of banks and bankruptcies around 20 per cent. This more dynamic structure affects and is affected by the attitudes of the supervisory authorities, shareholders and depositors. The threat of bank failure is more real in the United States. There is therefore some difficulty in putting forward recommendations for banking supervision that will be equally appropriate in the two regions or indeed equally acceptable to the decision-making authorities and the banks themselves. History has an important effect in shaping people's attitudes.

The nature of the changes stretches rather more widely as financial institutions run across sectors, with links between banks and insurance companies and with banks themselves becoming more universal in character. The trend is not entirely in one direction as some banks have sought to reduce the range of their

Table 3.2 Major acquisitions and mergers in Western Europe

Date	Banks involved	Countries
National		
1996	Credit Agricole/Banque Indosuez	France
1997	UBS/SBC	Switzerland
1998	Cariplo/Ambrosiano Veneto (Banca Intesa)	Italy
	Kredietbank/CERA	Belgium
	Bayerische Vereinsbank/Bayerische Hypothekenbank	Germany
	Credito Italiano/Unicredito	Italy
	Istituto Bancario San Paolo di Torino/Istituto Mobilare Italiano	Italy
	Banco Exterior de Espana/Banco Hipoteco/Caja Postal/Coporacion Bancaria de Espana (Argentaria)	Spain
1999	Banco Santander/Banco Hispanoamericano	Spain
	BACOB/Artesia Bank	Belgium
	Generale de Banque/ASLKCGER	Belgium
	BNP/Paribas	France
	Kapital Holding/FIH	Denmark
	Banca Intesa/Comit	Italy
	Den Norske Bank/Postbanken	Norway
2000	Royal Bank of Scotland/ National Westminster	UK
Crossborder		
	Merita/Nordbanken	Finland/Sweden
	Fortis/Generale de Bank	Netherlands/ Belgium
	Credit Locale de France/Credit Communale de Belgique (Dexia)	France/Belgium
	Den Danske Bank/Fokus Bank	Denmark/Norway
	ING/Banque Bruxelles Lambert	Netherlands/ Belgium
	Dexia/Banco de Credito Local	France/Belgium/ Spain
	ING/BHF Bank	Netherlands/ Germany
	MeritaNordbanken/Unibank	Finland/Sweden/ Denmark
	Deutsche Bank/Bankers Trust	Germany/US

Notes: Names in parentheses are those of the resulting entities.
Some major mergers predate this list, e.g. HSBC/Midland and TSB/Lloyds in the UK and ABN/AMRO in the Netherlands

activities, particularly in the face of difficulty, as in the case of Barclays and National Westminster in the United Kingdom.[2]

3.2   INCREASING SCALE, INTERNATIONALISATION AND CONGLOMERATION

The forces for fragmentation across national borders in Europe in the past have been considerable, in many cases more than geographical proximity would suggest. Colonial linkages have shown that multinational operations, even at the retail level, can be undertaken across major geographical divides. However, as the integration of the European market for financial services has increased so analysts have expected a consolidation of banks and other financial institutions both within the borders of the states of the EEA and across those borders. In the main the responses have in fact been limited, so it is realistic to question whether anything is going to be particularly different this time round. We have already seen a wave of consolidation within domestic banking industries, which has significantly increased banking concentration, particularly in smaller European countries (such as Austria, Belgium, Denmark, Finland, the Netherlands, Norway and Sweden). However, crossborder mergers or acquisitions between large universal banks still seem to be the exception rather than the rule, though things have started to change. Among the EU countries, it is probably only in the case of Belgium that there is now significant foreign ownership of the banking system. Further consolidation in Europe would largely have to involve an international dimension in countries where further reduction in the number of major banks would be questioned by the competition authorities.

However, it is somewhat surprising how great a concentration has been permitted. We had already thought (Mayes and Vesala, 1998) that the limits were being reached in mid-1998 before some of the largest recent mergers were announced. For example, in the Nordic countries three large banks control 70–80 per cent of bank assets (Koskenkylä, 2000). National authorities seem to have been prepared to see concentration as a means of increasing the security of the domestic banking system. Moreover, it is clear from the remarks of a number of national authorities (the Irish Republic, for example) that foreign ownership per se has been viewed with considerable apprehension. A further example is the blocking of the bid by Banco Santander Central Hispanoamericano of Spain to acquire Group Mundial Confianca of Portugal by the Portuguese Finance Minister in June 1999. The Commission of the EU challenged this move in July as running against the principles of EU competition law. It has also been instructive to observe the attitude of the French authorities, first in bailing out Credit Lyonnais and second in the contest for control over Paribas and Société General.

The creation of strong national institutions rather than European or international ones appeared the objective (see Graham, 2000, for example).[3]

There are other factors likely to encourage international consolidation in the years to come. Firstly, crossborder deals may be struck to achieve 'critical mass' for euro-denominated wholesale markets, which seem to exhibit significant economies of scale. Banks will need to process not just national financial market information but euro area-wide information. Secondly, the introduction of the euro will lower the barriers to entry into national banking markets yet further. In Stage Three foreign entrants no longer will need to use local currencies. They can fund their lending in euro from their domestic retail deposit base or from European money and capital markets. It will become easier and cheaper to conduct foreign businesses. Cross-border mergers or acquisitions would be the fastest way to acquire local expertise and customers. Although transnational operations are also traditionally a means of diversifying risk, the power of this incentive will probably fall as the EU economies become more integrated.

Since econometric studies have not typically found significant evidence of overall economies of scale in banking (at the company level), some have argued that national consolidation has occurred because of banks' desire to strengthen market position and monopoly power. Molyneux *et al.* (1997) provides a substantial survey of the results from research on European banks. However, the recent comprehensive European study, by Vennet (1996), concludes that in cases of large-scale domestic mergers of equal partners the major source of performance improvement has been through the reduction of costs, by elimination of duplication and exploitation of synergies (efficiency improvement) and also to some extent through economies of scale (and scope). Calomiris and Karceski (1998) provide strong methodological criticisms of estimates of the gains from mergers that are based on econometric cost/profit functions or on stock market data, primarily because the time horizon is too short. They present case-study evidence from the United States that mergers have increased efficiency and produced customer benefits. Bikker (1999) also suggests that there does seem to be scope for cost reduction from increasing scale in Europe

These changes have improved the competitive viability of the banks involved. The efficiency improvement motive for merger might continue to prevail but continuing improvements in information technology and the move to the euro may well increase the importance of the overall scale economies, not just in wholesale activities. Studies using more recent data tend to point to larger scale economies than before. Berger and Mester (1997) attribute this to technological change. IT development increases scale economies, because it increases the share of fixed and investment costs and reduces that of variable per transaction costs in the overall banking costs. The traditional results may underestimate the scale economies, as they do not often include the more up to date data nor the full consequences of recent IT developments and substitution of automation for labour in banking.

Up till now retail banking has remained largely in the hands of national banking organisations perhaps in part because legal and cultural factors and differences in payment systems constitute barriers to entry. Different conduct of business standards applicable in each domestic market also tend to encourage separation. Since the savings in direct costs from eliminating overlaps in the retail network (potential efficiency improvement) are likely to be limited and the managerial costs involved substantial, even with a single currency, the likelihood of cross-border mergers and acquisitions that are motivated by the access to local retail markets may still be low. At least this may be true in the short term, as the effects of the euro on retail markets is likely to be slower than on their wholesale counterparts.

Where cross-border mergers have taken place, the national operations have often remained separate (as in the Merita–Nordbanken case – what Matthews and Mayes (1993) describe as the 'multidomestic' as opposed to the multinational approach to organisational growth'. In Europe, corporate law seems to have supported this kind of structure, since merging two banks across borders would require the termination of one or both components and consolidation of assets, which would not be an attractive proposition to strong banks. There are prospects for the creation of an 'European corporation' through a Community Regulation that could abolish this problem and probably boost cross-border consolidation significantly. Moreover, the likely result of mergers and acquisitions could then be fully integrated banking firms (including retail banking) that operate through branches in different countries, since branching seems to be more cost-efficient than establishing or maintaining subsidiaries in the Single Market. In this case the supervisory concerns we highlight in this paper would be greatest.

3.3 THE STIMULUS FROM TECHNICAL CHANGE

Technological change, particularly in the case of information technology, has helped facilitate both competition and the ability to reap economies of scale from amalgamation. In the United Kingdom supermarkets such as Tesco and Sainsburys have set up banks, as has Virgin, the airline, rail, musical and other services conglomerate. By the 1980s (Berger *et al.*, 1998; Calomiris and Karceski, 1998; Rhoades, 1998) the bulk of econometric opinion was that the opportunity for economies of scale could be exhausted in banking. Incompatibility of computer systems and other forms of working meant that merged organisations either had to operate as largely separate entities or undertake major expenditures that offset the gains. As the pace of IT innovation has continued to grow, such expenditures and major changes become commonplace within the evolution of companies and hence make those required by acquisition less unusual. At the same time the pace of change has altered the way in which skills are acquired. Rewriting job specifications and retraining are becoming a normal facet of personnel development. Organisations have effective systems for such retraining.

IT also makes the location of the provider of services compared to the user much less relevant. Face-to-face contact is usually not necessary and transactions can be undertaken by telephone or over the Internet. Of course, a large proportion of trading on financial markets has taken place by these means for some time and the existence of physical markets making deals by 'open outcry' is largely a thing of the past. Since very large sums are transacted in this manner it has been necessary to develop a comprehensive system of verification and recording in order to ensure that the chance of making mistakes or misunderstanding is minimised. The development of these systems not only means that the established providers of banking and other financial services can use these methods but that other companies, which lack a local presence can also come into the market, particularly through 'e-commerce'. In many cases they are related to existing financial institutions, as is normally the case with telephone insurance, but other internet providers can also access such systems.[4] Service providers, including banks, can readily add on other services. Once banks become more remote from their customers this may reduce customer loyalty and lead to greater volatility between banks (and other financial intermediaries) in the future (Koskenkylä, 2000).

As these changes have been implemented we would expect to have seen margins fall. Indeed, the prior existence of high margins will have been one of the factors encouraging acquisitions to capture them and mergers to protect them. However, the evidence (Danthine *et al.*, 1999; Koskenkylä, 2000) is rather more mixed and margins have only fallen in some countries. To some extent this may have been the result of simultaneous improvements in efficiency.

Most analysts see more changes in the offing, particularly in Europe. One of the simplest lines of argument is to look at the more open US market and ask which of its characteristics will be transposed into the European market. One such possible trend would be a continuation of the move away from bank loans towards securitisation and the direct issuance of bonds and shares by the corporate sector as euro markets deepen. Such a move would be complemented by an increasing drive towards the accumulation of private financial assets both as real standards of living improve and as the public sector finds that the rapid growth of the elderly as a proportion of the population makes a 'pay-as-you-go' pension system more difficult to finance. The current preoccupation with holding down public sector debt levels, aided by the Stability and Growth Pact, the Broad

Economic Policy Guidelines and the popularity of privatisation as a means of increasing returns for the taxpayer, will advance these moves towards a more US-style structure for the banking system. However, the general expectation (see Davis (1998) and Danthine *et al.* (1999) for example) is that there will only be a partial convergence of the two systems over the next couple of decades.

Danthine *et al.* point out that the convergence in the various sectors of financial markets is likely to be different. In investment banking and asset management, for example, there is likely to be rather greater convergence and a move towards a genuinely global market with only the major institutions being able to offer experts in every sector of each market. In any case restructuring in the financial sector is not just within segments but across segments – with alliances between banks and securities companies, insurance companies, and so on.

There is naturally much uncertainty surrounding future banking structures, since only time will show how banks respond strategically. One of the strongest possibilities is that multinational banks or financial conglomerates will acquire important positions in the smaller European markets. Banks that are large by local standards and have a strong niche in their national-currency-denominated markets, but which are small by European standards, could be badly placed to cope with changes brought about by the introduction of the euro and be forced to adjust. The recent Merita–Nordbanken merger of the largest Finnish bank with the third largest Swedish bank and the subsequent expansion of the group to Denmark and Norway is an obvious example of the sort of response that can take place.

3.4   THE IMPLICATIONS FOR THE SUPERVISOR

All these changes pose problems for the supervisor. Indeed the more speculative or less identifiable the trends the more difficult it is for the supervisor to anticipate them adequately. The more complicated financial institutions become the more difficult they are to monitor. The faster the pace of innovation in financial products the more difficult it becomes for supervisors to keep up and to understand how these new products should best be regulated. These all pose the potential for new risks. Commonly the greatest threats come when institutions enter new markets and do not have adequate risk management procedures in place to govern them (as exemplified in the previous chapter with the impact of financial liberalisation on the Nordic countries). Increased competition may add to the incentive to take greater risks. Danthine *et al.* (1999) makes the nice point that if the promise of gains to shareholders from acquisitions proves as illusory in the banking sector as it has in acquisition booms in other sectors, banks may feel obliged to increase the riskiness of their activities in an attempt to provide the higher returns by another route. Boot *et al.* (1998) suggests that managers' incentives to engage in consolidation can be related to either building managers' own reputation, which would be a cause for concern to supervisors, or obtaining skills and other possibilities for competing efficiently in future market conditions, which tend to be viewed favourably. They show that managers' incentives to conduct 'skills-enhancing' deals are greatest when competition in banks' present activities is moderate, but keen future competition is expected. On these grounds growth in mergers and acquisitions in European banking can be expected with the introduction of the euro.

The sheer size of banks poses a number of problems, not just that of difficulty of monitoring because of complexity. Although this latter is exacerbated when banks are truly international and conduct transactions under a variety of jurisdictions. This raises particularly difficult issues for the authorities in the EEA which we detail below, because of the structure of regulation that has been set up by the EU to aid the 'completion' of the internal market in financial services. There are thus twin problems of co-ordinating multiple regulators. Not only may different parts of the financial sector be governed by different regulators within any given national boundary but the activities of a financial institution in a single part of the industry may be covered by different national regulators. International agreements on who should take the lead in co-ordination may help but it is clear from the latest proposals from the Basel Committee that the regulators themselves feel that these are currently inadequate.

While mega-regulators within national jurisdictions, such as the Financial Services Authority in the UK, may be a step towards trying to control the problem of conglomerates within a single jurisdiction, this does not at present seem to be a plausible route at the international level, even within Europe, where the framework for international co-operation is highly developed. In some respects the expansion of large banks into other countries may ease problems of supervision. For example, the expansion of Nordic banks into the Baltic states may ease the problems for the Baltic supervisors as not only does it increase the capital base of their banks dramatically, but it also means that other supervisors from the home countries are also actively involved in the supervision.

A second consequence of size is the implications of failure or distress for the financial system as a whole. On the one hand increasing size is a reassuring move from the point of view of regulators. Larger organisations acting in more markets and products have a greater ability to diversify risk. Risks in any single part of the business that would be large enough to bring down a smaller organisation, as in the case of Barings, for example, can be covered by other parts of the bank's operations. Moreover larger organisations stand a much better chance of developing the skills and expertise necessary to manage risk in an evolving and forward-looking manner. These factors therefore should reduce the chance of overall distress or failure. Set against that is the moral hazard that stems from the knowledge that the bank is 'too big to fail' and will not be allowed to go under by the authorities. This might encourage banks to take greater risks.

The changing structure of the banking system itself may lead to higher risks. If banks become more universal in character they will increase the amount of trading they do on their own account and will become more active in capital markets. This in itself will tend to increase their fragility. Although they will have to hold greater capital to support these activities, such active trading could greatly increase the vulnerability of banks to swings in asset prices.

3.5   WAYS FORWARD

The Basel Committee's latest proposals seek to cover an ever-increasing range of risks, but it appears necessary to tackle the problem from a number of directions if coverage is to improve. The primary aim should be to ensure that banks are well informed about the risks they face and have good management systems in place and in effective use to control those risks. Supervisors can play two roles in this regard. The first is simply to see that banks and all those involved with them are well informed about the risks that are faced by banks individually and by financial markets as a whole. An example of this is the six-monthly Financial Stability Report produced by the Swedish Riskbank, that not only provides a summary of the market as a whole and the banks within it but also provides detailed explanations of specific areas of risk on each occasion. One of the difficulties facing any individual bank is that their actions may appear prudent on their own but are in fact much more risky if all other banks in the market are similarly exposed at the same time. The second is to monitor the individual banks closely to ensure that they have and are using appropriate risk management systems. This last 'supervisory review' is one of the three pillars in the Basel Committee's recommendations.

The primary pillar of the Basel Committee's approach, however, is to try to insist on some minimum insurance against risk in the form of capital adequacy standards. Supervisors would be responsible for monitoring and enforcing compliance with these minima. The new proposals go a long way towards reducing the rather arbitrary nature of the original Basel Accord and to eliminating some of the anomalies that currently exist. However, more are created, such as the ranking of low-rated bonds below unrated bonds. While the final agreement will no doubt remove such problems it cannot hope to be complete nor to cover the full range of individual requirements of complex individual banks.

While there would be general consent over the third action that supervisory authorities can take through closer co-ordination and where appropriate the formation of higher-level co-ordinating bodies, our prime emphasis in this book is on a fourth mechanism – namely, public disclosure and greater market discipline. Authorities will themselves find it easier to monitor complex organisations if information is publicly available from other jurisdictions and the task of the public authorities will be assisted if the market itself imposes discipline through reacting to the disclosed information. However, as we go on to explain in later chapters the greatest discipline comes not from the actions of the market but from bank managements' apprehension of what adverse market reaction will imply for their share values, profits, salaries and indeed jobs.

One should take a wide view of the role of supervisors in safeguarding systemic stability. Although there is a tendency to separate out banking supervision from the traditional role of the central bank in providing adequate liquidity for the banking system this second role cannot be ignored. In the academic literature there is a tendency to use the term 'lender of last resort' in two different contexts. In the traditional context it takes the form of providing collateralised lending when big shortrun valuation swings in asset prices place banks under pressure to meet their immediate obligations. If they had to realise their long-term liabilities in these circumstances they could only do so at substantial loss. Since the system as whole is likely to be under pressure it is very difficult for some banks to obtain the necessary liquidity from the others. With a rise in active trading and an increasingly cross-border structure for banks in Europe it has been argued (Danthine *et al.*, 1998, for example) that the European central banks may individually have difficulty handling the problem. As part of the working rules for the operation of the ESCB the system has agreed a list of collateral that will be acceptable for lending. National central banks have traditionally given themselves rather more leeway. The ECB (Padoa-Schioppa, 1999) has been rather sceptical about the existence of any such deficiency. Indeed there is no reason to expect that the ECB could also not act swiftly in the event of a crisis of this form.

However, the second meaning of lender of last resort tends to confuse it with the bailing out of insolvent banks. This is a role which authorities are extremely reluctant to discuss in advance, not just because of the moral hazard involved in making any statement that might look like a promise, but because they normally do not want to be in the circumstances to have to exercise it. Because of the divide between monetary policy and government's responsibility to taxpayers it is unlikely that the ECB would acquire a role in this area of supervisory intervention. Although in a national jurisdiction this area of crisis resolution would be a related part of the overall system, in the EU set up the divide will inevitably be greater. This provides a problem for effective running of the system, which is an issue we return to in Chapter 10. However, it does point to five really rather separate issues in international co-ordination that are particularly pertinent in the case of Europe:

- the development of common rules or standards for registration as a bank;
- the development of common rules for the prudential management of banks;
- an effective system of co-ordinated monitoring to ensure compliance with the rules and the early detection of systemic problems and difficulties for individual banks;
- an effective means of providing liquidity in the role of lender of last resort;
- an effective means of resolving crises.

The European Union has from an early stage focused on the first of these issues, assisted by progress in the Basel Committee. The European Commission is heavily slanted towards the development of new rules and the stream of banking and financial services directives have sought to address these problems. While there are common rules for prudential management, this is an area where the member states have followed rather different routes and have different requirements, subject to minimum standards of capital adequacy and EU rules. Co-ordinated monitoring is less well developed and is the subject of much of the rest of the present chapter. The Eurosystem is alert to the problem of providing adequate liquidity. Unfortunately it will only be possible to judge if the mechanism in place will be adequate when a crisis occurs but the experience from the 1987 stock market collapse suggests that the lessons from earlier periods, particularly the 1929 Great Crash and the subsequent depression in the United States, have been learnt. It is argued (Friedman and Schwartz, 1963) that the severity of the depression was in part due to the failure of the Federal Reserve to provide adequate liquidity. Crisis resolution, when the problem is one of insolvency, is a different matter and this remains an area where there are many loose ends in Europe (and indeed elsewhere) as is addressed in Chapter 8 and initially in the present chapter.

3.6   A PARTICULAR EUROPEAN PROBLEM

There are some specific problems for the supervision of banks arising from the development of European integration. Normally national supervisors seek to regulate all banking activity taking place within their borders and banking activity undertaken by banks headquartered in their country. This can sometimes result in double regulation of subsidiaries and branches abroad or in some cross-border or offshore activities largely escaping regulation. However, in the case of the EEA there is a deliberate pooling of responsibility in order to try to reduce the effective height of national barriers to 'trade' in financial services. This sort of arrangement is not unique to Europe. Financial services between Australia and New Zealand, for example, are regulated by the country of origin if they are provided direct from one country to the other without the need for local branches – something that can be quite common in the case of stocks and shares. However, the treatment of foreign branches is different.

In the case of the EEA it is the responsibility of the 'home' country (the country in which the bank is registered for operation within the EEA) to supervise the activities of its banks, wherever they are operating via branches or remote supply across borders within the European Economic Area. We concern ourselves here only with issues of prudential supervision. Consumer protection and other aspects of regulation lie beyond the scope of this book (see Chapter 4 for discussion of the framework of regulation of the financial sector). It is the responsibility of the host country (the country where the transactions are taking place) to deal with the stability of its financial system and problems stemming from failure or distress. In this section, we address problems related to conduct and co-ordination of these two responsibilities.

The introduction of the euro may increase the incentive for cross-border merger and the supply of services across borders to the point where smaller countries, in particular, find that significant parts of the banking activities for their residents are no longer directly supervised by their own authorities. In these circumstances the responsibility of home authorities in conducting efficient consolidated supervision would increase considerably. Moreover, host supervisors could find that they have insufficient information either to monitor the health of the financial system to anticipate a crisis as well as they might or to be able to react to it as rapidly and effectively as they might. Until now the extent of this problem has been limited as the large majority of the banking systems are domestically controlled.

Establishing a single branch or a small number of branches in foreign countries could also be sufficient to attract customers when they are served through modern techniques, like phone- and PC-banking (also called 'direct' banking). There are also prospects for increased supply from outside the country, without establishment at all, using direct banking methods. The euro could constitute a significant catalyst for such investment, as the effective market size expands. Given the geographic structure of Europe such foreign suppliers can often be nearer than the major financial centres within the country. Direct cross-border banking from other countries, like the development of direct insurance and some other financial services, will be progressive and could develop rapidly. The Internet (e-mail) adds to the opportunities available over the telephone. To some extent, remote supply could be an alternative to cross-border mergers and acquisitions.

Although there will no doubt continue to be roles for banks of all sizes and ranges of facilities to play, the creation of any cross-border entity that controls a substantial proportion of a host country market, yet is supervised by a different home country, provides a challenge that must be addressed. Such an outcome is by no means impossible. All the significant banks in New Zealand are foreign-owned and substantial changes have been occurring in Belgium and other smaller EEA states. While it remains to be seen whether the introduction of the euro is the key change that triggers the creation of many such institutions, supervisors need to be alert to the prospect.

The potential internationalisation of banking, which could take place as the introduction of the euro breaks down the barriers in European financial markets still further, could pose problems for the efficient working of the present European supervisory system. The difficulty is likely to be greatest for small countries who continue to have responsibility for systemic risk but have less and less ability to manage that risk. They are likely to become less well informed (both about individual banks and the market as a whole), to be less able to take pre-emptive action and to have fewer means of resolving a crisis. Strengthening co-ordination between home and host supervisors so as to overcome these problems and supporting the host country's contribution to the overall supervisory process would be required. Home country supervisors will find their task more difficult to execute the more foreign operations they have to cover and will lack the more intimate knowledge of those markets possessed by the host supervisor.

In considering the consequences of the development of the euro area, there is a danger of focusing too directly on the banks themselves. The whole range of financial markets is changing. Short-term money markets have converged considerably, while bond markets are also moving towards the US pattern, particularly those focusing on government bonds. Equity markets have been integrating rapidly with a rapid reduction in the number of exchanges and a proliferation of alliances (Malkamäki and Topi, 1999). Derivatives markets are already more concentrated and Eurex exceeds the size of its US counterparts. Payments and settlement systems are also restructuring with the introduction of TARGET and the consolidation on Euroclear and Cedel. All of these changes in the financial infrastructure and those that are to come affect the environment that banks operate in, the risks and the task of supervision. In some respects consolidation both eases supervision and reduces the risk, insofar as supervision is concentrated in a smaller number of lead countries and the larger organisations have the resources to cover a wider range of risks. Size, of course, poses more of a problem when something goes wrong.

3.6.1 Possible Responses

There are three obvious ways in which the existing authorities could respond within the confines of the principle of home country control:

- greater co-operation and exchange of information among supervisors;
- strengthening the role of host supervisors;
- public disclosure of information.

This presumes, of course, that the current national structure of supervision is the way to progress. A more fundamental change that we consider in Chapter 10 is to introduce new regional or European-level authorities.

However, if we keep the focus on what can be done within the existing arrangements for the moment, implementing the first response in our list would entail encouraging the exchange of information and co-operation among supervisors further in a way that makes the best use of the 'comparative advantages' of the authorities involved. It is the efficient exchange of information that is the main purpose of the Memoranda of Understanding (MoU) that have already been signed bilaterally between many supervisory authorities. Within the EEA, bilateral agreements between national supervisory authorities MoUs concerning the exchange of information and the organisational aspects of co-operation have emerged after the implementation of the home country principle (Second Banking Co-ordination Directive). Such MoUs exist between all of the main supervisors who have concerns in each other's markets. They facilitate both formal meetings and informal interchanges. On current evidence, MoUs seem likely to be the main tool of bilateral co-operation in the future. Experience seems to suggest that they are effective in communicating information about institutions that are facing difficulties but less effective in providing a broad swathe of information where no stress has as yet been detected. There are also multilateral arrangements to discuss issues of mutual interest such as the Banking Supervisory Committee in the ESCB.

There are potentially difficult incentive issues, especially related to co-ordination in a crisis, that need to be resolved if this mechanism is to be efficient. Secondly, one might consider strengthening the role of the host authorities while, nevertheless, maintaining the principle of home country control and thus allowing cross-border activity to develop without unnecessary bureaucratic barriers. The host's contribution is especially valuable in assessing whether banks' problems are systemic (industrywide) or idiosyncratic, which is a key consideration when choosing the appropriate supervisory action. However, a third suggestion, which we espouse, is that the appropriate response should, in any case, seek to strengthen market discipline. Wider public disclosure by banks, so that all those potentially affected by banks' cross-border activities, be they supervisors, customers, creditors or taxpayers, can be informed of the risks they face, would both encourage prudent behaviour in general and alleviate the specific concerns over home country control identified here.

Thoroughgoing cooperation among supervisors would ease the problem of information but this may not be adequate. A more substantial prospect for improvement would be offered if banks' disclosure requirements were expanded and, especially, if credible penalties were installed to ensure prompt and correct disclosure. In this way not only will all supervisors gain access to information relating to their own and other markets promptly, but the market itself will exert discipline over the multinational banks. Such a move towards a disclosure regime is warranted in any case, as it will tend to encourage prudential behaviour in a world of increasing complexity and speed of transactions. It would also tend to be of net benefit to all stakeholders in the banks, especially the taxpayer, given that the chance of a bailout is reduced.

However, disclosure is not a panacea. Host countries will still lack power to act early and to prevent spillover losses in the event of a crisis. While in this area co-operative arrangements among supervisors are least problematic in less urgent cases, the need to act promptly and decisively as well as the existence of potential conflicts of interest would seem to argue for a wider role for a European-level body that could help to ensure efficient co-ordination in crisis resolution. The informational requirements of such co-ordination would naturally be quite substantial. If domestic banking systems become substantially foreign owned, the question of ensuring efficient crisis management becomes acute.

4 Principles of Good Financial Supervision

The fundamental premise of this chapter is that the legal and supervisory framework of the financial industry matters as a precondition for stability. An effective and workable regulatory and supervisory regime is forward-looking and anticipatory, so that those responsible for financial system stability ensure that the regime is adapted to forthcoming, or at least current, changes in the surrounding economy and can react flexibly. These aspects have often been given too little weight – if not forgotten entirely – during the regime shifts that preceded banking crises in many countries. As Llewellyn (1999) points out, when planning regime shifts, the authorities need to ensure that they have a supervisory system in place that can cope with the inevitable mistakes that financial institutions will make as they learn how to operate in the new regime.[1] The framework required for the transition is likely to be different both from that required for the old regime and from that for the new.

An analysis of how the financial infrastructure may have contributed to banking crises is complicated and politically unattractive to domestic policy makers. It is always easier to discuss somebody else's problems rather than one's own. It is certainly difficult to discuss the problems when they are emerging for fear of making them worse and causing just the crisis that one hopes to avoid. However, while the state of a country's financial infrastructure may not be the trigger for a banking crisis it is clear from past experience that it may affect the scope, depth and length of a crisis.

But what constitutes an effective regulatory and supervisory framework? Increasingly, global integration and the development of financial markets have put pressure on supervisors to focus their attention on the role of incentives alongside rules, as supervisory authorities struggle to keep up with the financial world they are supposed to safeguard. It is today quite widely accepted that the regulatory and supervisory framework should be based on incentives that make financial institutions, other market participants and supervisors act in a way that supports both the stability of the financial system as a whole and the efficiency of the financial sector.[2] However, there are different views on the practical features of such a framework.

Our aim is to highlight possible features of an incentive-based legal, regulatory and supervisory framework that would minimise incentives for excessive risk-taking in the business of banking and compensate for moral hazard generated by the existence of safety nets.[3] Much of the discussion referred to is based on developed countries, in particular Scandinavian countries, New Zealand and to some degree the United Kingdom. A helpful run down on where the literature has got to can be found in Bhattacharya *et al.* (1998).

We begin by explaining very briefly the theoretical background for incetive-based regulation, showing the link between the assumption of rationality in an individual's behaviour and legal rules. Section 4.2 highlights key elements of an incetive-based approach for a legal, regulatory and supervisory framework. We go on in Section 4.3 to paint the broader picture of what oversight of the financial system involves for the public authorities before considering how supervision and monitoring can be developed in Sections 4.4 and 4.5.

4.1 BACKGROUND

In giving recommendations for the most effective legislation we go beyond the positive analysis of economic effects of individual measures and take a view in favour or against various legal rules. Economics provides assumptions for the legal structure supporting the functioning of ideal markets. These are the assumptions of 'natural law'.[4] Natural law assumes that legal rules are defined in a hypothetical situation in which no one knows which individual will be subject to which legal rule. This ensures that legislation is just, meets the principles of freedom, equality and rationality, is acceptable to all members of a society and is in harmony with the interests of individuals and society. The natural rights of a free and equal society, and reflected by legislation, are stability of possession, its transference by consent and the performance of promises (see Hayek, 1982). They are also key assumptions of economics when it comes to basic institutions of the market economy and the assumptions form the fundamental basis for values of modern private law. 'The essential content of all contemporary systems of private law are freedom of contract, the inviolability of property and the duty to compensate another for the damage due to his fault' (Hayek, 1982).

Economics also provides suggestions on how those subject to regulation actually behave and what the incentive impact of legal rules is on their behaviour. The drafting of legal rules should take into account that individuals behave rationally – that is, in their self-interest. Under perfect market conditions this kind of behaviour leads to efficient outcomes (Pareto-optimality) which are in harmony with the objects of a society. In addition, this behaviour is also acceptable from an ethical point of view, but only under assumptions of ideal markets. This view can be linked to natural law and the concept of a social contract, which has been dealt with in depth by various contractarian schools of thought (moral, social and constitutional contractarians) (Boucher and Kelly, 1994).

However, the real world is not ideal. One of the most analysed deficiencies is the lack of perfect information and the issue of how this affects the actions and outcomes of rationally behaving agents – developed by economists as 'principal–agent' theory.[5] The assumption of rationality prevails even in the real world with information problems, but rationality now leads to outcomes that can be detrimental to financial stability. The key issue is how to build the regulatory and supervisory framework so that it allows markets to become as efficient as possible and – because conditions of ideal markets cannot be achieved – how to correct distortions caused by non-ideal conditions, such as asymmetric information and moral hazard.

The answer stems from the idea of legal rules as incentives for bringing about desired behaviour.[6] However, the problem is that an individual may not automatically obey the rules, particularly if they are not in line with his self-interest and failure to comply elicits only a minor sanction. This gives rise to an obvious tension between an obligation to obey legitimate rules and rationality-based behaviour (agent as law-taker). It is also possible that the agent – for example banks – will attempt to direct the course of legal amendments (agent as lawmaker). In the latter case, if a legislator does not act 'behind the veil of ignorance', i.e. he does not treat all parties on an equal basis, there is a danger that particular parts of the legislation may be amended in a way that is contradictory to the objectives of the entire piece of legislation.

For the legislator, this means that in drafting laws he must take into account the rational behaviour of individuals. It also means that in a 'proper' legal framework the pursuit of self-interest can be consistent with the interests of society, or public good. In other words, the idea of complete contracts should be transferred to legal rules so that the agents are responsible for their actions, receive the benefits of them and take part in risk-sharing. This gives us rules that are based on a clear and explicit division of responsibilities, but also explicit and exercisable rules on sanctions. This is how to maximise the agent's commitment to compliance with the rules, and minimise the distorting effects of asymmetric information and moral hazard. This is the basis of legal rules as incentives.

However, not all economists – let alone lawyers – share the above view on legal rules as incentives. Some argue that the concept of rationality aimed at the maximisation of self-interest of an agent is about the rationality of greed and suggest that in order to limit the pursuit of self-interest, agents must take into account moral and ethical principles. Thus, for example, incentives together with ethics form a sound basis for financial market stability (see Buchanan and Tullock (1965) and Friedman (1953)). There is, however, a danger here of confusing description and prescription (Friedman, 1953).

The link between ethics (the approach of equality, justice and fairness) and financial market legislation can also be viewed from the perspective of depositor protection (consumer protection) and financial stability. These two aspects form the basic rationale for the whole of banking legislation. Thus it is also the responsibility of the banks themselves, when pursuing their self-interest, to take into account the interests of other stakeholders and the stability of financial markets as a whole, not just the interests of the shareholders. Or, as the EU Council has noted, well-functioning financial markets must strike a balance between the interests of market players, consumer protection and the need to maintain a reliable regulatory framework that has the capacity to ensure the stability of financial markets while adapting to new developments.[7]

The theory does not tell us much about how to implement an institutional, legal or supervisory framework. Nor does it tell us much about the actual behaviour of particular agents because it is too general to model individual preferences. Rather it just gives a general prediction of the behaviour of agents, taking into account the intrinsic rationality and self-interest assumption in various principal–agent relations (Friedman, 1953).

What we can take from the basis of the theory is that, when structuring the legal and supervisory framework, we have to mimic complete contracts in rule setting, and mimic ideal market conditions by exploiting market discipline. Rules and incentives need not be seen as separate and distinct tools, which is the point of view quite often taken in economic or regulatory literature. Rules should also be based on incentives. Even so, the more market discipline there is in practice, the more we can count on an endogenous (self-imposed) governance system.[8] However, until perfect market conditions can be achieved with a self-imposed governance system – as the proponents of the free banking school have suggested – we need ex ante and externally prescribed rules by the legislator, regulator or supervisor. And we need an enforcement system for both legally binding and self-imposed rules.

4.2   KEY ELEMENTS OF AN INCENTIVE-BASED LEGAL, REGULATORY AND SUPERVISORY FRAMEWORK

The lawmaking process should be such that it leads to a sensible and well-reasoned division of responsibilities and to sound rules on disclosure of information and competition. Furthermore, the contents of legislation should not be affected by the interests of the parties subject to regulation, unless this can be justified on stability grounds. Similarly, considerations relating to the interests of banks should not influence supervision or the decisions of regulators, if they are not compatible with the stability of the financial system as a whole.

As was explained in the previous section the fact that the requirement of perfect information cannot be satisfied in the real world is one of the biggest drawbacks that the authorities have faced in banking regulation. Lenders can never be very clear about how likely borrowers are to repay. Not only is there an incentive for borrowers to cover up the full extent of potential difficulties but assessing the viability of projects is inherently uncertain and inaccurate. However, given this inherent opacity, bank management is always better aware of the bank's financial situation than the supervisor, shareholders, depositors or creditors. It is the 'mission' of the legislator to correct distortions caused by such asymmetric information. Rather than simply introducing some offsetting mechanism the most appropriate response is to try to reduce the distortion itself by improving the flow of information, in so far as this is possible. That is the first emphasis in this book but since this endeavour can only be partially successful, however well implemented, we go on to discuss offsetting the consequences.

When emphasising the importance of transparency in the business of banking, we normally consider the rules concerning disclosure of information on the financial status and risk exposures of the bank. From the supervisor's point of view transparency and disclosure requirements mean, above all, the minimisation of private information. Transparency may also be improved by disclosing supervisory decisions and actions – positive and negative (see section 5.4).[9]

In the following we identify the essential features of a regulatory framework that would underpin the stability of the financial system, provide effective incentives for compliance with legal rules and commitment to the legislator's objectives, and remedy the problems caused by information asymmetry and moral hazard. The proposal is presented in the form of a three-by-three matrix that examines three legal entities that are subject to regulation: bank management, owners and supervisors (Table 4.1).

However, this matrix is not complete, in the sense that there are at least six other groups affected by the regulatory framework: depositors (both insured and

Table 4.1   Key elements of efficient regulation

	Commitment	*Market discipline*	*Control*
Management	Responsibility	Obligation to disclose information	Efficient internal control
	Sanctions	Code of ethics	Efficient shareholder control
Owners	Responsibility	Take-over threat	Legal form of ownership
	Sanctions	Efficient competition	Control of abuse of legal form
Supervisors	Responsibility	Obligation to Disclose information	Supervision v. norm-setting
	Sanctions	Role as communicator	Control by legislator

uninsured); creditors, competitors, 'taxpayers', the employees and 'other' interested parties – analysts, auditors, etc. They play a key role in the process of market discipline. Regulators and supervisors are acting on behalf of those in society not directly in the specific transactions but nevertheless potentially affected, or at some clear informational or power disadvantage. Society at large benefits insofar as the banking system assists the process of economic growth but is harmed if a problem lowers incomes or redistributes wealth through bailouts. We return to the role of these groups later but for the moment concentrate on owners, managers and supervisors.

The matrix is based on the assumption that efficient regulation and supervision presuppose conditions where:

- the *commitment* of both principals and agents is taken into account;
- there is *market discipline*;
- actions of agents are subject to *control*.

This framework does not rely primarily on control; rather, we assume that legislation and regulation must be based first and foremost on commitment and market discipline.

Commitment refers to the existence of explicit rules concerning responsibility and sanctions in the event of non-compliance. It is the binding force. Legal rules should pursue the ideal of perfect contracts in which the agent bears full responsibility for performing the task specified in the contract, and an effective sanction is imposed for the breach of the contract.

Market discipline refers to the pressures that markets bring to bear on the actions of banks and all those involved with them. These include not just equity markets, debt markets and the markets for bank products but labour markets and the market for corporate control. However, our major focus is on the obligations to disclose information that depositors, investors, regulators and the markets in general can use as a reliable basis for assessing the activities of a bank and thus overseeing, for example, bank management. Here market discipline is associated with first-best solutions, which endeavour to eliminate the underlying causes of problems encountered in banking and banking regulation. The smaller the amount of private information a particular agent has,[10] the less that agent can act in a way that is at variance with the principal's objectives and the less is excessive risk taking. Disclosure of information imposes discipline but it is only effective if there is competition. In the absence of competition there is also a need for control.

Control is needed to support commitment and market discipline. Control would not be needed at all if there were perfect information. As this objective can never be fully met, the actions of agents must be supervised. However, control itself suffers from the very shortcoming that it is needed to deal with, namely imperfect information. Since the agent always knows more about his own actions than does the principal or his representative who exercises control, the potential for control alone to reduce moral hazard and excessive risk-taking is limited.

It is arguable that the matrix should be extended to include other stakeholders in the bank. In a corporatist model the workforce would have a role to play and indeed in some jurisdictions in Europe they currently have a prescribed role within the framework of corporate governance as members of the supervisory board of the bank. Clearly the principal–agent relationship that exists between the owners and managers can be replicated in a sense between each layer of management and its subordinates. In just the same way that directors want a relationship between themselves and senior management that will convince them that the bank is being run according to the precepts they have laid down, so will senior management want to be convinced that junior management will be doing their jobs in the prescribed manner – and so on down the chain of responsibility. Within banks, the mechanisms of commitment and control are likely to be explicit and the market discipline would come both through trying to design systems that made sure that information flows made the actions of subordinates transparent and from the simple forces of competition as employees seek to improve their earnings and move up the ladder of promotion. We concern ourselves purely with the responsibilities of management as a group to ensure prudential behaviour and do not go more deeply into the system.

In the same way we can look at the role of customers, whether as lenders or borrowers, and indeed at that of creditors. Much of the relationship with customers lies in the field of consumer protection, which is outside our study. However, as Llewellyn (1999) points out, consumers play an important role as electors who put pressure on the government and parliament to formulate and enact rules that safeguard their interests. Such pressures are often without regard to the costs of regulation – there is a tendency for consumers to assume that many regulations are virtually costless if they do not have to pay a charge at the time. Thus if deposits are insured but the depositor is not subject to a direct charge for that facility the cost is likely to be neglected.[11] We view customers in this framework as part of the force of market discipline through the markets for bank products. The wholesale and business customers are likely to be able to exert much more effective discipline than retail consumers through financial markets. We do not treat them or other agencies, such as credit rating institutions or auditors, as separate categories although their roles are very important in ensuring the effective functioning of the system as we explain in some detail.

4.3   THE FUNCTIONS OF FINANCIAL SYSTEM OVERSIGHT

There are three main sources of confusion in discussing financial supervision. The first is in the discussion of what such actions are intended to achieve, the second in the structures and methods used to achieve those objectives and the third is in the meaning attributed to the terms being used. The principal focus of this book is on one specific means for achieving one of the objectives – namely the use of more market discipline rather than supervisor intervention to improve the prudential management of banks. However, implementing such a scheme successfully involves a much wider range of regulatory activity affecting banks and this chapter seeks to set them out.

4.3.1   Objectives

The objectives of public sector involvement are perhaps the easiest to disentangle, although in most jurisdictions they tend to be implicit and hence have to be inferred from what has been implemented. Normally the public sector has *two objectives*:

- systemic stability
- consumer protection

(Goodhart *et al.*, 1998). The implications are simple. There are some respects in which the operation of the market system may not be totally satisfactory.

In the first case, problems in the financial sector, whether general or relating to some large institutions, may have adverse spill-over effects for the rest of society that are not adequately compensated within the system. By appropriate action the public sector may be able to reduce the overall loss. It may also be able to organise what is perceived to be a fairer distribution of the losses. However, most importantly it may be able to reduce the chance of these problems occurring in the first place, with very little cost. This is a key feature of most financial supervision – namely, that it seeks to prevent where it can rather than simply organise insurance and clearing up after the event. The balance of the choice will depend upon the costs of the two routes and their likely efficacy.

In the second case consumers tend to be less well-organised, less well-informed, less able to understand such a complex industry as financial services and less able to withstand shocks than banks.

The new Financial Services Authority in the United Kingdom has two additional objectives:

- promoting public awareness;
- reducing financial crime.

In a sense these are subsumed within the others. A system that is riddled with crime is scarcely going to inspire much confidence.[12] Public awareness is rather a route to helping markets work better and hence also a step in trying to reduce the occurrence of problems, particularly for consumers. A society that understands the concept of risk and what it means in practice is likely to be less exposed to shocks to the financial system. However, it is possible that the public sector may be better informed than much of the market about new risks and about risks that are occurring simply because the market players are tending to acquire the same risks at the same time, making their exposure much more than they might think purely from examining their own businesses.

This emphasises one important facet of the response by the authorities to their task – namely, that regulation is not the only thing that can be done. Authorities can provide information; they can provide the financial services themselves. Many countries try to produce a 'risk-free' retail asset that guarantees a real rate of return equivalent to the long-run rates that occur in the market so that small savers can feel protected. Others provide settlement and payment systems so that markets can have confidence in the fundamental system of transactions. Indeed the fact that the public sector is there as a potential competitor, regulator and policeman will itself act as a spur to the financial sector to pay regard to the needs of the system and consumers. Indeed there are some who argue (Dowd, 1996, for example) that the banks themselves need to create adequate market confidence and consumer protection if the system is to work effectively.[13] Hence the need for public intervention may be rather less than many people think. However, public authorities are rather reluctant to experiment in this area and support for this thesis rests primarily on data from the past or on limited examples like Hong Kong.

The UK FSA also phrases the idea of systemic stability rather differently – speaking in terms of 'maintaining market confidence'. In some respects this last is a rather neat way of explaining the problem, since 'maintaining systemic stability' does not imply that the impact of all shocks to the system should be neutralised.

4.3.2 Functions

In what is probably the most comprehensive recent survey of the problems and how they might be tackled in an embracing framework, the Wallis Committee distinguished *three* main *functions* in its report on Australia, *The Financial System: Towards 2010*:

(i)   the regulation of 'conduct' and 'disclosure' for financial institutions
(ii) prudential regulation (financial safety) and
(iii) systemic stability

and advocated the establishment of a regulator for each function ((i) Corporations and Financial Services Commission, CFSC, (ii) Australian Prudential Regulation Commission, APRC, (iii) Reserve Bank of Australia, RBA).[14] The RBA is also responsible for monetary policy and the regulation of payment systems in this framework. Payment systems are clearly a component affecting all three functions.

What this Australian approach does, is effectively divide up the consumer protection objective in two. However, effective prudential regulation also contributes to making the task of maintaining systemic stability easier. So the items are interrelated. The emphasis in the Wallis Commission discussion is on 'regulation'. However, it is not necessary to view the way that the public sector involves itself in these issues just from that perspective.

There are other approaches. Merton (1995) suggests distinguishing between *functions* in the sense of financial services: financial intermediation, risk management, etc.

4.3.3   Means

In a second recent comprehensive survey, Goodhart *et al.* (1998, p. 189) cut the cake slightly differently, distinguishing the approaches of:

Regulation (the establishment of specific rules of behaviour);
Monitoring (observing whether the rules are obeyed);
Supervision (the more general observation of the behaviour of financial firms);

as *means* of addressing the regulatory goal. Financial system oversight in the sense we are using the term covers all of these means and indeed most supervisory authorities are responsible for all three and not just 'supervision' in the specific sense defined above.

One of the interesting features of the new UK FSA is that their very first point in describing the new regime says it should be 'built on a clear statement of the realistic aims and the limits of regulation' (p. 3). It develops this by saying that it has to recognise 'the proper responsibilities of consumers themselves and of firms' own management, and the impossibility and undesirability of removing all risk and failure from the financial system'. The limits occur partly through costs. If the costs of regulation in terms of direct compliance and the restriction of business and innovation exceed the likely losses from unregulated operation then it makes more sense to apply ex-post compensation. However, the limits also occur through incentives. Both purchasers and providers need incentives to manage their risks. If these do not exist then the presence of rules may actually increase risk taking as it may be thought to legitimise all permissible behaviour. FSA (2000) goes on to say that the regime should create 'incentives for firms to manage their own risks better and thereby reduce the burden of regulations'.

4.3.4 Structures

There is no simple paradigm for implementing such systems in practice. Structures of financial supervision vary considerably across countries, even within the European Union. The effectiveness of the system and the effectiveness of a more market-based regime are affected by the structure chosen. The structure chosen often reflects decisions made in the past, usually implicitly rather explicitly, about the purpose of regulation.

Attitudes towards what should be done and how it should be organised tend to be heavily influenced by the prevailing regime and experience with it. There are several fundamental questions:

* Are banks separately regulated from other financial institutions?
* Is there a distinction between responsibility for the stability of the financial system as a whole and the supervision of individual banks?
* What functions of banks are covered by the specific regulator and what by regulators of general business practice – advertising standards, consumer protection, and so on?
* How far do the powers of responsibility for the stability of the financial system extend – into the degree of monopoly?
* What powers are there for crisis resolution?

It is unusual for all functions to be the prime responsibility of a single body and the Wallis proposals are well towards the neater end of the spectrum. In many jurisdictions, not only may different functions be assigned to different bodies but responsibility for a single function may be shared. Normally, if there is a 'conduct and disclosure' regulator much of that function will be to administer rules set for the whole economy in the particular instance of the financial sector. As the Wallis Report puts it, '[while a]s a general principle, and to avoid regulatory inconsistency, economy wide regulation should not exclude the financial system ... the complexity of financial products and the specialised nature of financial markets has led most countries to establish specialised regulatory arrangements for the financial sector' (p. 17).

Table 4.2 cuts the functions of supervisors identified by Wallis in a slightly different way in order to highlight seven aspects that affect the applicability and effectiveness of a more market-based regime. As an illustration, Table 4.3 sets out the position for Finland. The central bank (Bank of Finland) is responsible for the stability of the financial system and for the payments system but the supervision of financial institutions is primarily the responsibility of a largely separate Financial Supervision Authority (FSA), although responsibility for the FSA also lies with the Board of the central bank and the FSA shares common services with the Bank of Finland. Some financial institutions, such as insurance companies, lie outside the ambit of the FSA. Insurance companies play a special role in the Finnish financial system because they administer funds that are compulsorily contributed towards the payment of occupational pensions. Since responsibility for the pensions system lies with the Ministry of Social Affairs it is the regulator of insurance companies in this regard. The primary concern of the FSA is prudential issues but it does have a somewhat wider regulatory role for Finnish banks, spilling into other aspects of commercial behaviour as laid down in the Credit Institutions Act (1993), such as Chapter 10 on Consumer Protection.

Tables 4.2 and 4.3 are somewhat more extensive than might be expected because corporate governance is a key determinant of the effectiveness of more market-based supervisory regimes. If incentives are to work well there needs to be a clear identification of property rights and avoidance of conflicts of interest. However, the system of auditing and accounting needs to be such that market information is understandable, verifiable and comparable. To some extent the

Table 4.2   Functions of financial system oversight

1   Prudential management of individual banks.
2   Systemic stability – crisis resolution.
3   Supervision of other financial institutions –
    including payment and settlement systems.
4   Competition – regulation of entry.
5   Management of deposit insurance.
6   Fair trading.
7   Corporate governance:
       Reporting
       Structures
       Auditing
       Accounting standards.

Table 4.3 Responsibilities in Finland

	Function	Responsibility
1	Prudential management of individual banks	Financial Supervisory Authority[1]
2	Systemic stability – crisis resolution	Bank of Finland / Ministry of Finance / Financial Supervisory Authority[2]
3	Supervision of other financial institutions – including payment and settlement systems	Financial Supervisory Authority / Ministry of Social Affairs[3] / Bank of Finland[4]
4	Competition – regulation of entry	Financial Supervisory Authority / Office of Free Competition / EEA home country supervisors
5	Management of deposit insurance	Ministry of Finance / banking industry organisations
6	Fair trading	Financial Supervisory Authority / Office of Free Competition / National Consumer Organisation / Central Criminal Police Money Laundering Unit
7	Corporate governance	
	Reporting	Financial Supervisory Authority / Stock Exchange / National Board of Patents and Registration
	Structures	Financial Supervisory Authority / Ministry of Trade and Industry
	Auditing	Financial Supervisory Authority[5]
	Accounting standards	Financial Supervisory Authority / Ministry of Finance[5]

Notes:
[1] The FSA, although independent, has common services with the Bank of Finland and has a Board member of the Bank as its Chairman.
[2] The ESCB/ECB and the Commission of the European Communities also have responsibilities particularly for cross-border implications.
[3] The Ministry is responsible for insurance companies.
[4] The ECB/ESCB also has responsibility for payment systems.
[5] There are Accounting and Auditing Acts administered by the Ministry of Trade and Industry plus self-regulatory bodies, the Auditing Board of the Central Chamber of Commerce and the Regional Auditing Committee of the Chambers of Commerce.

Financial Supervisory Authority has jurisdiction in Finland over all of these and indeed the chapters relating to corporate structures and the keeping and auditing of accounts are among the most extensive in the Credit Institutions, Commercial Bank, Savings Bank, Co-operative Bank and Postipankki Acts (1993). However, the provisions fit within the overall framework of the Companies Act (1978, revised 1997) and the Accounting Act (1973 as amended).

In many respects the most important provisions concern the control of entry and exit. Banking licences provide a measure of rent to those permitted to be banks if the entry restrictions are at all onerous. They also provide a very important opportunity for the supervisory authority to exclude organisations over which it has any doubts. However, there are two restraints on this: first, when banks have already been registered; and, second, in the EEA, where other national supervisors make (or have made) the decision over initial registration. Thus while the Financial Supervision Authority recommends to the Ministry of Finance who shall be registered (or indeed be deregistered) the main function in practice at present purely relates to registration of:

- new Finnish institutions;
- extra-EEA institutions whose first point of entry to the EEA is Finland;
- EEA institutions who wish to set up a subsidiary rather than a branch in Finland (i.e. a very limited group).

Powers of compelling, managing or avoiding exit are, however, much more real and apply to all banks registered in Finland. In the event of insolvency and the failure of a bank to act voluntarily the FSA can have its licence cancelled and place it in liquidation. (Technically the actions are taken by the Ministry of Finance on the recommendation of the FSA.)[15]

Lastly the operation of market incentives will be affected by the nature of the insurance that the parties can take out to avoid the direct consequences of bank distress and misguided actions. How well the system of supervision works and the extent of moral hazard depend in part on the structure of the system of oversight of the financial system. If the prudential supervisor is readily able to organise a bailout then the moral hazard will tend to be increased. Following recent changes, deposits in Finland are now protected only up to a maximum value of 150 000 FM (about US$30 000). Legislation is currently in progress to remove implicit guarantees to other creditors by the public sector over and above their rights under liquidation. The main guarantee has taken the form of a parliamentary resolution. At the time of the banking crisis at the beginning of the 1990s, the Ministry of Finance had rather wider responsibilities for banking supervision (including responsibility for the FSA) and hence the explicit and implicit guarantees it offered through access to taxpayer funds were considerable. Much of the point of the changes in the supervisory structure that have taken place since (Table 4.4) is to help convince people that in any future case of bank distress the insurance available will be strictly limited. A more market-based system will help reinforce that (Bhattacharya *et al.*, 1998, p. 760).

However, it is not our purpose to make judgements about the appropriateness of the specific regime in place in Finland nor to recommend changes, although

Table 4.4   Main changes to the financial system in Finland since 1992

(a) Financial Supervision

Transfer of supervisor FSA from Ministry of Finance to
  Bank of Finland.
New banking legislation tightening up preconditions for registration as
  a bank.
Reorganisation and increase in size and resources of FSA and
  change in focus from compliance monitoring to risk assessment.
Issuance of new set of banking regulations.
Membership of EEA then EU and adoption of EU
  compatible legislation.

(b) Banking System

Wave of mergers encouraged by the authorities eliminating many
  small savings banks. Resolution of larger banks and assumption
  of non-performing assets by the state. Restructuring of
  co-operative banks.

---

the existence of some drawbacks will be evident as in almost any other existing system. The purpose is to explore the extent of the opportunity to introduce more market-based measures.

What the changes in Finland reflect is a tightening up after the crisis. The regime is therefore an amalgam of two processes – the transition and the new more open environment. The joining of the EU has, of course, complicated this process, as the regime has had to move on again. Indeed, as we suggested in Chapter 3, this might be taken to illustrate that the new, more open environment is one of much more rapid change and hence that the regulatory framework has to ensure that banks can cope with this faster process of change. While a regime for the transition set up ex ante might have had several of the characteristics of the regime set up ex post, it is unlikely that such a regime would have involved such an intrusive approach. The FSA itself has been easing some of the information requirements as the banks became better capitalised and confidence in their prudential management systems increased.

4.4   ELEMENTS OF AN EFFICIENT SUPERVISION REGIME

In the context of the EU and the wider EEA the problems of design of appropriate financial system oversight is more complex as the scope for regulation and the role of regulatory institutions is limited by the Treaty[16] and the *acquis*

communautaire. In Chapter 3 we highlighted our concerns for adequate information to monitor the ongoing health of the financial system and resolve and indeed
pre-empt crises under the principle of 'home country control'. However, to
understand the context of these issues we need to have a clear overall view of
what is required of a successful supervision regime that encourages prudent
behaviour.[17] Following the generally accepted principles (see Goodhart *et al.*,
1998, for example) the main ingredients of such a regime also include a third
requirement and are

1. careful control of the right of establishment as a bank,
2. a system of supervision substantially complemented by market discipline
   stemming from public disclosure,
3. an efficient system of handling banking problems and crisis management.

These three 'pillars' have to coexist if the regime is to fulfil its task efficiently
and need to be supported by regulations on licensing requirements, prudential
standards, disclosure requirements, safety net provisions, and accounting and
audit standards. The supervision regime involves monitoring that the regulations
are obeyed, observing the behaviour and exposures of institutions, and taking
care of problem situations in a predetermined manner.

Without exercising entry control it is difficult to have a proactive approach to
supervision in order to ensure that banking activities are conducted by institutions that have capable management, incentives to prudence and adequate internal controls in place and in operation. Entry control is also needed to ensure that
company structures and operations are and remain transparent to markets and
supervisors. Common rules to achieve this have been agreed and implemented in
the EEA (as discussed in the next section).

The most important part of the incentive structure embedded in an efficient
supervisory regime is that all parties understand the possibility of difficulties or
even failure associated with the risks inherent in banking. If shareholders (in
choosing management and management control practices), managers (in managing risk) and uninsured creditors of banks (in choosing banks) feel themselves
more at risk, both financially and for their reputations, they will tend to want to
manage their risks prudently.[18] Thus, public supervision and crisis management
practices and safety net arrangements should be devised to support the contention that shareholders and uninsured depositors and other creditors will not be
bailed out by taxpayers' money.[19]

It is widely accepted that supervision would be best consistent with this incentive structure if systemic stability and confidence in the banking system as a
whole, not the integrity of individual institutions, were the primary objective.[20]
While individual managements may be best suited to addressing the problems of

their own businesses a supervisor with information on all the market participants is in a better position to point out market-wide trends that may threaten stability. Supervisors also need clear procedures and autonomy for handling breaches of prudential rules and other types of misconduct. Forbearance of banking problems through adjustment in the interpretation of rules, or hesitation in supervisory reactions is likely to aggravate the existing problems and induce moral hazard.[21]

Vigilant supervision by a public sector agency is merited by the high social costs associated with the systemic banking problems. Concerns will always be greatest in periods of structural change, as at present, with banks having to adjust to the more integrated and competitive markets occasioned by the introduction of the euro. As pointed out by Estrella (1995), inter alia, prudential supervision needs to cover behaviour and cannot merely rely on limits such as capital adequacy. New markets and instruments have made it possible for banks (or their individual employees) to make easily and quickly huge bets that may drive a bank into insolvency.

However, banks and insurance companies also require special attention as they appear to be more opaque to than forms in other industries (Morgan, 2000).[22] It appears that the two main rating agencies in the United States, Moody's and Standard and Poors more often disagree over new issues in banks and insurance companies than they do over new issues by companies in the rest of the economy. This has two implications. First of all, if even specialist agencies are to be able to rate banks with the same efficiency that they can rate the rest of the company sector, the amount of information publicly available on banks needs to be greater than that customarily produced for the rest of the economy. This does not imply that banks are more effective in concealing information, simply that the nature of their business makes it more difficult to judge the likely risks and rates of return.

Secondly, this opacity helps justify the role of supervisors in trying to provide a more equal treatment of the risks to society across sectors. If the inherent risks from the banking sector tend to exceed those from other sectors then it might very well be that the amount of information that needs to be disclosed to try to right the balance will have to be greater. At one step removed, the pressure for less opacity on banks will push the banks themselves to try to reduce the opacity of borrowers.

The response of supervisors has already been to put more emphasis on the supervision of institutions' internal control mechanisms and practices, since innovation, internationalisation and increasing complexity of businesses make it increasingly hard for supervisory authorities to keep track of the risk exposures of individual institutions continuously. For this reason, there is also substantial support for putting more emphasis on public disclosure and forces of market discipline and corporate governance in order to strengthen the overall supervision regime.[23] That is, supervision not just by authorities but also by banks' clients (other financial institutions, firms and private customers) and shareholders. The precondition is that these parties are not insulated from losses in case of failure.[24] Insofar as depositors are insured then this group will have weakened incentives. Even so it is possible to build some degree of incentive into such insurance schemes both for depositors through keeping some element of exposure and for the banks through the premia charged (Chan *et al.*, 1992; Craine, 1995; Kupiec and O'Brien, 1998).

Increased transparency through public disclosure of information is thought to be most influential with respect to the enhancement of market discipline. The goal of disclosure from the supervisory perspective is to improve bank managers' incentives for prudent risk-taking and thus reduce the probability of failure. Cordella and Yeyati (1998) show that this indeed occurs when risk-taking is largely idiosyncratic and a bank can choose its portfolio risk. But when risks are largely exogenously given and the risk level of the banking system fluctuates within a wide range, disclosure of information increases the probability of bank failure. Our interpretation of recent banking problems is that idiosyncratic risk-taking has played an important role. For example, in the banking crises of Finland, Norway and Sweden, where the operation of the entire banking system was threatened, some banks actually managed to get through the crisis without major losses.

The analysis by Cordella and Yeyati implies that increasing disclosure is likely to produce the desired result in strong and developed banking systems. Opportunities for banks to hedge risks would also support this outcome. In these conditions disclosure can reduce the opaqueness of banks' asset values and thus reduce the negative effects of asymmetric information between banks and their clients. As with any change in regulation, the introduction of a greater emphasis on public disclosure should be timed in a period of financial system health so that the chance of unwelcome shocks to the market from what is revealed is limited.

Markets (credit rating agencies, counterparties, depositors and other creditors) can be expected to anticipate problems to some extent, and react accordingly when there is accurate and timely information. However, in our view, the major mechanism actually generating the incentives for prudence is the requirement to disclose problems quickly after they have emerged, which would expose banks to the possibility of adverse market reactions. Counterparties' and creditors' reactions are more likely to be 'exit' than 'voice' (public announcement of their judgement) to protect their own receivables, but this would affect the cost of borrowing and impose discipline indirectly.[25] The threat of adverse market reactions increases the accountability of the managers, and makes them subject to reputational penalties,[26] which encourages them to be well informed about the activities and risks of their organisation. For example, one would expect that management would be more inclined to have an independent audit committee.

Calomiris (1999), building on his earlier work, advocates building in a specific element of market discipline for all banks by compelling them to issue subordinated debt to the tune of 2 per cent of their risky assets. This debt would have a two-year maturity, would be placed on a readily traded market and 1/24 of it would mature each month so that the banks were faced with the costs of rolling it over on a continuing basis. These instruments would not, of course, be insured since that would defeat the purpose. While our view of the operation of market discipline is much broader than this, having such explicit arrangements would make sure that banks of all corporate structures face this discipline clearly.

Sufficient penalties are needed to enforce the mechanism in the case of a prolonged disclosure of problems (which tends to aggravate difficulties) or misleading information. If there were any attempt at deliberate obscuration of information, supervisory action against the bank and the managers in question would be called for.

Emphasising market discipline should not be viewed as washing one's hands of supervision in an increasingly complex world, but rather as an attempt to provide a supervision regime that increases the chance of prudential behaviour. The most important benefit of this approach to the supervisors is that they could concentrate more on the functions where they have clear advantages:

- assessing entrants' management quality and transparency of company structures (ensuring proactive supervision);
- identifying potential problems which relate to the banking system as a whole (e.g. exposure to particular markets or sectors) and focusing on potentially fragile institutions;
- prompting early corrective action or resolution of banking problems and ensuring that crisis resolution capabilities (contingency plans) are in good shape;
- ensuring that institutions comply with the disclosure requirements and providing relevant advice.

An additional advantage of effective disclosure is that it reduces the threat of supervisory arbitrage – that is, relocation of activities into jurisdictions where the supervisory standards and practices are looser.[27] Under effective market discipline, placing oneself under a 'weaker' regime would have little impact on prudent behaviour and quality of service. Indeed the incentives might be heightened if the market chooses to penalise such a move. We discuss disclosure in more detail in Chapter 7.

In the next section we move on to the more practical issue of the difficulties of implementing an effective regime in the context of the EU/EEA. Applying the principles we have developed is more difficult because it requires co-ordination across regimes. For this reason some would prefer to restore the problem to the dimension of a single jurisdiction and then the more simplified approach we have outlined could be applied. However, rather than join the debate about what sort of European institutions would be most appropriate we outline the current problems facing the member states in running supervision and monitoring and suggest how improvements can be made by applying the principles, whatever regime is ultimately decided upon.

4.5   ONGOING BANKING SUPERVISION AND MONITORING FINANCIAL SYSTEM HEALTH

4.5.1   General Supervisory Framework

The EU supervisory framework is based on the principle of home country control, which maintains that the competent supervisory authority of the home country, where the bank has received its licence, has the responsibility for the ongoing supervision of that institution. This responsibility covers the activities carried out by branches throughout the EU or by cross-border supply of services. If the establishment occurs via subsidiaries, the host authority is responsible for the supervision, since a subsidiary is a registered entity within the host country jurisdiction. Supervision of individual banks is complemented by the supervision on consolidated basis of groups of banks. Again, the home supervisor is responsible for the supervision on consolidated basis.[28]

A particular feature of the EU supervisory framework is that there is no separate licensing by the host authorities of branches of banks registered in other member states. This 'single passport' was devised to support the creation of the Single Market and increase foreign competition and hence the depth and efficiency of financial markets. This approach is viable, since the main body of prudential legislation has been harmonised in the EU and the supervisory practices are sufficiently similar to one another.

The current EU framework for prudential supervision is not affected by Stage Three of EMU because the Statute of the ESCB/ECB permits the national central banks (NCBs) to continue their supervisory duties or close co-operation with supervisory authorities.

According to the Core Principles for Effective Banking Supervision issued by the Basle Committee (on Banking Supervision) (1997), as the basic reference for supervisory authorities in all countries, the home supervisor must be in charge of the worldwide consolidated supervision of their international banks, including overseas branches, subsidiaries and joint ventures. However, the thrust of the Principles is to support the role of host country supervision as well.[29]

When a substantial part of banking activities is conducted by foreign-owned institutions ongoing supervision requires co-ordination. Within the scope of the general framework we have outlined, an efficient system would make the best use of the contributions and 'comparative advantages' of home and host supervisors. The accomplishment of this requires adequate and relevant information and sufficient incentives to all concerned authorities.

4.5.2   Contributions of Home and Host Supervisors

There are strong arguments for organising supervision by functions and risks in contrast to the traditional institutional approach where different institutions with de facto similar functions may be supervised by different authorities (Merton, 1995; Wallis Committee, 1997; Goodhart *et al.*, 1998). The functional approach has its own merits, like better guarantee of equal supervisory treatment of similar activities. However, there are also strong merits in having one authority in charge of monitoring the safety and soundness of entire institutions or groups, since the continuation of their business, and hence the systemic stability, hinges on the financial condition of the institutions as a whole. Prima facie, therefore, no single supervisor is likely to be able to handle all facts of prudential supervision efficiently and effective supervision will require co-ordination among supervisors.[30]

When the bulk of the activities of the institutions are conducted domestically, the home authority has the least difficulty in carrying out consolidated supervision. Home authorities have typically developed intimate knowledge of their institutions and close contacts with their personnel. In these conditions, host country supervisors see only a limited part of the overall operations of the foreign institutions within their territories.[31]

The internationalisation process, when it results in organisations having a substantial share or even majority of their operations in foreign countries, is almost bound to loosen these ties with their home supervisors. Moreover, with growing cross-border exposures, failures in foreign activities constitute an increasing threat to the solvency of the entire institution. However, this is not a one-sided issue. There is a clear benefit from internationalisation for systemic stability, when it enhances the diversification of banks' risks and capability to withstand country-specific shocks such as economic downturns.

As a result of internationalisation, home authorities' burden in getting and processing information for efficient consolidated supervision of the institutions for which they are responsible increases considerably, even if there are no specific obstacles to getting necessary information, as is the case within the EEA. Assuring timely corrective action can be quite hard. Banks' central management can have considerable problems in controlling foreign operations and supervisors are largely dependent on the second-hand information from the banks themselves. The lesson from the recent Barings and Daiwa incidents seems to be that the focus should be on the institutions' ability to produce and indeed use sufficient consolidated information for their own internal risk management purposes reasonably quickly (Goodhart, 1995). This information would then be disclosed to supervisors and markets. It would be the task of the home supervisor to ensure that banks complied with implementing and reporting on their risk management mechanisms in all their operations and not just those in the home country. Public disclosure should improve banks' incentives to invest in the respective risk management systems.

The informational requirements of efficient consolidated supervision are quite different when banks operate solely in foreign securities markets and only conduct wholesale activities from when they engage in widespread commercial and private customer lending. The former has been so far the major cross-border activity for banks in Europe and market risks have dominated in banks' foreign exposures. Extension of the latter activities, and hence foreign credit risks, would increase the importance of being familiar with the local market conditions.

Indeed, the significant contribution of the host supervisors is the view of the trends and areas of growing risks within their financial systems (strategic risks) that can seriously affect all institutions operating in that system. The more weight is put on the systematic assessment of the effects of the macroeconomic and sectoral developments[32] on banks and on the industry-wide developments within the banking system such as asset quality, lending growth and competition, the more effective this contribution ('macroprudential supervision').[33]

The supervisor responsible for such concerns needs to be well integrated with those involved with forward-looking assessments of the economy. Central banks or ministries of finance often provide such links. Deriving the view on the banking industry requires banks to produce information for supervisors in a manner that makes possible calculation of aggregate figures and comparisons across banks. 'Hands-on' knowledge and understanding of the local market conditions that cover the banks' business environment goes beyond the quantitative prudential supervisory returns on credit and market risks.

This kind of analysis would help supervisors to distinguish between idiosyncratic and systemic (industry-wide) banking problems, which is a fundamental consideration in choosing the appropriate supervisory action. Based on the arguments in Dewatripont and Tirole (1993, ch. 4) and Nagarajan and Sealey (1995), supervisory actions would best provide incentives for prudent behaviour when they penalise problems caused by idiosyncratic individual management decisions more severely than those caused by adverse market movements out of management's control. The goal is to contain the idiosyncratic problems in a timely manner before the spillover effects could jeopardise the stability of the banking system.

Idiosyncratic 'misbehaviour' can be twofold. Institutions may not respond promptly to economic and structural developments or financial market events (lack of effort), or they may engage actively in high-risk strategies. There have been clear cases of herding behaviour in banking, with many institutions having the same strategies at the same time. In these cases individual strategies may not necessarily entail excessive risk-taking, but the combined effect may be heightened systemic fragility.

Early communication of this information and analytical results based on it are crucial. The home authorities in charge of the consolidated supervision need to be able to add up the effect from the different markets. While the host authorities need information on the exposures of the foreign banks within their territory if they are to contrast these exposures to those of the rest of the industry and inform the home authority of possible concerns (of idiosyncratic misbehaviour). Hence, unconstrained sharing of the information between the home and host supervisors would be useful, perhaps through development of the current MoUs. Furthermore, multilateral contacts with supervisors to assess regional or global trends affecting the banking industry should bring a significant value added to the supervisory process, say, by expanding the role of the Groupe de Contact, which currently deals with multi-country problems involving individual institutions.[34] The ECB Banking Supervision Committee has already taken steps in this regard by setting up a process of macro-prudential surveillance aggregating information provided by the national central banks on a common set of variables on trends, risks, exposures and the health of the banking system.

The issue we highlight here is that the host country may be unable to detect a problem properly unless the home country makes the information about activities in its market available. It is true that host authorities can get some information from foreign branches' direct reports – for example, for statistical purposes – but host authorities' powers to impose reporting requirements are limited.

It appears to us that the MoUs which have been signed thus far in the EEA do not normally provide for the routine transfer of information among supervisors in the manner described but only in the case of suspected misconduct or other problems pursuant to 'BCCI' Directive. A host cannot pass back helpful market-wide observations to the home country if it does not have data on the whole market.[35] Here is a potential contrast between the needs of supervisors and the wishes of banks for public disclosure. Banks would expect to disclose on a consolidated basis only.

The same issue of 'detecting trends' and singling out 'idiosyncratic' problems arises in the context of supervising financial conglomerates. Namely, the supervisor that carries out consolidated supervision would benefit from information from the separate supervisory authorities responsible for particular sectors (for example, insurance), concerning the specific developments within that sector.

Since the host authorities work in close contact with the local markets and have responsibilities for supervision of business conduct, they might receive information that indicates problems in the organisational structure, management competence, internal control or business practices and reputation that could be present elsewhere as well and jeopardising the stability of the institution as a whole. These may be signs of the lack of the requisite expertise to conduct operations in foreign markets. The host authority should naturally communicate these signs to the home supervisor, as stipulated in MoUs.

With public disclosure the problem of what confidential information to communicate to other supervisors about individual banks is considerably reduced as supervisors have much less private information. Communications would then be more in terms of qualitative assessments and interpretations of the data. It may even so be that pure co-ordination among supervisors is not enough and that a new EEA-level organisation will be required to ensure that comparable information is available and that an adequate picture can be built up by authorities that can then act effectively to deal with the problems of highly multinational banks where the concept of 'home' is relatively weak. The co-ordination required is not just across countries but also across financial sectors.

4.5.3   Proactive Adjustment of Public Supervision

Perhaps the most important precondition for efficient consolidated supervision is that the company structures are always transparent and that no part of the organisation is omitted because it lies 'between' or outside the jurisdictions involved. The global structures should not be beyond reach and the internal controls and public supervision should to be adjusted at the same time as the company structures change to enable efficient consolidated supervision. This principle has been adopted in the Basle Core Principles and the EU Directive on Consolidated Supervision.[36]

A severe problem related to blocking structures that would make efficient supervision impossible could be that the supervisory authorities only have the available extreme threat of withdrawing the banking licence of the institution in question, on the basis that the licensing requirements are no longer met.[37] Exercising this extreme threat is not likely to be practicable in most cases. As a minimum, supervisors could have the right to require (for example, by issuing binding regulations) that, following changes in company structures, institutions must adjust their internal control systems in a way that ensures monitoring of exposures and capital adequacy at the consolidated level without significant breaks.

4.5.4 Incentive Issues

A distinct role and responsibilities and adequate accountability are necessary to ensure that any organisation has incentives to operate efficiently.[38] Host supervisors' incentives to monitor foreign institutions and deliver their input to the supervisory process may be blunted by the fact that they do not have the ultimate responsibility of overseeing the safety and soundness of these institutions. The concern could be pronounced in the EU supervisory framework, in which the formal obligations of the host authorities are limited when the foreign-owned banks operate through branches or remote cross-border supply.

One way of increasing the host supervisors' incentives would be to specify explicitly the inputs the authorities in charge of the consolidated supervision expect from the host authorities. It would be preferable for these agreements to cover explicit aspects of conditions in the host markets. Another way would be to increase the weight of the systemic banking industry-level issues at international fora, where host supervisors could base their contribution on their expertise of local market conditions. Finally, if home supervisors actively inform the host authorities of significant matters affecting the established institutions' overall performance, they could feel more committed to the overall supervisory process.

Public disclosure of information could reduce the incentive problems. Both supervisors would be concerned to see speedy disclosure so they can complete their analyses.

Specific incentive issues may also arise because of different market sizes. Establishments of small (country) banks in large financial centres might not receive so much attention from the host authorities, if their significance in the overall market is small. However, their exposures could be very important for their overall soundness, and the home country supervisor would benefit from comparative information on them.

If banking business becomes significantly concentrated in large pan-European or global banks in the future, supervisory responsibilities would accordingly tend to concentrate in the home authorities of these institutions. The host supervisors (without their 'own' multinational institutions) would face not only incentive, but also heightened resource constraints, since their tasks would become significantly reduced. These authorities would also lose funding directly to the extent that it is based on charges levied on supervised institutions.

4.5.5 Co-ordination of Supervisory Activities

The issue of implementing efficient co-ordination involves two dimensions: (i) bilateral/multilateral co-ordination of supervision at international fora; and

(ii) co-operation based on general guidelines/case-by-case agreements concerning individual institutions.

Clearly, the internationalisation process increases the need for both bilateral and multilateral co-ordination. Co-ordination and co-operation among supervisors has already increased considerably. The actual involvement of foreign institutions in the particular countries and the technical and organisational aspects of ensuring adequate co-operation largely dictate the extent of bilateral co-ordination. Multilateral co-ordination has its role, inter alia, in providing guidance and direction for arranging the bilateral relations and facilitating exchange of information and establishing systemic trends in financial markets. [39]

The supervision of large multinational institutions (or large conglomerates) seems to require case-by-case-agreed supervisory procedures. The duties of the various authorities involved could be unclear if they rest on general supervisory agreements alone. International consolidation (as well as conglomeration) increases the significance of this method of allocating tasks and responsibilities among supervisors (following the general principles stipulated elsewhere). The benefit of this is that agreements on supervisory co-ordination would then evolve in line with the actual changes in market structures.

The more radical solution, advocated by Lannoo (1999b) inter alia, is to create a European-level supervisory body specifically to handle cases where the degree of internationalisation makes it difficult for the home supervisor to carry out the overall co-ordinating task efficiently and difficult for the host country to form a clear view of systemic issues. A European-level body might also find it easier to solve conflicts of interest among supervisors. While such a body could be a full-blown executive regulatory agency an alternative could be a monitoring agency for issues of systemic risk (Aglietta and de Boissieu, 1998).

5 Corporate Governance and Financial Stability

Good corporate governance is a key element in a satisfactory framework for financial supervision. The financial system is only likely to maintain stability if there is a reasonable balance between the interests of the various stakeholders in banks. Shareholders (owners), depositors, borrowers, creditors, managers and supervisors all have a stake. If we make a crude division of the relationships, consumer protection covers the framework for the relationship between individual depositors and borrowers and the bank, while rules relating to liquidation and the like cover the relationship with all depositors and creditors. Corporate governance on the other hand relates primarily to the relationship between investors in the company and its management (Shliefer and Vishny, 1995, p. 773). The way in which the final relationship with supervisors seeking to maintain systemic stability should be conducted is dependent upon the framework for all of the others.

If the corporate governance arrangements are unbalanced then supervisors will be concerned to try to offset the problem. On the whole banks are treated like any other company and are subject to general legislation but, as discussed in Chapter 4, there are aspects where special treatment is usually thought appropriate. The most common ones are deposit insurance, the handling of distress with the prospect of undercapitalisation or even liquidation and prudential behaviour. However, corporate governance is one of the three key issues we identified in Chapter 4 along with the handling of distress and prudential behaviour. We have treated good corporate governance as being a precondition for the successful operation of financial supervision. If owners are able to divert the activities of the bank to channel deposits to their own use through inadequately collateralised lending or managers are able to run the bank for their own purposes then the chances of achieving systemic stability are small. Intrusive supervision will be necessary to try to substitute for the lack of checks and balances in the system. And, as we have argued earlier, we do not think that this intrusion is likely to be particularly successful, as the management will always have an information advantage over the supervisor.

For a system based primarily on market discipline, the requirements on each of the components and corporate governance in particular will be even greater. There need to be markets. There must be a product market in the sense of there being strong competition among banks. People must face an active choice among banks both as lenders and borrowers. However, as Shy (2000) points out, this is not just a matter of there being quite a large number of banks none of whom has a dominant market share. There are considerable costs to shifting balances for retail depositors and if banks choose to make it difficult for others to determine a customer's credit history the operation of the market may be rather weak. There also needs to be a market for the financing of banks. If the bank does not have to compete for funds then the discipline over its behaviour will be weakened. If there is no market for corporate control then the pressures on bank management and directors will be weaker.

In most countries banks can adopt a variety of structures. They can be wholly-owned, part of a larger group, state-owned, a co-operative or mutual institution, a savings bank, private, as well as the traditional textbook joint stock bank with many shareholders none of whom has control or one where just a few shareholders have a controlling position. All of these can have disadvantages from the point of view of effective corporate governance and hence elicit different supervisory responses. Our prime concern in this chapter is to set out the characteristics of forms of corporate governance that are likely to operate satisfactorily from the point of view of systemic stability and to suggest how specific further regulations need to be introduced by financial supervisors when the ideal does not apply. We concentrate on three prime areas: (i) the structure and responsibilities of corporate boards; (ii) the need for unambiguous financial information through accounting; and (iii) the role of independent auditors and audit committees in providing checks and balances. We suggest that current best practice as outlined by the three committees of inquiry in the United Kingdom, the OECD and the Basel Committee provide a suitable precondition for prudential behaviour by banks.

No single structure is likely to be agreeable or even appropriate for the European countries, so we do not attempt to advocate the introduction of a uniform EU regulation. However, we do point out that the voluntary nature of many of the existing codes will only be appropriate if there is some effective form of sanction for non-compliance. If non-compliance is thought likely then financial supervisors will wish to place binding constraints instead.

One of the key issues in these principal–agent problems is information. Unless the various stakeholders have access to accurate and comparable information on banks they will be unable to exercise market discipline effectively. Hence we identify the need for clear accounting standards and verification by auditors. Again we do not suggest that there is any need for modification to the current international financial reporting standards. However, these have not been implemented in many countries.

Much of our analysis is retrospective, pointing out how failure to adhere to the principles has led to financial instability in the Nordic countries and elsewhere in recent years. We structure our discussion in terms of providing a framework that provides adequate incentives for each of shareholders, managers and supervisors to play their role in providing the checks and balances to increase the chance of prudential behaviour, effective market discipline and consequent financial stability.

5.1 CORPORATE GOVERNANCE AND THE IMPLEMENTATION OF AN INCENTIVE-BASED FRAMEWORK

Corporate governance has become a topical issue worldwide in connection with efforts to structure and implement an efficient legal, regulatory and supervisory framework for financial markets. The banking crises of recent decades have highlighted the importance of a well-functioning legal, regulatory and supervisory framework in ex ante prevention of massive banking crises and the reduction of the resulting pain. The crises have clearly demonstrated that there can be serious negative outcomes in situations where the incentives influencing the behaviour of legislators, regulators, supervisors or banks (management, board, shareholders) are inappropriate. Corporate governance as part of a legal and regulatory infrastructure has been seen as a device to mitigate moral hazard problems and make bank management accountable to shareholders and other stakeholders, including supervisors. The need for accountability and for appropriate incentives also applies to regulators and supervisors.

We look at corporate governance from the agency perspective, seeking answers to the question of how to increase the commitment of management, owners and supervisors. However, before drawing conclusions, we shed some light on the definitions of the concept and key features of studies and concrete work on the issue of corporate governance (Sections 5.1.1–5.1.3). We also give some concrete country-specific examples, mostly from Scandinavian countries, and explore problems related to managerial discretion, shareholder control and supervisory discretion (Sections 5.2–5.4).

The view of corporate governance goes beyond just the relationship between management, board and shareholders and inclines towards the view of Tirole (1999), inter alia, who argues that focusing on shareholder value alone generates biased decision-making. Although it is better founded, say, with regard to income generation and the clear mission of management. He sees corporate governance as an arrangement by which institutions induce or force management to internalise the welfare of all stakeholders, not just shareholders. Supervisors implement rules and regulations and represent dispersed depositors. Thus they play the role of one important stakeholder in banks' corporate governance.

5.1.1 Definitions of Corporate Governance

There is no single or simple definition of corporate governance, and certainly no definition that all countries agree on. The concept relates to the relationships between a company's management, board, shareholders and other stakeholders. Problems related to corporate governance originate from the separation of ownership and control of a company, i.e. from the agency relationships between a principal (shareholder, investor) and an agent (manager, entrepreneur). The problems of control have changed in line with the changeover from entrepreneurial capitalism via managerial capitalism to shareholder capitalism,[1] where the interests of strong and demanding shareholders do not necessarily coincide with those of management. As a result, shareholders have to put control systems in place.

The question then becomes: what constitutes an efficient system for controlling management and how can incentives be set so as to make management behave prudentially? As noted earlier, corporate governance is not restricted to areas of managerial responsibility and relationships between shareholders and managers, but covers a wider range of principal–agent relations involving a corporation's business operations.

The focus of interest in comparative corporate governance has shifted from detailed formal mechanisms to the aims and the means of achieving the aims. However, different corporate governance systems have basic aims in common. They are to achieve efficient functioning of management, board and the whole organisation and to support the legitimacy of economic activity in general.

Corporate governance has internal and external elements[2] in directing and controlling the company, as outlined by the Cadbury Committee (1992). The Committee defines the corporate governance concept as 'the system by which companies are directed and controlled'.[3] Expanding on this, the OECD defines the concept from three points of view. The first point of view is a combination of an internal and an external element, the second an internal view and the third clearly an external view. According to the OECD,

1. Corporate governance is an instrument for:
    *   improved economic efficiency
    *   a set of relationships between a company's management, its board, and all stakeholders
2. Corporate governance provides the structure for setting:
    *   the objectives of the company
    *   the means of attaining those objectives
    *   the methods of monitoring performance
3. Corporate governance depends on the legal, regulatory and institutional environment as it is mostly through laws and institutions that sound corporate governance is promoted (OECD, 1999a).

It is to be concluded from this OECD definition that the relevance of legislation is indirect in the construction of sound corporate governance, i.e. legislation does not create sound governance but promotes the creation of it.

5.1.2 Studies Related to Corporate Governance

There is a vast body of literature on the corporate governance of ordinary companies,[4] but much less specifically on banks. However, the issue of bank corporate governance has become of greater interest to regulators, supervisors and economists, particularly over the last decade.[5]

The problems of corporate governance in ordinary companies are to a great extent applicable to banks, too.[6] However, banks operate under a legal, regulatory and supervisory environment that is substantially different from that of non-financial corporations. The rationale for banking regulation and supervision – which differs from that of ordinary companies – is based on the need for safeguarding the stability of financial markets and reducing the likelihood of bank runs.[7] (As we noted in Chapter 4, there are, however, criticisms the conventional arguments for banking regulation and supervision, particularly those by the proponents of free banking, who argue that, in the absence of safety net provisions, market forces ensure that banks aim at strong capital positions and manage to retain depositor confidence.[8]) The main differences relate to explicit and implicit insurance of banks' liabilities and, in practice, even equity capital (the too big to fail aspect, liquidation and bankruptcy rules). Other differences include the existence of strict prudential regulations (e.g. capital adequacy rules), supervision by public authorities and regulations restricting the corporate control of banks (takeover rules).

It is widely accepted that an unduly extensive safety net weakens the potential of market mechanisms to control and discipline management and set proper incentives for shareholders, depositors and other creditors. The supervisory and regulatory regime of the banking sector may, to some degree, substitute for weak market mechanisms and market discipline. However, intervention and preventative supervision by the authorities has turned out to be a costly and not an optimal substitute for market control mechanisms. This leads us to conclude that the effectiveness of corporate governance mechanisms in banks is weaker than it could be in a regime focused on incentive-based rules and regulations, be they externally imposed[9] or self-imposed by banks.

Most research on non-financial companies concentrates on the issue of ownership structures of corporate firms. The papers look at whether an Anglo-American (US, UK) structure or the so-called European structure (Germany, Japan) is more efficient from the point of view of the companies' shareholder value. The main features of the Anglo-American corporate governance structure relate to liquid capital markets, diffuse non-corporate ownership, strong and demanding institutional investors, strong minority protection, frequent takeovers, independent board members in a one-tier board system and strong management incentives to maximise shareholder value. Typical features of the German–Japanese system are relatively illiquid capital markets, concentrated (bank- or family-centred) ownership, cross-holdings and board representation between companies, weak minority protection, and a two-tier board structure with primarily insiders in the executive board. The European corporate governance structure also allows other stakeholders besides shareholders to take part in the decision making of the company. Companies are therefore considered to take into account wider interests than just those of the shareholders.

The studies note that neither of these structures is more efficient than the other in all respects.[10] Both systems have their pros and cons. However, there is a tendency to move towards the Anglo-American practice. Economists have warned that changing only a single characteristic within one of these systems runs the risk of making performance worse, not better. This is because the various characteristics of any corporate governance system are complementary.[11]

5.1.3 Different Practical Approaches to Corporate Governance

Several proposals have been issued by committees in various EU countries and by international organisations such as the OECD and Bank for International Settlements.[12] The trend in proposals put forward by individual EU countries is towards reliance on self-regulation supported by market-based enforcement.

A good example of this is the Code of Best Practice issued and codified by three UK-based committees. It includes recommendations on efficient board structures and division of responsibilities, disclosure of information on executive pay systems and voting procedures at AGMs, as well as control systems for reporting by setting up audit and remuneration committees. Although they are only recommendations, reference to the Code is part of the listing requirements for the London Stock Exchange. What makes this even more effective, is that UK-listed companies are requested to indicate the degree of compliance with the code in their annual reports and explain the reasons for any non-compliance. The ultimate efficiency of self-regulation of this kind depends very much on the actions taken by the Stock Exchange or other market players in the event of non-compliance. Voluntary rules lose much of their effect if they do not include or are not supplemented by adequate means of enforcement in the event of non-compliance. This is the situation with regard to the Viennot Report issued by the French Employers' Federation.[13]

The criticism of a loose enforcement system can be applied to the recommendations of the Helsinki Stock Exchange on corporate governance. The Stock Exchange supported the conclusions of the Corporate Governance Working Group by recommending that listed companies comply with the proposals of the working group. In the absence of an obligation to justify any non-compliance and in the absence of any indication of sanctions in the case of non-compliance, the incentive effect of the recommendation is quite small. Moreover, the recommendations are less far-reaching than, say, those of the UK committees.

The principles of Corporate Governance[14] issued by the OECD are non-binding and as such not meant to be implemented into national legislation. According to the OECD, principles of good corporate governance cover five key areas:

1. The rights of the shareholders;
2. The equitable treatment of shareholders;
3. The role of stakeholders;
4. Disclosure and transparency; and
5. The responsibilities of the board.

On the contrary, the OECD, favouring a laissez faire system, leaves it up to national governments and market participants to decide how to apply the Principles to each country's legal and regulatory framework, 'taking into account costs and benefits of regulation'. The value of the OECD guidelines lies in their material content, not in their judicial force or legal powers.

The Basel Committee on Banking Supervision has supported the OECD work and published a paper entitled 'Enhancing Corporate Governance for Banking Organisations' (September 1999). The committee wanted to 'reinforce the importance for banks of the OECD principles, to assist supervisors in promoting the adoption of sound corporate governance practices by banking organisations'. According to the Basel Committee, good corporate governance includes the following areas:

1. Establishing strategic objectives and a set of corporate values that are communicated throughout the banking organisation.
2. Setting and enforcing clear lines of responsibility and accountability throughout the organisation.
3. Ensuring that board members are qualified for their positions, have a clear understanding of their role in corporate governance and are not subject to undue influence from management or outside concerns.
4. Ensuring that there is appropriate oversight by senior management.
5. Effectively utilising the work conducted by internal and external auditors, in recognition of the important control function they provide.
6. Ensuring that compensation approaches are consistent with the bank's ethical values, objectives, strategy and control environment.
7. Conducting corporate governance in a transparent manner.

The committee, like the OECD, recognises that different structural approaches to corporate governance exist – and are allowed to exist – across countries.

Therefore the committee encourages any practices that can strengthen corporate governance under these diverse structures. As a result, neither of these organisations indicates a preference for a particular governance structure.

The European Union approach to corporate governance stems from the drive to create a single market area. Essentially, this means that the primary approach of the EU is to harmonise the legal framework at EU level.[15] In line with this, the European Commission has launched a Financial Markets Action Plan supporting a rapid progress towards a single market. As part of the Plan, the Commission will publish a review of existing national codes of corporate governance in order to identify potential legal barriers to the completion of a single European financial market.

It is clear that Europe has a long way to go when it comes to common rules on corporate governance. In view of the fact that legal frameworks associated with corporate governance differ significantly across EU member states and include very sensitive issues from political, social and economic points of view, it is hard to foresee rapid harmonisation in this area. A quicker way forward might therefore be a combination of national codes of best practices backed up by national stock exchanges as well as by supervisory, accounting and auditing bodies. On a cross-border level, the strengthening of the BIS role as regards guidelines for corporate governance of financial market institutions would be beneficial. Obviously there are other alternatives. An example that applies to corporate business in general is the Centre for European Policy Studies (CEPS) suggestion that a group of blue chip European corporations could show the way and adopt a European Code of Good Practices in directing and controlling corporate business at EU level.[16]

A critical question at EU level, and more generally, is the balance between promoting self-discipline and binding legal rules. As noted earlier, self-discipline may remain ineffective if not backed up by rules of enforcement. The self-discipline approach is, however, more flexible and quicker to realise. Political consensus for legal amendments could be more difficult to achieve than say consensus among supervisors.

5.2   SETTING INCENTIVES FOR BANK MANAGEMENT

A good governance system for bank management focuses on the questions of how to get management committed, how to exploit market discipline and how to control management. A suitable corporate governance structure will start with a clear division of labour and responsibilities among a bank's management and board, as well as clear and exercisable sanctions in the event of non-compliance. Thus, all responsible agents and bodies must face their responsibility in its positive (responsibility and power) and negative (responsibility and sanctions) dimensions.

In the following, we look first at the positive side of responsibility, Section 5.2.1 focusing on one particular aspect, that is the issue of a one-tier board structure versus a two-tier board structure. We cite some of the conclusions in the literature and use empirical evidence from Finland as a case to argue in favour of a one-tier board structure. Section 5.2.2 'Responsibility and Sanctions' explores the negative side of responsibility, and refers to empirical evidence from New Zealand and Scandinavian countries, mostly Finland.

5.2.1 Responsibility and Power

Research results are somewhat contradictory and studies have not been able to recommend a single optimal board structure. The structure of corporate boards varies greatly across the countries. It ranges from a two-tier supervisory and management board structure in Germany, to insider-dominated boards in Japan, and to mixed boards in the United States and the United Kingdom.[17] Sweden has applied a one-tier board structure with a strong presence of non-executive members. It is one of the forerunners in having a profession of expert non-executive board members.

All models are at least partly dependent on the corporate and political culture of each country and not a simple result of pure economic factors. Shleifer and Vishny (1997) refers to studies showing that there has had to be a real disaster, before boards, even in the US, have actually acted and removed top managers. Some studies refer to the fact that even US corporate boards are captured by management.

When it comes to the potential approach of the European Union in this respect, it is unlikely that there will be any strict ruling in favour of any particular one of the models. On the contrary, there are signs that Europe will allow both two-tier and one-tier board structures. This can be concluded from the EC draft on the Fifth Company Law Directive, from BIS guidelines, and from the OECD approach. Thus, it will be up to member states' own legal rules which model is chosen. This being the case, the need for a European-wide code of best practise emphasising crucial elements *within* different legal structures becomes even more important.

Empirical Evidence from Finland

If forced to a choice our inclination is to favour a one-tier board structure for both ordinary companies and banks. Empirical evidence from Finland for example points in this direction. Finland's banking crisis revealed major drawbacks in the internal governance structure of banks, both for commercial banks with limited liability and savings banks with a special kind of a thrift or mutual form.

In Finland the legal framework of ordinary companies differs in some crucial aspects from that of banks. The Companies Act (1998) allows, but does not require, a two-tier board structure for companies above a certain size (in relation to share capital, the trigger is EUR 80 000). The responsibilities of the supervisory board can be divided into those required by law, assumed by law, and permitted by law. The supervisory board is required to oversee the board of directors and managing director, to give a statement on the annual accounts and audit, and to give instructions to the board on far-reaching and crucial issues. The body is assumed to elect and decide the pay and bonus systems of the board. If stipulated in the articles of association, the supervisory board is, for example, entitled to decide on a major decrease or increase in the company's activities.

According to the Companies Act, the board of directors is responsible for the proper organisation of the administration and business of the company. More specifically, the board is ultimately responsible for accounting and financial management, while the managing director is responsible for running day-to-day business and is particularly charged with ensuring that the company's accounting satisfies legal requirements and that financial management is organised in a reliable manner. The board of directors is the key body of the company. The managing director may be appointed chairman of the board of directors in companies with a supervisory board.

When it comes to banks, the supervisory board is a compulsory body in commercial banks and co-operative banks, while in savings banks it is non-compulsory. The rationale relates to the fact that the board of directors is assumed to include, predominantly or solely, executive members, each of whom is responsible for various fields of banking business in day-to-day operations. The supervisory board is responsible for overseeing that the bank is run prudently in compliance with laws and articles of association. More specifically, the supervisory board is responsible for electing members of the board of directors, deciding on their pay and bonus systems, confirming general guidelines on strategic matters and issuing a statement on the accounts and audit of the company.

The responsibilities of the board of directors are very loosely regulated in the Banking Acts. The only rule is that the board of directors is responsible for the conduct of banking business in compliance with laws and the articles of association thus implying that the board is the key organ of the bank with a wide range of responsibilities. There are no specific provisions on the responsibilities of the managing director, thus leaving this area dependent upon general law and the articles of association.

The problems with the two-tier board structure relate partly to the laxness and obscurity of legal rulings and partly to problems caused by poor business practices.

Ordinary companies in Finland, with the exception of state-owned companies, are in the process of doing away with their supervisory boards and strengthening the role of the non-executive boards. An example of this is Nokia Plc, a Finnish-based telecom company with 80 per cent of its shares in foreign hands. The company adopted a market-oriented strategy in 1994, with the aim of building a global company with a clear focus on telecom business. The company now has a nine-member board with eight non-executives, two of which are non-Finnish.

Most of the state-owned companies in Finland have had, and still have, a two-tier board structure with a large (12–20-member) supervisory board. Some companies even have a supervisory board as well as a non-executive board, thus providing two overlapping levels of control. However, most Finnish academic literature sees a combination of a supervisory board and executive board as being problematic, even dangerous.[18] There have been serious discussions, and official committee recommendations, regarding the need for simplifying the governance structure in state-owned companies. The recommendations have only slowly led to any major changes mainly because of political resistance. Recent developments have, however, accentuated the problems associated with large and poorly informed supervisory boards. It has become increasingly obvious that supervisory boards are failing in their role of exercising control and decision-making.

The dangers from the two-tier structure are evident from the problems revealed in the Finnish banking crisis at the beginning of the 1990s. When it comes to their role in controlling the board and management, the supervisory board is highly dependent on information given by management. In this structure, the supervisory board becomes the only controlling organ in the bank because the internal board structure makes lines of responsibility between management and the board obscure. If the supervisory board is large (more than ten members) and simultaneously the duties are obscure or less relevant regarding the actual possibilities for controlling the executive board, the executive board (not the supervisory board) actually runs the business and even supervises itself. The vagueness of the agent-principal relationships between management and the board causes real problems. It is difficult to see how the board can critically and independently judge management in a situation where the board is comprised of members of management. The situation is also difficult in the sense that management presents company matters on the board to itself.[19]

The situation described above becomes worse in a bank where decision-making powers are widely delegated among members of the board of directors. Combined with the need to run the operational business quickly and flexibly, this may result in a situation where there is no single entity within the bank that is actually aware of and is controlling the total risk positions of the bank as a whole. There have been cases in the history of banking in some countries where the delegation of responsibilities within a board and the absence of sufficient control systems has offered a free rein to the most aggressive management-board-members, without any fear of actually being controlled by anybody. There is a Russian saying 'trust but verify', which sums up the desirable division of labour between management and board, as well as the division of labour within the board itself.

For Finnish savings banks, a two-tier board structure was made possible in 1991. However, a lot of the bad assets had already been taken on by the savings banks. Thus it is not a two-tier board structure that is to blame when it comes to problems in the performance of Finnish savings banks. The key problems relate to the uncertainty surrounding the division of responsibilities between the managing director, the board and delegates. The last-mentioned are the authorised representatives of the members of savings banks (i.e. the savers), mostly senior managers, to whom the board can delegate its duties. The managing director can also act as a delegate.

Supported by the statutory right to delegate authority, there was a shift in the control and decision-making in the day-to-day business of savings banks towards a powerful internal management (managing director and the delegates) on the one hand, and a soft non-executive board on the other. The situation was further exacerbated by the fact that board members represented local interest groups (customer groups, local economic and social groups) and thus lacked experience in banking or corporate business. The decision-making and control system resembled that of their central institution (the Skopbank). The only difference was that in Skopbank practically all powers were vested in the executive board, while in the savings banks it was the management team (managing director and the delegates) which wielded similar powers.

It was very much in the Skopbank's interests to favour a quick and flexible decision-making system in the savings banks (and obviously this has some merits in principle). But given an aggressive lending strategy, efficient control systems became even more relevant. The boards lacked both sufficient information and sufficient expertise, the need for which was not regarded necessary by management nor indeed by Skopbank. There was a feeling, during the late 1980s, that the mission of the board of savings banks was to trust, not to control. All in all, the delegation of responsibility for day-to-day operations to a savings bank's management, headed by the managing director, obscured the original division of responsibility between management and the board. The power of the managing director, in particular, increased, but he was not subject to effective scrutiny and control.

The more levels of control there are, the bigger are the agency problems. The Finnish experience provides support for a one-tier board structure approach with highly qualified non-executive board members forming a majority (even in banks and state-owned companies). A situation where non-executive members are in a minority on the board may cause problems.[20] The 'external' members can end up as hostages of the chairman and their independence can be questioned. The collegial legal responsibility, if also enforced by courts, should, however, act as an incentive for 'external' members to fight for a level playing field in comparison with 'internal' members.

In addition to a one-tier board structure, legal rulings should emphasise the clear division of responsibility between the managing director and the board, and distinguish the relevant areas of responsibilities for each of these parties. For example, banking legislation should mirror company legislation in addressing who is responsible, and how, for risk management and accounting. The confusion regarding the principal–agent relationship that results from delegation is a matter that should be given greater attention when defining rules of responsibility. The board can delegate its tasks, but the act of delegation should not reduce its own liability to oversee management.

5.2.2   Responsibility and Sanctions

The issues discussed above were connected with the positive side of responsibility – the 'responsibility and power' dimension. We now turn to the negative side of responsibility, namely the 'responsibility and sanctions' dimension. The idea of sanctions has to do with the incentive effect they have on management and board members by encouraging them to undertake their existing duties conscientiously. Thus in an optimal situation, there is no need to exercise sanctions. They act as a deterrent and a driving force for prudence. However, the real world is not optimal and the enforcement of sanctions is as important as the sanctions themselves.

Rules on Sanctions

We consider in some detail the New Zealand regime in the next two chapters as it is the main example of an existing scheme employing market discipline through public disclosure. However, at this point it is worth noting their approach to sanctions. New Zealand implemented a new system of banking supervision, following a four-year period of review, in 1996. The system entails a network of incentives to ensure that appropriate attention is paid to the management of risk by bank shareholders, directors, management, depositors, financial analysts and competitors. These incentives are applied by an extensive regime of quarterly disclosure of banks' assets, liabilities and exposures to risks, backed up by an attestation by all the directors, including also non-executive directors, that the bank is applying appropriate risk management procedures. In the attestation the board members confirm that the bank has put adequate systems in place to monitor and control risks and that these systems are being properly applied. Directors are liable to fines (up to $NZ25 000, equivalent to US$13 000) and periods of imprisonment (up to three years) for false or mis-leading statements – regarding both disclosure and attestation – and have unlim-ited personal civil liability for losses incurred by others as a result of these statements. Civil liability is possible in the case of losses sustained from sub-scribing to any debt security, including bank deposits, issued by the bank on the basis of false or misleading information contained in the disclosure statements.

The requirement for disclosure and attestation, together with a particular criminal or civil liability to provide true and fair information, is a clear incentive for prudent behaviour and ex ante commitment. It is also common in Sweden and Finland, for example, to have rules on sanctions in the event of overall neg-ligence. To give an example, under the Finnish Credit Institutions Act, members of the supervisory board and executive board are subject to civil liability for losses incurred by the bank and caused by negligent or intentional behaviour on the part of board members. The responsible bodies are also subject to a criminal liability (fine or imprisonment of up to six months) for providing false or mis-leading information to the authorities. Moreover, there is a penal law provision on intentional or gross negligence in connection with the drawing up of an annual or interim report that contravenes the law or regulations issued by the authorities.

The New Zealand approach is far better when it comes to ex ante efforts through legislation or regulation to get bank directors committed to prudent behaviour and control. The approach clearly highlights the key responsibility of the directors. A particular advantage of the New Zealand approach, as compared with that of Finland and Sweden, is that it addresses the key areas of responsibil-ity while in Finland and Sweden civil liability is limited to an overall duty to run the business in a prudent way. Another drawback of the provisions on special criminal liability in Finland and Sweden relates to their emphasis on gross negli-gence and intention, as well as to the emphasis on providing information to the authorities, not to the public. A more effective approach would be to specify the duties of the board and management to ensure true and fair disclosure as well as risk management procedures, and leave non-compliance with these duties sub-ject to a particular liability.

Enforcement of Sanctions

One consequence of the banking crises in Scandinavian countries was that direc-tors had to share the financial losses incurred by the banks as a result of their negligent behaviour. The procedures themselves differed quite markedly between Finland, Norway and Sweden. Sweden and Norway did not embark on long court processes. Rather, the authorities succeeded in agreeing with the directors amounts of damage compensation, together with the cancellation of retirement bonuses previously granted to the directors. Whereas in Finland, the authorities left it to the banks to raise damage compensation claims against former bank directors, 27 claims in total. The cases were raised on the basis of negligent behaviour in respect of an overall duty for prudent conduct and also in respect of the duty to comply with some specific legal rules, such as rules on large exposures and rules on limitations for non-collateralised lending. After seven years of ongoing trials, there are still some cases waiting for the verdict of the appeal courts. Thus the process has been a long one, has cost both sides a great deal of money, and resulted in quite low levels of compensation penalties, particularly for former board members.

It is by no means certain that these trial procedures will act as proper incentives against excessive risk taking in the future, although in theory this should be the case. When all the rulings have come out, the banking industry and supervisors should be better informed about the extent of accepted risk taking. Thus one can argue that legitimate rules for misconduct enforced by courts may increase the accountability of bank's management and board, and thus act as proper incentive for prudent behaviour in the whole sector.

However, the compensation processes have turned out to be burdensome, difficult to run, time consuming and expensive. They have also revealed features of unfairness from a human point of view. Although the court rulings may serve as codes of conduct for prudent banking business, the compensation processes are too costly ways for safeguarding prudent banking behaviour. Thus the experience has revealed the structural problem of the compensation processes. It is fair to conclude that the confidence of shareholders and supervisors in the compliance of prudent banking business cannot be built upon compensation processes. There is evident need for emphasis on clear-cut rules of responsibility as well as proper corporate governance culture.

Sanctions play a certain role in the incentive framework for prudential behaviour by banks. Sanctions and their enforcement are the last link in the chain beginning from clear-cut lines of responsibility in all agent-principal relations. An important aspect is progressive incentives before penalties are triggered. This latter aspect is also explored in connection with incentives for supervisors (Section 5.4).

Instead of traditional damage compensation types of sanctions there is need for sanctions marked by easy execution. An example of this could be an administrative or civil fine determined by a supervisory authority in the event of a clear breach of a legal norm. Compared with traditional and heavy mechanisms of civil liability, these types of sanctions would be most efficient from the point of view of ease of process. Other examples in this connection would be a statement or an admonition given by a supervisor.

5.2.3   Positive Incentives

There is a danger in focusing to strongly simply on the corporate structure of the bank. There is a parallel concern in the literature with trying to provide appropriate mechanisms for managers to share the same incentives as the shareholders. These usually come in the form of stock options or other elements of salary that are only paid if the company performs up to the shareholders' expectations. Although this is normally characterised in terms of encouraging effort on the part of the top management, in part this is a reflection of a fear that managers may be more risk averse than the shareholders. (There is, of course, the simple aspect of reward. Managers need to be given adequate incentive to stay with the bank. Otherwise in a competitive environment good managers will be enticed away to competitors.)

There are various ways in which this could occur. Since a manager's career may be at risk from ill-advised actions it may be much more difficult for them to diversify risk in the way in which corporate shareholders and funds can. It would not look good for a manager to have extensive shareholdings in competitor banks, for example, assuming they have the wealth to do so. Skills may be relatively sector specific, so the manager is more exposed to financial sector fluctuations. Shareholders' risks are limited to their investment. It may be therefore that the extra risks that the managers face are a help in trying to ensure the prudential behaviour of banks.

The evidence on where the balance lies in practice is mixed. Whidbee and Wohar (1999) argue that there is a clear link between the use of derivatives by the bank and the extent of insider shareholdings in the United States. Most importantly they interpret this as a deliberate shifting of the risk onto deposit insurance. Hedging is lower when insider holdings are larger. But there is a second finding that reinforces our emphasis on the structure of corporate governance, namely, that a higher level of monitoring by external directors also increases the use of derivatives as a means of reducing risk. While Houston and James (1995) find that CEOs in US banks tend to receive rather less in the way of options and stocks than their counterparts in other industries, this does not tell us whether the incentive is optimal from society's point of view. One of the main reasons for wanting to regulate banking in the first place is that the moral hazard is greater. Hence having lower incentives for managers to take risks would be wholly appropriate. The incentives do not have to substantial to be effective (Haubrich, 1994).

As we develop in the next section, if the system of banking regulation involves the explicit insurance of deposits then the insurance premium that banks (or their depositors) have to pay will depend upon the structure of corporate governance. Thus in this instance the nature of the management incentives will need to be priced into the premium (John *et al.*, 2000). Doing this would presuppose the ability to identify and price the risk profile that the incentive packages for the managers is intended to generate. If it is the insurer who determines the premium according to their view of the risk then the onus would be on the bank to make the scheme transparent if they are not to be charged the higher premium based on unknown risk. However, the same argument applies to pricing through the market. The bank's risk premium will depend upon its revealed capital provisioning and its risk management processes of which the compensation incentive structure is part.

5.3 SETTING INCENTIVES FOR SHAREHOLDERS

The issue of owners' incentives for efficient control of management relates to the amount of capital they have invested in the company as well as to the functions of market mechanisms in the case of the threat of liquidation or take-over by outsiders.

The literature in this area often refers to the fact that dispersed ownership together with too many small shareholders creates bigger demands for well-functioning corporate governance, although this view is also disputed. Some studies address the fact that large shareholders also cause costs (see Shleifer and Vishny, 1997). These studies note that large investors represent their own interests, which need not coincide with the interests of other investors nor with the interests of employees and managers. Japanese evidence offers a very different view of large investors, namely that they are too soft rather than too tough. According to various studies the same applies to German banks, who are not nearly as active in corporate governance as might be expected given that their influence in lending to, and control of, corporations is significant. Large banks are seen to be too soft in corporate control because of their own agency problems, and because they fail to terminate unprofitable projects they have invested in – continuation is preferred to liquidation.

The United States and the United Kingdom are among countries where large shareholdings, especially majority ownership, are relatively uncommon (Shleifer and Vishny, 1997; Yla-Anttila and Ali-Yrkko, 1999; Dewatripont and Becht, 1998). In 98 per cent of US companies voting powers of individual shareholders are less than 50 per cent and in 53 per cent of companies less than 5 per cent. The respective figures for German companies are 36 and 1 per cent. The median size of the largest ultimate outside voting block in Germany, France, Italy, the United Kingdom and the United States are 52, 20, 52, 10 and 0 per cent respectively. We can conclude from this that large shareholdings in one form or another are almost the norm in countries other than the United States and the United

Kingdom. The same applies to the banking sector, although the high concentration in the banking sector in several countries also reflects the small number of significant banking institutions.

There are additional ways to increase owners' incentives to control management than purely through concentration of ownership. The importance of adequate capital includes factors that reduce the quality of capital. Besides formal capital requirements, true and fair financial statements, which enable determination of whether the actual capital base corresponds with the officially reported capital, are also crucial. Sufficient actual and reported capital is necessary for preventing excessive risk taking. Firstly because it comprises a necessary buffer against risk realisations. Secondly, a sufficient capital requirement gives owners the proper incentive to upgrade their monitoring, which again lowers the probability that they will lose substantial amounts of their investments. Sufficient legally mandated capital is also an important offset to excessive risk taking that might result from the moral hazard generated by deposit protection and other safety nets.

Consequences of differences in the accounting rules of Scandinavian countries provide lessons for the crucial features of well-functioning accounting rules that support the build-up of 'true' capital. ('True' in the sense of there being capital of the size stated readily available to use in the event of adverse shocks to the bank.)

On the whole, the capital adequacy requirements laid down in Finnish banking legislation did not meet international standards as regards their contents and timetable for their adoption.[21] The situation did not change until the end of the first half of the 1990s. When deregulation got under way in the mid-1980s this structural distortion in the legal framework became more pronounced since banks could operate with levels of capital that were too low and the rules on capital adequacy underestimated the true extent of risk taking. This was particularly true for local banks – savings banks and co-operative banks.[22]

In addition to the overall framework of capital adequacy mentioned above, there were some particular features, which in fact eroded the hard core of equity capital. The widespread use of revaluation reserves to meet the requirements of capital adequacy was one of the major distortions, which led to a situation where savings banks' formal capital adequacy did not correspond to their actual capital adequacy. In contravention of the Accounting Act and good accounting practice, the revaluation reserves among banks have from the very beginning aimed at increasing the level of equity capital, rather than being an exceptional and extreme instrument for re-pricing the value of real estate assets, for example. The revaluation reserves were key, for example in the 1980s, when competition among the different banking groups increased. The situation was preceded by a long boom period and liberalisation of capital markets. In this new situation there were no impediments to increased lending to customers. Thus the pressures to increase the level of equity capital became bigger and bigger. In hindsight, the distorted incentive effect of this particular accounting practice can easily be discerned: instead of prudent risk taking, efforts focused on finding artificial ways to meet the legal requirements of capital adequacy.

The accounting rules and practices of Denmark are an example of efficient rules that have resulted in the disclosed amount of capital being in line with the actual amount of capital. The Danish accounting rules for banks are basically based on a mark-to-market principle. Banks have for years had to value their assets, including loans to customers, according to the market value or present value. The latter can be applied if there is no actual market value for a particular loan. In line with this principle, the banks have had to make loan loss reserves for both obvious and potential losses. In general, the Danish loan valuation rules are among the strictest in the world. The Danish authorities and banks share the opinion that the strict rules for loan losses were one reason for the fact that Denmark escaped a systemic crisis in their financial markets, unlike its Nordic neighbours Norway, Sweden and Finland.[23] Of equal importance is also the requirement of an adequate level of capital – Denmark met international standards years earlier than Finland, Sweden or Norway.

When it comes to Finnish accounting rules, particularly before the 1990s, the loan loss provisions were based on taxation rules rather than on accounting rules. Taxation rules specifying the maximum tax-deductible amounts of annual provisions for loan losses (0.6 per cent of the lending) have dictated the level of loan loss provisions in accounting. This led to a situation where too little emphasis was given to the true value of banks' loan stock, which may have increased the potential distortion between the actual value of own capital and the formal value. As a consequence, the profitability and solvency of savings banks reported in their accounts did not give sufficient, if any, warning signals before 1991, although the problems that ultimately culminated in a severe crisis were present in balance sheets during the late 1980s.[24] As a curiosum, Skopbank was apparently one of the most solvent banks in Finland at the start of the 1990s. However, the bank was taken over by the Finnish central bank in September 1991. All in all, loosening the close links between taxation and accounting has been a key issue since the 1980s and some progress has been made, but a lot still remains to be done.

The accounting rules on asset valuation and loan loss reserves in Sweden and Norway have also by tradition been less strict than in Denmark. However, the Norwegian accounting rules for loan loss reserves, for example, cannot be blamed for the country's banking crisis. Although reliable, true and fair accounting rules for valuation of lending activity are an important instrument for describing the real economic situation of banks. In addition to well-founded and forward looking accounting rules for loan loss reserves, there is a need for banks to create adequate reserves for potential future problems during years of good economic performance. This highlights the importance of a strong capital base as a buffer against potential future problems. In line with Finland, the capital adequacy of many Norwegian banks was insufficient for covering any big losses. According to the report to the Norwegian Parliament, the legal requirements regarding solvency ratios were, at least to some extent, too lax in order to prevent excessive risk-taking. This criticism applies, for example, to rules on subordinated debt, which enabled the Norwegian banks to increase their capital base without any actual external capital infusion.

5.3.1 Limited Liability

One specific factor that may lead to moral hazard among shareholders is the existence of limited liability. Once the share value has reached zero there is nothing worse that can happen. There is thus a clear division of interest between the shareholders and the depositors and other creditors, who will lose when the bank is unable to meet its obligations. Their loss will only be total when the bank has no assets with which to meet its liabilities, a step far beyond simple insolvency. Insofar as there is some seniority ranking among creditors then there also there will be difference in attitude with those that get paid out first tending to take a rather more lenient view than those who are paid out last.

Clearly, if depositors were sufficiently concerned about the risk they would prefer to bank with institutions that offered unlimited liability. An analogous situation applies in insurance where Lloyds of London was able to offer unlimited liability as part of its attraction. However, such arrangements are only attractions if they remain believable. In the case of Lloyds it became clear that many of the 'names' had not treated the prospect of unlimited liability seriously. Being bankrupted or at best severely affected by the unexpected risks incurred by their syndicates was not what they had in mind in subscribing capital to what had previously been a fairly reliable source of income. (Lloyds has responded by moving away from unlimited liability.) Similarly in the case of the unlimited liability banks in Scotland in the nineteenth century it was the failure of the City of Glasgow Bank in 1878 that brought the system down (Evans and Quigley, 1995). Ultimately calls of £2750 per £100 share had to be made, bankrupting all but 254 of the 1819 owners.

Introducing greater liability for shareholders is not a realistic option even if it were a sensible means of improving the incentive for shareholders to manage their risks more prudently – by monitoring the behaviour of management much more closely. There are other disadvantages of unlimited liability in that not only are the monitoring costs of the managers by the owners more costly but so are the monitoring costs by the shareholders of each other. Each shareholder needs to be reassured that the others can meet their obligations if the bank fails, as the remainder have to find the necessary funds when a shareholder defaults or is brankrupted.[25] There are, however, two important corollaries from these observations. First, one of the main responses to the increased risk for the depositor from decreased shareholder liability has been deposit insurance. This does not remove the risk but it shunts it one step further on – to the non-insured depositors and onto the insurers. There is then more moral hazard for the insured depositors who have little reason to be concerned about the management of risks by the bank, as their exposure to loss (from a period of restricted access to their funds) is small. For this reason some deposit insurance schemes, the United Kingdom for example, impose a 'haircut' on all depositors, which both puts some pressure on them to monitor and covers some of the administrative costs.

It is easy to see how this cycle works if it is the state that is the implicit or explicit insurer. It is they who will have the main incentive to monitor the banks, through the supervisory authorities. If they give signals that they are likely to bail out banks with taxpayers' money then this increases the incentive for everybody else in the circle to run higher risks. O'Hara and Shaw (1990) show the extent of the bonus to the share price, when the Controller of Currency in the United States admitted to Congress that he regarded the 11 largest US banks as in effect 'too large to fail' (Morgan, 2000).

The second important corollary for our purposes is that the main feature that led to the development of effective limited liability was the increased transparency and hence ability to monitor the behaviour of our banks offered by publication of bank balance sheets and the introduction of independent audits required by the Companies Act of 1879 (Lewis and Quigley, 1995). Between them these two implications illustrate key characteristics of our proposals: all those involved as stakeholders in the bank need to have incentives for seeing prudent risk management by the bank; increased transparency, through public disclosure, is required to enable the stakeholders to monitor the bank sufficiently to judge that risk management.

5.3.2   The Role of 'Charter' Value

One further incentive that applies to bank shareholders, or at least a different perspective on the incentives that exist, is the 'charter' value of the bank. This is in effect the value to the bank of having a banking licence and the value of the private information it has about the quality of its borrowers. This will accrue in part from the barrier to entry and in part from the availability of insurance, whether explicit for depositors or implicit for the bank itself through the expectation of a bail out. The charter value will also depend on the bank's perceived position in the market, as it is effectively a capitalisation by the market of the expected 'rents' that the bank can earn (i.e. profits above the normal for the economy).

The greater the charter value then the more the bank has to lose, hence higher charter values themselves act as a deterrent to risk taking (Bhattachrya *et al.*, 1998).

5.4   Setting Incentives for Supervisors

One of the key lessons of banking crises in several countries is that regimes of detailed supervision have major drawbacks not only in relation to cost but also in relation to systemic stability.[26] Another key lesson is that supervisors tend to be overly forbearing when detecting signals of distorted behaviour or imminent problems.[27] Supervisors may also have a tendency to buy time to solve the problems, rather than getting to grips with the very problems themselves.[28]

The responses in relation to detailed supervision and forbearance are that supervisors should commit to ex-ante-defined procedures and disclosure of supervisory actions, positive or negative. Commitment to procedures, rather than to licence-based detailed supervision, underscores supervisors' commitment to the objectives of rules and procedures. Striving for the increased disclosure of supervisory findings is a way of increasing the accountability of supervisors, of letting other market participants assess the effectiveness of supervision and also of increasing the commitment of bank management, directors and owners to prudent behaviour and risk control of banking business.

The above-mentioned commitment to ex ante procedures is not unanimously shared by all participants in the field of supervision.[29] However, commitment to ex ante procedures does not necessarily mean a reduction in overall supervisory discretion. But it does mean the limitation of arbitrary discretion by supervisors. Commitment to procedures makes supervisors more accountable to the public and other market participants. It also implies incentives for supervisors themselves to comply with the objectives of legislation and supervision, which helps to promote systemic stability. And last but not least, it implies incentives for bank management to take deliberate remedial actions before being subjected to legal actions taken by authorities. At the end of the day, there also is a possibility that the amount of detailed, private information provided to supervisors can be reduced. It is, however, noticeable that most suggested 'incentive' systems for supervisors are actually regulatory constraints. Some authors, such as Campbell *et al.* (1992) have discussed a system of financial reward and penalty for monitors according to the quality of the job they manage. This would be a profit-making exercise undertaken by a private institution, in effect on behalf the institution that is insuring depositors. Such an open contract would certainly make the point of the exercise clear and would require a very explicit evaluation of priorities.

An example of ex ante procedures is the system of Prompt Corrective Action in the US, which gives the FDIC wide rights and duties in the event that the capital adequacy of a credit institution falls below each prescribed limit as the position worsens. This emphasises the accountability of supervisors and their duty to commit themselves effectively to the objectives of legislation.

5.4.1 The Approach of the Finnish FSA

The Finnish Financial Supervisory Authority (FSA) provides an example of a supervisory approach aimed at increasing the accountability of supervisors and promoting market-based supervision (to exploit market discipline).

As a response to the 1990s banking crisis, the FSA has thoroughly revised its values, objectives and strategic approach with a view to achieving objectives in harmony with the accepted ethical values. The FSA's main values are independence, transparency, effectiveness and expertise in supervision (as set out on its webpage, www.rata.bof.fi). Its main objectives are to promote the stability and reliability of financial markets. Its main aims as an organisation are to be an independent, reliable, transparent and respected part of the domestic and international network of supervisors. The FSA's strategic approach is built on the twin aims of promoting market-based supervision and increasing the disclosure of relevant information. It also promotes the efficiency and reliability of financial markets, as well as co-operation with relevant domestic and foreign participants. The FSA's market-based approach to supervision is expressed in the way it promotes the efficient and ethically accepted functions of the financial markets.

The principles set out above could be applied to any supervisor operating in developed financial markets with a reasonably well functioning financial infrastructure. Our main interest here, however, is not in general objectives and values, but rather to point out some concrete methods and procedures for increasing the commitment and accountability of the supervisor himself to the above-mentioned objectives.

To implement the market-based approach in supervision, the FSA has split its concrete objectives into six areas:

1. to contribute to correct and sufficient information on financial services and products;
2. to contribute to a true and fair view of entities subject to supervision;
3. to achieve an effective combination of self-control and supervision;
4. to promote effective corporate governance, in particular effective shareholder control;
5. to control the suitability of the administration (risk management and 'fit and proper' aspect) of entities subject to supervision;

6. to increase the accountability, consistency and predictability of the supervisor himself.

As part of objective (2) (to contribute to a true and fair view of entities subject to supervision) the FSA is endeavouring to increase the amount of public disclosure of relevant information on financial sector institutions' performance and risk exposures. Of particular importance in the context of incentives for supervisors, the FSA is aiming to disclose its key supervisory decisions and actions. The main aim of disclosing ex post supervisory actions is not to increase the accountability of the supervisor, but rather to provide the public with a true and fair view of financial institutions. However, the disclosure of supervisory actions by definition also increases the accountability of the supervisor. Still, while the main aim is elsewhere, the need for ex ante disclosure (such as, for example, disclosure of internal ratings used by the supervisor and disclosure of findings on the basis of on-site inspection) is not emphasised. The latter aspect is one of the most problematic issues by far. One can, with good reason, argue that disclosure of ex ante findings creates more ambiguity and problems than it resolves. It might encourage highly rated institutions to take more risks. However, if, as suggested in Chapter 7, the burden of the supervisory regime is greatly increased should banks fail to live up to their high rating, it is possible to encourage banks both to try to raise their ratings and to maintain them, as they provide a clear benefit in indicating quality and reducing the cost of capital.

A basic principle underlying the FSA approach is to publish, whenever possible, all supervisory actions and decisions. Supervisory actions subject to disclosure are defined as legally binding actions authorised to be taken by the FSA, be they disciplinary (sanctions, prohibitions, etc.) or just the implementation of the legal rights of the FSA (to call for a general meeting or a supervisory board meeting). The interpretations of particular rules are not treated as supervisory actions, but the nature of them is such that it is in the interests of all parties that they be published. However, at this stage, the plan does not include actions relating to liquidation procedures. As one specific exception, the FSA is not going to disclose its decision to run a special audit of a bank.

The discretion relates to situations where the outcome could have extremely adverse consequences (unreasonable harm or threat of collapse) for the institution subject to disclosure. The aim is not to cause instability in the markets, but rather to strengthen the stability. However, the judgement involved in exercising discretion can be problematic, given the fact that short-term and long-term consequences can be different. The FSA has not defined closely where discretion might start, which leads to the assumption that discretion will be exercised to a rather limited extent, as the starting point is to disclose all decisions or legal actions taken by the FSA.

At the beginning of December 1999, a new Act on Publicity of the Actions of the Authorities came into force. The Act gives a clear signal in favour of transparency, stating that the documents of the authorities are public unless otherwise stipulated in the Act. The criteria for secret documents or secrecy are spelt out in the Act. In the field of financial markets supervision, documents concerning information on activities of financial markets are considered secret if the release of the documents would impair market reliability and stability. Documents containing findings on on-site inspection are also defined as secret if disclosure would jeopardise supervision or, without justifiable reason, have harmful effects on the institution subject to inspection. Thus the Act leaves the disclosure of the findings of inspection reports to the discretion of supervisors.

As part of objective (6) (to increase the accountability of the supervisor) the FSA is aiming to inform (through organised meetings) institutions subject to supervision of the requirements imposed on them as well as of any forthcoming projects. All this is seen as a way of making the supervisor commit himself to ex ante principles and enabling supervised institutions to assess the fairness and impartiality of the supervisor. As regards an active role in the financial markets, the aim of the FSA is to take a stand on the developments in the sector as a whole and from the stability or systemic risk point of view in particular.

5.4.2 Comparisons with other Regimes

The Finnish FSA is in the process of disclosing ex-post, rather than ex-ante supervisory actions, both positive and negative. The disclosure approach is based on two principles. The first is to make the supervisor committed to ex ante procedures and keep financial institutions informed about the procedures. The second relates to the 'real' disclosure of supervisory actions. It remains to be seen which cases will turn out to be the most important ones from the disclosure or commitment point of view, and how far-reaching the consequences of the FSA approach will be. The forthcoming Act on disclosure requirements of public authorities also lays the ground for increased transparency, although it is too early to anticipate the real consequences of the Act as that will depend on case-by-case interpretations.

The Act on Financial Supervision does not include any legal mechanisms for increasing the accountability of the FSA. The actions described above are based on voluntary decisions made by the FSA. In addition to the requirements of the forthcoming general Act on disclosure of documents of public authorities, the only statutory requirement relates to the obligation to disclose the annual accounts of the FSA. This approach differs markedly from that of the draft Bill for the UK statutory requirements.[30] Given that the proposed Financial Services and Markets Bill gives the UK FSA substantial discretion in the use of its rights and powers, the accountability of the supervisor is clearly emphasised in the Bill. The accountability mechanisms include:[31]

- the scope of judicial review
- public reporting mechanisms to the Treasury
- requirements for consultation
- the creation of Consumer and Practitioner Panels
- independent review of the rules and decisions of the FSA
- independent investigation of complaints against the FSA
- independent appeals and enforcement procedures

One reason why the aim of disclosing the supervisory actions of the Finnish FSA is to contribute to a true and fair view of supervised entities, rather than to increase the accountability of the FSA itself, might be the lack of statutory requirements for accountability. In this respect, the UK approach is preferable.

The other reason for less emphasis on the accountability of the supervisor relates to the Finnish legal tradition of limitations of supervisory discretion. The smaller the amount of discretion is, the smaller is the need for mechanisms of supervisory accountability. By contrast, the legal tradition of countries with common law jurisdiction (e.g. the United Kingdom) allows for wider discretion, which has to be balanced by mechanisms of accountability. However, the need for wider supervisory discretion is extensively emphasised in today's financial regulation. An example of this is Basel Committee's latest proposal for amended capital adequacy rules and especially its supervisory review element (pillar II). The accountability of the supervisor is an important element in the regime of forward-looking and anticipatory supervision where the supervisor has wide discretionary powers.

However, Finland, like most other countries, still has quite a long way to go in establishing new disclosure regimes for supervisors' activities. In addition to decisions on what and to what extent to disclose, the supervisor has to decide on the timing of disclosure. The supervisor may be faced with certain situations, particularly when it comes to critical findings that come to light in the course of supervision or inspection, where immediate disclosure would create problems for the institution being inspected. However, the sooner action is taken the better are the chances for well-timed corrective measures. Disclosure supports effective action by disciplining management to respond immediately to restore confidence in the institution.

There is no cut and dried answer to the question of where and when disclosure creates more problems than it solves. Lessons from the past nevertheless show that those required to disclose tend to take be reluctant and use the threat of potential negative consequences as an excuse for not disclosing information.

Supervisors should therefore take a sceptical view of proponents of non-disclosure in an effort to uncover the real motivations behind their arguments.

5.5 THE APPLICABILITY OF THE INCENTIVE-BASED CORPORATE GOVERNANCE FRAMEWORK TO DIFFERENT COUNTRIES

The incentive-based corporate governance framework we described functions best in well-developed markets, where market discipline functions effectively to provide incentives for various agent groups. Without effective and competitive markets, market-based disclosure loses most of its effect.

However, the incentive-based corporate governance approach remains an effective tool for achieving a more stable financial system, even in less developed markets, for example those of the transition economies. Individual rationality will still apply. Legal rules should be based on the premises of clear-cut rules of responsibility and sanctions in the event of non-compliance. Formal sanctions should be preceded by step-by-step tightening procedures to give parties a chance to take corrective actions before legal penalties are imposed.

There are problems in applying the framework we have described to economies with a different level of market efficacy but we do not draw a comprehensive picture of good corporate governance for countries in various stages of economic development here. We raise questions and point out issues that are of more importance than others. For instance, the ranking of importance of various actions and their appropriate sequencing may be different in emerging markets from that in advanced market economies.

In the absence of effective enforcement systems in the form of competitive markets it is not possible to emphasise market discipline and ways in which governance should mimic market discipline. Reliance on disclosure will fail, not only because actual legal constraints against misbehaviour are weak but also because external economic, cultural and market-based constraints are weak or absent.

This puts pressure on basic legal rules and institutions as well as on efficient implementation of those rules and enforcement systems. One feature that the legal systems of some transition economies share, especially in relation to their financial markets, is that legal rules (e.g. rules on capital adequacy) may give an impression that systems are very much in line with OECD standards. However, in the absence of well-functioning implementation and judicial enforcement, the actual impact of legislation remains very weak. Thus the existence of adequate corporate and banking legislation, accounting standards and auditing requirements are not alone sufficient. Rather, there is a great need to increase the integrity and credibility of the accounting and auditing profession, supervisors, regulators and even courts.

One way to increase integrity is to increase the accountability of the above mentioned bodies. This leads to the need for increased disclosure and assessment requirements concerning the duties and decisions of different bodies. It also increases the need to limit the discretion of authorities by making them commit to ex-ante procedures. The question of 'who monitors the monitors'[32] is a thorny one in advanced economies but exacerbated still further by the weakness of general oversight capabilities in transition economies, be it a question of the capabilities of laws, institutions, authorities, information or codes of conduct.

Thus, there is more need for an intrusive regime with incentive-based rules rather than self-imposed codes of conduct. Where self-regulation applies, the codes must be backed up by effective enforcement.

5.6 THE ROLE AND RESPONSIBILITY OF THE CENTRAL BANK

One of the primary responsibilities of central banks is the maintenance of financial market stability. However, there are differences in the implementation of this responsibility in practice. The differences are mainly due to the basic functions of central banks as well as to the institutional structures of supervision. The purpose of this chapter is not to delve into the issue of the role of central banks in promoting financial stability[33] but rather to raise some concrete questions as to what might be the optimal way to promote well-functioning corporate governance.

The starting point is the fact that corporate governance, as part of the legal infrastructure, is seen as a key factor promoting financial market stability. The importance of incentive-focused corporate governance has been accentuated in connection with the financial markets' crises of the last decade. The problems of emerging-market economies provide further support for this view, and emphasise the implementation and enforcement aspects. Thus we are concerned with the question of whether central banks should take a more active role in ex ante promotion of robust structures or whether (in many countries) the established division of labour between, say, the Ministry of Finance and the FSA, can be regarded as optimal.

The procedures established in Nordic countries provide examples of the somewhat different roles of central banks in the oversight of financial markets. These countries are not an entirely homogenous group owing to their different status in the European Union. However, all of their central banks have 'the promotion of financial stability and the reliability of financial markets' as one of their main functions, either in practice or specifically stated in their governing acts. The promotion of the stability of the system is interpreted as meaning that the central banks are responsible for financial markets oversight, while the separate supervisory authorities carry out supervision of individual institutions. Finland, Sweden and Norway publish somewhat differing reports on financial system stability while Iceland and Denmark do not publish anything. Sweden has chosen the most transparent approach. On the basis of a semi-annual 'Report on Financial Stability', they state the views of the central bank on strategic risk, credit risk, and counterparty risk, together with an assessment of macroeconomic developments. Openness is considered to be a way to increase the accountability of the central bank and make banks take corrective actions more quickly than would be the case if there were no open discussion. However, it is not clear what the reactions would be of, say, the Swedish central bank, if they anticipated systemic problems in financial markets.

All in all, it is not even clear how policy-oriented (including the legal policy approach) the oversight role of different countries' central banks is. And it is impossible to say how policy-oriented their role should be. Intuitively, and being aware of the strong macroeconomic expertise of central banks, one would assume that central banks are more inclined to use economic indicators for assessing financial stability, rather than analysing legal policy implications based on research work using both law and economics. A conventional view is to regard this issue as falling within the remit of the Ministry of Finance and whoever carries out financial supervision, as opposed to central banks. However, if we accept the key role corporate governance plays in financial sector stability, this area should be of particular interest to central banks, too. The more ex ante preventive central banks want to be, the more focus they should put on policy studies and recommendations with regard to well-functioning corporate governance as part of financial stability.

5.7 IMPLICATIONS

This chapter is based on the premise that corporate governance, as part of a country's legal infrastructure, is highly relevant for the stability of financial markets. This view has gained more and more supporters after the lessons learnt from the financial crises of the last two decades. It is widely accepted that a framework of good corporate governance should be based on incentives to induce various agent groups to be committed to their duties. Problems arise, however, in the actual implementation of an incentive-based corporate governance framework in different economies, and even within one country. This is because studies have not been able to demonstrate that one single framework is clearly better than another. What we do know is that the more efficient financial markets are, the more we can rely on market discipline as an effective incentive for bank directors, management, shareholders and supervisors.

As regards the incentives of the management for prudent behaviour, banking crises have taught us, among other things, that the confusion regarding the principal–agent relationships between the management and the board can result in serious negative outcomes, such as unsound risk taking by management. The more levels of control the bigger the agency problems. We therefore support the approach of a one-tier board structure with highly qualified non-executive board members as a majority. This applies both to banks and ordinary companies, be they private-owned or state-owned.

The accountability of supervisors should also be emphasised as a response to lessons from banking crises. This can be done in several ways, as the examples of the Finnish and the UK FSA show. However, the disclosure of supervisory decisions and actions as well as statutory requirements for accountability mechanisms need not be seen as mutually exclusive but rather as complementary for the overall increase of the effectiveness of supervision and the stability of financial markets.

The promotion of well-functioning corporate governance should also be in the interests of central banks. The more ex ante preventative approach central banks adopt the more one would expect them to focus on promoting well-functioning corporate governance as part of financial stability.

6 The Rationale for a More Market-based Regime

In this and the following chapter we explore the possibilities for introducing a more market-based regime for financial supervision. This analysis will be based primarily on an appraisal of the characteristics of the best-known example of such a regime that is currently operating – namely, that in New Zealand. The key feature of our proposals is that we advocate a rather more comprehensive approach to exposing banks to market pressures in order to improve their prudential behaviour than has typically been the case in the existing literature. There the focus has been on trying to ensure that banks have to raise at least some of their capital from the market on a continuing basis. As mentioned earlier, Calomiris (1999), for example, suggests that every bank should have to raise at least 2% of their risky assets in the form of uninsured subordinated debt. This debt would have a two-year maturity and 1/24 of it would mature each month. In that way banks would continually have to face the market, whatever their corporate structures.[1] We noted in the previous chapter that one of the major problems in some banking crises came from banks – particularly small banks with a mutual element to their corporate structures – that were largely rather immune to market pressures.

We, therefore, consider a range of market pressures, starting with pressure in the product market through competition among banks and competition at the margin between banks and other financial institutions. Clearly the whole opening up of the European Single Market and the euro area, along with liberalisation of financial markets in the member states since the beginning of the 1980s will act as a boost, particularly in some of the smaller countries where domestic banks have exercised substantial monopoly power. As we noted in Chapter 3 there is continuing pressure for consolidation at the national level not just in Europe but in North America and Japan as well. The pressure from retail depositors and borrowers will depend a little on how high the barriers are to switching among banks.[2] Furthermore, insofar as their deposits are insured the market pressure will be blunted. In any case small retail depositors are typically ill-informed about risks, however transparent the system. It is therefore the large customers, the financial analysts, media and, above all, competitors, who will exert the real pressure.

Secondly, financial institutions are somewhat different from many commercial sectors in that they have to have extensive transactions with each other on a continuing basis and can be exposed to risks from imprudent behaviour by them. There is thus peer pressure from a different direction as well.

By discussing consolidation we have already mentioned a third area for market discipline – namely, the market for corporate control. This market can operate in a number of different ways. For widely quoted companies it will operate directly through the equity market, while for less traded institutions it will operate more through the pressure of the principal owners. We have already discussed in the previous chapter the importance of having structures of corporate governance that allow managers and directors of banks to be responsible for their prudential actions by being exposed to internal and regulatory sanctions.

Various aspects of market discipline will be blunted in each particular case. By establishing a variety of routes for this discipline the authorities can seek to ensure that, taken together, these pressures have effect. The New Zealand system is unusual in that all of the routes we have described are in operation. Its banks are exposed to the share market, the market for corporate control, retail depositors are not insulated by an insurance scheme and no bank has a dominant position in the market. Financial markets are typically quite deep and well-traded and the authorities have put considerable effort into increasing financial 'literacy'. The general picture is as follows.

In 1996 New Zealand implemented a new system of banking supervision following a four-year period of review. This new system has attracted considerable international interest as it represents a major step away from the prescriptive and intrusive systems that have normally been implemented elsewhere. It is an innovative response to the unfortunate fact that in recent years there have been substantial bank failures in the Nordic countries, Japan and the United States, among many others.

The principal feature of the new system is that it puts the responsibility for the prudent management of banks firmly on the directors and management of the banks themselves. It makes it the responsibility of the supervisor to concentrate on the stability of the financial system as a whole, not on the viability of any individual bank. Under this view, the 'moral hazard' present in banking systems should be reduced and taxpayers' money should not be put at risk. Individual banks should expect to fail if they become insolvent, whatever their size.

This system is based on incentives to try to ensure that all those actually or potentially involved in the business of the bank have a keen regard for the management of risk. This includes not just bank shareholders, directors, management and depositors but analysts and competitors as well. These incentives are provided by a regime of quarterly public disclosure by banks. They are required to disclose their assets, liabilities and exposure to risks. The disclosure is backed up by an attestation by all the directors including the non-executive directors, which every bank is required to have, that the bank is applying appropriate risk management procedures. Directors can be fined or even imprisoned for up to three years for false or misleading statements and have unlimited personal civil liability for losses incurred by others as a result of these statements.

However, as explained earlier, disclosure is one of three pillars that support the system. The second is that the structure, ownership and management of the banks should be such as to encourage prudential behaviour. There is thus a series of wide-ranging prior conditions that have to be met before a bank can be registered, relating to capital adequacy as laid down by the Basel criteria, size, standing and corporate governance. The third pillar is the Reserve Bank's extensive powers to act swiftly and effectively in a crisis, including the ability to place an insolvent bank under statutory management.

New Zealand, being a small country, with a small number of banks, almost all of which are foreign-owned and undertake only limited business overseas, is not typical of many of the other OECD countries. In particular it is unusual in having no deposit insurance. However, while having deposit insurance may limit the bite of the market discipline it does not invalidate the applicability of any of the main principles. These principles can be readily applied in the EU countries, consistent with their existing directives, including those on capital adequacy and protection of depositors. Indeed the idea that market discipline can place a substantial incentive on banks to run themselves prudently will have a significant appeal as regulators struggle to keep pace with the rapid internationalisation of banking operations and the rapid rate of innovation of financial products and IT systems.

This chapter and the one that follows, therefore, appraise the New Zealand regime, suggest improvements and indicate how it might be introduced to European Union countries. Their structure is as follows. Sections 6.1 and 6.2 explain the role of more market discipline and how it might improve the incentives towards greater systemic stability. Section 6.3 sets out the framework for bank regulation and section 6.4 then goes on to explain in the light of this what the key ingredients of effective market-based regimes appear to be. Then Chapter 7 examines the key feature of the New Zealand regime – the system of public disclosure. Section 7.2 asks how far the New Zealand regime is transferable, while Section 7.3 considers barriers that have to be overcome for successful implementation of a similar regime in the EEA before concluding. The relevant legislation is not discussed in detail but excerpts from actual disclosure documents are set out in the form of Appendices.

6.1 THE ROLE OF INCENTIVES AND MARKET DISCIPLINE IN REDUCING SYSTEMIC RISKS

Following ten years of discussion and consultation, in 1996 the Reserve Bank of New Zealand introduced a new system of banking supervision designed to improve the prudential operation of banks and the soundness of the financial system. The Reserve Bank sought, by imposing requirements for the public quarterly disclosure statements of their health on registered banks, to obtain much more discipline from the market on banks to run their businesses prudentially. Secondly by heightening the role and accountability of the directors of the registered banks in attesting to the veracity of these disclosures it hoped to improve the management of banks, in particular, their identification, monitoring and management of risks.

As by-products the Reserve Bank expected to reduce compliance costs for the registered banks and improve their business freedom. Furthermore, it expected that this regime would reduce the risk to the taxpayer of ever being called upon to rescue a bank. By eliminating the traditional monopoly of information that supervisors have on the banks' financial condition this should both heighten the public perception that the management and directors of a bank have the sole responsibility for the management of their bank's affairs and assist future governments in resisting the pressures to rescue a bank in distress or insulate its creditors from losses.

6.1.1   The Need for Banking Supervision

The changes to the system of banking supervision stem from an extended period of revision of the regulation of the company sector and financial institutions in particular. Although the detailed changes resulted from the four-year review of banking supervision, which began in late 1991, the basis for change was set out in the mid-1980s and the enabling legislation incorporated in the Reserve Bank Act of 1989. The review and the wholesale changes were motivated by the fact that traditional banking supervision arrangements in other countries, while costly, have not been very effective in forestalling banking crises or identifying banks in difficulty.

While, by and large, the Reserve Bank would prefer that banks be regulated like other trading bodies, there are some respects in which banks have a special position and hence require more explicit supervision. These include the traditional feature, that banks play a special role in the working of the economy by accepting short-run and very liquid deposits and providing business stability by lending long and hence creating assets which cannot readily be liquidated (George, 1996). As a result they are vulnerable in a crisis; yet removing the vulnerability by changing their role would greatly reduce the value of banks to the economy.

Furthermore, banking crises tend to occur at times of overall difficulty for the economy, exacerbated by the fact that, compared to some other financial institutions, the assets underpinning banks' balance sheets, such as property, can be subject to wider swings in value. The appropriate valuation of assets relating to businesses, particularly small businesses, will depend upon private information held by the bank and will be difficult to establish rapidly in a crisis.

There are also particularly large externalities from bank failures. Not only is there the domino effect where a failure in one bank can cause problems for others and undermine the public's confidence in the banking system as a whole but failures in the banking sector will knock on to the rest of the productive economy, reducing activity (Goodhart, 1995).

It is thus important to understand that in making the changes to the system of banking supervision in New Zealand, the Reserve Bank was not washing its hands of its responsibilities for the soundness of the financial system but seeking to exercise them more effectively. The Reserve Bank continues to regulate the system and increase the chance of soundness for the system by:

- regulating entry;
- insisting on internationally accepted capital adequacy standard; and
- requiring bank structures that create incentives for bank managements to ensure that their bank has good risk management systems.

Disclosure alone is not enough. There is also continuing consultation with the senior management of the registered banks and the Reserve Bank retains a wide-ranging capacity to respond to bank distress or failure where the stability of the banking system is threatened.

At the same time the Reserve Bank has continued to reduce the risks inherent in the operation of the financial system, for example, through introducing RTGS, which covers over 90 percent of transactions by value. Improved arrangements on netting (Zodgekar, 1996) have also been implemented. Taken together these measures should lessen the exposure for other banks should any particular bank fail or get into difficulties.

However, as explained in Section 7.2, although the supervision arrangements are more detailed and comprehensive for banks the same principles regarding the importance of disclosure apply to legislation relating to all trading companies and to other financial institutions in particular. Some parts of the regime are still being developed, such as that for insurance companies.

6.1.2 Assigning Responsibility and Reducing Moral Hazard

One of the Reserve Bank's concerns with the traditional system has been that it blurs the responsibility of the management of the registered bank and that of the supervisor in ensuring that the bank is well run. With intrusive supervision, including site visits, there will be an expectation, among both directors and the public, that if there is something wrong the supervisors will pick it up. Furthermore there will be a greater expectation that if, despite the close supervision, a bank fails or gets into difficulty the government will have an obligation to intervene, as in some sense this would imply failure by a public authority in its duty. This introduces a 'moral hazard' that both depositors and those running banks will tend to take greater risks because there is a safety net limiting the adverse consequences of their actions for them.

The more that depositors and bank directors have at risk the more effective are market disciplines likely to be. With the absence of deposit insurance in New Zealand those incentives for the depositor may be rather greater than in most other OECD countries. However, it is not possible, even in these circumstances, to eliminate moral hazard altogether. If the central bank stands ready to prevent a spill-over into the rest of the financial system and retail depositors also form a significant portion of the country's electors there will always be the expectation that some form of safety net exists, however, strong the words denying it are. Even so, the new regime in New Zealand should clearly reduce any moral hazard that did exist.

In their summary of the issues facing the financial sector, the OECD (1997) put the point very clearly:

> A key and recurrent question is what induced banks to lend so heavily on the basis of real estate collateral particularly in the late stages of booms when prices had reached historically unprecedented levels. The experiences suggest that 'moral hazard' incentives arising from deposit insurance or the implicit insurance afforded by the likelihood of state support in the event of failure of a large institution ('too big to fail') encouraged institutions to assume excessive risks (relative to returns that could reasonably have been expected) while lowering incentives for depositors to adequately monitor the risks of banks in which their funds were placed. (p. 27)

They come to a similar conclusion about the appropriate way forward for supervision:

> Financial reform also necessitates fundamental changes in prudential policies, in particular to foster effective market discipline and adequate risk management by financial institutions including strong corporate governance regimes; to improve disclosure and transparency; and to harmonise oversight policies in similar market segments. (pp. 37–8)

6.1.3 Market Discipline through Disclosure of Information

The quotation from the OECD makes it clear that the appropriate system for reducing risk includes not just disclosure but good corporate governance, as we discussed in the last chapter. However, if there are to be effective pressures from the market they can only come about if the individual bank's actions are transparent and the relevant information is readily available.

Naturally there will be some who view such a change with apprehension. Indeed there may be circumstances where a scheme of open disclosure could pose a disadvantage, for example, when a bank is in temporary difficulties. Under a more closed system the problem would be known only to the supervisor (let us assume) and to the bank itself. The bank might then have time to sort the problem out before the difficulty became publicly known. With public knowledge, depositors and creditors will attempt to protect themselves and that action in itself will worsen the problem, possibly turning a difficulty into failure. The knowledge that a safety net exists might reduce the chance of a 'run' on a bank, as all insured depositors would expect not to lose their money and there would be no need to try to rush to get to the front of the queue.

It is not quite clear whether there is in practice a net disadvantage in these circumstances. There might well be more disadvantages from a system where public knowledge was more limited and hence rumour and misinformation were more prevalent. This could harm banks that did not in fact have difficulties but had disclosed insufficient information to satisfy market fears. The New Zealand approach creates incentives for the bank to present solutions at an early stage and hence reduce the risk of a run on the bank.

In any case the sheer knowledge that disclosure means that the opportunity to cover up problems is very limited may in itself lead the management of banks to act much earlier to head off problems or to implement more effective systems which will prevent such problems emerging in the first place. This in itself will tend to reduce the cost of finance for banks.

It is not, of course, realistic to expect that every ordinary depositor will be rushing into the nearest branch of every bank, reading the various disclosure statements with enormous care and then making wise and well informed decisions about where to place their funds. It is the financial news media, financial analysts, investment advisers, major creditors and the competing banks who will digest and publish the results of their analysis. Most ordinary depositors will rely on this secondary information and the fact that it will be spread rapidly by word of mouth.

The ability to make comparisons across banks has several advantages. The banks themselves have a twofold interest in each other's performance. First of all they have major transactions with each other through money markets and, second, they want their own positions to be compared favourably with those of competitors. The fear that banks might be able to take advantage of each other's weakness as a result of disclosure does not appear to have been translated into a problem in practice, although their positions are more transparent.

It is already clear from initial experience (Brash, 1997) that the financial media and particularly competing banks are scrutinising disclosure statements and there has been some public comment about issues such as the breach of exposure limits.

In any case, the point of the system is to have prudently run banks in the first place and the main incentive structure and discipline lies firmly on directors and bank managers whose livelihoods and reputations are at stake if a problem arises. Brash (1997) claims that there are already signs that directors of banks are exercising 'greater scrutiny of their banks' risk positions' (p. 11). Signing-off procedures by management need to be rigorous and transparent if non-executive directors, in particular, are to be willing to sign the quarterly attestation. Furthermore the increased auditing requirement helps provide a greater independent confirmation of the banks' performance.

6.2   THE RATIONALE FOR A MORE MARKET-BASED REGIME

The successful implementation of a more market-based supervision regime is expected to offer benefits on a wide front (Ledingham, 1995). Not only are gains expected for banking supervisors in the effective and efficient execution of their tasks but also for all the stakeholders in the banks themselves: owners, managers, depositors, borrowers and creditors. Most important there are benefits to the public at large both as taxpayers and as employees and consumers through the reduced risk of banking crises and the consequent difficulties for the economy as a whole. Of course, no system of banking supervision is a panacea. Banking inherently involves taking risks, but it is the prudent management of those risks that defines a successful bank. A successful supervision regime will provide effective incentives to keep the quality of management of risks by banks above the minimum acceptable level and should ensure that, in the event of difficulty in one or more individual banks, this does not spill over to the detriment of the banking system and economy as a whole.

In other words, it is the aim of a successful regime to focus supervisors and the supervised on the aspects of the task that they are best equipped to handle. Thus the responsibility for the prudent management of any individual bank should lie not with the supervisor but with the managers and directors of that bank themselves. They are the only people with the information and opportunity to run an individual bank well. An outsider, however well qualified and however good the information system, cannot hope to do as well. If one is not prepared to accord this responsibility to the banks' management then the obvious alternative would be to opt for a publicly owned banking system and to reject the hypothesis that the disciplines and incentives of a well-operating market stand the best chance of maximising welfare for society.

It is the role of the supervisory authority, to quote the Reserve Bank of New Zealand's *Commitment to New Zealanders* (RBNZ, 1998) '[to] do everything in our power to build national and international confidence in the stability and integrity of New Zealand's money and monetary system by:

- operating monetary policy so as to maintain price stability;
- *promoting the maintenance of a sound and efficient financial system*; and
- meeting the currency needs of the public',

where the italicised phrase provides the key remark. In this view it is not the job of the supervisor to support any individual bank. Indeed if it were thought that the supervisor would provide such support this would increase the moral hazard that bank managements might run greater risks as owners and depositors would not have funds at risk.

A more market-based system operates by revealing publicly the sorts of information that would previously have been disclosed only to the supervisor and by providing a system of incentives that encourages banks to operate in a prudent, efficient and indeed profitable manner. Although the supervisor needs to lay down the minimum of information to be disclosed, the practice in New Zealand has been for banks to disclose more as they seek to demonstrate their strengths compared to their competitors to depositors, actual and potential shareholders, counterparties and other customers. There is a trend towards increasing voluntary disclosure as companies in the United States move towards quarterly accounts and a trend among supervisors to encourage more disclosure both through the Basel Committee and within the EU.

Some people view public disclosure as a support to the traditional regime of the collection of detailed undisclosed information by the supervisor. However, this belt and braces approach is not advocated here and it is anticipated that the supervisor would follow the New Zealand approach of only seeking more information if the disclosure statement seemed inadequate or unclear or in the event of a difficulty emerging. Even in the event of difficulty the emphasis would be on openness and revelation as soon as possible as to how the problem would be solved.

6.2.1 Increasing Effectiveness of Supervision

Putting the emphasis on public disclosure and the forces of market discipline is not washing one's hands of supervision in a difficult world of technical change and international business. It is an attempt to provide a system in jurisdictions where the banks are strong and accounting and auditing rules adequate, which increases the chance of prudential behaviour. It is clear from experience that current regimes of detailed supervision cannot 'succeed' in the sense of stopping banking crises but then nothing can, because we are talking about managing risk prudently not eliminating it, which is impossible. There are downsides to any approach and detailed supervision can be costly and inhibit banks in undertaking profitable business. As explained in Chapter 4, an advantage of this arrangement is that it allows the supervisor to focus on the parts of the problem where it has a clear advantage:

- Assessing the quality of new entrants.
- Ensuring that banks comply with the disclosure rules and following up problems.
- Oversight of the system as whole – identifying potential problems which relate to banks as a whole, e.g. exposure to particular markets or sectors – considering social costs and risks.
- Resolving problems when they emerge and ensuring that crisis resolution capabilities are in good shape.
- Advising banks that have not as yet managed to get to the stage where they can comply with a full disclosure regime.

These comments all relate to prudential supervision, corporate governance and disclosure but not to other aspects of conduct such as fair-trading. It is an open question whether this last should be covered by a special financial sector or banking regulator. OECD countries show a variety of decisions.

6.2.2   Reducing Costs of Banking Supervision for the Taxpayer, Customers, Banks and the Supervisor

It is a relatively trivial consequence that the scale of supervision necessary will be reduced and hence the cost of supervision, which in most countries is borne by the banks themselves, or more literally by their customers, rather than the taxpayer, is reduced. Given the scale of other bank costs, the effect on interest rates and other prices will be difficult to detect. Secondly, if it is more costly for the banks to comply with the disclosure regime than it was with detailed supervision then this gain will have been lost. However, if the New Zealand approach, of trying to align what is disclosed with what banks need to compute for internal purposes, both for decision-making and monitoring, is followed, then any extra costs are likely to be small and not sufficient to offset the gains from reduced detailed supervision costs. The New Zealand banks report that possibly one or two more staff may be involved and that extra printing may be required. On the whole, however, the extra printing replaces the costs that would otherwise have been incurred in printing prospectuses and annual or other reports in order to inform potential investors or depositors (Mayes, 1997).

The bigger gains come because banks are now able to run their businesses in a less constrained manner. Rather than having to conform to specific ratios or limits to exposures in particular sectors laid down by the supervisory authority, their requirement is simply to disclose the risks they have taken on. They are therefore able to pursue opportunities for profit and to differentiate their business from that of competitors as they think appropriate provided they can convince markets that they are managing their risk satisfactorily when they do so. The New Zealand banks reacted particularly well to this freedom (Mayes, 1997). They use the disclosure documents as an opportunity to convince customers that they manage risk well.

Customers are also able to benefit, not just because costs are reduced but because they can choose institutions whose business more closely reflects their own needs. The efficient assessment of the quality of banks is thus largely assigned to the market and to competing private sector analysts and rating agencies. The role of the supervisor is to ensure compliance with the law. Disclosure thus can permit a rather wider range of choice rather than a clustering of bank behaviour close to but above the minimum standards that the supervisor requires.

Secondly if the risk of bank failure is reduced through better incentives for prudential management then the potential cost to the taxpayer is reduced in addition to any small costs that could not be passed on by the supervisor to banks. Given the scale of the bailout in the banking crisis at the beginning of the decade then this would be the largest single source of gain, totally dwarfing those relating to compliance costs.

6.2.3 Focusing Supervisor on Systemic Risk

Governments do not seek to protect people from all risks but they do wish to act where the public benefit and the private benefit diverge. If banks are in general well supervised, there is insurance available, particularly for the small depositor, and a wide range of choice, then the main concern is that a problem in a specific bank spills over into the rest of the system and causes a loss to society as a whole that could be reduced by public action. Otherwise one set of individuals who have taken a specific risk are going to be bailed out by the community at large who take a general risk over which they have little control.

6.2.4 Placing Responsibility for the Management of Banks on the Management of Banks

The people who can ensure prudent management are the directors and managers of banks themselves. Disclosure will help achieve this because markets and customers will penalise banks that are not well run. The cost of raising capital will tend to rise and banks will have to cut margins in order to attract customers. This information on how the market views moves by banks will also help them in running their business. However, this information alone is not likely to be sufficient. Directors and managers need to be held accountable for their actions, both within the framework of the firm, for poor performance, and legally in the event of fraud or failure to conform to disclosure or corporate governance standards. The shareholder always faces a difficulty in knowing whether the management it has appointed is doing an adequate job. Disclosure assists this assessment because it is more readily possible to compare the performance of banks with their competitors and, indeed, with banks in other jurisdictions. (Of course, with the exception of large shareholders, it will be analysts and market commentators who will provide much of the advice. If there are problems then competitors will be only too keen to point out the difficulty and their own success in countering it.)

In the New Zealand system all bank directors, whether or not executives, have to sign an attestation on the accuracy of the accounts and on compliance with the rules for prudential management. Thus it is not just that such rules be in place but they actually be followed.

6.2.5   Establishing Incentives for All 'Stakeholders' in Banks

For this regime to work well there needs to be as comprehensive a set of incentives as possible. This comes not just from setting out regulations and having penalties for not following them. It is not possible to specify in sufficient detail what any individual organisation should do in order to manage its risk 'properly'. It is, however, possible to lay down general principles and then get banks to disclose enough of what they are doing so that people can decide whether they like the specific risks involved. We do not expect banks to be identical. People are prepared to take different risks. The concern of supervisors is to limit the risk to the system as a whole and for that reason they insist on minimum standards.

All those involved therefore need to have appropriate incentives: not just managers but owners – shareholders, depositors, borrowers and, of course, the supervisors themselves. The key ingredient of the disclosure system is that it provides the basis for people to take informed decisions. One requirement of an effective market-based regime is that there is a sufficiently large group of professional analysts crawling over the information to provide advice for the rest of customers and investors to act on. Clearly the message will be more limited if the shares in a particular bank are not actively traded or if shareholders do not have much say in the way the bank is run.

A feature of a market-based regime is that it makes it easier for incentives to be progressive rather than there being simply penalties for stepping over a specific line. The size of the changes in market prices will reflect the extent of the strengths and weaknesses in banks as they are perceived.

6.2.6 Reducing Moral Hazard from Implicit and Actual Guarantees

One of the main problems is that the public at large may feel that there is no risk from bank failure. Even if they know that banks can fail they may have the expectation that the bank will be bailed out. Experience supports this view. As a result (Llewellyn, 1995) retail customers will tend to choose the banks that offer the most favourable terms, as they treat all the risks as being effectively zero, not recognising that higher returns are normally associated with higher risks. Worse still this view can extend to creditors, shareholders, directors and managers. Bailing out a bank may mean for them that they do not lose as much financially as they would with a commercial company. It may mean that reputations and future employment are not expected to be harmed substantially by bad performance. One could scarcely give a worse signal than show that someone who has been held responsible for major losses by others in the past continues to prosper personally.

The moral hazard may extend to the banks themselves if they regard interbank risk as zero. They might, for example, prefer a 'cheaper' netting system to real-time gross settlement systems that effectively eliminate the exposure.

6.2.7 Precommitment – Focusing Supervision on Banks with Potential Problems

In most circumstances bank failures are fairly isolated and in a well-regulated system only some institutions will have difficulties even for common risks associated with the macroeconomic cycle. There is a role for a supervisor to focus on those institutions and help see how the problems can be resolved. Here an extra step is required that was not a concern for the introduction of the New Zealand regime, because European countries are not starting with a clean slate. It is not a matter of being able to choose just strong banks for registration. Some banks have been in difficulty and may not yet be fully out of the wood. The decision to allow them to continue and work their way out of the problems has already been made. The supervisor may therefore want to keep an especially close eye on them until they are either closed, taken over or move into satisfactory performance. There will be a strong incentive for a bank to move as quickly as possible out of the problem category, if the position is public knowledge, as being there will affect its cost of capital and business adversely.

Section 7.4 suggests that within the group of 'strong' banks it could be possible for individual banks to make precommitments to avoid actual exposures to market risk exceeding a given level and to provide capital cover of at least that amount. This would enable them both to use their own risk assessment methods and to choose the appropriate level of cover, instead of following some predetermined rule applied to all banks irrespective of the particular characteristics of their business. It would be up to the market to judge the quality of these commitments ex ante and for the supervisor to decide if they were to be allowed to continue in future if either the commitment were violated or the standing of the bank fell.

It would be possible to invert this idea and allow banks to choose the level of supervision. In this case a bank might feel that it could enhance its standing by exposing itself to more vigorous inspection. It could balance the increased cost of supervision against the benefits from the expected improvement in reputation in the market. However, different supervisory regimes may have rather more hidden costs. If such inspections were thought to imply validation of the bank by the supervisory authority then it might be argued that the supervisor should bear some share of the responsibility if the bank subsequently fails. Simply charging the bank for the costs of the extra supervision would not cover the cost of any increased potential systemic risk from its subsequent failure or bailout.

To some extent this choice of supervisory regime can take place if the area of competition from non-banks is increased, say, by permitting entry into e-money without a banking licence.

6.2.8   Comparability

The disclosure regime needs to require banks to report on a basis where they can be compared with a standard and with each other, otherwise the necessary transparency for informed market judgements would not be achieved.

Somewhat ironically, disclosure means that there is much less incentive for banks to try to choose one supervisory regime rather than another as their position is clear and can be compared across borders wherever they are located. With the advent of the euro area comparison is greatly facilitated.

6.3   THE FRAMEWORK FOR BANK REGULATION IN NEW ZEALAND

The changes to bank regulation in New Zealand have been harmonised as part of a much wider revision of the regulation of trading activities in the economy. Most importantly, the Reserve Bank's disclosure regime has been developed in tandem with the accounting standards for financial reporting (Financial

Reporting Standard (FRS) 33). The Companies Office accepts the disclosure documents as meeting their requirements. Hence banks are spared multiple reporting standards within New Zealand. Similarly these standards apply to other institutions so that disclosure is becoming a feature for the rest of the financial sector as well.

Bank regulation in New Zealand is covered by a number of very simple principles, which were derived after an extensive review that took place in the early 1990s. (These principles are set out in RBNZ (1999).) The new regime came into full effect from the first quarter of 1996. However, the framework for the Reserve Bank's regulation of the banking system is contained in Part V of the Reserve Bank Act 1989. Sections 67 to 156 cover the registration and prudential supervision of banks out of total 192 sections in the Act. Indeed one of the main reasons why it has been possible to implement the new regime so successfully is that it has been introduced only after extensive consultation over many years.

The principles supporting the regime can be summarised as follows:

- only financial institutions of appropriate standing and repute can become registered banks;
- impediments to entry of qualifying institutions be kept at a minimum in order to encourage competition in the banking system;
- that the incentives in the system encourage prudence on the part of registered banks and their customers and that normal market disciplines are not impeded.

Thus while outside interest has tended to focus on the disclosure regime that underpins the application of the third of these principles, an important precondition for its success is that there is a screening process to try to ensure that all participating banks are of a high calibre and likely to follow prudential behaviour (section 73 of the Act). Furthermore, these principles recognise that competition can bring significant benefits to users of the services provided by registered banks. New Zealand has lower margins and a higher quality and range of services than in some other small countries, which may in part be due to competitive pressure. It is the combination of these three aspects which provides the full flavour of the New Zealand approach.

The series of criteria, which the Reserve Bank applies in deciding whether to register a bank in the first place, are straightforward but wide-ranging. They are set out in more detail in Appendix 6.1. They entail:

- that the Reserve Bank satisfy itself that the applicant's business will substantially consist of the borrowing and lending of money, or the provision of financial services, or both;

- and that it have regard to:
  - incorporation and ownership structure;
  - size of business;
  - ability to carry on business in a prudent manner;
  - standing of the applicant in the financial market;
  - law and regulatory requirements in an overseas bank's country of domicile;
  - any other matters prescribed in regulations.

It is worth emphasising that these provisions include compliance with the Basel criteria for capital adequacy, restriction of connected lending exposure, separation from the other interests of the owners and adequate internal and accounting controls.

The incentive system to encourage prudent behaviour has two main elements:

- a system of quarterly public disclosure statements and attestation by directors;
- the avoidance as far as possible of any implicit guarantees against bank failures or of the protection of creditors. Supervision is aimed at encouraging the soundness and efficiency of the financial system as a whole.

In the event that a bank should fail – and there have been no bank failures in New Zealand in 'living memory' (Ledingham, 1995) – the Reserve Bank will seek to minimise damage to the financial system, in a way that does not involve taxpayer funding. The Bank has extensive powers of crisis management under the Act including the power to put registered banks under statutory management (a statutory manager has a broader set of powers than a receiver). This aspect of having a crisis management system, which not only has strong powers but seeks to limit moral hazard, is a key pillar in the system.

Furthermore, an open system of this form, with precommitment to respond in specified circumstances (as Goodhart (1996) puts it), is likely to minimise any possible potential conflict of interest between the supervision and monetary policy functions of the Reserve Bank. This requirement to act when banks become undercapitalised and the effective means for doing so lie at the heart of our proposals in the last part of this book.

Chapters 7 and 8, which follow, cover two main ingredients of the New Zealand system:

- disclosure statements;
- crisis management;

as they have most to offer for changes in the European system. There are, however, important preconditions for a disclosure regime; the most important of which are fully functioning of markets, a good system of corporate governance and the rule of law. The next section reviews the key ingredients of a more market-based regime and their importance.

6.4 THE INGREDIENTS OF EFFECTIVE MARKET-BASED REGIMES

6.4.1 A Well-Functioning Market

The market itself needs to operate well, in the sense of there being

- an active share market;
- good market analysts;
- rating agencies;
- effective competition among banks; and
- an effective market for corporate control;

if the disclosure is to mean something. Clearly if banks do not need to raise capital in the open market and if their customers have no effective choice the system will work poorly. Disclosure tries to overcome some of the problems of asymmetric information that may inhibit the effective operation of the market.

While most EU countries reflect these five characteristics to some extent there are frequently limitations. Some banks are not actively traded. Setting aside those that are actually private, there are substantial numbers of government controlled banks. There are also savings and co-operative banks that face relative inactive members, whose disciplining effect on the institutions has been relatively limited (as illustrated in the Nordic crises of the last decade, for example, where these banks got into serious trouble when they went outside their previous experience and expertise). The United States has had similar difficulties with Savings and Loans. Lastly it is not clear how competitive the European market is in practice. Some banks have very large market shares to the extent that they can act as market leaders. Others have privileged positions, as the European Commission is alleging for the German Landesbanken, or have been the beneficiaries of substantial state injections of capital (Credit Lyonnais being a well-known case in point).

6.4.2 Good Corporate Governance

Establishing a structure for the governance of financial institutions which maximises the chance of good prudential management is clearly an important starting point for an effective supervision regime. The New Zealand system focuses on four key features:

- incorporation and ownership structure;
- size;
- ability to carry on business in a prudent manner;
- standing in the financial market;

which between them cover the likely range of issues. However, much of the relevant legislation for ensuring good corporate governance is not in banking law but in company law. This is an area where the European Commission has had only limited success in ensuring convergence and considerable national diversity prevails.

6.4.2.1   Ownership Structure

It is a simple starting point that the ownership structure needs to be transparent. This is particularly important in the case of conglomerates, where one might question the role of the bank compared to other parts of the company, and to international institutions where the network of ownership may be obscure. The BCCI debacle has been very helpful in sharpening the mind in this regard.

The principles that need to apply within an institution are fairly commonplace and include that the ownership structure needs to provide incentives for owners to monitor the performance of the bank closely and seek to ensure that it is managed prudently. If owners have a substantial stake in the business and are among the first to absorb the losses from poor performance then this will tend to be the case. However, owners and the board of directors need to be separated, as the interests of the bank and the interests of the owners may not always be identical.

Private banks and joint stock banks with dispersed ownership present contrasting difficulties. The worry in the case of the private bank is that activities could be run in the inappropriate interest of the owners, providing them or friends with cheap or inadequately collateralised loans. In the case of a diffuse ownership no single owner will be able to exert any effective control and the holding in the bank may only form a very small proportion of their total assets, thus tending to leave the company to the interests of the management and ineffectively monitored. In savings and co-operative banks the interests of owners and customers are not clearly separated and the position of the managers and directors vis-à-vis the owners may also be somewhat unclear in practice.

One of the key features of the New Zealand system is the role of independent directors. All banks are required to have at least two independent directors and an independent chairman. These will offer not only the benefit of outside experience but will also tend to have a more independent and dispassionate view of the running of the business. Since they, like the rest of the board, will be personally liable for the accuracy of the disclosure statements, they will have a particular interest in being convinced that the bank is applying all the appropriate risk management measures. A common arrangement is for one of their number to chair the audit committee, for example (Goodhart (1996, p. 64) sets out a similar suggestion). Their presence on the board will tend to give comfort to small shareholders, depositors, creditors and indeed the supervisory authority that the business is likely to be run prudently. This is very much the sort of banking system that is common across the Anglo-Saxon world.

The boards of some European banks have a somewhat different structure. They tend to be divided into two in a manner similar to that in Germany, with an executive board on which there not normally independent outsiders and a supervisory board where the majority are outsiders. Clearly, the members of the executive board would need to attest to the correctness of any disclosure statement. To mirror the role of external directors or to demonstrate the supervisory board's confidence in the activities of the executives then a matching action would be for the members of the supervisory board to sign the attestation.

Resolving the problem of the blurred distinction between owners and customers in co-operative and savings banks is also difficult. New Zealand faced this problem potentially with the trustee savings banks but they voluntarily changed their structure shortly before the introduction of the new regime (with the exception of the small Taranaki Savings Bank) and have since been acquired by one of the larger banks. However, while this was seen as a difficulty it was not viewed as being insurmountable. The main difficulty is a lack of any public quotation and hence clear expression of view by shareholders and the market as to the performance of management that is incorporated in a price. However, views would still be reflected in the action of depositors so market pressures, although perhaps a little weaker, would still exist. The worry would be that depositors might not be very well informed particularly if they were largely individuals and not corporate entities. However, difficulties would be reflected in the costs of any market finance required by the bank.[3]

6.4.2.2   Accounting and Auditing Practice

Secondly, an essential feature of good corporate governance is independent verification of the accuracy of the accounts and statements made by the directors. This role of independent auditors is crucial both for reassuring the directors themselves and for external purposes. It was simultaneous developments in financial reporting standards that made the development of the New Zealand system possible. The innovations were already being made in the United States and the accounting profession in New Zealand based its changes on them.

The Reserve Bank was a party to the discussions (through membership of the professional association) but implemented its proposals ahead of the final decisions of the association, as their progress was too slow. However, only very limited amendments had to be made when the Financial Reporting Standard (FRS33) was actually published.

The key changes related to the frequency of the production of accounts – quarterly – and to the valuation of financial assets. There is already a trend towards quarterly accounting in Europe. Moreover, companies commonly produce considerable detail at even greater frequency for internal purposes. Valuation, however, does pose a clear problem, as there is some variety of opinion on the best way forward. Mark to market is becoming the accepted way of determining fair values in Europe and the discussions within the profession appear to be going in the same direction. At present practice varies with use of historical cost, revaluation and mark to market. As noted in Chapter 2, revaluation to current prices proved one of the factors assisting the banking crisis in the Nordic countries in the early 1990s when some property portfolios were revalued to prevailing prices shortly before the asset price bubble was pricked (Bordes *et al.*, 1993). As a result the value of the liabilities incurred against those property assets did not fall. Indeed where they involved foreign currency borrowing the liability actually increased substantially, emphasising the solvency crisis in the banking system.

The passage of time since New Zealand's implementation of the disclosure regime means that there is now a clear model to follow from international accounting standards, should others wish to adopt a similar approach. However, the IASB standards follow the 'Anglo-Saxon' approach to accounting, which many continental European countries do not, so adopting a more transparent valuation basis will involve a complication to the way in which accounts are presented. As things stand the additional information would need to be presented in the form of notes to the accounts. This is the same sort of procedure that is being followed in the agreement on accounting standards within the EU to which all member states will have to conform. There, although there is a general preference for the international standard, the pressure for the retention of the 'continental tradition' is sufficiently great that both systems will be permitted with an encouragement to follow the international standard in the form of notes to the accounts. Thus while the necessary standard will not be compelled, it will be permitted. (See also the discussion in Chapter 5.)

Of course, the accounting bodies are not the only relevant organisations as others accepting accounts for official purposes, such as the tax authorities, would need to agree to the changes if the system were not to become unduly complex.

6.4.2.3 Size

In one sense size is an important issue. The minimum size for registration as a new bank in European countries is similar to that in New Zealand and follows the EU standards. There needs to be a reasonable minimum size in order to make sure that organisations really are going to operate as banks and are on a scale such that they can reasonably be expected to have the resources to operate proper risk management. In practice most new entrants lie well above the minimum and banks from elsewhere in the EEA opening branches in other member states are likely to have very substantial asset backing. The reservation comes from the large number of small savings and co-operative banks that already exist – not so much that their small size makes prudential behaviour more difficult but simply that their sheer number makes the process of analysis and comparison complex and less valuable. The ordinary depositor or investor is not going to be considering the whole range of banks but just those that can readily operate in the relevant region. This immediately reduces the comparison to a small dimension, as the small banks are mainly regionally concentrated.

One problem not present directly in the case of New Zealand is that of large-scale banks. Some of the European banks are very large indeed and with such complex operations it might be legitimate to question whether the limited disclosure proposed would be adequate for outsiders to form a view of the risks faced by the bank. The problem for New Zealand is that the parent bank may be large as in the case of Citibank, Deutsche Bank or Lloyds TSB, for example. If, like Deutsche Bank, the New Zealand operation is undertaken through a branch then it is the viability of the whole organisation that determines much of the risk involved in New Zealand. The issue is therefore not evaded but can have the ironic result that more is being disclosed in New Zealand about the parent than is normally readily available in the home country.

6.4.2.4 Prudential Potential

Assessing the potential for the applicant to exercise prudence in management is a complex issue but one where there is considerable agreement among supervisors. The simplest is capital adequacy. Here there are accepted rules through the Basel criteria, which the EEA countries apply, so all banks operating in the EEA could be expected to meet these minima. However, it is a separate issue whether these criteria are adequate in all cases or indeed necessary in others (Mayes, 1997). For banks operating very cautious lending strategies, such as those specialising in house mortgages, where loans involving high percentages of valuation of the property require further security, the necessary capital levels could be quite small. For some wholesale institutions the risks could be large and the

142	*Improving Banking Supervision*

appropriate backing larger as well. Indeed this is one advantage of a disclosure system as a bank facing relative high risks can demonstrate that it has adequate capital over and above the Basel minimum. For example, Bankers Trust (1998) in New Zealand went out of its way to explain that it had more than the minimum cover, as this was appropriate for its business.[4]

Capital adequacy alone is, however, is thought to be inadequate by most supervisors. The main areas of contention are:

- loan concentration and risk exposures;
- separation from the interests of owners;
- internal controls and accounting systems;
- fit and proper persons.

New Zealand does not impose exposure limits but does seek to get disclosure so that concentration of loans to particular parties, sectors or countries is known. It is then up to the market to decide whether these exposures are acceptable. Clearly before registering a bank a supervisor has to form a view. However, some supervisors are more prescriptive and set limits. This, of course, begins to reintroduce the moral hazard as it could be taken to imply that exposures up to the limit are in some sense satisfactory. The EU already imposes requirements for exposure limits on own funds to a single customer, to a parent or subsidiary and to large exposures in total. Individual regimes impose other restrictions, such as on net overnight exchange risk exposure. While these may not be necessary under market disclosure, many are unlikely to impose any great inhibition on banks' activities. It would be for the banks to make a case that such restrictions were important but, where the limit is imposed by EU agreement, the regulations will have to stand.

The existence of adequate controls is a much more difficult subject. There are several important structural steps that can be taken, separation of front and back offices, establishing a strong internal audit function and audit and risk committees that are chaired by external directors, for example. Within reason it is possible to get banks to describe what they do but such descriptions, where they do not relate to well-known products, will tend to be rather inexplicit and will convey little information. A good example of what can be done is the disclosure statement by Bankers Trust in New Zealand (Bankers Trust, 1998), where the description covers some four pages and deals explicitly, inter alia, with how they were handling the Year 2000 problem. Bankers' Trust had its own proprietary system RAROC, which is well known, as well as the Daily Price Volatility assessment. (This includes their statement on risk management procedures.) In any case it is not the existence of systems alone that matters but the effectiveness with which they operated in practice as well. The supervisor, large counterparties and analysts can use the disclosed information to enquire further.

For an existing organisation one can see the track record but that is a combination of the operation and the risks encountered. Indeed for an existing organisation, based abroad but coming to an EEA country for the first time, it is possible to get a view on its success in the existing jurisdiction from both supervisors and markets. For a new organisation it may be possible to see the track record of the individuals concerned but the validity of that also depends on the environment in which they then were. It is difficult to go beyond the New Zealand solution of getting the directors to attest that the appropriate systems are in place and effectively applied and to make them liable should that statement be shown to be untrue.

Similarly if one wants to vet the appropriateness of bank directors one can only look at their record. The criteria applied by the European countries vary considerably. However, the aim is at least to comply with the BIS recommendations on what constitutes a 'fit and proper' person. As a result a bank will tend to choose its directors and senior management with a view to their external reputation as well as their internal competence. Otherwise there is a danger of adverse selection, where only those people who are not trustworthy will be prepared to commit themselves in advance to sign disclosure statements when they do not expect to be sure whether the bank is following prudent risk management policies.

It is, of course, always helpful if there are strong independent credit rating agencies that can give their own view of the quality of banks.[5] Indeed if a bank wants to give an idea of its quality to outsiders it will promote its rating in its statements in the same way that commercial companies are concerned by their ratings. Such ratings are also of considerable value in supporting a disclosure regime to which we now turn. International agencies operate in the European countries but a wider development of domestic agencies could also be helpful to extend the range of assessments.

6.4.3   Transparency – Availability of Information – Disclosure

The public availability of meaningful information sufficient for people to make informed decisions about the likely standing of banks both individually and relatively is the keystone of market discipline and this is therefore subject of a chapter of its own to which we pass next. However, before doing so we should note that two further aspects of the New Zealand system are still to be discussed – namely, the existence of sanctions in the event of non-compliance and the powers that exist to resolve crises should banks actually get into difficulties.

The topic of sanctions forms part of the next chapter and crisis resolution is the subject of Chapter 8. However, it is worth noting that the process of crisis resolution is itself part of the regime as a means of sanction and contributor to the effectiveness of market discipline. If banks in difficulty are bailed out or expect to be bailed out then market discipline will have a more limited effect. The expectation of bailout will impose a moral hazard on the system. Banks must expect to fail if they cannot keep trading and the private sector will not rescue them. They must also expect that private sector rescues are likely to take a harsh view of shareholder value and that wholesale management changes will be required. Thus owners will expect to lose their assets and managers their jobs and reputation if the bank gets into difficulty.

However, the point of market discipline is not merely to avoid ever getting into these extreme circumstances, but also to provide continuous and graduated pressures for better performance. The bigger the difficulty the bigger the penalty the market will extract. Even where financial liability is legally limited those involved will be open to charges of fraud and negligence. So while the system may be bounded those bounds should cut in at penalties that those involved find unattractive.

APPENDIX 6.1   CONDITIONS FOR REGISTRATION OF BANKS IN NEW ZEALAND

In fulfilling the requirement that the Reserve Bank be satisfied that the applicant's business will substantially consist of the borrowing and lending of money, or the provision of financial services, or both the applicant has to set out what business it intends to conduct, including any business through subsidiaries. There are no requirements to provide particular financial services nor any explicit list of which services are deemed to be 'financial'. Financial services are defined by the common practice of other banks in New Zealand and other similar countries. Application would be refused where it was clear that these services were not primarily to be provided in New Zealand. The Reserve Bank does not want to provide a refuge for banks that are seeking to evade the vigour of supervision elsewhere by registering themselves in New Zealand.

1   Incorporation and Ownership Structure

The Reserve Bank seeks to ensure that the ownership structure is such that the owners have incentives to monitor the bank's activities closely and influence its activities so as to keep a high level of soundness. This is likely to occur when the owners have a substantial stake in the bank and where they are the first to have to absorb any losses stemming from poor performance.

Furthermore the incentive to encourage sound management will increase if the owners have reputation to lose from any problems which may arise. However, there does need to be sufficient separation between the board of directors and the owners as the interest of the bank and its owners may diverge.

If the application for registration is from an overseas not a local entity, they will have to demonstrate that

- they have bank status in their home jurisdiction;
- that the supervision regime in that jurisdiction is adequate or that disclosure requirements or market disciplines exist.

Otherwise they will probably be required to incorporate locally. In any event the views of the supervisor of the parent would be sought before granting registration.

2   Size of Business

Locally incorporated banks require minimum capital of NZ$15 million, while the branches of overseas banks are expected to operate off the capital on the parent's total balance sheet, which must exceed that sum.

3   Ability to Carry on Business in a Prudent Manner

For prudence the applicant must meet criteria for:

- *Capital adequacy*
  This criterion follows the Basel framework. Thus, at all times, the minimum capital ratio is 8 per cent with a tier 1 capital ratio of 4 per cent for the banking group. However, regard is also paid to any restrictions on access to further capital and the need to hold capital for risks not covered by the Basel framework. Furthermore the applicant must be in a position to disclose information on capital adequacy both for itself and, where applicable, its parent.
  It is worth noting that the Reserve Bank viewed these specific requirements as unnecessary in a disclosure regime but felt they were desirable for international credibility. 'Although the Bank considers that disclosure alone, without minimum requirements, should provide sufficient incentives for banks to at least adhere to the international norm of 8 per cent, it believes that retention of the capital requirement offers benefits in terms of international credibility, at little, if any, marginal cost to banks' (RBNZ, 1995b, p. 76). However, the Reserve Bank took careful account of international opinion in its consultations before implementing the new regime.
  It is interesting that the US Fed (as set out in Kupiec and O'Brien (1995) for example) is adopting an approach where systems operated by the banks themselves may give a better indication of the specific sorts of risks that they face, in particular, because of the ability to take full account of the inter-relationship among risks. The Basel Committee (1997) seems to be moving in this direction.
- *loan concentration and risk exposures*
  Applicants have to show that they have adequate mechanisms for monitoring and preventing excessive exposure to risks from single parties or sectors and that they will be able to comply with the disclosure requirements in this regard. Otherwise there is a danger that a single party or groups of related parties could bring down the bank.
- *separation from other interests of the owners*
  (This section does not apply to branches or guaranteed subsidiaries of overseas banks because creditors will have a claim on the assets of the parent.) Applicants are required to have at least two independent directors and a non-executive chairperson in order to ensure that there is a degree of objective scrutiny of:
  - exposure to the parent or related parties;
  - exposures to unrelated parties undertaken at the request of the parent;
  - other matters where the interests of the bank and parent or management could conflict.

Secondly exposure to related parties (excluding risks layoffs to a parent bank) must be limited to 75 per cent of tier 1 capital and within in this limit, aggregate exposure to non-bank connected parties to 15 per cent of tier 1 capital. In addition, banks must not adopt a constitution that would allow directors to act in the interests of a holding company where to do so would conflict with the interests of the bank in New Zealand to the detriment of creditors.

- *Internal controls and accounting systems*
  For overseas banks these requirements will normally be met by adopting the parent's systems but elsewhere the Reserve Bank will need to be satisfied of the nature of the controls especially in areas outside the bank's normal experience.

The nature of the corporate governance of the bank is thus a key concern in determining its suitability for registration.

4   Standing of the Applicant in the Financial Market

Unless the institution, executive board members, senior staff or owners have proven good experience in financial markets it is unlikely that the application will be approved. However, there is no 'fitness or properness' test for a bank's directors and senior management. It is the role of the shareholders to appoint directors and of the directors to appoint the senior management. Here the concern is with the standing of the bank as a whole – clearly the presence of a notorious individual in a position of trust would call the organisation into question.

5   Law and Regulatory Requirements in an Overseas Bank's Country of Domicile

Where the requirements of the parent's supervisors or the legal framework in the home jurisdiction may cause problems in New Zealand the applicant may have to be locally incorporated. (This might include preference for foreign creditors for example.)

6   Any Other Matters Prescribed in Regulations

(Currently none.)

7 A Disclosure Regime

Disclosure is a word without any accepted detailed meaning. Increasing transparency is very much in vogue at present. The IMF, for example, adopted the 'Code of Good Practices on Transparency in Monetary and Financial Policies: Declaration of Principles' in September 1999. Buiter (1999) and Issing (1999) both espouse the cause of transparency for the European Central Bank, but with strongly conflicting views about what such transparency entails. The same applies to transparency in financial markets. Few would argue against it, as this would be taken to imply that they had something to hide but there is only limited agreement on what should be disclosed.

There are no obvious answers as to what should be disclosed, although, of course, there are some simple requirements for making the disclosures useful and fair in competitive terms across banks. The obvious requirement for fairness is that there should be common rules that do not discriminate against any particular class of banks. Indeed it is important to make sure that the requirements for banks are not so onerous compared to other financial institutions that business is driven outside the scope of the regulation designed to cover it – offshore, for example. The obvious requirements for usefulness are that the accounting conventions used should be both common to all reporting organisations and provide valuations that are comprehensible, comparable and meaningful. An independent check on quality would also seem to be appropriate as provided by independent auditors appointed by the shareholders or some other body independent of the management.

Adequate assessment requires the disclosure of sufficient information about a bank to be able to determine the structure of its assets and liabilities and the riskiness of that structure. However, it is insufficient merely to show account and balance sheet information because the assessor also needs to know how risks are managed. It is thus not just information about the past that is relevant but any indicators that are available as to the risks that are likely to be encountered in the future and how they will be managed. As in other areas there are some clear factors that need to be disclosed. Seven obvious sets can be listed:

1. information on the structure of the institution and its relationship to others in any interest grouping;
2. information on the nature and reputation of those responsible for the running of the bank;
3. information on the financial standing of the bank and its recent track record;

4.   information on capital adequacy;
5.   information on risk exposures – these need to be peak exposures and not just averages or end-period values;
6.   information on the systems used to manage risks;
7.   information on how independent sources such as rating agencies and auditors view the procedures and riskiness of the bank.

Additionally the information needs to be up to date and revised at frequent intervals.

In a sense it is the assessors who will be judges of the adequacy of the disclosures. If they are unhappy about them, then the natural reaction will be to rate the bank rather lower, by selling its stock, withdrawing deposits, lowering credit ratings, making sell recommendations and so on. However, experience suggests that it is unlikely that the market system will itself be able to generate sufficient self-discipline to ensure that the minimum – or, rather, common – standards are adequate for the purpose of assessment. The banks themselves may have an incentive to limit the information available in a concerted manner.[1]

The result is not obvious, as healthier institutions will have an incentive to disclose their health while those that are in difficulty will have an incentive to disguise their problems. Hence greater disclosure will itself be an indicator of quality. Nevertheless it seems likely that the supervisor will feel the need to intervene and set standards, even if these are largely determined by accepted international conventions.

One of the simplest ways to go about this would be to ask what information the banks' managements deem necessary for monitoring that risks are being managed satisfactorily. This information may be daily, weekly or possibly monthly. However, even in the most transparent companies information is currently usually only released quarterly. Nevertheless, it is notable that requirements for statistics about the operation of markets and indeed the economy at large are usually provided rather more frequently – continuously in some cases.

One of the major criteria to be applied in these cases will be the cost. Particularly if some external assessment is required. Frequent statistics may tend to be rather less accurate and subject to revision. This is a typical principal–agent problem. The 'principal' – in this case the outside assessor – wants to be convinced of the health of the bank, while the agent, the bank's management, wants to undertake the job in the least costly – that is, the most profitable – manner. The relationship exists because the principal does not have the time, resources or skills to do the management's job. It merely wants to be convinced that the agent is going to do the job adequately. This will come from a combination of the agent's track record, the knowledge of the quality of the systems being employed and their use, a structure that makes mismanagement less likely, the ability to monitor and exit so as to limit losses and the views of credible third parties. In other words a list akin to the seven points we have outlined above.

However, rather than develop some suggestions ab initio, the approach of this chapter is to describe and appraise the best-known disclosure regime that is in current operation and has been employed since the beginning of 1996, namely that of New Zealand. New Zealand is in some respects unusual. Although having a well-developed financial system it is a small country of some 3.8 million people with only 17 registered banks, almost all of those being foreign-owned. We therefore argue that amendments to the system are necessary where the country is larger, where financial markets are less developed and in particular where there are large numbers of banks that do not have publicly quoted or actively traded stock.

Nevertheless these amendments are matters of detail compared to the strength of the principle of disclosure. The uniqueness of the New Zealand position is not in our view an argument against the general applicability of a disclosure regime but a ready explanation of why the system should have been introduced there first. Changes are often easier to implement in a small country. Small open economies are used to being at the mercy of shocks from their larger neighbours in the outside world and hence have to have robust systems. Furthermore, countries with a single-chamber parliament run by majority governments are able to pass new and indeed radical legislation rather more readily than others. They are therefore likely to be well motivated in seeing the good management of risk.

7.1 THE DISCLOSURE REGIME IN NEW ZEALAND

There is likely to be considerable debate over the level of detail to be disclosed. New Zealand has made a decision about the level of information that it feels is necessary (see Table 7.1). These are laid out in detail in the *Banking Supervision Handbook* (RBNZ, 1999), which is provided for registered banks on the Reserve Bank's web page www.rbnz.govt.nz.[2] It has also chosen to go for quarterly accounting periods, although a full audit is only required half-yearly. This approach has been made in conformity with emerging practice in the United States and international accounting standards – international standards have now caught up with the New Zealand practice with the interim proposals developed by the IASC. (Clearly in implementing any proposals one should try to align them with standards in a forward-looking not backward-looking manner, otherwise they will be rapidly outdated.)

As far as possible the disclosure statements have been designed to fit with modern accounting practice. The legislation also puts the treatment of directors of banks very much on a par with the treatment of directors of other companies

Table 7.1 Disclosure requirements in New Zealand

- the income statement and balance sheet (including a five-year summary of key financial data
- directors and their interests
- asset quality and provisioning
- the number of large exposures (including interbank exposures) as measured relative to the bank's equity
- related party exposures as measured relative to the bank's tier one capital
- sectoral exposures
- capital adequacy, including off-balance-sheet items
- market risk exposures
- credit rating (if held)

---

that issue securities under the terms of the Companies Act 1993, the Financial Reporting Act 1993, the Securities Act 1978 and Securities Regulations 1983 (Mortlock, 1996). Indeed, bringing financial accounting and auditing practices into line was an essential part of ensuring that disclosure statements could be externally verified to a standard that would satisfy shareholders and depositors (and the Reserve Bank as supervisor).

Although the disclosure requirements might seem onerous at first blush, they are designed to do no more than encourage directors to undertake their existing responsibilities conscientiously. It makes directors accountable; it encourages them to be well informed about the activities of the bank and the risks to which it may be exposed. In particular, it encourages them to make sure that the systems in place in the bank are adequate to monitor and manage those risks.

In taking this last step, the Reserve Bank has sought to get round a problem that entraps more traditional supervision systems, which lay down a set of procedures that should be followed. It is easy to find out whether the bank has actually put the procedures in place but it is very difficult, as an outside observer, to find out how well they are followed and whether it is the spirit of their purpose which has been implemented. The system of incentives encourages directors and managers to satisfy themselves that both the letter and the spirit are being followed, because they will be held accountable if there is a problem.

Since these statements should correspond closely to the quarterly information that banks would wish to produce to ensure their own good operation the compliance costs should be reduced compared with other supervisory regimes – although no doubt there are transition costs as the new arrangements are implemented. The Reserve Bank has stopped charging banks for the costs of supervision and banks now have increased business freedom through the reduction of direct controls.

The costs of supervision are thus reduced directly in three respects: the costs to the supervisor are lower; the compliance cost for the bank is likely to be lower; and there is likely to be an efficiency gain. Should a crisis occur it is unlikely that the supervisory costs will be much affected but since the intention is to reduce the chance of such a crisis the expected value of these costs should also fall.

Although banks expressed fears of increased costs in advance they have not reported any substantial increases now the regime has bedded in. Much of the information now disclosed is similar to that provided previously in private to the Reserve Bank. Furthermore, anyone, including banks, issuing securities was required by the Securities Commission to produce an extensive prospectus – an obligation now rescinded for registered banks.

The system is particularly designed to take full advantage of the role of independent directors. (The disclosure statement itself covers conflicts of interest.) Such directors bring a different perspective to the management of the business. This additional and, probably, more objective scrutiny should help ensure that dealings with controlling shareholders and related parties are not contrary to the interests of the bank in New Zealand. They will be particularly concerned to be certain that the risk management mechanisms and internal controls are effective as they are not party to the day-to-day activities of the bank. For example, one would expect that the board would want to have an effective audit committee chaired by a non-executive director.

These arrangements will encourage banks to appoint directors who are not only skilled in their own right and have established reputations but who have an incentive to see that the bank's management has the necessary skills and experience. By having these reputational penalties and encouraging a regime which makes early identification of problems more likely it is hoped to provide at least some safeguard against 'go for broke' strategies (Kupiec and O'Brien, 1995). That worry is that managers, having breached the criteria for prudence, have no greater downside penalty from following increasingly risky strategies. In the New Zealand regime the penalties for trying to cover up and get through a difficulty may be greater than those from disclosing an impending problem in the first place.

What is being sought here is a 'contract' between the supervisor and the registered bank, where the incentives are such that, for the minimum cost, the bank keeps the risks of imprudent behaviour below some minimum acceptable to the supervisor. (This is analogous at one remove to the sorts of optimal contracts discussed by Diamond (1984), inter alia, between lenders and borrowers, where the borrower is faced by a set of disincentives to fail to produce the required return for the lender.) Registration criteria help screen out high risks and the range of risks to be covered in the disclosure statement help ensure that the identifiable facets of risk are covered. Managing the risk is achieved through a combination of specified minima and pecuniary and non-pecuniary disincentives, where the required standards cannot be expressed in any such directly quantitative form. Market disciplines are likely to be more effective than threat of fines and other similar penalties. It is not possible to draw the appropriate line for prudent minima or for the appropriate level of the disincentives with any precision. Furthermore, supervisors wish to avoid conducting any experiments that demonstrate what incentives are insufficient. The Reserve Bank of New Zealand's system is thus not designed to test the margin of adequacy but to operate at a level where risks are low at the best international standards for supervision.

7.1.1   Key Information Summary

The disclosure statements are published in two forms. A *Key Information Summary* (KIS) is required to be displayed prominently in every bank branch and is available on demand. (See Appendix 7.1 for an example of a KIS.) As its name implies it contains the core information in the statement presented in a manner that is accessible to the ordinary bank customer, normally in the form of a single folded card placed in a pamphlet rack (it is now also available on bank web pages, which can also be accessed through the Reserve Bank website www.rbnz.govt.nz). It includes:

- the bank's credit rating (or statement that it does not have one);
- capital ratios;
- information on peak exposure concentration, asset quality, shareholder guarantees (if any) and profitability.

The KIS is primarily aimed at the retail customer. However, the practice is that most individuals do not look at the documents and the numbers used are small. There are several reasons for this. The documents are not particularly simple to read. They are written in financial reporting jargon and hence most people would have difficulty interpreting them. Retail customers tend either to take the quality of the bank on trust or rely on others. The reader who can cope with the jargon readily is also likely to be interested in more detail.

Thus the idea of the KIS, while appealing in principle, has not really achieved its aim in practice of meeting the needs of those who walk into bank branches.[3] Other information documents produced by the Reserve Bank to try to deal with the main practical questions concerning risks have also had a relatively low take up, although internet access widens the availability substantially. As a result the Bank has tried to adopt a different approach to trying to increase financial and economic literacy by providing resource packages for schools that form part of the main curriculum (RBNZ, 1995a; 1996).[4]

7.1.2 The General Disclosure Statement

The other publication is the *General Disclosure Statement*, which contains the full list of information described above in a manner aimed principally at the professional analyst.

These documents can vary fairly substantially between the banks in terms of presentation. The KIS is usually two to four pages in length but the GDSs are much more substantial (ANZ 48 pages, BNZ 66 pages, Countrywide 41 pages, Westpac 52 pages for the six months ended February or March 1997).

Appendix 7.2 contains excerpts from the most recent statement we had received, Deutsche Bank's June 1999 GDS (61 pages), as an illustration of the regime in practice. The Appendix shows:

1. the contents of the financial statement
2. an example of the detail shown in the statement of financial position
3. an example of the cash flow statement
4. the notes on accounting policies, including valuation of derivatives and treatment of market risk
5. related party transactions
6. risk management policy for derivatives and statement of on- *and off-*balance sheet risk
7. statement on fair value and concentration of credit risk
8. market risk management and exposures to market risk (including peak exposures)
9. the attestation statement by the directors

Much of the financial information is fairly conventional and by not presenting the exposure information in ratio form it is not as helpful to the reader as it might be. Around a quarter of the document is explanation. It is probably the last two items that are of greatest interest.

New Zealand requires the disclosure of peak exposures not just some quarterly average or end period value. This enables the disclosure of the full extent of the risks that have been run. Disclosure would clearly be of much less market value if it did not also include peaks or the number and nature of the greatest exposures. It is quite possible that peak exposures will exceed either limits prescribed by the authorities or limits voluntarily imposed in advance by the banks on themselves, but this is not a problem for disclosure as such. It is up to the bank concerned to explain the overshoot in a manner which the market finds convincing. As it happened the illustration of a disclosure document shown in Mayes (1997) for the National Bank of New Zealand (NBNZ) included an overshoot of the limits to exposure to related parties laid down by the RBNZ. The NBNZ explained that this exposure – to its parent – occurred as the result of a failed transaction and when this was publicly disclosed it went completely without comment or noticeable reaction by the market. (The overshoot was notified immediately to the supervisor without waiting for the next public disclosure date.) If an overshoot were the result of an internal system not working properly not only would the bank wish to correct that but it would want to do so in a manner that convinced outsiders. Disclosure of excess risks does not therefore place obligations on banks that they would not wish to place on themselves.

An issue that arises from the New Zealand context is the need to bring as much as possible of the bank's activities into the frame for disclosure and not just to consider what is on the conventional balance sheet. It is risks associated with market activities and in well-known cases with derivatives that have provided the crucial source of risk for some banks. It is therefore necessary to go rather further than the traditional accounts. Thus off-balance-sheet as well as on-balance-sheet risks are included.

The Reserve Bank has gone rather further than the Basel accord in requiring disclosure of Value at Risk not just for the banks' trading book but for the whole of their balance sheet (Harrison, 1996; RBNZ, 1999). It has set out a common framework for the calculation of risk so that banks can be compared and assessed relative to a standard. (Banks can use their own systems to measure exposures provided that this does not generate results materially below those obtained from applying the Reserve Bank's standard.) The market risks cover interest rate, exchange rate and equity exposures. The Basel 'standard model' forms the basis for the assessment, with interest risk decomposed into directional, yield curve and basis risks. Both end of quarter and peak risks during the quarter have to be disclosed. As from the end of 1998 these market risks have had to be externally audited along with the rest of the disclosure document.

The Reserve Bank has been opposed to laying down uniform quantitative risk limits. If such limits are to be effective in restricting risk in all normal circumstances they would tend to have to be set rather low, inhibiting some prudent business. While, when they are normally set fairly high so as only to exclude imprudent behaviour, they will implicitly offer an endorsement of behaviour up to those limits, which could in some circumstances result in the taking on of undue risk. The problems of moral hazard are thus reintroduced and the Reserve Bank has limited such ratios to the minimum number that international standards require.

Similarly, the Reserve Bank does not prescribe particular internal control mechanisms. If it did it would again face the twin dangers: that such controls might be thought to be adequate in all circumstances and hence allow the emergence of greater risks than banks would be prepared to tolerate of their own volition; and that such controls would be felt mandatory and hence their imposition might impose unnecessary costs on some banks, whose business does not require them. (Section 7.3 contains suggestions for improving on the New Zealand system in this particular area.)

By following this Value at Risk approach the New Zealand supervision system should be well adjusted to the advances being reported (see Jackson *et al.*, 1996, for example) in bank-based systems which can be 'back-tested' for accuracy compared with the unadjusted Basel criteria. By using a disclosure route it is possible for concerns over capital adequacy to be expressed before the bank reaches any specific limit. As Goodhart (1995) points out there is no material difference between capital adequacy of 8.000 and 7.999 per cent. Triggers for concern should be progressive and take into account an evaluation of the bank's whole business, as well as the wider state of the financial system and the economy as a whole at the time (Benston and Kaufman, 1994). Disclosure enables concern to be expressed with varying intensity at any juncture.

To some extent New Zealand requires the disclosure in public of what other authorities collect in private and do not disclose. One obvious approach for introducing disclosure elsewhere would be to say that everything which is currently (or planned to be) disclosed to the authorities should be disclosed in public, as clearly the authorities feel that all that information is necessary in forming a view about the standing of the institution. This criterion might, however, be too detailed and banks would feel that some of this information is too sensitive.

It is also likely that in the discussion with the banks over what should be disclosed the authorities may find information that has been collected more for historical reasons than current benefit and hence can be dropped with little loss. Some of the information that is currently provided to the authorities by banks, such as the detailed quarterly country risk, is collected for international statistical and surveillance purposes on behalf of the BIS and IMF and so would not directly indicate the appropriate level of detail that should be disclosed. Similarly, daily foreign exchange transaction information is collected for reasons of financial system management rather than for prudential supervision and hence would not be affected by a change in the supervision regime. Nevertheless it is to be expected that the burden on banks would be reduced and the specification of the disclosure requirement such that they could use the data that they collect for internal management purposes for public disclosure and not need to collect information for disclosure alone.

The European Commission (DG Markt) has also been discussing Disclosure of Financial Instruments. The detail being discussed there is also greater than that required in New Zealand and fairly similar to that currently required by EEA supervisors. It is therefore likely that a disclosure regime implemented in the EEA would at least meet the level of detail in these draft proposals, assuming that is that an agreement is likely in the reasonably near future. It is anticipated that in due course there will be an EU recommendation advocating a similar level of public disclosure (but probably at annual rather than quarterly frequency).

In the New Zealand case it is probably the attestation by the directors that is the most important single item in the document. All of the directors, including the non-executives have to sign stating not just that the financial information is correct and that the bank has complied with the requirements on capital adequacy, risk exposure and reporting but that the necessary risk management procedures have been properly applied. (See item 9 in Appendix 7.2.)

7.1.3 Rule of Law – Responsibility

A disclosure system is only going to work if compliance is the norm and, in general, breaking the regulations is by accident and not fraudulent intent. The system of penalties needs to act as a deterrent and as an adequate punishment in society's eyes. For large institutions like banks, penalties have to be huge to be effective. However, if they are to be administered at a time when the bank is in distress they may end up being levied, in effect, on creditors and depositors not on the management and shareholders of the bank. It is therefore difficult to get them to be very effective. New Zealand tries to get round this by imposing penalties on the individual directors who have signed the disclosure statement. Here jail terms and unlimited civil liability can have a very real impact, as they apply to the individual and not the institution in difficulty. If the prospective penalties are such as to act as a genuine incentive to prudence by bank directors and are believed to act as such by the public then the system is likely to function.

Of course, the penalties must not be so harsh that they deter reputable people from becoming bank directors. This is not the case in New Zealand where the penalties are:

- a fine of up to NZ$25 000;
- a jail term of up to three years;
- unlimited personal civil liability for losses sustained by reason of subscribing to any debt security (including bank deposits) issued by the bank in reliance on false or misleading information contained in a disclosure statement.

It is well known in economics that the system that maximises welfare is a compromise and not just one where all fraud is deterred (Acemoglu and Verdier, 1998; Tirole, 1996).

Penalties also need to be progressive. If the only effective threat is deregistration as a bank then the transgression of the regulations would need to be correspondingly drastic and persistent. The authorities need not merely to be able to deter infringements at the margin but also to discourage banks from thinking that once they have broken a regulation there is no greater stigma from a large rather than a small breach. In general, the EU has not been very active in trying to establish market-wide minima for effective penalties and incentives for prudence.

However, the importance of a reliable legal framework stretches rather wider than just compliance with regulations. Property rights need to be clearly established for incentives to be effective. Not only does the valuation of assets have to follow a generally agreed system but the ownership of collateral needs to be clear if risks are to be properly assessed.

7.1.4   Banks can Fail

Perhaps the most important part of the incentive structure is the understanding by all parties that bank failures are possible, even in well-managed organisations, because banking involves the taking of risks. *And* those banks that do become insolvent will be allowed to fail by the authorities. If that is understood then shareholders will know that they will be the first at risk if the bank fails. They will then seek to ensure that the directors that are appointed are suitable and that the information disclosed is adequate for them to be convinced of the sense of their decisions. Customers, counterparties and depositors (who are not otherwise insured) will be keen to satisfy themselves about the strength of the bank. The directors and management themselves will be keen to ensure that they do not lose their jobs.

Unfortunately it is impossible to set up a completely credible prior commitment not to bail out insolvent banks, but the system can be set up in such a way as to make it difficult and the extent of prior reassurances to the contrary can make reneging very expensive. Credibility of course breeds credibility. If people believe that there will be no bailouts and hence banks are run in a more prudential manner the risk of insolvency falls and the authorities' resolve under pressure is not so tested. Even in small markets, where there are many small banks, the chance of testing the authorities resolve may be small. Small banks in difficulty either present little public problem if they fail or, more likely, they can rapidly be reconstructed by one or more larger banks through voluntary agreement. It may be some time before a larger institution whose failure would have a noticeable impact (in political as well as economic terms) gets into a difficulty that cannot be resolved within the banking sector.

Similarly if a bank actually fails and is not bailed out this will also increase the authorities' credibility in the future. Some parts of the EEA obviously face a problem of history, having bailed out the banking system in the last crisis. In such cases it is necessary to be even more effective in designing a system that makes it look less likely in the future. There are some simple structural aspects that will assist this:

- making sure that those responsible for resolving the crisis do not have direct access to public funds;
- making sure that those who resolve the crisis are completely independent of those who have funds at risk.

7.1.5 Good Effective Systems to Handle Systemic Risk

The final requirement for the successful operation of a more market-based system of banking supervision is that there should be arrangements for the resolution of difficulties that enable the incentive structures to be effective. Namely, it must be possible to resolve a bank that is either insolvent or unable to meet the capital adequacy or other requirements for registration rapidly and without the need to bail out the shareholders. Liuksila (1998) suggests that there are some question marks over whether this is possible without shareholder agreement in the EU (which could effectively preclude a rapid resolution).[5] In the New Zealand case there is no such barrier 'a statutory manager has, and may exercise, in the case of a body corporate, all the powers of the members in general meeting and the board of directors of that body corporate' (Reserve Bank Act, 1989, section 129). The statutory manager can also:

- Carry on the business (section 130);
- Pay creditors and compromise claims (section 131);
- Sell the bank (section 132);
- Petition to wind the bank up (section 136).

By following the route of statutory management there is a clear separation between the process of resolution and any access to government funds. The Reserve Bank of New Zealand also shall if it 'considers it necessary for the soundness of the financial system, act as lender of last resort for the financial system' (section 31). There has been no explanation either of the conditions that would merit such lending or the terms under which such lending would be made. Clearly it will weaken any incentives if the banks believe such facilities will be readily available or that the prospect of failure of any large bank would be thought to be an unacceptable threat to the soundness of the financial system as a whole.

A key feature of the New Zealand regime is that the idea of any implicit guarantee for registered banks should be minimised. Unlike most OECD countries, New Zealand does not have any system of depositor protection, even for small retail deposits. Nevertheless, it is impossible to dismiss the idea that the government might step in the event of the failure of a major retail bank, however much the authorities wish to precommit themselves not to act in that manner. The system is designed to permit individual banks to fail, whatever their size, and purely to try to make sure that the knock on consequences for the financial system as a whole are minimised.

It is important to distinguish between liquidity and solvency problems. The Reserve Bank has the power to provide whatever liquidity is necessary to maintain the confidence in individual banks and hence the system as a whole. This guards against the consequences of shocks, either to the economy as a whole or to individual banks, which have a short run adverse effect on liquidity, spilling out into a wider problem. (It would also prevent market participants driving some of their number into difficulty by cornering markets.) However, the Reserve Bank will not provide liquidity to banks that are either insolvent or likely to become insolvent and will instead recommend to the Treasurer that the bank be placed under statutory management. Such a recommendation would also be made if a bank in difficulty refused to consult, comply with a direction or behaved in a manner prejudicial to the soundness of the financial system.

The statutory manager has wider powers than a liquidator. There is a moratorium on legal proceedings. The manager can suspend payment on money owing and can convert a branch of an overseas bank into a locally incorporated entity. The statutory manager is subject to direction by the Reserve Bank. The prime regard of the statutory manager is the need to maintain public confidence in the operation and soundness of the financial system and to avoid significant damage to the financial system. However, consistent with that, they are also required to try to resolve the difficulties as soon as possible while preserving the position and maintaining the ranking of creditors' claims.

The more common occurrence will, it is to be hoped, not be crises but breaches of the capital adequacy requirements. Here (RBNZ 1995b, p. 78) the Reserve Bank has implemented a version of what Goodhart (1996, p. 647) has described as 'a precommitted graduated series of responses in face of capital erosion':

- If tier 1 capital falls below 4 per cent or total capital below 8 per cent of risk-weighted exposures a bank must submit a plan for restoring its capital at least to the minimum to the Reserve Bank and to publish that plan as soon as possible in a disclosure statement.
- The plan would have to include:
  - no distributions are made to shareholders till the minimum position is regained;
  - no increase in the exposure to a related party from that prevailing at the time of the breach.

- If tier 1 capital falls below 3 per cent gross credit exposures must not be increased above the level prevailing at the time of the breach.
- The Reserve Bank can, if necessary, enforce this policy by giving a 'direction' to the bank under the provisions of section 111 of the Reserve Bank Act.

7.2   HOW FAR IS THE NEW ZEALAND SYSTEM TRANSFERABLE?

New Zealand is a small country with only 17 registered banks all but one of whom, with a very small market share, are foreign-owned (Table 7.2). It is thus relatively easy to keep tabs on the whole of the financial system and to be relatively well informed about what if going on. However, it is sometimes argued (see Brash, 1997) that New Zealand is to some extent piggy-backing on the more traditional supervision regimes in other countries as home country regulators normally require reports on the whole operations of the banking group, including those in New Zealand.

To some extent this is true, in that if the supervisors in the parent's jurisdiction were to do a poor job and allow the parent to fold the chances are that the New Zealand subsidiary and certainly a New Zealand branch would fold with it. New Zealand is thus reliant on adequate supervision of the parent. However, this reliance only extends to supervision within New Zealand in a rather limited sense. The Reserve Bank will normally place a lot of stock by the parent's supervisor's views of the standing of the institution and of the bank's compliance with the requirements imposed by the home supervisor. However, if the Reserve Bank were not able to place that reliance it would have to make up its own mind.

However, the success of the system within New Zealand does not rely on external supervision but on the rules for registration, disclosure and crisis management.

Secondly, the position would be very different if there were a large number of New Zealand registered banks which were doing substantial business in third markets. In these cases the Reserve Bank would in effect be supervising a parent and it is likely that the nature of disclosure would have to change to take account of substantial overseas operations.

Thirdly, it is worth noting that financial markets in New Zealand are highly developed. Information about financial institutions and those who run them is good. There is fortunately no history of corrupt or suspect behaviour. Where a central bank has far more doubts about the quality of those wishing to run banks or the public lacks confidence then a more intrusive regime and a wider system of guarantees may be appropriate. The nature and adequacy of corporate law, the adequacy of accounting standards, auditing requirements and even the integrity

Table 7.2   Registered Banks as at 30 September 1999

Registered Bank	Owner(s)
(a) New Zealand incorporated banks	
ANZ Banking Group (New Zealand) Limited	Australia and New Zealand Banking Group Limited
ASB Bank Limited	Commonwealth Bank of Australia (75%), ASB Community Trust (25%)
Bank of New Zealand	National Australia Bank Limited
BNZ Finance Limited	National Australia Bank Limited
Rabobank New Zealand Limited	Rabobank Nederland
The National Bank of New Zealand Limited	Lloyds TSB Group plc
TSB Bank Limited	TSB Community Trust
(b) Overseas incorporated banks	
ABN AMRO Bank N V	
AMP Bank Limited	
Bank of Tokyo-Mitsubishi (Australia) Limited	
Banque Nationale de Paris S.A.	
Citibank N.A.	
Deutsche Bank A.G.	
Hong Kong and Shanghai Banking Corporation	
Kookmin Bank	
Rabobank Nederland	
Westpac Banking Corporation	

of the accounting profession will all affect the efficiency of a disclosure based regime – as indeed will freedom and ownership of the press. As in so many circumstances this is a matter of weighing up the costs and benefits of the different regimes and there is no reason to expect that precisely the same conclusion will be drawn in each jurisdiction. Where the banking system is largely owned by the state, disclosure may be less meaningful as the implicit guarantees will be substantial. Even so a robust disclosure regime may encourage better risk management.

Furthermore, the regulation of the banking sector has to be balanced against the regulation of closely related sectors. If the regulation of banks is too harsh, in relative terms, then some of the task of intermediation undertaken by banks will tend to migrate to less regulated sectors. This migration may itself tend to lessen the stability of both the financial sector as a whole and the banking sector in particular. In New Zealand the whole system of financial regulation has been developing in parallel, with some steps, outside the banking sector, still to be completed.

Lastly, regime changes can always lead to uncertainty. Even if a disclosure-based regime might be more effective in the long run, introducing it at a time of fragility in the financial system might be ill advised.

It is also worth noting that while we may appear to have focused on systemic risk, this does not mean investor protection is neglected by the New Zealand approach. The absence of any public or private insurance schemes for depositor protection does not mean that depositors are not protected. The system is designed to provide sufficiently strong incentives to prudential management that such schemes are unnecessary. Indeed, it is argued that the presence of such schemes would themselves weaken the incentives and increase the chances of a failure and hence the need to bail out depositors.

Not all jurisdictions might feel that they had the confidence to operate such a scheme. Ultimately the fallout from losses by retail depositors will be political, as they are also electors. As Goodhart (1995, p. 27) points out, there is one sense in which the contract between depositors and banks differs from that with other transactions. Here one cannot inspect the goods before parting with the money. The depositors part with their money now in return for the promise of more later under various conditions.

In some respects it is the treatment of deposit insurance that provides the clearest difference between the New Zealand regime and the progress towards greater disclosure occurring in other OECD countries. The New Zealand system does offer a substitute for deposit insurance in that the incentives in the system should encourage more prudent behaviour by the banks and depositors in the first place.

Others (Diamond and Dyvbig 1983, for example) have suggested that the lender of last resort facility to deal with liquidity problems for banks that are basically solvent but faced with a crisis of confidence can act as an alternative to deposit insurance. There it is hoped that the existence of the facility will provide the necessary confidence and that hence runs would not occur in the first place. As with government-backed deposit insurance schemes, where the payout can be covered by taxation, no cost is incurred if the facility is not called on. (There are, of course, severe practical problems in distinguishing between liquidity and solvency problems in a crisis, as action has to be swift. The quality of the decisions made will depend upon the accuracy of the knowledge available to the central bank at the time.)

However, comparable economies are not starting from a clean slate. Most have deposit insurance already. It is probably unlikely that countries with deposit insurance would feel inclined to remove it, although changes in form in order to focus on the depositors with the greatest difficulty in obtaining information on the risks to banks – that is small retail depositors – might occur. In no way does this mean that a disclosure regime only makes sense if there is no deposit insurance. All of the other incentives on directors, shareholders and non-insured depositors still apply, as do the incentives for competitors to highlight difficulties – they may have to pick up some of the bill should there be a call on the deposit insurance – and for analysts and the media to search for value and for stories.

In choosing an appropriate regime one needs to balance out the costs. A detailed regulatory regime would impose heavy compliance costs on the participating banks and to this would have to be added the costs of the regulator (which could be charged back to the banks as used to be the case in New Zealand) or financed out of more general taxation (for example, through central bank surplus not passed on to the taxpayer). To these costs need to be added two forms of efficiency loss. The first stems from the need to maintain any excess margin against risk but the second relates to the need to resort to higher cost methods of finance outside the banking system. These costs may be not just in terms of direct costs but flexibility as well.

Against this must be offset the increased security of the system as a whole. In so far as the risks are perceived to be lower then this will have a downward effect on borrowing costs. However, the largest cost normally only occurs in the event of failure. These failures are fortunately sufficiently few that it is very difficult to build up a clear assessment of the size of this cost. That cost extends beyond the direct cost, in terms of lost deposits or insurance paid out, to the reputational cost to the system as a whole and higher costs that will be incurred until confidence returns. The higher the protection for banks then the greater the incentive to use other forms of finance and the risk may be transferred rather than reduced.

In the New Zealand case the direct costs are clearly reduced by the new system and efficiency is likely to increase, as banks are able to take a more flexible view in assessing risks. The Reserve Bank clearly thinks that the risks of bank failure are also reduced. It is difficult to prove that one way or the other. The absence or occurrence of failure under one regime will only have clear implications for the other if it is possible to point to events that would not otherwise have happened. For example, the supervisor may have detected a problem or the disclosure regime may have led a bank to implement improved procedures that closed an opportunity for a dangerous risk. Such unrecorded events are either unknowable in principle or not publicised in practice. There must, however, be a supposition in favour of the New Zealand changes, suggesting that not merely may the risks have been reduced but the costs reduced as well. In so far as this has implications for investment there could be small 'supply-side' benefits for economic growth as well as the static efficiency gain.

7.3   THE MAIN BARRIERS

The discussion so far has identified five main issues that need to be addressed if greater market discipline is to be introduced successfully in EEA countries:

1. accounting and auditing standards;
2. the structure of the banking industry with high concentration on the one hand and a string of small banks on the other;
3. the role of deposit insurance;
4. the powers of crisis resolution; and
5. the treatment of market risk.

The last of these is qualitatively different, as, unlike the first four, it is not just a question of whether existing experience in successful supervision regimes can be emulated but whether existing regimes, and the New Zealand one in particular, can be improved upon. We therefore turn to this point next, along with the issues of 'too big to fail' and deposit insurance.

One further problem that does not affect New Zealand or other jurisdictions is the requirements of EU legislation. One issue has been clearly identified in this regard:

6. the problem of *home country control.*

The single European market legislation, as expressed in the Second Banking Directive (1989), required that, subject to a set of minimum prudential requirements that must be applied by all member states, a bank headquartered in one member state and meeting the requirements to be registered as a bank in that state has the right to set up branches in other member states. Furthermore, although some data will be collected from branches in other host countries supervision will be exercised on a consolidated basis by the authorities in the home state. (The issue of home country control is treated in more detail in Mayes and Vesala (1998).)

The host authorities may thus have limited information on banks operating in their market but headquartered elsewhere in the EEA and even more limited powers of action should those banks get into difficulty. While the host authority has the responsibility for the systemic implications for its own market, the authority with the power of resolution will have responsibility only for its own financial system. Thus small member states may find they have banks with significant implications for systemic stability in their market yet rather less importance for the financial stability of the home market.

Secondly, if multinational banks have an element of choice of where to be headquartered and registered within the EEA, they may move away (towards) a jurisdiction that introduces a less (more) favourable regime.

Clearly the EEA, like other countries, is facing the consequences of trends in financial markets, such as the rapid growth of information technology, improved payment systems and the introduction of new products, especially derivatives. All of which will have an influence on the introduction of changes to the supervision regime. These will be exacerbated by the completion of the single European market and the innovations involved with participation in Stage 3 of EMU. In general these forces either increase the need for introducing greater market discipline or make its introduction rather easier, such as the improvements in payments systems. So we do not deal with them explicitly here.

7.3.1 Market Risk

The New Zealand authorities had wanted to introduce a regime that required the banks to disclose how they handled market risk and to ensure that the quality of that management at least met the latest Basel standards. This latter did not imply that these standards were thought to be either ideal or adequate but that they were likely to become the international standard and New Zealand was concerned that its banks would face difficulties in capital markets if standards were perceived to be below the norm.

The problem is simply that assessment of market risk is not a simple task and assessment methods are complex and difficult to describe. Disclosing the methods used would therefore be a substantial process and one only assessable by a very small group of specialists. In other regimes it has only been supervisory authorities that have been prepared to assess alternative risk management models against the standard, through methods such as 'back testing'.

The Reserve Bank therefore found itself pushed into setting out a version of the emerging Basel standards as a description of the sort of regime that would be acceptable (RBNZ, 1999, part 6).[6] A bank could then apply that model of Value at Risk and disclose the outcome without any need to justify the method being used in the disclosure statement. However, the RBNZ did not want to compel banks to use that specific model, as it might very well not be appropriate to their specific businesses. For example, covariances might be important either in reducing or increasing the overall risk. The RBNZ did not want to impose a compliance cost on the banks by compelling them to use one model for disclosure while they actually used another in managing the risk in practice. Having different internal models and disclosure models is suboptimal in two further respects. Not only does it mean that banks do not demonstrate that they are employing risk management methods that they think are superior to the standard model but it may also mean that banks have to have cover in excess of the risks they perceive internally, thereby inhibiting the business and imposing further costs (on customers). However, one point to note in the New Zealand system is that there is no requirement to hold capital against the disclosed Value at Risk. That is a commercial choice for the banks. The market can observe what capital they do hold. It practice the retail banks have not always held enough capital (in addition to the capital adequacy requirements) to cover this risk fully in the manner normally advocated (see Ruthenberg, 1997, for example). Wholesale banks, on the other hand, have normally exceeded it, sometimes by a substantial margin, which could be interpreted as a demonstration of the prudent management of risk in relation to the specific business.

The result of specifying the standard model as a guideline was that all banks disclosed using that model, irrelevant of whether they used the model internally. While this has the advantage of comparability, it did not really reflect the intent of the regime. Some of the banks claimed that they preferred not to disclose their internal models because this revealed more about their competitive strategies than their competitors were revealing. This is a classic prisoners' dilemma. If all the banks revealed their internal models then the playing field would be even again, the disclosures would be more meaningful and the banks could demonstrate a competitive edge over each other in terms of the quality of the methods they used. The incentive structure would tend towards encouraging greater quality of risk management not the bare minimum.

Kupiec and O'Brien (1997) offer an alternative approach, which might get round this difficulty, by suggesting that banks could 'precommit' themselves to cover value at risk. They would use their own VaR models and choose what capital they wish to hold against the computed risk. If the capital held turns out to be inadequate then the bank is faced with having to recapitalise itself to meet both the capital adequacy standards and the market risk for the future under what are likely to be adverse conditions. The market will be aware of why the self-imposed capital cover has been breached because the bank will have had to disclose it. If that reflects bad luck rather than bad management then the market may be relatively tolerant but if, in the opinion of the market, the risk should have been identified then the bank will be penalised in terms of the costs of recapitalisation. It will also expect to have to take appropriate measures for improving procedures and probably dispensing with the services of those responsible in order to secure the new capital backing. This regime would reflect clear market discipline.

It also has the advantage that it is progressive. The self-imposed limits do not have to be breached for the market to start raising the cost of capital for the bank. Indeed, prudent behaviour can also be rewarded as investors seek to provide capital to a well-managed bank.

In the literature surveyed by Kupiec and O'Brien (1997) it is usually suggested that the supervisor might wish to impose some penalty on the banks in addition to market discipline if the precommited value is breached. This could take a number of forms. The idea of a fine seems rather inappropriate as it would be eroding the bank's capital base just at the time it needs to replenish it and would make resolution of the problem more difficult and increase the chance of turning a difficulty into failure. A more appropriate threat, which is also suggested, is to relate the supervision regime to the past performance. Thus a bank that fails in its precommitment could expect to have to face a much more intrusive supervisory regime until the supervisor is convinced that the new processes and management are adequate for a return to precommitment. (Indeed some market valuation approach could be used so that the regime switch is in effect dictated by the market.)

There is some attraction in this latter approach particularly if market discipline is being introduced (see Mayes, 1998b, for an application to the transition economies). A supervisor could progressively grant banks the freedom to operate under market discipline instead of detailed supervision as it became confident of their standing, an idea that is being trialled in the United States (Kupiec and O'Brien, 1997). This is relatively easy under the US framework as the Fed assesses the quality of banks regularly according to a battery of criteria. A cutoff value could be established at which the regime shift could take place. However, this assessment is not published at present.

It is also the case that in the US system the Federal Reserve assesses the adequacy of the VaR system that is being used. Any such assessment would tend to reintroduce an element of moral hazard in the sense that it could be taken both by the management of the bank and by the market as an endorsement that the risk management system is appropriate. It also exposes the authorities to an implicit obligation that, should the system be shown to be inadequate, they should prevent the failure of the bank or ease its recapitalisation in the event of difficulty. It would be up to the authorities to make it clear that they recognised no such obligation under a disclosure regime and that any individual bank would be allowed to fail. Nevertheless, either the VaR model itself or its properties relative to the 'standard' would have to be disclosed, if the market is to be convinced and adequately informed in the absence of an official 'acceptance' of an undisclosed model.

7.3.2 'Too Big to Fail'

The system of market discipline works well in New Zealand, first because all of the main banks are quite large and are publicly quoted either themselves or through their parents. Secondly, not only are there five main banks competing for retail deposits but none of them has a dominant position. Competition is thus very real.

Some EEA countries are not so fortunate in the structure of their markets. In some cases one or two banks have a dominant position, while in others some banks are government-owned. This leads one to question the extent of the effect that external pressures, whether from the market or from government, would have. However, such problems remain whether or not more market discipline is introduced.

Thirdly, when there are many small banks, the degree to which the market would monitor them effectively is limited. They are mainly regional and therefore would attract interest in the region but perhaps not much from the main national or international money markets. Lastly, since many of the banks are co-operative in structure the nature of the incentives varies from the traditional model. Owners are not so readily divorced from customers. Nevertheless, the management still has the same incentives if they are personally at risk.

Small banks pose problems for appropriate supervision. On the one hand should any of them fail the systemic consequences will be negligible. Larger banks can afford to acquire them. Hence there is less 'need' in some senses to spend major effort in supervising them. On the other hand smallness makes it less likely that sophisticated risk management methods will be applied, often because the business is sufficiently simple that it can be monitored by more direct means. The risks of poor management could therefore be greater but by the same token the risks in the type of business may be less with no extensive trading in derivatives that could bring the bank down. There is a general danger in supervision systems that small banks may have more than proportionate attention paid to them compared with their importance in order to ensure equal treatment of banks irrespective of size. While large near-bank financial institutions, whose demise would propose substantial problems, may receive attention less than proportionate to their importance. Such near banks normally do not have so much reliance on assets that are difficult to value in a crisis or realise without substantial penalty.

All supervision regimes face a test of credibility. In a crisis there are enormous pressures to bail out a bank in difficulty with taxpayers' money, particularly because far-reaching decisions have to be made at high speed. If there is a history of such bailouts it is even more important to give a clear signal that a different approach will be followed in the future. Regrettably the most convincing way of giving that signal is to allow the first bank which encounters difficulties to fail (and to hope that it is not so large that it presents serious systemic problems) (Mishkin, 1998).

7.3.3 Deposit Insurance

In New Zealand there is no deposit insurance, so in one sense the moral hazard is reduced as bank managements and owners can expect that they will have to face the full responsibility for the loss incurred even by small depositors. However, it is not clear how much this is a realistic difference from the EU schemes, which have insurance up to some limit. It is unlikely that it will be politically viable to allow large numbers of small depositors – who are also voters – to incur losses that amount to a substantial proportion of their small resources. Indeed it may be better to have explicit rules, which are known in advance and cover the political risk, than to leave the position open for people to guess. Their uninformed expectations may be rather larger than could be agreed beforehand at a time when there was no crisis and hence no specific people who were about to become losers unless the authorities acted.

With the partial insurance provided in the EEA, at least some depositors know their funds are at risk. Since these are the larger deposits there is a good chance that their holders appreciate the risks involved. With only limited insurance there is less of a barrier to entry for banks in terms of the funds they must hold against the risk.

What is more interesting in the EU environment is whether the hazard is affected by the nature of the insurance system and the relationship between the insurer and the authority responsible for deciding upon how the problem should be resolved. If the public provides the insurance then the insurer may want to try to trade off the costs of a bailout against the insurance. Certainly any insurer will want to trade off the costs of the resolution against the costs from paying out on the insurance, as in the case with the FDIC in the United States. Hence industry-based insurers would increase the chance of the industry itself mounting a rescue for the bank in difficulty. Here the incentive structure is quite complex. If banks think their colleagues will bail them out then they may be less prudent. However, they do not want to be pushed into acquiring their competitors' assets at a time when the market as a whole is under pressure. There could be an incentive then to weaken a competitor that is having idiosyncratic difficulties in order to pick up its assets at a discount. This would strengthen the case for having a resolution procedure based purely on avoiding systemic risk and one where the concerns of those with assets at risk are only treated relative to each other and not in some context of the wider good or the interest of one specific group. Mishkin (1998) has recently made some interesting additions.

7.3.4 Home Country Control

As we noted at the beginning of Section 7.3, there are co-ordination difficulties for home and host country supervisors in obtaining the appropriate information that they require from banks under the principle of home country control. If much of the information they require is available rapidly through public disclosure then the problem is reduced to following up signs of difficulty and asking questions where the results are unclear.

The key question is whether shifting emphasis to disclosure could provide the necessary information in the EEA. Unfortunately the onus for implementation of disclosure rules lies not with the host countries that could have the severest informational problems, because of a lack of information through substantial foreign control of their banks, but with the home countries of those banks. However, implementation by a host country would encourage foreign banks to comply voluntarily if they did not want to face a competitive disadvantage. If domestically controlled banks are providing a wide range of information that permits depositors, creditors and other involved parties to assess their quality, foreign controlled banks that remain silent on the subject will find it more difficult to demonstrate that they are in some real sense 'better'. In this case foreign controlled banks may decide to get themselves locally incorporated so that they can benefit from the same regime and perhaps save on compliance costs.[7] They may also press their own authorities to adopt a similar regime, so that the bank as a whole is not at a competitive disadvantage.

The content of banks' disclosure requirements and their international harmonisation has been recently addressed at the main international fora (EU, IASC, Basel Committee on Banking Supervision, IOSCO). At present, countries' disclosure requirements show considerable differences. The focus of the discussions has been on increasing public information about risk taking strategies, risk exposures and risk management tools, where advances would seem to be mostly needed. Qualitative information has received a lot of emphasis and there has been a move toward valuing assets in terms of their likely realisation values (implying mark-to-market when applicable).

Development along these lines would certainly increase the ability to assess the risks of individual institutions. Although the international accounting conventions relating to financial reporting now cover the presentation of the information required for disclosure in a manner that enables both comparability across banks and an adequate quality for a meaningful assessment, EU accounting requirements only permit this approach to reporting, they do not compel it. The valuation of assets on a mark-to-market basis is by no means universal outside the Anglo-Saxon countries and auditing conventions do not necessarily provide for the appropriate independent cross checks at present (Mayes, 1998). Quarterly accounting is becoming steadily more common in the United States and indeed financial companies produce substantial unaudited information monthly to assist monitoring and decision-making. The practice is less common, though increasing, in Europe. Without quarterly disclosure within a few weeks of the end of the quarter it is unlikely that the quality of the information will be sufficient for either supervisors or markets to form an adequate up-to-date view of the quality of the bank.

Increasing the role of disclosure, and meeting the preconditions for it to be efficient, could achieve two aims simultaneously as Stage 3 of EMU develops. It could strengthen banking supervision in general by enhancing market discipline in a world of rapid innovation and growing cross-border activity, where the work undertaken by public supervisors becomes increasingly difficult. As we have argued here, it could also overcome some of the present and, especially, envisaged information and co-ordination disadvantages of the present supervisory framework, without the need to make formal changes in the framework of existing EU law. Supervisors could then be able to focus their attention more where their advantage lies, in handling the problems of systemic risk – to which we now move. However, rapid progress in this area is hard to achieve. As Mayes (1998a) points out, negotiating the necessary changes in legislation can consume a lot of time, even if the main preconditions are already in place.

Although there are agreements on minimum requirements for aspects of financial supervision among the member states considerable scope remains for individual jurisdictions to decide to improve upon them. The risk that banks would indulge in 'regime shopping' is fairly small for the major retail banks but rather higher for the more specialised banks operating in a variety of EU markets and rather higher for the EU subsidiaries of large non-EU banks, which may be rather more flexible about where they headquarter their activities. On the whole the larger concerns have chosen one of the established financial centres, but as the case of BCCI illustrates the choice of a less regulated centre may attract those who intend to act outside the rules. By and large the main regime shoppers are likely to present relatively limited systemic risk.

The major concerns in the present circumstances are not from the point of view of the systemic risk that may occur within a country with 'lower' supervision requirements but from the sheer complexity of having banks operating under several different regimes in the same member state and from the problem facing the authorities in the host country when a bank headquartered elsewhere has difficulties. This latter problem has two facets: (i) The home country authorities are unlikely to view depositors, shareholders and creditors in other member states as being equally important as they do not represent the same political risk. Although EU legislation limits the extent to which there can be any home country preference there is no requirement to concentrate attention in the state where the systemic risk is greatest. (ii) A bank may be a smaller systemic risk in its state of incorporation than it is in some of the other states where it operates. If a substantial proportion of the banking system were to be foreign owned this would pose problems that are not present in New Zealand.

In the New Zealand case the RBNZ continues to supervise the local branch or subsidiary and needs to be convinced that branches provide adequate arrangements, otherwise it can demand local incorporation. Thus while New Zealand banks may face the problem that the New Zealand supervisor requires one disclosure regime, the home country supervisor a second and both of these differ from the information and risk management systems used for internal purposes, the problem would be the other way round in an EU country with substantial foreign ownership. In this circumstance, customers would face one level of disclosure from banks that are locally incorporated and different levels from those headquartered elsewhere. This could weaken the effectiveness of market discipline. However, if banks find that there are benefits from disclosure, it is likely that those headquartered elsewhere within the EEA will voluntarily disclose similar information to that required of the domestic banks, if they are not to suffer a competitive disadvantage. 'Competition among rules' could emerge with some banks trying to offer the reputation of their home supervisors as a substitute for disclosure (Mayes, 1997).

7.4   CONCLUDING REMARKS

It is easy to exaggerate the differences between the New Zealand scheme and that in place in many other jurisdictions. One way to view it is that the New Zealand arrangements are a more direct interpretation of the principles that others also espouse – take the Bank of England (1997) 'Standards for Supervisors', for example. Paragraph 4 reads 'We are predisposed to market solutions, and believe in the benefits of fair competition and market disciplines.' The latest Basel Banking Supervision Committee Proposals follow a similar line – 'supervisors should encourage and pursue market discipline by encouraging good corporate governance and enhancing market transparency and surveillance' (p. 3). Again on page 4 it suggests 'Supervision cannot, and should not, provide an assurance that banks will not fail. In a market economy failures are part of risk taking.' and on page 10, '*Effective market discipline* depends on an adequate flow of information to market participants, appropriate financial incentives to reward well-managed institutions and arrangements that ensure that investors are not insulated from the consequences of their decisions.'

Sufficiently flexible powers are necessary in order to effect an *efficient resolution of problems in banks*. 'Where problems are remediable, supervisors will normally seek to identify and implement solutions that fully address their concerns, where they are not, the prompt and orderly exit of institutions that are no longer able to meet supervisory requirements is a necessary part of an efficient financial system. Forbearance, whether or not the result of political pressure, normally leads to worsening problems and higher resolution costs.'

Some prefer to view the New Zealand regime as being, if anything, rather towards one end of a spectrum of possible approaches to banking supervision than representing a complete paradigm shift which others would find it difficult to emulate (Nicholl, 1996). What they have done is unwind the process that George (1996) notes – that there is a danger that every time there is a failure of supervision there is a temptation to ratchet regulation a notch tighter. There is still an essential role for supervisors to play and the Reserve Bank still thinks it important to publish annual surveys of the banking system each June in its *Reserve Bank Bulletin*. It is able to flag developments that it can see in the system as a whole, which may not appear from the scrutiny of individual disclosure statements. For example, as OECD (1997, p. 38) puts it: 'Caution flags should be raised by the regulatory authorities when financial market participants begin to assemble on the same village green.'

New Zealand's experience with the new regime will be studied closely by supervisors in other countries. Subject to the requirements for capital adequacy and depositor protection, there will be considerable incentives for the authorities in the EU countries to increase the role of market discipline and of public disclosure as increasing cross border operation makes it more difficult for national supervisors to keep track of the operations of large international banks.

Stumbling blocks for the implementation of more disclosure would be posed by the principle of home country supervision as substantial differences in requirements faced could emerge for competitors in the same market. As a result banks might feel encouraged to change the jurisdiction that applies to them. Secondly harmonisation with accounting standards, regulation of the rest of the financial sector and regulators of other aspects of banks' behaviour may be difficult.

Thirdly, substantial changes in legislation may be required if crisis management powers are to be strengthened to make credible the threat that insolvent banks will be allowed to fail and the viable business restructured and transferred (see Chapter 8). Implementation of the new regime in New Zealand was greatly facilitated because the Reserve Bank already had all the necessary powers under the 1989 Act. With a small exception (Reserve Bank Amendment Act 1995) new legislation was not required. Registration and crisis management powers were already in place and the disclosure regime could be implemented by Orders-in-Council, without recourse to parliament. However, given that New Zealand already has the necessary legislation and orders in place, other countries have a precedent to follow and could draw up the legislation they need and implement a regime involving more market discipline much more rapidly than in New Zealand, even after allowing time for adequate consultation with the banks.

APPENDIX 7.1   DEUTSCHE BANK AG NEW ZEALAND

General Short Form Disclosure Statement

Key Information Summary as at 30 June 1999

Introductory Information   The purpose of this Key Information Summary is to provide customers and potential customers with information about the financial condition of their bank. Neither the New Zealand Government nor the Reserve Bank of New Zealand guarantees or insures bank deposits. The information contained in the Key Information Summary is explained in the Reserve Bank publication "Your Bank's Disclosure Statement -What's In It For You?" which can be obtained from the Reserve Bank.

Corporate Information   The full name of the Overseas Bank is Deutsche Bank AG which is domiciled in Germany. The Overseas Banking Group is referred to as Deutsche Bank Group.

Credit Rating   Deutsche Bank AG has the following general credit ratings applicable to long term senior unsecured obligations payable in any country or currency and applicable in New Zealand, in New Zealand dollars.

	Current rating	*(If changed in the two years)*
Moody's Investors Service, Inc	Aa3	Aal (to May 1999)
Standard & Poor's Corporation	AA	AA + (to May 1999)
IBCA Limited	AA	AA + (to May 1999)

Profitability

Deutsche Bank Group Corporation	*Six months ended 30 June 1999 euro millions*	*Six months ended 30 June 1998 euro millions*
Net profit after tax and extraordinary items	1802	1242
As a percentage (annualised) of average total assets	0.49%	0.40%

Deutsche Bank NZ Group	*Six months ended 30 June 1999 NZD millions*	*Six months ended 30 June 1998 NZD millions*
Net profit/(loss) after tax and extraordinary items	4	1
As a percentage (annualised) of average total assets	0.23%	0.21%

Size

Deutsche Bank Group	30 June 1999 euro millions	30 June 1998 euro millions
Total assets	847 568	621 578
Percentage increase from previous year	36.36%	22.04%

Deutsche Bank NZ Group	30 June 1999 NZD millions	30 June 1998 NZD millions
Total assets	5578	1406
Percentage increase from previous year	297%	196%

Capital Adequacy

Deutsche Bank Group	30 June 1999 unaudited	30 June 1998 unaudited
Tier One capital as a percentage of risk weighted exposures	5.4%	5.1%
Minimum Tier One capital as a percentage of risk weighted exposures	4%	4%
Total capital as a percentage of risk weighted exposures	11.0%	10.3%
Minimum total capital as a percentage of risk weighted exposures	8%	8%

Capital adequacy ratios listed above for the Deutsche Bank Group are based on the calculation according to BIS-rules and are publicly available from the Financial Statements released for the Deutsche Bank Group. Ratios for Deutsche Bank AG are provided to the Bundesbank based on the German Principle 1, however, these are not publicly available and have not been disclosed here.

Asset Quality

Deutsche Bank Group	31 December 1998 euro millions audited	31 December 1997 euro millions audited
Total impaired assets (non-accruing exposures)	3119	2863
Total impaired assets as a percentage of total assets	0.50%	0.54%
Total specific provisions	5650	5807
Total specific provisions as a percentage of total impaired assets	181.2%	202.8%

Peak Credit Exposures Concentrations Deutsche Bank AG, New Zealand and its Associated Banking Group has no aggregate credit exposure to an individual counterparty or group of closely related counterparties which equals or exceeds 10% of Deutsche Bank Group's equity.

The calculation of Peak Credit exposures excludes exposures to any OECD Government.

Ranking of Local Creditors in a Winding-up   Deutsche Bank NZ will have full access to the capital of Deutsche Bank AG. The rights of creditors located in New Zealand in a bankruptcy of Deutsche Bank AG would be governed by the German Bankruptcy Act. Subject to all claims of secured creditors and creditors mandatorily preferred by law, all unsecured creditors of Deutsche Bank AG would be treated equally in a bankruptcy of Deutsche Bank AG. Ordinary unsecured claims by creditors of Deutsche Bank NZ would not be subordinated to the ordinary unsecured claims of any other creditor of Deutsche Bank AG in the bankruptcy and winding up of Deutsche Bank AG under the German Bankruptcy Act. Under section 207(1) of the German Bankruptcy Act, Deutsche Bank AG is required to always hold an excess of assets over liabilities. Deutsche Bank AG has complied with all provisions of the German Bankruptcy Act throughout the year.

The Federal Association of German Banks operates a system of deposit protection called the Deposit Protection Fund. While this is a private and voluntary system, almost all commercial banks in Germany are members (including Deutsche Bank AG). The Fund protects all deposits with a bank by non-banks irrespective of the location of the depositor or its claim up to a protection ceiling of 30% of the liable capital as defined in section 10(2) German Banking Act KWG and stated as per the last approved annual statement of accounts; for measurement of the protection ceiling, the supplementary capital as defined in section 10(21b) KWG shall only be taken into account up to an amount of 25% of the core capital as defined in section 10(2a) KWG. In the case of Deutsche Bank NZ this means that at present the Deposit Protection Fund would protect individual depositors (whether in New Zealand or elsewhere) up to an amount in the order of NZD 10.016 billion.

Deutsche Bank NZ is unable, because of systems limitations or because of circumstances beyond its control, to disclose whether there are any material legislative or regulatory restrictions of all countries in the world other than Germany ('Other Countries') which subordinate the claims of any class of unsecured creditors of Deutsche Bank NZ on the assets of Deutsche Bank AG in a winding up of Deutsche Bank AG. An explanation of the circumstances is:

(a)   Deutsche Bank AG operates in 30 Other Countries,
(b)   while any bankruptcy of Deutsche Bank AG would be governed by German law as a general principle, it is impossible to predict whether anyone in any Other Country would seek to allege that any law of that Other Country should be applied in respect of any asset or liability of Deutsche Bank AG in that Other Country in preference to the law of Germany;
(c)   whether a court in one country may apply the laws of that country in preference to laws of another country usually involves complex issues of public international law or private international law as well as complex and technical principles of the domestic law of the relevant country which are usually referred to as conflicts of laws rules. The interaction between principles of public or private international law and the conflicts of laws rules of any particular country is even more complex and uncertain in the context of insolvency where significant issues of public policy may arise. Therefore it is impossible to predict whether, if someone was to allege that the law of the Other Country should be applied in preference to the law of Germany, a court in the Other Country would accept the allegation and apply the law of that Other Country instead of German law, and

(d) given that the matters referred to in paragraphs (b) and (c) above are beyond the control of Deutsche Bank NZ and impossible to predict, Deutsche Bank NZ cannot tell whether there are any material laws or regulatory restrictions of any Other Country which subordinate the claims of any class of unsecured creditors of Deutsche Bank NZ on the assets of Deutsche Bank AG to those of any other class of unsecured creditors of Deutsche Bank AG in a winding up of Deutsche Bank AG.

In the opinion of Deutsche Bank NZ, the closest available alternative to disclosing whether there are any material laws or regulatory restrictions of any Other Country which subordinate the claims of any class of unsecured creditors of Deutsche Bank NZ on the assets of any other class of unsecured creditors of Deutsche Bank AG in a winding up of Deutsche Bank AG is to disclose that:

(e) as at 30 June 1999 approximately 44.7% of the total assets of Deutsche Bank AG were located in Germany and approximately 0.17% of the liabilities of Deutsche Bank AG were located in New Zealand, and

(f) unsecured depositors of Deutsche Bank NZ would have the benefit of the Deposit Protection Fund as outlined above.

In the opinion of Deutsche Bank NZ these facts indicate that, if:

(g) there was a legislative or regulatory restriction of an Other Country which could have the effect of subordinating the claims of any class of unsecured creditors of Deutsche Bank NZ on the assets of Deutsche Bank AG located in that Other Country to those of any class of unsecured creditors of Deutsche Bank AG in a winding up of Deutsche Bank AG;

(h) anyone alleged that such a law of that Other Country should be applied in preference to a contrary law of Germany in the winding up of Deutsche Bank AG; and

(i) the court of that Other Country accepted that allegation,

any effect on unsecured creditors of Deutsche Bank NZ would be unlikely to be 'material' as that term is defined in the Registered Bank Disclosure Statement (Full and Half-Year-Overseas Incorporated Registered Banks) Order 1998.

Financial Statements of the Overseas Bank and Overseas Banking Group Copies of that part of Deutsche Bank AG, New Zealand's most recent Supplemental Disclosure Statement, which contains a copy of the most recent publicly available financial statements of Deutsche Bank AG, being 31 December 1998 and of Deutsche Bank Group, being 31 December 1998, will be provided at no charge, immediately to any person requesting a copy where the request is made at the Auckland office of Deutsche Bank AG, New Zealand.

Reference to Disclosure Statements Copies of Deutsche Bank AG, New Zealand's most recent General Disclosure Statement and Supplemental Disclosure Statement will be provided at no charge, immediately to any person requesting a copy where the request is made at the Auckland office of Deutsche Bank AG, New Zealand.

General Information and Definitions In the Key Information Summary the following definitions have been used for the four main reporting groups:

• Deutsche Bank AG refers to the worldwide business of Deutsche Bank Aktiengesellschaft (Deutsche Bank AG) excluding subsidiary entities.

• Deutsche Bank Group refers to the worldwide business of Deutsche Bank AG including subsidiary entities.

- Deutsche Bank NZ refers to the business conducted in the Deutsche Bank AG New Zealand branch only.
- Deutsche Bank NZ Group refers to the business conducted in the Deutsche Bank AG New Zealand branch consolidated with the business of other New Zealand subsidiary entities of Deutsche Bank AG.

The comparative figures provided for Deutsche Bank NZ Group are extracted from the audited accounts of Deutsche New Zealand Limited (formerly Deutsche Morgan Grenfell New Zealand Limited) a subsidiary of Deutsche Bank AG.

Independent Examination Report
To the Directors of Deutsche Bank AG, New Zealand
    We have examined the interim financial statements including supplementary information included in the General Disclosure Statement for the six months ended 30 June 1999. Our examination was conducted in accordance with the Review Engagement Standards issued by the Institute of Chartered Accountants of New Zealand. A review or examination of the information extracted from the General Disclosure Statement is limited primarily to enquiries of Banking Group personnel and analytical review procedures applied to financial data, and thus provides less assurance than an audit. We have not performed an audit and, accordingly, we do not express an audit opinion. In our report dated 24 September 1999 we expressed an unqualified statement on those interim financial statements and supplementary information.
    The Key Information Summary has been extracted from information contained in the General Disclosure Statement for the six months ended 30 June 1999.
    We have examined the Key Information Summary and based on our examination:

- the Key Information Summary has been completed in accordance with the Registered Bank Disclosure Statement (Full and Half-Year-Overseas Incorporated Registered Banks) Order 1998, and
- the information contained in the Key Information Summary has been properly taken from the information contained in the General Disclosure Statement.

For a better appreciation of the scope of our examination, and of the Banking Group's financial position and the results of its operations for the six months, this report should be read in conjunction with the General Disclosure Statement.

KPMG

Note: The original format was a folded card with three panels, each half A4 width, on each side. We have not reproduced the covering panel nor the exact font.

APPENDIX 7.2   DEUTSCHE BANK AG NEW ZEALAND GENERAL
                          DISCLOSURE DOCUMENT 30 JUNE 1999 – EXCERPTS

1 Financial Statements Contents

FIVE YEAR SUMMARY OF FINANCIAL STATEMENTS
STATEMENT OF FINANCIAL PERFORMANCE
STATEMENT OF MOVEMENTS IN EQUITY

STATEMENT OF FINANCIAL POSITION
STATEMENT OF CASH FLOWS
NOTES TO FINANCIAL STATEMENTS FOR THE SIX MONTHS TO 30 JUNE 1999
Note 1 – Statement of Accounting Policies
   Statement of Financial Performance Notes
Note 2 – Interest
Note 3 – Other Operating Income
Note 4 – Operating Expense
Note 5 – Income Tax Expense

Asset Notes
  Note 6 – Due from other banks
  Note 7 – Due From Corporates
  Note 8 – Trading Securities
  Note 9 – Reverse Repurchase Agreements
  Note 10 – Available For Sale Securities
  Note 11 – Other Assets
  Note 12 – Loans
  Note 13 – Fixed Assets
  Note 14 – Income Tax Assets

Liability Notes
  Note 15 – Due to Other Banks
  Note 16 – Deposits
  Note 17 – Trading Securities
  Note 18 – Repurchase Agreements
  Note 19 – Other Liabilities
  Note 20 – Imputation Credit Memorandum Account
  Note 21 – Investments in Subsidiary Companies
  Note 22 – Related Party Transactions

Other Notes
  Note 23 – Interest Earning and Discount Bearing Assets and Liabilities
  Note 24 – Derivative Financial Instruments And Financial Instruments With Off-Balance Sheet Risk
  Note 25 – Fair Value of Financial Instruments
  Note 26 – Segmental Analysis
  Note 27 – Commitments and Contingent Liabilities
  Note 28 – Capital Commitments
  Note 29 – Lease Commitments
  Note 30 – Capital Adequacy
  Note 31 – Concentration of Credit Exposures to Individual Counterparties
  Note 32 – Asset Quality
  Note 33 – Risk Management
  Note 34 – Securitisation, Funds Management and Other Fiduciary Activities
  Note 35 – Exposures to Market Risk
  Note 36 – Foreign Currency Positions

2 Statement of Financial Position as at 30 June 1999

Dollars in millions	Note	Deutsche Bank NZ Group			Deutsche Bank NZ Branch		
		Unaudited 6 months 30/06/99	Unaudited 6 months 30/06/98	Audited 12 months 31/12/98	Unaudited 6 months 30/06/99	Unaudited 6 months 30/06/98	Audited 12 months 31/12/98
Assets							
Due from other banks	6	10	61			1	
Due from corporates	7	34	–		18		
Trading securities	8	239	21	77	151		
Reverse repurchase agreements	9	–	1118	–	–		
Available for sale securities	10	2794	37	–	2603	37	
Amounts due from related parties	22	1952	11	55	802	116	93
Other assets	11	141	2	15	127	1	3
Loans	12	340	155	374	308	95	373
Investments in subsidiary companies	21	–	–	–	–	–	–
Fixed assets	13	14	1	1			
Income tax assets	14	54	–	1	(1)		
Total assets		5578	1406	523	4008	250	469

Liabilities

	Note						
Due to other banks	15	945	–	–	947	–	–
Deposits	16	655	130	94	310	130	94
Trading securities	17	174	21	11	122	–	–
Repurchase agreements	18	–	1010	27	–	–	–
Amounts due to related parties	22	3623	237	383	2514	117	372
Other liabilities	19	135	4	3	112	2	2
Total liabilities		5532	1402	518	4005	249	468

Equity

	Note						
Paid in capital	20	20	–	–	–	–	–
Retained earnings		26	4	5	3	1	1
Total equity		46	4	5	3	1	1
Total liabilities and equity		5578	1406	523	4008	250	469

The accounting policies and other notes form part of, and should be read in conjunction with these financial statements.

3 Statement of Cash Flows for the Six Months Ended 30 June 1999

Dollars in millions	Note	Deutsche Bank NZ Group			Deutsche Bank NZ Branch		
		Unaudited 6 months 30/06/99	Unaudited 6 months 30/06/98	Audited 12 months 31/12/98	Unaudited 6 months 30/06/99	Unaudited 6 months 30/06/98	Audited 12 months 31/12/98
Cash Flows from operating activities							
Cash was provided from/ (applied to):							
Interest received		119	16	34	88	9	21
Fees and commissions		17	–	4	4	–	–
Trading income		399	–	6	89	–	6
Dividends received		–	–	–	–	–	–
Movements in net amounts due to and due from related parties		(786)	–	–	(622)	–	–
Movements in net trading securities and deposits		537	169	71	665	111	75
Movements in net repurchase and reverse repurchase agreements		(171)	(109)	–	–	–	–
Interest paid		(130)	(15)	(28)	(90)	(10)	(21)
Other revenue		–	2	–	–	–	–
Other expenses		–	(2)	(7)	1	2	–
Operating expenses		(42)	–	–	–	–	–
Income taxes paid		(3)	–	–	–	–	–
Net cash flows from operating activities		(60)	61	80	135	112	75
Cash flows from investing activities							
Cash was provided from/(applied to):							
Movements in net available for sale and available for purchase securities		(1010)			(2603)		

Disposal of fixed assets	–	–	–	–	–	–
Decrease/(Increase) in loans	(312)	(56)	65	(329)	(66)	121
Purchase of fixed assets	–	–	–	–	–	(4)
Increase in investment securities	–	(37)	–	–	(37)	–
Net cash flows from investing activities	(312)	(93)	(2538)	(329)	(103)	(893)

Cash flows from Financing activities

Cash was provided from/(applied to):

Increase in deposits	–	–	162	–	–	145
Decrease in equity (refer to Statement of Movements in Equity)	–	–	–	–	–	(239)
Disposal of fixed assets	–	–	–	–	–	1
Increase in due to related parties	237	(18)	2058	242	96	1050
Supplementary dividend paid	–	–	–	–	–	(38)
Net cash flows from financing activities	237	(18)	2220	242	96	919
Net increase/(decrease) in cash	–	1	(183)	(7)	54	(34)
Opening cash and cash equivalents includes Bankers Trust NZ Group	–	–	–	7	7	(121)
Closing cash and cash equivalents	–	1	(183)	–	61	(155)

The accounting policies and other notes form part of, and should be read in conjunction with these financial statements.

4 Notes to Financial Statements for the six months to 30 June 1999

Note 1 – Statement of Accounting Policies

Basis of Reporting

The financial statements are for the reporting entity DBAG NZ and the aggregated financial statements of The Group comprising DBAG NZ, Deutsche Management New Zealand Ltd (formerly Deutsche New Zealand Ltd) and Deutsche New Zealand Ltd (formerly Bankers Trust New Zealand Ltd) and its subsidiaries.

The financial statements have been prepared in accordance with the requirements of the Companies Act 1993 and the Financial Reporting Act 1993, and the Registered Bank Disclosure Statement (Full and Half-Year Overseas Incorporated Registered Banks) Order 1998.

The financial statements have been prepared in accordance with historical cost concepts with the exception of certain items for which specific accounting policies are identified.

Particular Accounting Policies

Basis of consolidation   The Deutsche Bank NZ Group's financial statements include Deutsche Bank AG New Zealand Branch aggregated with all New Zealand subsidiaries of Deutsche Bank AG.

The consolidated financial statements of Deutsche Bank NZ Group have been prepared using the purchase method including the profits and losses of all subsidiaries since their dates of incorporation. All inter-company balances and transactions have been eliminated.

Currency of presentation   All amounts are expressed in New Zealand currency and all references to $ is to New Zealand dollars unless otherwise stated.

Loans   Interest on loans is recognised on an accruals basis. Interest ceases to be taken to account as income if repayment of a loan is considered doubtful, or if:

1. payment of principal and/or interest is overdue by more than 90 days; and/or
2. the total amount outstanding including accumulated interest on secured loans exceeds 85% of the collateral value; and/or
3. with respect to loans which are being repaid and interest being added to principal, the total sum outstanding including accumulated interest reaches the lending limit established by management.

Accounting for securities   All securities are accounted for on a trade date basis.

Trading securities   The Banking Group has holdings in various debt and equity securities, which are held for trading purposes.

These securities are shown at market value, and the unrealised profit or loss is taken to account in the Statement of Financial Performance. This is a departure from the historical cost convention, but is considered to be a more appropriate method of accounting for results arising from trading in highly liquid financial assets and is consistent with generally accepted accounting practice in the banking industry.

Available for sale and available for purchase securities Available for sale and available for purchase securities are public and other debt securities which are purchased or sold with the intention to be held for an indefinite period of time, but not necessarily to maturity. Such securities may be sold or repurchased in response to various factors including significant changes in interest rates and liquidity requirements. These securities are shown at face value less unearned discount remaining to maturity.

Investment securities Investment securities are public and other debt securities which are purchased with the positive intent and ability to hold until maturity. Such securities are recorded at original cost adjusted for the amortisation of premiums and accretion of discount to maturity. In the rare event that investment securities are sold prior to maturity, profits or losses on sales are taken to the Statement of Financial Performance when realised and separately disclosed in the notes to accounts.

Certificates of deposit and commercial paper Certificates of deposit and commercial paper contract orders are shown at face value less unearned discount remaining to maturity.

Fixed assets Fixed assets are recorded at cost less accumulated depreciation. Depreciation is charged using the diminishing value method based on depreciation rates issued by the Inland Revenue Department. The following range of depreciation rates is used.

Motor vehicles	20.00–31.29%
Leasehold improvements	10.00–33.09%
Computer equipment	20.00–48.0%
Furniture, fixtures and office equipment	5.00–60.0%

Income Tax Companies in the Banking Group have adopted the liability method of tax effect accounting applied on a comprehensive basis, whereby the tax expense or benefit for the period is matched with the accounting surplus after allowing for permanent differences. Future tax liabilities and benefits have been provided at current tax rates.

Transfers of income tax benefits and liabilities between group companies are treated as permanent. Future income tax benefits are brought to account when their realisation is virtually certain.

Foreign Currency Translation Companies in the Banking Group in the normal course of business have entered into contracts as principal for the forward purchase and sale of foreign currencies. At balance date these contracts have been revalued at the market rate for contracts of those maturities and the unrealised profit or loss on revaluation has been included in the Statement of Financial Performance.

Assets and liabilities denominated in foreign currencies are translated at period end rates, while foreign currency revenue and expense items are translated at the exchange rate current at the date at which those items were recognised in the accounts.

Foreign currency monetary assets and liabilities are current assets and current liabilities. Exposures to foreign currency market risk are detailed in Note 35.

Futures   Futures contracts held as principal for trading purposes have been revalued to market value at balance date and the resulting profit or loss has been included in the Statement of Financial Performance. Profits and losses relating to revaluations of futures contracts held as principal for hedging purposes are brought to account on the same basis as the income or expense, which is recognised in relation to the hedged instruments.

Options   In the normal course of business the Banking Group grants and purchases option contracts. As at balance date unexpired trading option contracts have been revalued at market rates and the resulting profit or loss has been included in the Statement of Financial Performance.

Provision for Doubtful Debts   All receivables held by the Banking Group are regularly reviewed and a specific provision is raised for any amounts where recovery is considered doubtful.

Dividend Income   Dividends on investment shares are brought to account as income when declared except for dividends on investments in preference shares and unit trusts, which are recognised, on an accrual basis.

Swap Transactions   The Banking Group has exposures arising on swap transactions hedged by financial instruments. These transactions are traded by the Banking Group and are carried at their fair values as either trading assets or trading liabilities. Fair values are based on quoted market prices or pricing models, which take into account current market, and contractual prices of the underlying instruments, as well as time value and yield curve or volatility factors underlying the position. Profits and losses resulting from these positions are included in the Statement of Financial Performance.

Derivatives Valuation Adjustments Policy   Derivatives positions are valued using the derived mark to market method, whereby all future cash flows arising from the contracts are brought to a present value using appropriate discount rates derived from current mid-market data. Future cash flows are determined from the appropriate valuation model on which the specific contract details are booked. Models range from simple deterministic derivations of forward interest rates to vanilla and exotic option pricing models.

Principal Valuation Adjustments   In its 1993 report entitled "Derivatives: Practices and principles" the Global Derivatives Study Group of the so-called Group of Thirty (G-30) recommended that mid-market valuations were used together with adjustments for expected future costs such as unearned credit spread, close-out costs, excess investing and funding costs, and administrative costs. The bank's existing methodology follows the same categories of Market Risk, Credit Risk, Financing Risk, and Administrative costs.

Market Risk – Liquid   Two principle portfolio level adjustments are calculated to reflect the costs expected to be incurred in reducing the level of open market risk within the portfolio:
Delta Close Out

The cost of closing out interest rate delta exposure is quantified with reference to market bid/offer spreads and current risk positions, as measured by DV01's. The bid/offer spreads used are a best estimate of what the bank should easily be able to achieve on transacting the necessary hedging trades and may be within externally observable market spreads.

The assessment of portfolio risk is made separately by the main product types and the close out costs determined for each product class. The DV01 risk is by market point across the whole term structure, though this is bucketed within certain maturity bands to reflect the high level of correlation between neighbouring parts of the yield curve.

The adjustment is made at trading portfolio level but allowance for offsetting risks across portfolios is made at the business level.

Vega Close Out

In a similar fashion to delta risk, a bid/offer spread is applied to portfolio vega risk positions to determine the cost of eliminating first order vega risk within the vanilla option portfolios.

Market Risk – Less Liquid (Product/Trade Specific)   Within the OTC portfolios are some trades which may require adjustments for additional risks not captured by the above adjustments. Additional risks may arise for a variety of reasons, the majority arising from the inherent subjectivity and calibration compromises within the mathematical valuation models used for more Exotic structures.

Although such valuation models do provide a best estimate of the fair value of the contracts, in many cases it is sensible to make additional adjustments for possible future hedge re-balancing costs for example by a prudent marking of pricing parameters.

Further adjustments are considered necessary where positions are held in highly illiquid market areas such as long dated Swaptions where no suitable hedge exists and it is not feasible to observe current market pricing parameters for the positions.

Credit Risk   An adjustment is included for the expected credit loss arising from counterparty defaults. The adjustment is based on current credit exposures (PVs) by counterparty, utilizing the Standard & Poors credit default probabilities for the appropriate rating class applied to the current exposure, amortized over the remaining life of the trades. In addition, collateral, mutual termination clauses and potential recovery rates in the event of default are incorporated to arrive at the final adjustment.

Administrative Costs   The present value of the expected administration costs of all derivative transactions in a portfolio is accounted for through a valuation adjustment. The adjustment is currently determined on the basis of USD 500 for each new swap entered into, regardless of maturity. This figure is based on an ISDA estimate of an average administration cost.

Statement of Cash Flows
(a)   *Basis of preparation*   The statement of cash flows has been prepared using the direct approach modified by the netting of certain items as disclosed below.
(b)   *Cash and cash equivalents*   Cash and cash equivalents reflect the balance of cash and liquid assets used in the day-to-day cash management of the entity, which are unconditionally convertible at the investor's option within no more than two working days and include the interbank balances arising from the daily Reserve Bank settlements process.
(c)   *Netting of cash flows*   Certain cash flows have been netted in order to provide more meaningful disclosure as many of the cash flows are received and disbursed on

behalf of customers and reflect the activities of the customers rather than those of the entity. These include customer loans and advances, customer deposits, certificates of deposit, parent company funding and trading securities.

Repurchase and Reverse Repurchase Agreements   Repurchase agreements and reverse repurchase agreements are treated as collateralised financing transactions and are carried at the amounts at which the securities were initially acquired or sold. The difference between the sale and repurchase price represents interest expense and the difference between the purchase and sale price represents interest income. Both the interest expense and interest income is recognised in the Statement of Financial Performance over the term of the agreement.

Right of Set Off   The Banking Group reflects unrealised gains and losses on foreign exchange and interest rate contracts for counter-parties where a master netting arrangement has not been entered into as gross positions.

Trustee and Funds Management Activities   Certain entities within the Banking Group act as Trustee and/or Manager for a number of investments funds and trusts. These funds and trusts have not been included in the consolidated financial statements as the Banking Group does not have direct or indirect control of the funds of these trusts. The Trustees hold a right of indemnity against the assets of the applicable funds or trusts for liabilities incurred in the capacity as Trustees. As the assets are sufficient to cover liabilities, the liabilities are not included in the financial statements.

Note 22 – Related Party Transactions

During the period there have been dealings between DBAG NZ, Deutsche New Zealand Limited and subsidiaries, and other members of the Deutsche Bank AG Group. Dealings include on-balance sheet activities such as funding, accepting deposits and management fees and off-balance sheet activities such as foreign exchange and derivative transactions. These transactions are subject to normal commercial terms and conditions.

The financial statements of Deutsche Bank AG, New Zealand should be read in conjunction with the financial statements of Deutsche Bank AG, Frankfurt for the year ended 31 December 1998.

Dollars in millions	Note	Deutsche Bank NZ Group			Deutsche Bank NZ Branch		
		Unaudited 6 months 30/06/99	Unaudited 6 months 30/06/98	Audited 12 months 31/12/98	Unaudited 6 months 30/06/99	Unaudited 6 months 30/06/98	Audited 12 months 31/12/98
Due from related parties							
Call		948	11	55	–	116	93
Term		895	–	–	715	–	–
Commodity Swap		–	–	–	–	–	–
Unrealised gains on off-balance sheet financial instruments		109	–	–	87	–	–
Total due from related parties		1952	11	55	802	116	93
Due to related parties							
Call		953	237	383	–	117	372
Term		2526	–	–	2432	–	–
Unrealised losses on off-balance sheet financial instruments		144	–	–	82	–	–
Total due to related parties		3623	237	383	2514	117	372

Note 24 – Derivative Financial Instruments and Financial Instruments with Offbalance Sheet Risk (continued)

Credit Risk   The Banking Group manages the credit risk of its derivatives portfolio by limiting the total amount of arrangements outstanding with individual customers;

- by monitoring the size and maturity structure of the portfolios; by obtaining collateral based on management's credit assessment of the customer; and
- by applying a uniform credit process for all credit exposures.

In order to reduce derivatives-related credit risk, the Banking Group enters into master netting agreements which incorporate the right of set-off to provide for the net settlement of covered contracts with the same customer in the event of default or other cancellation of the agreement.

Derivative transactions create dynamic credit exposure, which changes as markets move. The credit risk of derivatives arises from the potential for a customer to default on its contractual obligations. Accordingly, credit risk related to derivatives depends on the following:

- the current fair value of the contracts with the customer; the potential credit exposure over time; the extent to which legally enforceable netting arrangements allow the fair value of offsetting contracts with that customer to be netted against each other;
- the extent to which collateral held against the contracts reduces credit risk exposure; and
- the likelihood of default by the customer.

The Banking Group monitors and manages the credit risk associated with derivatives by applying a uniform credit process for all credit exposures. The credit risk of derivatives is included in the Banking Group's centralised credit management system. In order to reduce derivatives-related credit risk, the Banking Group enters into master netting agreements that provide for offsetting of all contracts under each such agreement and obtains collateral where appropriate. The Banking Group monitors credit risk exposure on a gross and on a net basis and on a collateralised and an uncollateralised basis as appropriate.

The international bank regulatory standards for risk-based capital consider the credit risk arising from derivatives in the assessment of capital adequacy. These standards were issued under the Basle Capital Accord of July 1988. These standards use a formula-based assessment of customer credit risk and do not reflect the credit risk-reducing impact of legally enforceable master netting agreements. However, these standards reflect the credit risk of derivatives on a conservative basis, as the calculation of the "add-on" component for potential future credit risk exposure caused by price volatility does not reflect the benefit for the reduction of future credit risk obtained from master netting agreements.

Market Risk   The market risk of derivatives arises principally from the potential for changes in interest rates, foreign exchange rates, and equity prices and is generally similar to the market risk of the cash instruments underlying the contracts. The market risk to the Banking Group is not measured by the price sensitivity of the individual contracts, but by the net price sensitivity of the relevant portfolio, including cash instruments. The Banking Group generally manages its exposures by taking riskoffsetting positions. Therefore, Deutsche Bank NZ Branch believes it is not meaningful to view the market risk of derivatives in isolation.

Liquidity Risk   In times of stress, sharp price movements or volatility shocks may reduce liquidity in certain derivatives positions, as well as in cash instruments. The liquidity risk of derivatives is substantially based on the liquidity of the underlying cash instrument, which affects the ability of the Banking Group to alter the risk profile of its positions rapidly and at a reasonable cost. The Banking Group mark to market practices for derivatives include adjustments in consideration of liquidity risks, where appropriate. These practices are consistent with those applied to the Banking Group's trading positions in cash instruments.

Note 24:   *Derivative Financial Instruments and Financial Instruments with Off-balance Sheet Risk (continued)*

	Deutsche Bank NZ Group Fair value			
	Notional amount unaudited 6 months 30/06/99	Assets unaudited 6 months 30/06/99	Liabilities unaudited 6 months 30/06/99	Credit equivalent unaudited 6 months 30/06/99
Derivatives				
OTC **Financial Instruments**				
Foreign exchange contracts				
Forward foreign exchange contracts	6962	112	192	107
Currency swaps	111	–	21	–
Cross currency and interest rates swaps	37	–	22	5
Currency options purchased	2215	113	–	152
Currency options written	2215	–	113	n/a
Interest rate contracts				
Forward interest rate agreements	780	–	–	–
Interest rates swaps	7722	642	631	510
Interest rate options purchased	238	1		2
Interest rate options written	45	–	1	n/a
Swaptions	–		–	
ETO **Financial Instruments**				
Interest rate contracts				
interest rate futures	3817	n/a	n/a	n/a
Interest rate options purchased	78	n/a		n/a
Equity contracts				
Equity futures written	–	n/a	n/a	n/a
Commodity Swaps	80	6	6	6
Total gross fair values		874	986	782
Impact of netting agreements		698	698	
		196	288	

Note 25 – Fair Value of Financial Instruments

Financial Reporting Standard 31, Fair Value of Financial Instruments, requires the disclosure of fair value information about financial instruments, whether or not recognised in the balance sheet, for which it is a practicality to estimate that value. Quoted market prices, when available, are used as the measure of fair value. In the cases where quoted market prices are not available, fair values are based on present value estimates or other valuation techniques. These derived fair values are significantly effected by assumptions used, principally the timing of future cashflows and the discount rate. Because assumptions are inherently subjective in nature, the estimated fair values cannot be substantiated by comparison to independent market quotes and, in many cases, the estimated fair values would not necessarily be realised in an immediate sale or settlement of the instrument. The disclosure requirements of Financial Reporting Standard 31 exclude certain financial instruments and all non-financial instruments, e.g., franchise value of businesses. Accordingly, the aggregate fair value amounts presented do not represent management's estimation of the underlying value of the Banking Group.

Methods and Assumptions   For short-term financial instruments, defined as those with remaining maturities of 90 days or less, the carrying amount was considered to be a reasonable estimate of fair value. The following instruments were predominantly short-term:

Assets	*Liabilities*
Cash and call balances with central banks	Due to other banks
Due from other banks	Deposits
Due from corporates	Repurchase agreements
Trading Securities	Available for purchase securities
Reverse repurchase agreements	Amounts due to related parties
Available for sale securities	
Amounts due from related parties	

For those components of the above listed financial instruments with remaining maturities greater than 90 days, fair value was determined by discounting contractual cash flows using rates which could be earned for assets with similar remaining maturities and, in the case of liabilities, rates at which the liabilities with similar remaining maturities could be issued as of the balance date.

As indicated in Note 1, trading assets and trading liabilities (including derivatives) are carried at their fair values.

Other assets consisted primarily of cash and cash margins with brokers and accruals on trading assets. Other liabilities consisted primarily of accounts payable and accrued expenses. Carrying value is considered to be fair value.

The fair value of investment securities (if any) is determined by discounting contractual cash flows using rates, which could be earned for assets with similar remaining maturities.

Loans, which are secured by real estate, appraisal values for the collateral were considered in the fair value determination.

Standby Letter of Credit   BT Futures New Zealand Limited is a member of the Sydney Futures Exchange Clearing House. A requirement of this membership is to provide a financial commitment to support the obligations of the Clearing house. This is currently $1.3 million (31/12/98: $1.3 million).

Notice has been given to the Sydney Futures Exchange Clearing House of relinquishment of membership effective December 2000.

Concentrations of Credit Risk   The Banking Group, as required by Financial Reporting Standard 31 has identified two significant concentrations of credit risk: OECD country banks and OECD country central governments, their agencies and central banks. The Organisation for Economic Co-operation and Development (OECD) is an international organisation of countries which are committed to market-orientated economic policies, including the promotion of private enterprise and free market prices, liberal trade policies, and the absence of exchange controls. The OECD consists of 26 individual nations, primarily the countries of Western Europe, North America, Japan, Australia and New Zealand. For risk-based capital purposes, domestic and foreign bank regulators generally assign OECD country central governments, their agencies and their central banks, a credit risk weighting of zero or ten percent. OECD country banks are generally assigned 20 percent by these regulators. The following table (p. 194) reflects the aggregate credit risk by groups of counter-parties, relating to on and off-balance sheet financial instruments, including derivatives.

Note 33 – Risk Management

Risk Management Policies   The Deutsche Bank/Deutsche Australasia group applies an integrated risk management strategy to all market risk exposures across all divisions including the Deutsche Bank NZ Group. Market risk resides within the Global Markets Division and the Equities Division and is a result of taking positions in traded financial instruments, securities and their derivatives.

The risk management function works hand-in-hand with a risk control function to ensure that appropriate risk management practices tie in with suitable risk limit structures and with an independent market risk reporting process. These functions ensure that dealer, trading heads and executive management are well informed on all aspects of transactions that incur market risk.

An extensive risk limit structure has been developed to provide suitable constraints for trading activities to allow revenue budgets to be met along with a prudent approach to risk taking. The market risk limit structure addresses Value-at-Risk exposures (i.e. Expected capital risk due to trading activities), operational risks as used by front office risk management staff and possible liquidity risks. These limits cover four asset classes: foreign exchange, interest rates, commodities and equities along with their related derivative products and are determined by global business heads in conjunction with local trading heads and the local risk management group.

Risk management practices ensure that all market risks are managed against limits on the following exposures:

Value-at-Risk: the expected gain or loss in risk capital based on statistical assumptions of market rates and prices.

Yield curve risks: the gain or loss resulting from movements in the entire interest rate curve, portions thereof or related hedge positions.

Nominal/Position risk: the gain or loss resulting from the change in price of equities, foreign exchange positions or commodity contracts.

Dollars in millions

Deutsche Bank NZ Group

	On Balance Sheet Unaudited 6 months 30/06/99	Off Balance Sheet Unaudited 6 months 30/06/99	Total Unaudited 6 months 30/06/99	On Balance Sheet Unaudited 6 months 30/06/98	Off Balance Sheet Unaudited 6 months 30/06/98	Total Unaudited 6 months 30/06/98	On Balance Sheet Audited 6 months 31/12/98	Off Balance Sheet Audited 6 months 31/12/98	Total Audited 6 months 31/12/98
Credit Risk by type of borrower									
Banking and Finance	4088	670	4758	198	6	204	296	7	303
Electricity, Gas & Water	264	9	273	–	–	–	140	–	140
Government & Local Authority	304	1	305	1022	–	1022	41	–	41
Total significant concentrations	4656	680	5336	1220	6	1226	477	7	484
All other	654	254	908	183	–	183	28	–	28
Total	5310	934	6244	1403	6	1409	505	7	512
Credit Risk by geographical area									
Within New Zealand	3465	379	3844	1141	2	1143	384	2	386
Overseas	1845	555	2400	262	4	266	121	5	126
Total	5310	934	6244	1403	6	1409	505	7	512

Liquidity risk: the risk of failure to meet commitments of on-balance sheet assets and liabilities and off-balance sheet settlements.

Independent reviews of these types of risks are undertaken by Internal Audit on a regular basis. No reviews of the Deutsche Bank NZ Group's risk management systems have been conducted by parties external to the Deutsche Bank Group.

Credit Risk   Risk Management function within the Deutsche Bank Australasia Group is located in Sydney and Auckland and is responsible for all credit risk in both the Australian and New Zealand operations. Credit Risk Management operates as an independent unit as part of Global Corporates & Institutions Division and reports directly to London. Credit risk includes both on and off balance sheet credit exposures to individual borrowers or agreeable groups of borrowers. Credit risk is controlled through a disciplined approval process which includes delegated authorities being exercised by authorised officers up to predetermined levels based on risk factors and in some cases tenor in accordance with established credit policies. Where these levels are exceeded credit exposures are referred to other Credit Risk Management offices or the Group Credit Committee in Frankfurt and beyond its authority to the Board of Deutsche Bank AG.

Credit exposures are the subject of active and ongoing review. Where deemed necessary adequate and appropriate security is obtained for credit exposures. Overall credit quality and the establishment of credit policies are the responsibility of the Credit Risk Management functions in London and Frankfurt.

Audit   Regional Head Office Audit for Australia and New Zealand is located in Sydney and is responsible for the audit of the organisation's activities in Australia and New Zealand. The audit group has a direct reporting line to the General Auditor, Asia Pacific and United Kingdom, based in London. The General Auditor reports to the Global Head of Audit who reports to the Deutsche Bank Board in Frankfurt. This offshore reporting line ensures the independence of the local audit function. The Regional Head of Audit also presents quarterly reports and updates to the Deutsche Bank Australasian Group Board.

The Audit process includes a complete review of all key business processes and systems for each audit area. Audit steps are continuously updated to reflect changes in the business and internal external regulations.

The scope and frequency of audits depends on the assessed level of risk associated with each business area. Higher risk areas are audited more frequently (generally annually) and low risk areas are audited on a rotational basis (minimum three years). To the extent possible, regional audits are performed that cover the relevant operations in Australia and New Zealand. Otherwise, stand alone audits are conducted at each location.

Note 35 – Exposures to Market Risk

Aggregate interest rates, foreign currency and equity exposure have been derived in accordance with Schedule 8 (1)a (8)a and (11)a of the Registered Bank Disclosure Statement (Full and Half-Year Overseas Incorporated Registered Banks) Order 1998.

Dollars in millions	Deutsche Bank NZ Group					
	Unaudited		Audited		Unaudited	
	As at 30/06/99	Quarterly Peak	As at 30/06/98	YTD Peak	As at 31/12/98	YTD Peak
Exposures to Market Risk						
Aggregate interest rate exposures ($millions)	6.9	9.7	1.7	–	0.5	2.6
Aggregate interest rate exposures as a percentage of the equity of Deutsche Bank Group	0.011%	0.016%	0.002%	–	0.001%	0.007%
Aggregate foreign currency exposures $millions	0.1	16.7	3.9	–	0.4	0.4
Aggregate foreign currency exposures as a percentage of the equity of Deutsche Bank Group	0.0002%	0.027%	0.006%	–	0.001%	0.001%
Aggregate equity exposures ($millions)	0.3	0.5	0.8	–	–	–
Aggregate equity exposures as a percentage of the equity of Deutsche Bank Group	0.001%	0.001%	0.001%	–		

Peak exposure not available for quarter ended 30 June 1998.

The calculation of exposures as a percentage of the equity of Deutsche Bank Group are based on the equity of Deutsche Bank Group as at 30 June 1999.

9   STATEMENT BY THE DIRECTORS ON BANK REGISTRATION

Each director of Deutsche Bank AG, being the members of the Board of Managing Directors, after due inquiry by them, believe that:

• The General Disclosure Statement contains all the information that is required by the Registered Bank Disclosure Statement (Full and Half-Year – Overseas Incorporated Registered Banks) Order 1998 as at the date on which the General Disclosure Statement is signed.

- Deutsche Bank AG, New Zealand Branch has complied with the conditions of registration over the interim accounting period.
- Deutsche Bank AG, New Zealand Branch had systems in place to monitor and control adequately the Banking Group's material risks, including credit risk, concentration of credit risk, interest rate risk, currency risk, equity risk, liquidity risk and other business risks, and that those systems were being properly applied over the interim accounting period
- This General Disclosure Statement is not false or misleading as at the date on which the General Disclosure Statement is signed.

Signed under Authority on behalf of the Directors at Sydney, the 24th September 1999.

8 Robust Exit Policies to Underpin Market Discipline

Two main issues relate to the appropriate handling of problems and crises. The first concerns the incentives suggested for banks to avoid getting into difficulties in the first place. The second relates to the issues addressed by the authorities in running a system where such difficulties can be handled swiftly and smoothly without damaging the credibility of the financial system as a whole. However well run the banks and however vigilant the authorities, problems will still occur, because banking involves taking risks. Even with well-managed risks and good information about borrowers one can be unlucky. Financial accidents will occur, but their size and incidence can be reduced by robust exit policies. There is, a distinction between those general measures aimed at preventing bank failure in the first place, and the exit policies that address the problem of preventing further losses, in the event of default or failure on the part of a bank. A role for government is warranted in minimising the costs to society and organising the means for a fair distribution of the loss.

The key incentive in setting out an exit policy in advance is that banks will run themselves in the knowledge of what will happen when they get into diffculty. The authorities face a classic time-consistency problem. To have a system that provides credible incentives for banks to avoid getting into difficulty, the authorities need to precommit themselves to be very tough with any bank that ecounters problems. However, should a bank get into difficulty, despite these threats, then there may very well be a smaller immediate cost to society from leniency in that specific case. A workout or bailout may be less costly than closure, taking that case on its own. In these circumstances the authorities feel they gain by reneging on their commitment. However, everybody knows that this temptation will exist, with the authorities ignoring the additional cost of encouraging other banks to run greater risks. Hence if the rules set in advance do not prevent the authorities from exercising leniency in the interest of systemic costs, the banks will be inclined to take more risks and hence generate potentially much bigger costs for society. The net benefit then disappears and society is not getting the more prudent behaviour it is seeking.

The system can never be completely credible because the government has the power to change the rules in the future. Nevertheless, making action mandatory and not discretionary for the banking supervisors, and giving them the independence from political concerns to exercise it, will increase believability. In the next three chapters, we explore the problem and set out a possible way to improve the chances of prudence.

8.1 THE NEED FOR EFFICIENT BANK EXIT

In the current chapter we begin by exploring the need for exit policies to underpin market discipline. Removing unsuccessful banks from national banking systems requires treating banks differently from nonbank firms. Indeed, modern banking is not a free profession, but a highly regulated industry, which shares a range of public benefits and burdens.[1] There are many characteristics that make banks 'unique' but the key facets that underlie the changes in exit policies to complement market discipline, we recommend are:

- Any individual bank's financial condition is difficult to monitor.
- Though markets drive nonprofitable firms out, markets do not, for various institutional reasons, drive out weak banks in the same manner.
- Without adequate information, the failure of one bank can lead depositors to withdraw their funds from other banks as well (contagion), and may cause a run on a country similar to a bank run as investors, expecting other investors to sell off, cause a rapid and large scale sell off of assets (currency).
- Bank regulators supervise banks solely in the public interest, and, therefore, are called upon to withdraw authorisations to protect public confidence in the banking system as a whole, on occasion subordinating the rights of individual depositors and creditors of individual institutions to considerations of public policy.
- Historically, preventing a bank's failure and depositor losses by allowing it to continue operating when insolvent, encouraged excessive risk taking by that bank and other banks resulting in still larger losses down the line, which were ultimately paid for by the public treasury (taxpayers).
- Discouraging bank runs by guaranteeing all creditors of deposit-taking institutions has eliminated important market incentives for owners and uninsured creditors to monitor bank soundness, thus placing an unrealistic responsibility on regulators and supervisors, and, ultimately, on the taxpayer.
- The best way to preserve and enhance market discipline, while protecting the confidence of depositors on the soundness of banks, is for the regulators and supervisors to intervene early, while the problem bank still has sufficient assets to cover deposits, and to do so with such speed that depositors' access to funds is not seriously interrupted.

The characteristic strength of a bank should be an ability to manage risk. However, instead of reducing adverse selection and moral hazard in financial markets, a bank may easily become the problem itself. Usually, those firms that systematically act impulsively or underestimate the risks of investment are quickly replaced by those that calculate risks better. This kind of exit is less likely to occur with banks.

The owners and managers of low net worth and insolvent banks have a financial incentive to take excessive risks in the hope of restoring solvency (if they lose, their depositors, deposit insurance and/or the taxpayer bears the cost) (Kupiec and O'Brien, 1995). Typically, the outcome of excessively risky schemes is a growing net cumulative loss. This diverts deposits from other banks, which distorts the allocation of financial resources. Loss of confidence means shrinking the size and contribution of the banking sector in the overall economy.

If insolvent banks do not leave the industry there is a danger that other banks will take greater risks too, in order to be able to offer competitive rates to high-quality customers. Spreads between deposit and lending rates will be greater than necessary and inefficient intermediation may slow the pace of economic growth. Ultimately bank insolvencies can create large fiscal costs in rescuing a range of institutions and may trigger capital flight. Furthermore, as national financial markets integrate, financial weaknesses in one country can more readily spill over to another.

8.2   CAPITAL ADEQUACY AND MARKET DISCIPLINE

It is the vast mass of private decisions that is banking, and not the workings of the official apparatus that is engaged in a continuous review of private decisions under administrative and judicial systems of remedies and sanctions, and in continuous revision of the terms and conditions under which similar decisions will be made in the future. Generally, therefore, operating in the shadow of law and policy, it is for banks alone to work out their problems of capitalisation with other members of the public comprising their shareholders, borrowers and lenders, as well as any other third parties.

The maintenance of adequate bank capitalisation to meet the needs of business, market confidence and regulators is a continuous process of market-based allocation of resources. It is thus a form of 'endogenous governance'. Market-based allocation of resources presupposes competitive pricing by the market of the availability of legal capital (common or preferred stock), and of capital to meet regulatory requirements.[2] A bank's franchise is a tradable (and perishable) good. A bank's position, business policies, and prospects affect its value as a target for possible merger and acquisition by other banks.

In the event of a shortfall, regulatory capital requirements work like minimum (legal) capital requirements in that they require increased contributions from equity holders. However, regulatory capital requirements may also shift risks and costs to the holders of subordinated debt.[3] Subordination occurs where creditors otherwise would rank equally. The depositor preference of the kind prevailing in the United States would be another way to reduce risks and costs of insolvency for depositors. This axiomatically increases risks and costs of insolvency to those ranking lower. Subordination, therefore, sharpens the incentives in the capital market compared to those for depositors.

Where banks capitalise themselves through the market, the market can drive a bank into inadequate capitalisation or distress, providing a clear signal to the authorities of market perceptions regarding the condition of that bank. Where the market fails to provide a solution to the bank's problem, it becomes an official concern because the impending outcome may have significant social and systemic risks and costs.

This raises the issue of the appropriate role for intervention by government, or by the administrative and judicial authorities (an exogenous process of governance), and of the form such intervention should take. Here we challenge the doctrine of constructive ambiguity. These issues cannot be resolved during a crisis but must be settled well beforehand.

8.2.1 Pricing of Capital

In the foregoing discussion we have emphasised that for market discipline to be fully credible banks must expect that if they get into difficulties and need recapitalising, they will not be bailed out. The penalties will be progressive depending upon the scale of the problem. Under such circumstances, if the problem is limited, the banks in difficulty will either have to try to raise capital on the market, presumably at higher cost, as the problems will harm their credit rating, or through an injection of equity. Again the equity injection is likely to entail some costs, not just because it may dilute the position of the existing shareholders if they do not provide it but because the new shareholders may very well insist on management changes as a condition for providing the funds. In the case of a resort to capital markets, existing shareholders are also likely to insist on management changes. If the problem is more severe then so will be the resulting ownership change, leading to merger or takeover. Ultimately, the problem may be so bad that there are no willing providers of the necessary capital and the bank has to be liquidated.

If the market system works well then the role of the authorities will be limited. They will need to ensure that the process is conducted under a set of rules that appear fair and they will need to be satisfied that the new capital and ownership structure complies with the rules for the registration of banks. The key issue here is likely to be speed. Banks in difficulty cannot continue trading long, as they will be faced with a run. Any protracted decision-making by the authorities will risk turning a resolvable difficulty into a crisis. The rules to be applied in these circumstances therefore need to be simple, clear and well known in advance by the market participants. In practice, this reduces the list of options quite sharply. New owners and managers need to be already acceptable to the authorities. New ownership structures need to be very transparent and the new capital needs to be clearly of adequate quality so there is no question about the viability of the new arrangements.

However, in a properly functioning market system, many banking problems are resolved well before a bank gets into real danger of failing to comply with regulatory capital requirements or exposure limits. If profitability and returns to shareholders begin to lag behind the banking sector as a whole then this will start to be reflected in the share price and the bank will become of increasing interest as a takeover candidate. At the same time, the bank itself will be looking for ways of restructuring in a manner that will be more attractive to the existing management. Action is therefore likely well before there is any need to involve the authorities. It is (almost by definition) only large shocks that are likely to cause unexpected problems for what appear to be sound banks. The exception will be problems that the management has succeeded in shielding from the information disclosed, particularly in the case of fraud.

If the market is not transparent, say, because the bank is privately owned, or state-owned or the market thin, then both the signals and the incentives may be weaker and difficulties may well become larger before the bank or its owners may feel obliged to act on them. As we have argued earlier, the authorities will wish to try to ensure that the opportunity for these incentives to be muted is as limited as possible. One such possibility was the requirement, suggested by Calomiris (1999), that all banks should have to have a substantial amount of marketed subordinated debt so that the chance of signals coming through was greater and that there should be more real penalties for poor performance. Even so, private, savings, co-operative, government and 'post-office' banks are likely to face rather weaker pressures than traditional joint stock banks.

However effective the functioning of the market and however assiduous the authorities have been in trying to ensure efficiency by demanding substantial disclosure of information, deep markets and good assessments of both idiosyncratic and systemic risks, ultimately the authorities will face problems where they could or should act. Where that dividing line falls is open to debate. Some authorities fear that the market system may not operate well when a financial market participant is in difficulty and that they should at least act as a marriage broker, helping the parties get together and work out a quick solution involving only private funds. This was certainly the case with the intervention of the Federal Reserve in the case of Long Term Capital Management (LTCM) in the

United States in 1999. It is more difficult to justify intervention if the 'market failure' would not result in any systemic problems. In the case of LTCM there were two main issues. On the one hand, a failure that perhaps could have led to LTCM filing for protection under chapter 11 of the US Bankruptcy Code, would have had serious consequences because of the extent of the exposures. On the other the parties involved had both the resources and the self-interest to resolve the problem out of court provided that each of them could be sure that the others would provide their fair share of the total cost.

This latter is a classic prisoners' dilemma. If some partners can achieve lower costs by early exit (at the expense of the others), then all of them will opt for that outcome and incur higher costs than if the problem were resolved with all taking shares in the cost. Here the regulators and supervisors can play a role in ensuring both lower social costs and convincing the partners that all will participate. Unfortunately it is likely to be a judgement call for the authorities whether the market will 'work' well in any particular instance. They do not have the option of waiting to see whether the specific case works out, because, if it does not then it will be too late and distress will be turned into failure. Some authorities will be more predisposed to act than others, often depending upon how well the 'club' of bankers (if any) works. Of course, the more that market participants expect the authorities to take the lead then the less likely it is that the market will 'work' or a completely private sector solution emerge unaided.

We are predisposed towards the less interventionist end of the spectrum, primarily for a second reason, which is that the greater the active role of the public sector the greater is the chance that public funds may be called upon. However, the appropriate structure does depend upon the nature of the explicit obligations that exist. For example, if some deposits are insured the insurer becomes an interested party on behalf of the insured should there be a risk of bank failure and its having to pay out insured depositors. A capital injection to keep a bank trading might be a lower immediate cost than meeting the requirements to pay out to the depositors but the implications for greater risk-taking by banks in the *expectation* of this bailout still have to be taken into account.

We have not discussed in any detail who among the authorities should be involved in decisions over how to treat distress. Clearly, the central bank will have an initial role to play as the ultimate provider of liquidity. It will have a further role if it is the guardian of systemic stability. Secondly, the supervisory authority will have a role in validating whether any new proposed arrangements comply with the regulatory framework for operation as a bank – corporate structure, capitalisation, fit and proper persons, etc. However, if at any stage public money could be called upon, say, in case of an assisted merger, then it needs to be the government that can authorise the use of such money that needs to be involved. This could be the insurer, if like the FDIC it is an independent administrative agency with financial autonomy and not a bank consortium. It could be the Ministry of Finance if the use of public funds is to be more direct.

The traditional argument (Goodhart *et al.*, 1998) is that there should be a clear distinction between supervisors and access to public funds. It is much more difficult when it comes to the judgement about systemic stability. It depends upon the regulations as to whether the central bank can use its own funds, even though it may judge that the appropriate response to ensure systemic stability is a capital injection. There is something to be said for a German style arrangement, where the use of such funds is at arm's length and is much more like a form of insurance where a separate decision by an independent body is required before action can take place. The more arm's length the arrangement then the less that prospective beneficiaries may believe it will be used and hence the greater the incentive to come to other arrangements.

The key step in the process is to try to encourage banks to act early and for difficulties to be resolved before they become serious, particularly before they threaten the system. On the whole, market penalties encourage this because the penalty increases with the seriousness of the offence. A fixed penalty, such as loss of job, can encourage a 'go for broke' strategy. If there is a small chance of avoiding the crisis by taking further risks but no greater cost to the risk taker from doing so then the chance of small problems being enlarged is much greater. In the same way, if there is a floor to the system because ultimately it is expected that the public sector will intervene financially then this may encourage an expansion of risks once difficulties set in. This is somewhat different from the standard moral hazard argument, that having any procedures that might imply a bail out, even if it is 'too big to fail', will tend to lead people to take higher risks more generally. The discipline of the market, in ensuring that people first of all start to lose remuneration if the bank under performs and ultimately their jobs, will argue against this even if the organisation can survive in some form. However, once job loss seems likely this progressive threat is largely removed, although re-employment prospects will be affected by the depth of the disaster that the manager has presided over, perhaps continuing the progressivity a little further.

The greater the lack of access to public funds then the more credible the authorities will be in the role of brokering purely private sector deals. If the private sector thinks that public money may be available then there may be a reluctance to incur costs. True, it makes sense for the private sector to ask the public sector to make the initial capital injection and organise the restructuring of the bank with taxpayers' money and then only step in when the public sector eventually attempts to dispose of the investment. In this way the risks and costs of the transaction are minimised for the private sector and conversely for the public sector. However, if public money is to be used it should fill residual financing gaps only on a last-in-first-out basis.

8.2.2 Forced Exit Policy

However, the theme of this chapter is not so much whether the public sector should intervene and how but rather, given it does wish to act, does it have the necessary instruments or tools to do a good job? More importantly, for market incentives to work well these processes must be believable to those who will be affected and must include a very real possibility that the effects may be adverse. We argue in following chapters that in the European context, in particular, the national authorities may lack the necessary tools in three respects. There is a danger of them being insufficiently informed to be able to act early, let alone pre-empt some crises. Secondly, also because of the problem of home country control they may be unable to act to resolve crises in banks that are primarily outside their jurisdiction, despite their systemic consequences. Lastly, even if the bank is totally within their jurisdiction, we argue that governments and administrative authorities may well lack the necessary powers to be able to resolve difficulties before they reach crisis proportions. The last point will be discussed in this chapter.

Bank regulators and supervisors can reduce moral hazard and adverse selection problems only if legislation lays down a legal basis for a robust exit policy for removing unprofitable banks from the industry, and, even more important, that government proceeds on that authority to take over and restructure institutions that are critically undercapitalised and do not have positive net worth. To be effective, this approach requires not only clear and efficient procedures for removing economically insolvent institutions from the industry, but also powers to take over and restructure them. Subject to notable exceptions, the latter powers have been missing in EEA countries.

In particular, governments (and even less regulators and supervisors) have no effective legal power to intervene if a bank becomes critically undercapitalised or its net worth turns negative. What is missing is a delegation of legislative authority to government or its designated agents to take over and restructure undercapitalised or insolvent banks. Findings by regulators and supervisors of a bank's failure to observe a prescribed financial benchmark should trigger the consideration of structural actions, remedies or sanctions. The triggering of such responses should not be dependent on conduct by the bank, which presupposes findings of fault. If another solution cannot be found the administrative authorities can only force it into judicial reorganisation or liquidation by withdrawing its banking licence, resulting in a lengthy administrative or judicial process. Ideally, administrative authorities would like to intervene early before all shareholder value had disappeared and while routes to exit could be found that do not result in depositors having to take losses – except in the sense of delays in payment due to temporary stays on individual legal actions that would force the insolvent bank to perform financial obligations on a, 'first-come-first-served' basis.

8.2.3 Qualified Applicability to Banks of Bankruptcy Law Qualifies Market Discipline

Experience in EEA countries shows that bankruptcy and other general insolvency proceedings are inadequate for the task of an expeditious, effective, and economic reorganisation or liquidation of insolvent banks (or of other deployment of their assets) in cases where the authorities are concerned about the wider costs to society or about unwelcome systemic consequences. Even where the authorities have no such concerns about an individual bank, there is the worry that procedures that are costly for those exposed, such as prolonged inability to access funds, may result in a lack of confidence in banking as a form of financial intermediation. Thus the rules themselves can be a systemic cost.

Where taxpayers have bailed out banks, the laws have failed the tests of expedition, efficiency and economy. It would appear that current laws do not wipe out the shareholders of an insolvent bank as a prerequisite of a bailout by the taxpayer, as would happen if the bank had been liquidated as of the date of intervention. Indeed, the liquidation of an insolvent bank is unlikely in systemic cases. The authorities are likely to continue insolvent banks in legal personality and entity, at the expense of the taxpayer. With a bailout being a probability, there is little prospect of voluntary contributions from an insolvent bank's directors, managers and employees, or shareholders or other owners, or indeed from its uninsured creditors, holders of its contingent liabilities, its landlords and so on. The chances that the government will rescue the bank are augmented for four intertwined reasons in EEA countries:

- The inability of government to proceed, without delegation of legislative authority, to seize the insolvent bank (that is, by 'taking' its worthless outstanding shares), in order to keep it open and operating for the time being (irrespective of whether it would be liquidated or reorganised later);
- The inability of the authorities to recapitalise an insolvent bank compulsorily without approval by a general meeting of shareholders;
- In many EEA countries, banking laws place restrictions on the filing by the bank itself of voluntary petitions for reorganisation or liquidation, as well as on the filing by their depositors and other creditors of involuntary petitions for the opening of judicial insolvency proceedings precluding access to judicial process to vindicate private rights and interests; and
- The availability of state aid for a bank's recapitalisation (at least) in the case of a bank of some size or in systemic cases, both to re-establish the solvency of the beneficiary of taxpayers' money, and even to recapitalise it to the point at which it would meet applicable legal and regulatory capital requirements.

Of course, the exposure of the taxpayer could be reduced, were the applicable law to reduce the insolvent bank's indebtedness to the point at which its assets would meet its liabilities, and to wipe out pre-existing shareholders' (worthless) interests to enable the private acquirers of the newly solvent bank to recapitalise according to applicable capital and solvency benchmarks. As a corollary, based on a hypothetical liquidation valuation of an insolvent bank's assets and liabilities, the law would preserve any liquidation rights and interests that existed as of the day of intervention by the authorities.[4] Ideally, a compulsory asset, debt and equity restructuring serves as a structural condition concurrent with any seizure, bailout or compulsory replenishment of capital the authorities may carry out.

There are powerful reasons for believing that there is a superior way to deploy bank assets than to rely on the opening of judicial insolvency proceedings as the only course of action. Generally, government intervention is necessary because courts are likely to fail to obtain individual assent by subject banks themselves, and their owners and creditors, to perform discretionary administrative functions. In law and reality, the court cannot take over and restructure an insolvent bank acting on the account of government, including the sale of equity or assets to new owners (e.g., through an 'assisted' merger). Discretionary powers, including the government's own financial powers to offer compensation to pre-existing owners, cannot be vested in judicial authorities, and, ultimately, in the hands of court-appointed individual accountants or lawyers acting under their supervision. Ideally, courts should be removed from the supervision of insolvent banks that are kept open and operating, and of the supervision of the liquidation of assets and liabilities of closed banks. Courts would be restricted to the performance of essentially judicial functions such as those pertaining to the resolution of disputes or issues involving adversary parties and matters appropriate for judicial determination, including (where required) review of any administrative decisions that affect, modify or annul private rights and obligations in restructuring.

8.3 OPERATION OF CAPITAL AND SOLVENCY REQUIREMENTS

Regulatory capital requirements may impose a higher level of capital adequacy on banks than they would have adopted in the absence of regulation. However, the Basel Committee has been wary of advocating any extreme form of rule-based regulation and supervision of capital requirements, such as the US approach. There, regulators and supervisors are mandated to take prompt corrective action as the level of a bank's regulatory capital falls below the prescribed benchmark (2 per cent of risk-weighted assets). However, the second pillar of the Basel Committee's new policy outlined in the 1999 Consultative Document, relating to 'supervisory review', is explicit in encouraging early action. Principle

4 reads '*Supervisors should seek to intervene at an early stage to prevent capital falling below prudent levels.*' Thus the Basel Committee recommends action *before* capital adequacy standards are breached.

It is a bit difficult to envisage quite how this might be done beyond exhortation and advice without effectively raising the limits themselves. It would not be easy to introduce a banking equivalent of prosecution for dangerous driving that did not involve substantial discretion for supervisors and rather soft ground for imposing any harsh remedies. Nevertheless it emphasises the point that the particular levels chosen by the Committee do not have any exact intrinsic merit but that lines have to be drawn somewhere. As capital gets lower so the remedies have to be increasingly drastic and the penalties for inadequate response increasingly severe.

In its Consultation Document 'Regulatory Capital Requirements for EU Credit Institutions and Investment Firms' (18 November 1999), the European Commission takes this even further and argues that supervisors should set capital ratios above the minimum for each individual bank based on a set of indicators, as a 'prudent level'. Pre-emptive action could thus be required above 8 per cent. However, because banks cannot readily improve their capital position 'overnight', a degree of discretion is inevitable. After all the existence of the capital is to act as a buffer in the event of a shock, so that the shock only results in a problem not failure. It is therefore to be expected that banks will have to be given a reasonable opportunity to recapitalise after a shock but under a tight timetable. In the case of a generalised shock to the system too drastic a reaction would generate a credit crunch.

In the US case there is no authority for temporary deferment of the action in case of a bank that passes the intervention point, particularly if it is insolvent. At that point, a mandatory exit policy triggers the takeover by the authorities, placing the bank in conservatorship or receivership.[5]

A survey of existing law in EEA countries suggests a rather different position exists from that under Federal banking and bankruptcy laws in the United States. An insolvent bank that continues payments can remain – practically or legally – immune both from administrative (forced) liquidation proceedings, as from the opening of judicial reorganisation and liquidation proceedings, for at least two institutional reasons. First, banking laws do not mandate regulators or supervisors to suspend or revoke authorisations of inadequately capitalised or even bankrupt banks forthwith. To protect the rights of individual depositors or other creditors they have discretion to defer making (or supporting) petitions for the opening of judicial proceedings by reason of their discretionary powers to pursue public interest particularly where there are systemic concerns. Insolvent banks may therefore remain open and operating. However, regulators have drawn up rules to compel action by banks in these circumstances. (As we argue in Chapter 5, the more transparent the regulator has to be the more difficult it is to do anything other than apply the rules diligently.)

The EEA approach is consistent with the objective of bank deregulation, which suggests the existence of a legislative preference for an enlarged freedom of action for banks to operate subject only to prescribed rules of conduct. As legal rules do not incorporate financial benchmarks directly (other than bankruptcy rules), the observance by banks of regulatory capital requirements is only a condition of continuing authorisation and hence normally a discretionary function performed by regulators and supervisors. By using a case-by-case approach, employing threats of withdrawal of authorisations, supervisors run the risk of micro management of the affairs of individual banks and their customers. In reality, where withdrawal of authorisation is the only remedy, the sanction may be but an empty threat, however intrusive the supervision may be.

In EEA countries, the idea of deregulation was to authorise the banks to carry out their business as financial market participants subject to general banking laws which in themselves are an expression of the stipulated purposes that fall within the public interest, without the banks having to run the risk that the laws themselves would be circumvented for other than prescribed purposes. Since 'deregulated' general banking laws now determine both the permissible range of private decision and the conditions under which the decisions are made (that is, the sphere of private autonomy of each individual bank), regulation and supervision is significant in shaping the general character and direction of banking industry, as well as the characteristics of individual firms operating as banks within that industry. Legislatures have put strong emphasis on endogenous governance in the EEA.

Under the regulatory theory, banks are deemed to be private firms first and foremost, like other such firms that are subject to general law, and to the jurisdiction of general courts. In the sphere of general law, banks are treated on a par with nonbank legal entities. For example, as public limited liability companies, banks are subject to a common body of European company law, including the permissible national variations of it. Remedies and sanctions that address the non-observance of legal capital requirements address the problem of limited liability of shareholders, as opposed to the regulatory capital requirements, which address the social or systemic risk, and costs of bank failure. For instance, capital increases and decreases require voting in shareholders' meetings: in the case of a public limited liability company, general corporation law confers the powers of capitalisation directly on shareholders' meetings, and prohibits their delegation to any other corporate organ.[6] Government orders as such cannot increase capital.

Another example of the strong emphasis on private autonomy would have been the applicability of bankruptcy and other general insolvency laws to banks in distress. On paper, insolvency entails at least a loss of authorisation for the bank in question, and probably constitutes a compelling case for regulators and supervisors to turn it over to the protection of independent and impartial courts and tribunals. However, this discrepancy between law and reality is resolved almost invariably by deposit guarantees and a taxpayer bailout. Market discipline in respect of banks is highly qualified in a number of EEA countries on paper, too. It would appear that restrictive general banking and/or insolvency laws, may preclude – taken as a composite – private actions and petitions in respect of banks in the following ways:

- Involuntary petitions by individual depositors and other creditors may be impermissible, with the law then reserving the right of initiative for regulators and supervisors.
- Voluntary petitions by banks themselves for the opening of insolvency proceedings (to obtain an automatic stay against actions by individual depositors and other creditors) may be impermissible.
- Privileges of voluntary liquidation to be carried out under the supervision of regulators may be restricted in the public interest.
- Powers of regulators and supervisors to carry out administrative (forced) liquidations of banks are restricted to apparently solvent banks excluding, by necessary implication, insolvent banks, which are subject to the operation of general insolvency laws.
- Where involuntary petitions by individual depositors and other creditors are permissible, insolvency proceedings are triggered by a default or failure (non-payment or impending nonpayment), not by contentious net worth estimates.

In the case of banks of some size and in systemic cases, therefore, it is not surprising that banks in distress remain subject to the 'out of court' jurisdiction of regulators and supervisors. It is hard to identify any mandatory exit policies whereby regulators and supervisors relinquish jurisdiction by withdrawing authorisations in the face of an impending bailout. This would carry some assurance that judicial authorities would declare the bank insolvent or appointed a receiver if, in the end, no public money were made available. Mere economic insolvency does not serve as grounds for bankruptcy with the exception of Germany where courts are not permitted to second-guess the supervisory authority on the question of observance by banks of a range of prescribed financial benchmarks (including 'overindebtedness'). Having no authority to carry out takeovers, reorganisations or liquidations by administrative means instead, bank regulators and supervisors are likely to appeal to government for a political decision.

8.4 FORMULATION AND IMPLEMENTATION OF EXIT POLICY

Existing exit policies are generally predicated on the threat of denial or withdrawal of authorisations, and of the opening of judicial insolvency proceedings, in respect of banks, and not on placing them in public administration for reorganisation or liquidation.

Traditionally, exit was the policy followed by the authorities in licensing institutions. General banking laws typically express the conditions of granting and withdrawal of authorisations in such a broad manner that they would appear to cover a range of financial benchmarks in that discretionary actions by regulators and supervisors are triggered by threats of capital impairment or insolvency. While withdrawals of authorisations serve as structural actions or sanctions, in themselves such decisions are mere status decisions. Typically, legal consequences such as an eventual takeover, reorganisation or liquidation attach to the subject bank. Of the familiar financial benchmarks, the legal solvency requirement is the only hard one because of its incorporation into bankruptcy and other general insolvency laws.

8.4.1 Binding and Enforceable Financial Benchmarks

There seems to be no particular reason why a range of financial benchmarks could not be made hard by the formulation of appropriate exit rules whose execution would be triggered solely by their non-observance. This can be done in two ways:

- On the condition that the legal rule incorporating the specified benchmark includes precise or objective elements that are stated or defined in such a way that departure from them will be obvious to the subject bank and the authorities, the prescribed legal consequences could attach to subject banks quasi-automatically without the need for the exercise of judgement. Banks would then be assured that they would not be taken by surprise. Such a rule would be harsh like the bankruptcy, based on a debtor's absolute and unconditional obligation to pay debts, which does not treat errors of legal judgement on the side of the debtor as *bona fide* errors. It might not operate in the public interest in all cases, as wider consequences are not considered.
- In addition to precise or objective elements that are stated or defined in such a way that departure from them will be obvious, the rule could require the exercise by government of informed judgement to determine whether the legal consequences of its application would be within the public interest. In the light of all the costs and benefits the rule would not so much impose a duty on banks as govern the performance by government of a discretionary

(executive) function. If government acted on public interest grounds, therefore, creditors and owners would have maximum assurance that they would be compensated on an appropriate valuation of the bank's assets and liabilities as of the date of takeover (for manifest division and valuation errors, respectively). At worst, the depositors and other creditors would receive what they would have received in liquidation.

There are examples of the latter kinds of rules. In Greece under a special law enacted in 1951 and subsequent banking legislation, administrative authorities retained a power to order a bank to increase capital, and to set aside the legal effect of pre-existing shareholders' pre-emptive rights until 1996 when that law was held contrary to the Second Capital Directive.[7] In Norway, infringement upon legal capital requirements may trigger intervention by the authorities from 1985 when the 1961 law on Commercial Banks was amended to permit government to recapitalise a bank as and when shareholders did not proceed to do so and order it to decrease its capital to cover the loss and to increase its capital to ensure the continued operation of the bank.[8] In Sweden from 1998 and as long as the universal deposit guarantee was in effect (it was withdrawn in 1995), government could, as and when regulatory capital fell below 2 per cent of risk weighted assets, engage in a compulsory redemption of outstanding shares of a critically under capitalised bank, or place it under compulsory administration. These techniques triggered the surrender of the outstanding shares of a corporate form bank to government, and the compulsory administration by the government of mutual savings banks.[9]

The opening by courts of bankruptcy and general insolvency proceedings gives rise to a drastic sanction, usually contingent on the withdrawal by regulators or supervisors of banking authorisations. However, no equivalent is available to governments, regulators and supervisors under the public law of banking. Indeed, in EEA countries, the role of regulators and supervisors is typically limited to withdrawal of authorisations, on the one hand, and to lodging a petition with the competent court to open judicial proceedings in respect of a bank in distress, on the other. Except in a few countries (including Sweden and the United Kingdom), the prescribed procedures preclude or restrict petitions by individual depositors and other creditors.

Market-based solutions are meant to substitute for official apparatus (substituting endogenous for exogenous governance), but for them to work banks would have to be completely 'privatised'. Making workouts successful probably entails the lifting of any vestiges of immunity that banks may enjoy *inter alia* from petitions lodged by individual depositors and other creditors. In the case of LTCM, which was cited above, the legal consequences of the failure to carry out the private workout were obvious from judicial practice under chapter 11 of the

US Bankruptcy Code. Nothing stood then between participants and the competent US Bankruptcy Court had LTCM or any individual creditor chosen to proceed. Analogous situations do not obtain in the field of banking in EEA countries, hence, any reliance on the competent court alone would be misplaced.

In contrast to cases of legal insolvency, which give rise to conduct-based remedies and sanctions, the court cannot proceed on mere findings of negative net worth. Generally, the non-observance of benchmarks such as regulatory or legal capital requirements, or net worth requirements (economic insolvency), triggers no actions, remedies and sanctions under general debtor-creditor, corporation, insolvency or other general laws. They may trigger actions by private parties (for example, by individual shareholders) against directors, auditors or managers of the bank, but typically they do not give rise to conduct-related actions by the authorities against the bank itself. Of course the administrative authorities will have a set of powers to require banks to act and restrict additional risk taking as the capital ratio falls but such powers alone are often not sufficient to prevent the slide into insolvency.

In EEA countries, banks are not subject to harsh breakdown actions in the case of criminal conduct. The law tends to criminalise the conduct of members of its organs and that of its managers rather than the resulting conduct of the bank itself making it liable for damages. Damages assessed on directors and managers may figure, however, if so determined by the court, as part of the bank's general indebtedness. It may be unique to the US law that that criminal proceedings can be commenced against an insolvent bank engaged in criminal activity resulting in seizure and forfeiture of assets upsetting expectations about finality of transactions, and removing assets that would otherwise be distributed to creditors.

Therefore, it is probably safe to say that as long as an insolvent bank makes payments and transfers in keeping with its financial obligations, the jurisdiction over the bank is unlikely to shift for any non-observance of capital or maintenance of net worth requirements, to a court which could proceed with its reorganisation or liquidation. EEA banking laws do not mandate any prompt corrective action of regulators or supervisors as the financial condition of a subject bank deteriorates. Generally, insolvent or bankrupt banks have remained immune from legal proceedings as long as they retain their authorisation or licence. More specifically, existing legislation does not appear to lay down any mandatory exit policy of the kind that would place regulators or supervisors under a duty to relinquish jurisdiction over subject banks in distress at a prespecified financial benchmark.

Relying on financial benchmarks typically involves highly technical assessments regarding the position of the subject bank. Hence, regulators and supervisors are equipped to deal with the flip side of capital adequacy, which is the pathology of capital inadequacy and negative net worth. Events such as: (i) the critical undercapitalisation of a subject bank in terms of regulatory capital requirements; (ii) the incurrence by subject bank of losses of (legal) capital; and (iii) findings of negative net worth, do not in themselves manifest fault on the side of the bank, but, because of the threat they present, justify immediate action and give rise to further inquiries regarding the circumstances of the bank. The point is that financial benchmarks should not be formulated in a conduct-related manner because they may refer to events that are largely beyond the immediate control of a subject bank. For example, events such as critical under capitalisation or negative net worth may be attributable to market developments, and nothing whatsoever turns upon the conduct of the bank or its directors or managers. Actions that take the form of remedies or sanctions presuppose a pre-existing duty to avoid certain financial results, and can never be applied without further administrative or judicial review to ascertain that there indeed was a failure by a subject bank to comply with an obligation incumbent upon it. In the event of a crisis, conduct-related rules afford no immediate recourse against auditors, directors, managers and employees. Indeed, authorities can never assume that because a bank was under duty to do a thing (or to refrain from doing it), it will be liable for doing (or not doing) it, but must await legal proceedings.

8.4.2   Specification of a Solvency (Net Worth) Requirement as a Financial Benchmark

It is unfortunate that courts do not test economic insolvency up-front upon the opening of insolvency proceedings in respect of banks, but do so only at the end following the distribution of proceeds of liquidation of assets. Judicial reluctance to carry out an up-front valuation to confirm a finding of fault in payments, in effect shifts the risk of initial valuation of the debtor bank's assets and liabilities, and of any subsequent changes in the value thereof to those holding claims and interests.

Hence, no revealed recovery rate can ever validate findings of legal insolvency to constitute findings of concurrent economic insolvency.[10] Negative net worth and other economic concepts of insolvency are not based on a finding of fault in payment; rather, they are predicated on a hypothetical liquidation valuation of a subject bank's assets and liabilities. Indeed, as opposed to testing maturities of assets and liabilities (or the debtor's conduct when actually presented with a demand for payment), negative net worth concepts refer to a hypothetical liquidation valuation as of now of a subject bank's assets and liabilities. For example, administrative authorities may use such valuation to withdraw an authorisation. Any concurrent judicial finding of insolvency must come within the bankruptcy law meaning of insolvency, however.

Possible advantages attach to a use of administrative concepts of economic solvency, as opposed to the judicial testing of the nonpayment, or any impending nonpayment, of obligations of which the payment may demanded currently: under traditional jurical, a debtor bank would be insolvent if its available assets did not match liabilities that must be paid forthwith. The implications have been noted by Hadjiemmanuil (1996, p. 271):

> [T]he conception of solvency as an ability to settle immediately all debts currently due which underlies this decision [by the UK court in *Re Goodwin Squires Securities Ltd. (1983)*] is unsatisfactory in the case of banking institutions, whose role as intermediaries depends on maturity transformation, i.e., the transformation of short-term deposit resources into longer-term earning assets, whose immediate realisation may be economically and legally impossible. Essentially, banking involves the practical ability to meet repayment demands as they are actually made in normal circumstances, not the theoretical ability to repay the full deposit base of the institution immediately. Accordingly, the legal concept of insolvency should be confined to situations where an institution's net present economic value is negative or where the institution has been unable to repay debts which have been actually called for repayment.

Undoubtedly, an appropriate financial benchmark would cover those 'situations where an institution's net present economic value is negative', and its non-observance by the institution (debtor bank) could be subject to structural actions such as takeover and restructuring or the withdrawal of its authorisation, the release of deposit insurance funds, and so forth. As a result of government having administrative powers, which are equivalent to those available under bankruptcy and other general insolvency laws, banks could be exempted from conduct-related actions, remedies and sanctions under general insolvency laws. The government could take over an insolvent bank, as long as it offers compensation and its actions are warranted by purposes that are within the public interest, subject to review by an impartial and independent body (other than government) of requisite administrative actions that affect, modify or annul private rights and obligations.[11]

9 A New Approach to Orderly Bank Exit

There are two polar regimes for the enforcement of insolvency law in respect of banks. By comparing and contrasting their salient features, this chapter provides the basis for a new approach that requires the authorities to act early as banks get into difficulty and gives them the powers to do so. This requirement for early action should reduce the chance that taxpayers have to be called upon and sharpen the incentive for bank management themselves to act early to protect their own interests.

At one pole, the US system includes a range of powers for the deposit insurer to handle bank insolvencies and crises. At the other, the system in the EEA countries distributes the responsibility for handling bank insolvencies among the administrative and judicial authorities.[1] In EEA countries, functions of deposit insurers are limited to dispensing cash in the event of default or failure on the part of depository institution. The former is a general insolvency (private) law approach, while the latter is an administrative (public) law approach. The new scheme for bank reorganisation and liquidation, which is set out below, is based on public not private enforcement of the law.

9.1 ADMINISTRATIVE AND GENERAL INSOLVENCY LAW APPROACHES

Bank insolvency laws in EEA countries are a part of general insolvency laws that are predicated on the principle of private autonomy. This presupposes the existence of impartial and independent courts or tribunals that decide upon the merits of each case on the basis of the record as established by the individual parties involved. States are not parties to bank insolvency proceedings. They do not, therefore, intervene as successors to an insolvent bank, or to its assets or liabilities, in insolvency proceedings before courts. (Although they may appear as interested non-parties, through having an exclusive right to file reorganisation or liquidation petitions, as in Germany.) As holders of claims and interests in respect of banks, governments intervene, like private shareholders and creditors, under private law. Private law distributes the losses and allocates the entitlements, according to the material general law (general property, contract and corporation laws), and the insolvency law (classified as civil procedure in some countries). The decision-making by which the process functions is carried out by courts, without review by governments.

In the United States, the government charters and terminates banks. Designated administrative agencies takeover (seize) problem banks, and then, as successors in interest, liquidate their assets and liabilities for their own account (and not for the account of depositors and other creditors). Their successor liability is limited to the value of the 'receivership estate', a misnomer.[2] Under the prescribed rules of succession, they also succeed to the shareholders' interests, and to the creditors' claims with respect to the bank and its assets. Except to the extent the liabilities are supported by the hypothetical liquidation valuation of the seized bank's assets (including any amount available to the bank under the obligation that the FDIC owes to the insured institution), the law discharges as 'moot' any further liability that the government might have incurred as successor. These powers to carry out seizures of banks and their assets, to terminate the seized banks in legal personality and entity, and to limit successor liability vis-à-vis those divested of their property and assets, have not been successfully challenged, for example, on constitutional grounds.[3]

9.2 GENERAL INSOLVENCY (PRIVATE) LAW APPROACH

9.2.1 Constructive Ambiguity

In EEA countries the authorities typically do not tie their hands regarding contingent events in the field of banking. Such 'constructive ambiguity' is normally justified on the grounds that, in the face of uncertainty, people will fear the worst and hence do their best to avoid ever getting into difficulty where they have to appeal to the state for help. The state can then afford to offset any systemic risks that may appear, because the event is rare. The drawback is that people appear to have placed exactly the opposite construction on the ambiguity and assumed that in the case of difficulty they will be bailed out. (The evidence suggests this belief is often correct.) In these circumstances ambiguity both increases the risk and the cost to the taxpayer. It is anything but constructive.

In cases of insolvency of banks of some size and in systemic cases where public interest comes into play, governments lack an discernible legal basis to takeover, reorganise or liquidate them and are unable to predicate their performance of functions of lender (or investor) of last resort on mandatory restructuring and burden-sharing. As long as the observance by banks of applicable legal or regulatory capital requirements has not been made the absolute legal duty of subject banks themselves, the authorities have no remedies or sanctions to apply in the face of non-observance. It follows that situations in which a bank's net worth turns negative, are treated as questions of withdrawal of authorisation, or as fresh political questions.

Indeed, the lack of legal basis for non-fault structural actions in respect of insolvent banks is a constraint which leaves regulators and supervisors with the one option which is to remove case administration to judicial authorities to be carried out under bankruptcy and general insolvency laws. Almost invariably, however, regulators and supervisors have considered the latter course of action unrealistic and have not closed banks where they are large or there are systemic implications. Bailouts have been the only way to go.

In comparison, Federal banking and bankruptcy laws in the United States contain far-reaching powers for bank regulators and supervisors to takeover and resolve critically undercapitalised, insolvent banks in 'prompt corrective action' programmes under a comprehensive Federal *lex specialis*. The same is true of New Zealand, where the law also contains powers for regulators and supervisors to apply structural sanctions such as the appointment of a statutory manager with sweeping powers in the event of nonobservance of regulatory capital requirements.[4] In EEA countries, in contrast, supervisors and regulators have no like powers to engage in compulsory takeover, restructuring, or liquidation of insolvent banks.

Whether facing a banking crisis or not, government is dependent on the legislature for operating authority and budgets. According to the tripartite doctrine of checks and balances, the government, as well as government institutions and administrative agencies, which wish to set and enforce policy must await the delegation of powers, and operating authority and the authorisation and appropriation of resources from the legislature. Conversely, powers and resources not expressly conferred on government, administrative or judicial authorities, are vested in the legislature so that it can decide whether and to which organs to delegate the powers and transfer resources. Generally, legislatures can delegate any residual (unallocated) legislative powers to the government, except the power for government to review its own or other actions that affect, modify or annul private rights or obligations. Legislature can delegate such powers of review to administrative tribunals or courts.

Without authority for the valuation, takeover and restructuring of insolvent banks, there is no law for administrative authorities to apply as they investigate and resolve bank insolvencies in EEA countries. Although insolvency is sufficient grounds for revoking an authorisation forthwith on grounds of the deteriorating financial condition of a subject bank, the finding may not suffice for the court to open insolvency proceedings, at least not without further review.

Indeed, dormant legislative powers are exercisable solely by legislature, even in crises. Authorities in those EEA countries where there have been threats of large scale, system-wide bank failures had to negotiate with banks in a legal vacuum. This experience shows that the options were limited to withdrawal of authorisations and the opening of judicial insolvency proceedings, worked against governments rather than for them in such negotiations. Unable to substitute valid, legally binding orders for the missing individual assent from creditors and owners, the government could only bail out banks and their owners and creditors. Thus, the latter were treated better than they would have been had the bank in question been liquidated up front.

As in the United States, legislatures in EEA countries might have bypassed the government and delegated broad powers of administrative action and review in respect of banks to specialised administrative agencies (regulatory and supervisory authorities and central banks). In addition, to expedite the process of restructuring, they might have assigned the review of the decision-making to the extent private rights and obligations are affected to independent and impartial administrative tribunals (as opposed to courts). They might have centralised conduct-related and structural remedies and sanctions in government or specialised agencies (e.g., deposit insurers) and equipped them with appropriate financial powers.

9.2.2 Why Did the Courts Remain Unused in Recent Banking Crises?

Bank insolvencies tend to fall in the cracks between two jurisdictions: (i) regulators and supervisors wish to retain jurisdiction over insolvent banks under general banking laws; and (ii) banks that are legally insolvent in the bankruptcy law sense fall under general insolvency laws, which prevent their administrative or 'voluntary' (forced) liquidation.

Forebearance by regulators and supervisors can suffice to keep an insolvent bank open and operating. However, they cannot exercise jurisdiction over insolvent banks under general insolvency laws, as this belongs to the competent court. Only judicial authorities can act under general insolvency laws, which permit the carrying out by the court of a bank's reorganisation (without allow-ing its creditors to succeed to its assets) or the liquidation of its assets and liabilities, as the case may be. However, the courts cannot proceed on their own initiative.

General banking laws, and the bankruptcy and other general insolvency laws, are different legal systems for case administration, with no one to remove insolvent banks from the jurisdiction of regulators and supervisors in case of unwillingness to cede jurisdiction to the judicial authorities. The constructive ambiguity about the identity of the institution that might unlock an insolvent bank's access to the competent court, meant that the courts were available to declare banks insolvent and appoint receivers to administer their assets but this power was not called upon. The failure of legislatures to prescribe mandatory exit points may have turned bank insolvencies into political questions for governments to resolve with the legislature.

9.2.3   Problems of Contingent and Concurrent Jurisdiction

Legislatures everywhere can delegate exit policy powers exclusively, contingently or concurrently. Experience shows that, due to the particular design and drafting of general banking laws, general insolvency laws apply only contingently to banks, as their applicability is vested in the discretion and right of initiative of bank regulators and supervisors. Moreover, in case of a bank of some size, as well as in systemic cases, the EU Commission has been prepared to approve state aid to keep them out of courts. Where things go badly wrong because of deadlocks caused by conflicts of jurisdiction, legislatures can change the delegation or distribution of powers as and when they see fit. So far, however, legislatures in EEA countries have not made any changes in the distribution or delegation of powers over banks in distress.

Artificial as it may be, the respective formulations of general banking and insolvency laws make a distinction between two legal situations. Bankruptcy and general insolvency laws are triggered in those cases in which insolvency is manifested by fault (nonpayment or impending nonpayment), whereas economic insolvency, which is demonstrated by opinions based on the valuation of assets and liabilities belonging to the debtor, does not constitute a default or failure by the debtor.[5] The distinction is not a mere quibble. In the latter case of a bank that is economically insolvent and, nevertheless, continues trading by selling assets, the bank may well remain open and operating, as any insolvent firm can by discharging its demand liabilities on a first come first served basis.

There are three reasons for this situation. First, general insolvency laws are triggered only in the event that individual depositors, creditors, or the authorities react by petitioning the court. Without a requisite finding of nonpayment, the court cannot proceed. Second, the judicial reorganisation and liquidation powers do not necessarily reach undercapitalised or economically insolvent banks – that is, banks that have negative net worth. Third, in the event of bank insolvency of a bank of some size, as well as in instances with systemic implications, regulators and supervisors almost invariably want to retain control, and in that process of 'active' forbearance end up imposing enormous risks and costs on the taxpayer.

9.3   ADMINISTRATIVE (PUBLIC) LAW APPROACH

9.3.1   Government Role in Case Administration

As the apex of the executive branch, government is the appropriate organ to be charged with the formulation and enforcement of exit policies as well as with the performance of functions of lender or investor of last resort, with respect to insolvent banks.

Unless the government has requisite powers to takeover, reorganise and liqui-date insolvent banks, there can be no robust exit policy. The performance by government of financial functions on an ad hoc basis has imposed large losses on the taxpayer for lack of any pre-prescribed burden-sharing. Rules of restruc-turing should authorise debt and debt service reduction, as well as the wiping out of pre-existing shareholders, as a precedent or concurrent condition for the avail-ability of public financial assistance in bailouts and approval by the EU Commission of state aid.

In their legal nature, structural actions that may be imposed upon the eco-nomic insolvency of a bank, encompass actions to be taken by government in the public interest. These may include individual measures such as the succession of the government to shareholders' interests in the bank, the taking or divestment by government of the property (assets) of the bank, and the taking or divestment by government of private property in the debt of the bank.

If the requisite actions are not those needed to ensure the succession of depos-itors and other creditors to the assets of an insolvent bank, they are necessarily expropriatory actions. The latter actions cannot be challenged, however, if car-ried out for purposes that are in the public interest, based on delegation of leg-islative authority for the purpose, and with the payment of appropriate compensation. Provided that the amount of compensation is subject to review by independent and impartial administrative or judicial authorities.

Unlike conduct-related remedies and sanctions, structural actions robust exit policies may be triggered by financial benchmarks, especially where they oper-ate in conjunction with the performance by government of its functions of lender or investor of last resort.[6] Appropriately, therefore, the process by which the decision-making functions under robust exit policies belongs to government and not to administrative authorities, except as executing agencies. It is for govern-ment to decide upon any compulsory acquisition of private property, rights and interests (or liabilities relating to them) in the first place. For example, if valua-tion errors are made by regulators and supervisors, resulting in takeover of a bank that appears insolvent but is not (as it turns out), compensation must be paid to the previous owners.

Of course, there are risks and costs involved, in that government has no power to review its own decisions that may affect, modify or annul private rights and obliga-tions in individual cases. Imposing a duty on the part of government to compensate for private loss means that any delegation by legislature of robust exit policy pow-ers is tantamount to the delegation of the power of the purse. Administrative and judicial authorities cannot engage on their own account in structural actions that commit the State to pay compensation, as determined by the competent court or tribunal. As bailouts are not entitlements belonging to insolvent or bankrupt banks, bailouts can hardly constitute nondiscretionary expenditure under the budget.

The key decision involved in the takeover and restructuring of a bank is the valuation of its assets and liabilities, which tells whether the condition of insolvency is fulfilled. Lawyers always argue that there is no such thing as 'final' insolvency until the termination of a debtor because future 'enrichment' cannot be excluded as long as the debtor continues in legal personality and entity. However, legislature may confer the power to make the determination of insolvency on, say, an administrative agency. Based on its determination, government may proceed, keeping in mind that any review of actions taken by government or administrative authorities belongs to independent and impartial administrative tribunals and judicial courts.

Legislatures may attach automatic legal consequences to administrative findings of economic insolvency based on a hypothetical liquidation valuation of a bank's assets and liabilities. Negative net worth, as such, implies no fault, which precludes the application of conduct-related remedies and sanctions. Law need not treat situations of negative net worth as transitory conditions, but may dispose of the case on such a finding. Here, the US courts have solved the problem of finality of determination of insolvency, in two ways under the FDI Act:

(1)   owners of banks cannot complain of confiscation because they should have read the law that says that the FDIC would step into their shoes if things go badly wrong (e.g., the bank becomes insolvent);
(2)   creditors of banks cannot complain that their claims were held worthless because the 'prudential mootness doctrine'.[7]

Maximum liability of the FDIC in its receivership capacity on creditors' claims is limited to what would have been received in liquidation. The court has stated, the FDIC 'will never have any [other] assets with which to satisfy unsecured claims'. Therefore, such a determination establishes the 'impossibility of any effective relief' by courts (ibid., pp. 426–9). All litigation thereafter by owners or creditors typically stops on summary judgment. In other words, the determination of insolvency may become final solely because of the legal consequences that are attached to the finding itself.

Bank insolvency that threatens the stability of financial markets permits the legislature to construct a legal theory for compulsory taking and restructuring by government of insolvent banks, without even having to attach to banks any conduct-related duty to avoid insolvency. Although individual depositors and other creditors of an insolvent bank are not at fault, the law may cancel their claims above the point at which its assets equal its liabilities on hypothetical liquidation valuation. As has been noted above, this 'solvency point' can be determined by way of official hypothetical liquidation valuation.

Indeed, technically, the solvency point determines the loss of creditors in the takeover, reorganisation and liquidation of the subject bank. An appropriate principle and method of valuation eliminates any negative net worth by way of debt restructuring. In equity restructuring nothing whatsoever turns upon any conduct of shareholders, which is the same point that applies in debt restructuring, where nothing turns upon conduct of individual depositors or other creditors. In most cases banks become insolvent without, and almost certainly against, the will of shareholders or creditors.

The liability of shareholders for loss of their interests would flow immediately from the threats that insolvency poses. Similarly, the liability of creditors would flow immediately from the mootness of their claims on a hypothetical liquidation valuation of the bank's assets and liabilities, as of the day of its takeover. The protection of public interest is a necessary and sufficient ground for this and may serve as an outright legal basis for the takeover and restructuring of an insolvent bank.

Omitting to impose any duty on a bank to avoid insolvency has advantages. We can say directly that a bank, if determined to be insolvent by regulators and supervisors on a hypothetical liquidation valuation of its assets and liabilities, becomes liable for prescribed structural actions by government. Otherwise, the government would have to show breach of duty making the bank liable for insolvency. Instead, the question of liability turns to the conduct of the government itself. Here the public law of expropriation places at least a general hypothetical duty on the state not willfully to take and convert private property, or to divest ownership of private property, except subject to delegation of legislative authority for appropriate compensation and for purposes that are within public interest.

Under the public law of expropriation, acting in the public interest, government may proceed with a takeover, reorganisation, or liquidation of an insolvent bank without having to await the commencement of insolvency proceedings by the court. Such structural actions can be distinguished in that they serve purposes that are within public interests. Nothing whatever turns upon any conduct of the owner. All that is needed is that the government has legislative approval, and compensates the divested party on the basis of appropriate valuation by the government of the object (as reviewed by competent courts or tribunals). Delegation by the legislature of authority for the government for this constitutes necessary and sufficient legislative approval.

9.3.2 How Might It Work?

Economic efficiency and depositor confidence suggest that intervention takes place immediately upon the event of 'economic insolvency', in order to maximise the value of the assets of the bank (i.e., minimising losses to all creditors). The opacity of valuation of bank assets means that criteria for the decision over what constitutes economic insolvency can be generated by particular levels of financial indicators. Restoring the depositors' access to funds calls for the distribution of losses at the very beginning of the intervention, through an up-front restructuring of an insolvent bank. The distribution of losses (as of that date) and the allocation of entitlements would be concurrent under a reorganisation plan, listing the restructured creditors' rights and assigning pre-existing shareholders' interests to new owners.

Clearly, a solution to the problem of an up-front distribution of losses is to make the subject bank solvent again. Examples are:

- augmentation of its assets through the usual legal techniques that are there to swell assets of bank debtor in reorganisation or liquidation ('asset restructuring');
- reduction of its debt and debt service to the point at which its liabilities equal its assets ('debt restructuring' or 'haircut reorganisation'), and
- carrying out of a forced acquisition of its outstanding shares that are worthless without compensation (equity restructuring).

Generally, continuing a bank in legal personality and entity, under new ownership and management, is a solution to the problem of closing and liquidating the bank piecemeal. The latter option of closure and liquidation can be only a solution of last resort, rarely a practical option for all but the smallest banks. The re-establishment of solvency is, of course, a prerequisite for continuing a bank as a legal entity for the time being.

The ability of the government to seize an insolvent bank, succeeding to its shareholders' interests or to its assets, would represent a fundamental change in the legal nature of exit policies in EEA countries. Having an option to transfer the ownership of the bank from its shareholders to the government, or to a designated specialised agency, allows the authorities a free hand to dispose of the shares and assets attached to the bank to the greatest advantage (that is, to maximise their value and to recoup the expenses of the rescue).

Of course, the government incurs an obligation to compensate those divested of their rights and interests, based on a hypothetical liquidation valuation of the subject bank's assets and liabilities as of the date of intervention. Taking by government of title to the subject bank, as well as any divestment by government of any depositors and other creditors of their rights of succession to the bank's assets, is inconsistent with bankruptcy and general insolvency laws, and, thus, requires exemption from the provisions of the bankruptcy and other general insolvency laws, which do not authorise such conversions of creditors' rights in liquidation.

An asset, debt and equity restructuring is necessary since seized banks would generally be deeply insolvent, making it impossible to sell them at a positive price. If such a restructuring is not carried out up-front at the point of takeover, the government may become liable as successor for the losses of the subject bank, which would undo the advantages of the proposed scheme.

In order to pass title to the bank to the eventual new owners (whether through public offering or private placement), the authorities must be able to take unencumbered title to the bank's outstanding shares. Its shares would be sold to an acquirer that is able and willing to recapitalise the newly solvent bank up to the applicable legal and regulatory requirements. Since banking supervisors have no particular expertise in running or administering banks, the bank will need to be sold (in whole or in part) very quickly in a newly solvent condition.

The designated agency could also dispose of the bank through a sale of the whole bank as an economic entity. This can be done by selling its assets and liabilities. The executing agency may also arrange for a purchase and assumption of a substantial part of the bank and liquidation of the rest. Thus it is necessary for the agency to acquire title on its own account to the bank.

Thus, the bank would remain in public ownership and administration during only a short period from the date of takeover. Takeover would therefore preclude the operation of traditional bankruptcy procedures, which froze the pre-petition claims of depositors and other creditors (by imposing an 'automatic stay'), and subordinated them to post-petition claims that permitted reorganisers and liquidators to operate the bank at the expense of pre-petition creditors.

If financial assistance is needed (whether from the government budget, deposit insurance fund, or reductions in the claims of creditors) to make the sale possible, it would be inappropriate (both in terms of fairness and economic incentives) for the owners of the insolvent bank to benefit from such assistance. Any reliance on the budget as a source of such assistance would also be inappropriate, both in terms of taxpayer acceptance and market discipline. For both these reasons, the takeover of an insolvent bank, if continued in legal personality and entity, presupposes comprehensive restructuring.

In order to carry out a forced acquisition, the designated agency must be able to determine the hypothetical liquidation value of the subject bank's assets and liabilities in a manner that disposes of the case without any second-guessing by administrative tribunals or judicial courts. The role assigned to the latter would be confined to determining compensation for private parties for manifest valuation errors, without having any power to reverse decisions on grounds of the initial determination of the value of assets and liabilities. Annulment would not be a prerequisite for compensation awards (if any).

The problem of valuation is heightened in court-conducted corporate reorganisations. No objective figure is available in judicial proceedings under general insolvency laws for the value of the firm that is subject to reorganisation, and such laws consign the determination of the size of the 'reorganisation value' to bargaining and litigation among classes of creditors (including even shareholders). This may take years, usually involves costs of litigation, and almost invariably produces an inefficient capital structure for the reorganised form. There the value of the assets and liabilities of subject firm is revealed at the end of the process as of the date of voting by creditors (and shareholders) of a reorganisation plan.[8] The courts generally approve (confirm) a plan if the prescribed majorities of all classes approve it.

In contrast to judicial reorganisation models under which the reorganisation value of a firm is subject to bargaining and litigation, our proposed scheme presupposes that the reorganisation value is determined, in terms of monetary value, up-front as a subject bank is determined to be economically insolvent. Using the same rankings of claims and interests that apply in judicial process, we can arrive at a division of the cake that is perfectly consistent with participants' entitlements, based on any remaining private property, rights and interests in the subject bank or its assets. Claimants will receive what they would have received had the bank been liquidated as of the date of takeover. Conversely, those debt and equity holders determined to be under water by official valuation would receive nothing.

The takeover by government of an insolvent bank is really just a fictional 'forced' sale of the bank to the government at the price prescribed by the government. Somewhat analogously, in judicial reorganisations there is a fictional sale of the debtor company to its creditors, except that the court can provide neither an objective, indisputable figure, nor any other figure, for the value of the assets and liabilities in question. Generally, in judicial reorganisation proceedings there is no official estimate for parties to work on, but each and every creditor (or shareholder) votes on his or her subjective estimates which, due to strategic manipulation, are pitched up by those who rank lower (shareholders, subordinated creditors, general creditors), and down by those who rank higher. Shareholders, whose shares are worthless in case of an insolvent company, even so hope to inflate asset values to support their continuing participation, a flaw of the bargaining model.

Moreover, it is unrealistic to think that judicial reorganisation models would permit a bank to continue trading in the same way as nonbanks can continue trading. While suppliers and other creditors of a manufacturer may tolerate debt and debt service reduction and the suspension of repayments while profitable production continues, a bank's business is the taking of deposits repayable in currency, at par and on demand. The vast numbers of depositors and shareholders of a bank of some size would not be interested in bargaining and litigating to keep a bank open and operating. They are unlikely to be able to make bargaining and litigating decisions by arriving at any informed subjective estimates of the bank's reorganisation value. They would protest for having to await access to deposits for long periods of time. The banks' assets would diminish, and its liabilities would increase, and its reorganisation value would probably fall below what its liquidation value would have been had its assets and liabilities been liquidated up-front as of the day of the opening of the proceedings (perhaps, years earlier).

Under our scheme, the process of establishing the value of assets and liabilities of a subject bank and, derivatively, the value of each claim supported by the assets can be completed later, as of the date of takeover. The process is pure arithmetic if the authorities follow the absolute priority principle. The valuation provides a key to the selection of claims and interests for cancellation. In addition to the ratable reduction of liabilities (haircuts), the privilege of cancellation would extend to contingent liabilities and to the selective repudiation of the bank's future liability on a range of possible claims (including repudiation of outstanding labour and rental contracts) as well.

The legal provisions for the seizure of an insolvent bank, its financial restructuring up-front, and its sale to new owners must be carefully designed and drafted to ensure that they are not confiscatory of private property of its owners or creditors. The law must ensure due process in settling claims, in case, for example, the apparently insolvent bank is not, in truth, insolvent, as of the date of intervention. In the event of any under valuation of assets or overvaluation of liabilities, the law could provide that the net profit remaining in the agency's books after administrative expenses could be returned to those divested of their rights or interests.

The requisite legal issues differ from country to country because there is no uniform bank insolvency law. The fact that some countries follow civil law and others follow common law complicates the analysis. The next sections examine these problems and propose an approach that would appear to be legally sound and economically efficient.

9.4   OUTLINE OF THE NEW SCHEME

The objective of the scheme is to provide the legal means for taking an insolvent bank from its owners, financially restructuring it (up-front and without significant interruption in the access of depositors to their funds) if needed in order to sell it or its assets to new owners. Such a process would improve the prospect for prompt action by the supervisory authorities, thereby reducing the moral hazard and ultimate cost to the taxpayer of forbearance and bailouts.

Under the new scheme the administrative authorities would remain in control of the legal consequences that licence revocation or other similar intervention bears on the depositors and other creditors of an insolvent bank. Thus, in lieu of simply revoking the licence of an insolvent bank (and, indeed, remaining indifferent to litigational outcomes), the authorities would carry out a seizure and restructuring. Their succession to the ownership of the subject bank would ensure a speedy conversion of the ownership of the bank in reorganisation from pre-existing shareholders to new owners. Alternatively, their succession to the ownership of the assets of the bank would ensure their speedy conversion into cash to satisfy the claims of its depositors or other creditors. The latter option would be always available if the authorities wish to skip finding a new owner, and, hence, proceed to an outright liquidation of assets.

In other words, the seizure of ownership of the bank (as opposed to a seizure of its assets) under the new scheme, implies that the bank continues in legal personality and entity, and does not change its status from a bank to a nonbank. Compare this with the seizure of assets from the insolvent bank, which removes, by the operation of law, the bank's competence to dispose of them. In the latter case, the bank may well survive as a corporation under EEA-type general corporation laws, which may continue its existence, for the time being, in legal personality and entity as an empty legal shell. Under the US banking laws, having been placed in receivership, the insolvent bank cannot continue. Although the government succeeds – by the operation of law – to its shareholders' interests, the mandatory pulling of its charter terminates it in legal personality and entity forthwith. As a result, the US law, unlike the new scheme precludes bank reorganisations.

Moreover, the purpose of a new system is not to underwrite the losses incurred by an insolvent bank. A concurrent asset, debt and equity restructuring of an insolvent bank upon its seizure would limit its indebtedness to what is supported by its assets, on a hypothetical liquidation valuation carried out as of the date of intervention (that is, as if the bank had been liquidated on that date). Such a restructuring, which would be carried out by the operation of law, as of the date of intervention, would re-establish the solvency of the bank. Thus, upon its seizure by the government, the bank's net assets would be zero, limiting the bank's and the government's successor liability (if any) to meeting the post-seizure losses arising during the agency's ownership of the bank. Any successor liability of the state would be limited accordingly.

Unlike the US scheme, the new scheme offers the option of keeping a bank alive (if it is worth more alive than dead), which means continuing it in legal personality and entity. This cures the defect of the FDI Act, which is the categorical requirement that each and every bank must be resolved upon seizure. This would not be a realistic move where the costs and risks of converting an insolvent bank's assets into cash through judicial insolvency proceedings would be exorbitant, especially if the deposit insurance covers only small claims or a fraction of all claims. Outright policy reasons may disqualify buyers, say, to prevent the largest bank from absorbing all others. Normally, a bank's assets are worth much more if sold as a going concern to other banks than if sold piecemeal to nonbanks, where there are few or even no nonbank buyers with both accurate information about the quality of assets and sufficient resources to acquire them.

In consequence of its inability to reorganise banks, the FDIC must unnecessarily create 'new' or 'bridge' successor banks (as asset managers) whenever bids come in too low.

The proposed new scheme allows for the exercise by Government of expediency, efficiency and economy in carrying out of the diverse mandate of regulator and lender or investor of last resort in the event of bank insolvency. The scheme seeks to eliminate:

1. the costs and risks that the taxpayer might otherwise incur in the event of bank insolvency;
2. the moral hazard that always attaches to extending state aid to insolvent banks; and
3. the undue delay that causes losses of bank assets which typifies negotiations with banks in distress and any of the rather (theoretical) alternative judicial reorganisation and liquidation proceedings.

These objectives can be realised through the following six key features that make the proposed scheme preferable to most existing systems of private or public enforcement:

1. It authorises the government to take over an insolvent bank, as and when the government determines that the bank is economically insolvent or, in other words, has negative net worth. As a bank's financial condition deteriorates compared to the prescribed minimum regulatory capital standards, so it becomes less relevant to value its assets and liabilities on the basis of its continuing as a going concern. The appropriate basis becomes that which would be used in a liquidation.
2. The seized bank would retain its franchise to conduct banking business and may be kept open and operating through the process. By becoming an owner of the bank, the government will have plenary competence to control the bank and to dispose of its interests in the bank. Acting on its own account, it would carry out a merger, sale or other disposition of the bank as a going concern.
3. It is self-financing in the sense that each insolvent bank that comes under the scheme is restructured up-front, as of the date of takeover, through asset, debt and equity restructuring (including the wiping out of the interests of pre-existing shareholders and subordinated debt-holders). In reverse order of priority the claims of subordinated debt-holders and other junior creditors are eliminated up to the point that claims equal the value of the subject bank's assets as determined by the hypothetical liquidation valuation of its assets and liabilities.

4 . The remaining depositor and other creditor claims are then fixed and guaranteed by the government. Thus the division of the cake among claimants, follows the 'absolute priority principle', which is pure arithmetic, for the purposes of the distribution of losses and, conversely for the allocation of guaranteed entitlements. This way the scheme avoids collective proceedings or out of court bargaining among creditors and shareholders. Hence the newly solvent bank can be continued by government in legal personality and entity, ensuring the prompt settlement of claims held by depositors and other creditors to the extent supported by assets.

5. The revaluation of the assets and liabilities of a subject bank eliminates the Government's successor liability through the imposition of the cut-off or 'solvency point' (under (3) above) in respect of all liabilities (including contingent, nonbook and undiscovered liabilities). This is subject to the exception that, if the valuation erroneously wipes out debt or equity that turns out to have positive value as of the date of takeover, the government must pay compensation to those divested of valuable rights and interests. The residual exposure of the government is limited to solvency support after the date of takeover during the prescribed short period while the subject bank remains in public administration pending disposition.

6. If the newly solvent bank cannot be disposed on terms and conditions acceptable to the government in transaction with a third party able and willing to recapitalise it to meet legal and regulatory capital requirements within the prescribed maximum holding period, its assets and liabilities would have to be liquidated by the government. Here again, government would be acting for its own account, which may involve a gain or loss.

9.7 CONCLUSIONS

The preceding sections build on a comparative examination of current national legislation in the United States and in the EEA countries pertaining to: (i) the distribution of losses and, conversely, the allocation of remaining entitlements in the reorganisation and liquidation of insolvent banks; and (ii) the administrative and judicial decision-making by which the process functions. The question is whether or not there are overriding or hard legal constraints that prevent the adoption of more expeditious, effective and economic bank insolvency laws than the existing laws. We conclude that the answer is no.

The European Human Rights Convention (EHRC) requires no judicial review of administrative acts that affect, modify or annul civil (or common law) rights and obligations.[9] Indeed, case law under the Convention shows that the requirement can be met by setting up a dispute settlement body inside an administrative agency, or a separate administrative tribunal. The Convention imposes no maximum speed for the conduct of insolvency or like proceedings before a dispute settlement body, on the condition that the body is impartial and independent, and that its decisions are final and binding (that is, they cannot be reviewed by the government).

It appears that no hard legal constraints prevent the delegation of legislative authority for bank exit, reorganisation and liquidation to government or a specialised agency, although there lingers a perception that the actions in respect of insolvent banks belong to courts. No such constraint can be identified in EEA countries. In the United States their seizure belongs to an administrative agency that settles, in its capacity as successor to their assets, any claims for its own account under a *lex specialis*. The US Constitution does not permit the agency to settle debt disputes by entering conclusive factual and legal findings. The agency is 'no more an adjudicator than an insurance company authorised to disallow any claim not proven to its satisfaction'.[10] Nevertheless, by assigning the settlement of claims to an administrative agency and the settlement of disputes thereof to courts, the US banking laws greatly gain in speed and efficiency.

Moreover the chapter is concerned with the principles of hypothetical liquidation valuation of an insolvent bank's assets and liabilities and the relative and absolute priority principles which come into play in the allocation of entitlements in judicial bank reorganisations (e.g., debt and equity instruments). The latter are not predicated on a multilateral burden-sharing between the public treasury (as it may be claiming reimbursement of costs and indemnity for risks), and the shareholders, depositors, and other creditors. We show that current law does not extract mandatory concessions from the latter, or require the assignment of an insolvent bank's future earnings to the public treasury as a prerequisite of a bailout. Asymmetric rules apply to the 'who gets what, how much, and in which order' in the distribution of the proceeds of reorganisation, as opposed to the absolute priority that creditors should have over shareholders in the reorganisation of the assets of an insolvent bank.

The chapter is also concerned with the scope and content of the administrative and judicial decision-making by which the process of bank reorganisation and liquidation functions. What is it that the owners and uninsured creditors of an insolvent bank have in the back of their minds as they turn into potential free-riders and holdouts? The answer is that they know that bailouts by the government do not generate legal consequences for them except by their own assent (for example, in collective proceedings). The government cannot (unless it can show intentional wrongdoing) make pre-existing shareholders discharge any of the obligations of the subject bank, or make them meet the losses incurred by it. For example, the EU Commission's approval policy regarding state aid for problem banks does not condition its approvals of infusions of public money on the making of prior concessions by pre-existing shareholders or creditors.[11]

The state aid provisions of the EU Treaty do not appear to preclude permanent legislation that wipes out pre-existing shareholders of insolvent banks, re-establishes the solvency of the bank by debt or debt service reduction, or authorises the State to recapitalise the newly solvent bank. According to the private investor principle, the State may subscribe to share issues on the same basis as any investor.

In conclusion, efficiency, expedition and economy speak for taking insolvent banks out of the supervision of courts and vesting the decision-making by which the process functions in the administrative authorities under a public law *lex specialis*. Appropriate procedures for the seizure, reorganisation or liquidation of insolvent banks could be put in place.

10 Exit Policy Co-ordination at EU Level

Those national legal systems that served as points of reference for the design of our proposed new scheme for orderly exit are sufficiently incompatible in case administration to make it difficult to contemplate the adoption of any single set of international rules and standards on exit policies in the near future. The need for a prior reform of national law to remedy the observed lack of convergence of national legislation accounts for the current lack of agreement between countries on reallocation of authority or jurisdiction over cross-border banks and financial conglomerates. However, even without resolving the fundamental issues it should be possible to get agreement on three problems of allocation of home and host country authority and jurisdiction. These are inadequate information, conflicts of interest, and lack of power for the authorities to do what is required of them under the Basel code, given the current division of responsibilities between home and host countries. There is a compelling case for a modest interim regime, as any ideal agreement on a full range of issues will take years to negotiate and implement. If no such progress is made, efforts to deal with cross-border bank insolvencies in an orderly manner will be thwarted.

10.1 THE PROBLEM OF HOME COUNTRY CONTROL REVISITED

Banks with branches abroad (hereinafter 'cross-border banks')[1] are, by definition, subject to the concurrent authority and jurisdiction of two or more countries where the head office and branches are located. Generally, exit policies of both home and host countries apply, but the exercise of authority and jurisdiction may be qualified by understandings reached between countries. These typically cover effective consolidated supervision, including the assignment of the responsibility to the home country supervisor in determining whether the cross-border bank meets its minimum capital requirement. It may also be the responsibility in the host country to be satisfied that banks that enter its market are supervised by home country authorities that perform consolidated supervision consistent with certain minimum standards for the supervision of cross-border banks.

Understandings between countries appropriately include detailed arrangements for collaboration between supervisors (exchanges of information, prior notices of bank closure, timing and extent of closures, designation of channels of communication, and so forth), as well as understandings on a long list of

233

desirable legal reforms (e.g., even permitting courts to appoint foreign liquidators). Additionally, in the EEA countries, the Second Banking Directive provides for the exclusive licensing by home countries of branches in other EEA countries and the Deposit Guaranty Directive extends the home country's deposit protection scheme to branches in host countries worldwide. However, no international agreement has been reached multilaterally or between the EEA countries on making the home country's authority and jurisdiction exclusive for exit policies, nor on conferring exclusive powers on the home country regarding takeovers, reorganisations and liquidations.

More generally, in their very nature as legal entities under common control and ownership, banks and bank holding companies with bank subsidiaries abroad, and banks that are owned by nonbanks with bank affiliates abroad ('cross-border groupings'), are at least for some purposes subject to the above problem of concurrent authority and jurisdiction. In other words, in the event of default or failure (nonpayment) by a debtor bank, whether a true cross-border bank or member of a cross-border grouping, its depositors and creditors may pursue their claims worldwide. In principle, national law can confer no immunity on a debtor bank from legal process in respect of its property and assets wherever located and by whomsoever held outside the home country.

Local bankruptcy and other general insolvency laws that might restrict the institution of civil actions and lodging insolvency petitions against a local bank in the competent local court do not protect (locally unauthorised) foreign banks, wherever they do not have an authorised local bank branch or agency. Typically, local laws restrict the institution by private parties of insolvency proceedings against a locally authorised bank, and the institution of any debt collection actions against that bank, as a result of an automatic stay from the moment of the opening of insolvency proceedings. But such restrictions and limitations do not prevent the filing by creditors of actions and petitions abroad against its property and assets.

The core of the problem we address here is that a host country with substantial responsibility for the activities and establishment of a foreign bank faces potential difficulties from three sources:

1. inadequate information;
2. conflicts of interest;
3. lack of power.

The problem may not be completely asymmetric. A home country will also suffer from a lack of information about the detail of what is going on in the various foreign markets and will have to 'freeride' substantially on second-hand information from host countries. In order to interpret this foreign information and reduce the information to a manageable size a lot of processing and analysis is required in the home country, and it is difficult to ensure when doing this that the interests of all possible users are borne in mind. These will include the interests of the headquarters of the foreign banks themselves, which must have detailed information about all of their operations and transactions abroad, including access to reports on their foreign establishments, to ensure that they are well managed.

More generally, the number of markets, and the range of businesses to be covered by regulators and supervisors (and by deposit insurers that are not regulators or supervisors in EEA countries) may be very large. While they could all be well informed about some situations, it will require a complex organisation to be well informed about developments in a number of markets and range of businesses on a continuous basis. Where two or more countries are involved, it is not clear that the kind or degree of the problem for the various parties will be identical or common. Cross-border activities and establishment are not likely to be geographically balanced so the respective supervisors would not be facing exactly the same problems.

It is the home supervisor who normally has the more comprehensive view, and can tackle the cross-border bank or grouping as a whole, having the first call over whether the organisation should be broken up. Only subsequently would the host supervisor be able to consider resolutions that involved activities and establishments under its authority and within its jurisdiction. The perceived or revealed lack of power on the side of a host country easily explains its lack of access to information and conflicts of interest, and it is here where the main lack of symmetry typically lies. In reality it may be neither host nor home country that has the bargaining power in casu to do what is required of it in the event of difficulty.

Although the division of authority and allocation of jurisdiction on paper favours the home country in bank insolvency, distributional outcomes may be largely attributable to circumstances beyond its control. For example, the relative economic size and political weight of the countries involved plays a role, so that the authorities in smaller countries may not be able to operate at equal advantage, whether they are the home or the host, even when they are subject to the more serious problems. The larger the host country in economic terms, the less likely that individual foreign players dominate at all. Thus, countries in groupings such as the EEA, which comprises many countries of good size, may have common concerns vis-à-vis sizeable third countries. Even in such a grouping smaller countries may have common perceived and revealed international concerns, take the Nordic countries for example.

Here again the two polar regimes for the enforcement of insolvency law in respect of banks suggest respective strengths and weaknesses in the cross-border dimension of the problem of achieving exit for insolvent banks. The United States authorises the deposit insurer (the FDIC) to take over and resolve insured institutions in the event of threats of insolvency, or upon declarations of insolvency by the Comptroller of Currency, and to extend open bank assistance in other cases (under statutory least cost criteria).

In contrast to the United States, under the kind of system that prevails today in the EEA, countries have delegated or distributed exit policy powers among the administrative authorities (for authorisation of banks, the supervision of solvent banks, and for the lodging of petitions to the competent court for the opening of judicial insolvency proceedings) and the judicial authorities (for supervision of the reorganisation or liquidation of insolvent banks). Countries have not assigned any exit policy functions to independent deposit insurers, whose role is confined to financing the losses of insured depositors, say, upon the finding of default or failure. Deposit insurers in EEA countries are called upon to dispense cash in the event of default or failure on the part of depository institutions wherever the branches are located.

The home country's exposure involves deposit insurance payouts arising from foreign branches' deposit liabilities payable abroad under the Deposit Guarantee Directive,[2] whereas the Federal banking laws in the United States explicitly remove the US$100 000 per depositor coverage in respect of deposits that are payable outside the United States. In contrast, if the branch of a bank that carries the single EEA banking licence, suspends payments abroad, it is the responsibility of the home country's deposit insurance system to protect the depositors. The logic effectively is to shift the risk of insolvency to the home country as the locus of the regulation and supervision of the bank as a whole. Hence the home supervisor has an incentive to contain bank insolvency wherever it might occur in its banks. (Foreign banks' subsidiaries are part of the host country deposit insurance scheme under both the two polar systems for bank regulation and supervision.)

However, our main concern with lack of power in this chapter applies equally to all regulators and supervisors in EEA countries. They do not have the power to intervene in a resolute manner in the event of cross-border financial problems or to undertake drastic actions to prevent distress becoming a major or system-wide crisis. In the sections that follow, therefore, we deal first with the problem of information and then with conflict of interest and lack of power in the context of host country control over local activities, offices and branches of foreign banks, before suggesting how this institutional problem might be resolved at the EEA level. However, the largest part of the chapter concerns how to resolve the problem of lack of power for EEA authorities more generally relevant to the problem of cross-border banks' activities.

10.2   INFORMATION

The problem of information is relatively straightforward. The host supervisor will not be the primary recipient of information furnished to the home country, including that by third parties from or about the host country. There is some danger that the efficient flow of information from home to host authorities may be impeded when the continuation of the business of a foreign institution operating in host territory is threatened. The home authority may be reluctant to reveal unfolding problems, because it might fear that widespread knowledge risks adverse market reactions that could actually take the problem bank under.[3] In the same way the home supervisor will only receive information about problems in the host market second-hand.

The home supervisor is the obvious source of information and analytical expertise on the institution as a whole, while the host supervisor is the obvious source on financial market participants under its authority or within its jurisdiction. The problem is to be able to put together these information flows in an efficient manner. Currently centralisation of information is attempted at three levels.

First of all there is a trend among supervisors to publish Financial Stability Reviews or similarly titled documents that summarise the state of the banking system in their countries and address various systemic risks. On the whole the information contained in them is relatively limited and relates to aggregates and not to individual banks. The Bank of England's Financial Stability Review is a substantial journal with over 200 pages, half of them devoted to high-quality specialist articles. Only five percent of that is devoted to the UK financial sector directly. Although the extensive assessment of risks round the world is a very useful source of information for readers who want a summary picture. The Swedish Riksbank's Review goes rather further into explicit detail, while the Reserve Bank of New Zealand publishes a comparative table of information that is available publicly. As Chapter 7 sets out, this last set of information is considerably more detailed than in other countries as a result of the disclosure regime.

Secondly, there are several fora for exchanging information in Europe. The Group de Contact (among supervisors) is probably the most relevant as this involves the exchange of information on individual institutions and other matters at a practical level. The Banking Supervision Committee of the ECB is explicitly gathering what it describes as 'macro-prudential' information from its constituent national central banks. This involves aggregated information on risk concentration, competitive conditions, profitability, capital adequacy, financial fragility, asset prices macroeconomic indicators. Lastly the Banking Advisory Committee for the European Commission provides the main body for putting together advice on regulatory matters.

However, the most direct relationship between supervisors comes through the operation of 'Memoranda of Understanding' that have been signed bilaterally between the member states to exchange relevant information on individual institutions and markets and to meet periodically. These do not necessarily have a common format and reflect the extent of the financial interaction between the economies. Opinions vary as to how well these arrangements work and their usefulness clearly depends both on the exact nature of the agreement and the extent of the goodwill between the partners. Outside observers have, however, tended to be sceptical about how well such informal arrangements might work and have tended to press for explicit pan-EEA arrangements (Lannoo, 1999b, for example, advocates a 'European Board of Financial Supervisors').

Three main routes have been suggested. One is simply to have a monitoring organisation that collects information from the national supervisors and puts it together in a comparable and comprehensive manner. Aglietta and de Boisseau (1998), for example, suggest the creation of a European Observatory of Systemic Risk. This would then form a bridge between the sort of information collected by the ECB Banking Supervision Committee and the specific institutional data that supervisors are seeking. Such a body could oversee whether the bilateral exchanges of information were functioning properly.

An obvious alternative would be simply to expand the role of the ECB. This is permitted under the terms of the treaty. However, there is little pressure in this direction at present and resistance from the ECB for doing so. In any case since most banking supervisors in the EEA are not central banks, such an agreement might be difficult to achieve.

The third suggestion is to create a new European level organisation that would co-ordinate supervision. It could, in particular, take on the task of putting together data about the more important cross-border banks and groupings. Simply elevating banking supervision to being an EU level competence does not seem a likely way forward. Not only would it be debatable in the context of the subsidiarity principle but it would run the danger of creating such a bureaucracy that could not function efficiently. The new Financial Services Authority in the United Kingdom is finding it difficult to put its various different regulators into a single framework – and this relates just to one member state. The 'cultural' gaps at the European level are likely to be even greater, making aggregation and comparison difficult. Indeed simple convergence of supervisory practices seems some way off; although that is an activity that the existing EU banking advisory committee could try to pull together.

We are rather apprehensive about developing yet another administrative level. A balance has to be found between the benefit to those involved and the cost of regulation. The pendulum has swung a long way towards greater regulation in almost all member states and extending it still further would add very clearly to the costs. Lannoo (1999b) suggests that there might be some helpful regulatory competition between the national and the EU authorities. Currently there is already regulatory competition within the EEA, namely competition among rules. Also substantial changes in cross-border ownership of the banking industry may be taking place at present, and the new entities may shop among regimes, as was mooted for the Merita–Nordbanken (Finnish–Swedish) merger.

While corporate tax was an important issue in deciding location of the joint activity, the nature of the supervisory regime could also have been a concern. However, the idea that banks might regime shop is only part of the way in which the system can operate. Customers can also decide which regulator they prefer by appropriate choice of bank with which to do business. However, with limited exceptions it is currently only the larger corporate customers who have this sort of freedom, although this could change as internet and telephone banking develop. The need to have anything much in the way of a local branch may disappear for many customers, provided they can get access to cash and payment services. Llewellyn (1999) takes this even further by suggesting that different supervisory regimes could exist even within member states. Customers could then choose between banks subject to different levels of supervision. Since supervision has costs, presumably these would be passed on to the customer and hence they would pay for what they perceive as greater security.

Taken together then this might appear to suggest that a monitoring and co-ordinating agency might be the appropriate way forward as an increased role for the ECB seems unlikely and creating a supranational supervisor might be rather burdensome. However, we suggest that a major part of the problem lies simply with the fact that the information that is required by supervisors is confidential and 'private' to the original authority to which it was supplied. The more such information is shared among other parties the greater the chance of the confidence being breached. Authorities become increasingly reluctant to pass the raw information in such detail that it would disclose affairs of individuals or corporations, on the largely unfounded fear of being held liable by courts on actions for economic damage. They, therefore, aggregate data. If the information were public in the first place and disclosed by the banks within whatever jurisdictions they were covered, then much of the problem of lack of information would be substantially diminished. There would certainly be no question of one authority keeping information from another or failing to pass on information that it wrongly thought was unimportant.

We have already set out in Chapter 7 what the information to be disclosed might be. It would certainly meet the macroprudential concerns of the ECB and since the bank by bank data would also be known it would go a long way towards filling in the gaps in host supervisors' knowledge. However, it would not be complete. Supervisors will still be having detailed discussions with individual banks and, where they have concerns, will be asking for further information. This will continue to generate some private knowledge. Furthermore one would need to decide whether the authority's opinion of the bank were also made public. Indeed, in some respects, purely publishing the CAMEL rating that the Fed has applied to the banks it supervises might be more informative than the detailed disclosure we propose. Rather like a rating agency, part of the information value lies in the opinion of the experts making the judgment.

This of course provides a difficulty for regulators, as their opinions as such are taken to be facts that, if revealed, will have commercial implications for the banks they judge. Banks are keen to publicise high credit ratings and in the same way would be keen to benefit from high assessments by supervisors. This therefore would increase the incentives for banks to run themselves in a very prudent manner. However, it would also open up the regulators to complaints from individual banks that they had been incorrectly classified or indeed that the system as a whole was biased against some sorts of financial institutions. If regulators have any grounds for complaint or concern, however, then they ought to voice them. Initially perhaps this should be to the bank itself, to see if there is a satisfactory explanation and then publicly, so that all those involved are properly informed. Any breach of the rules will have to be disclosed by the banks in any case, as will their subsequent actions and intentions in the light of it. Supervisors will want to satisfy themselves that such breaches are being dealt with appropriately, in addition to levying any fines that may be required.

In any event disclosure would reduce the problems of lack of information and would make the task of co-ordination between supervisors rather easier and less burdensome, whether it takes the form of more effective bilateral exchanges or an EEA level body.

When disclosure requirements are efficient and cover emerging problems, host authorities' concern about the adequacy of information is reduced. Moreover, with timely disclosure of problems it is more difficult for a supervisor in the home country to exercise forbearance. It is then less likely for forbearance to be a source of conflict between home and host countries or for resolution to be delayed to the point that assets are fully depleted. We therefore move on to discuss these potential conflicts directly as they also affect the ways in which the various authorities might beneficially co-operate.

10.3   CONFLICTS OF INTEREST

More than anything, in recent banking history, the BCCI saga demonstrated the need for more appropriate formulation and implementation of national exit policies in the future. Arguably, some better co-ordination of prior supervisory activities between the countries might have prevented the licensing of some 380 BCCI offices worldwide, with the respective authorisations having come from some 70 countries, before the Bank of England discovered it to be a criminal enterprise in June 1991.

Case administration in respect of the BCCI in the United States was successfully finished off by the liquidation of BCCI-related assets in July 1991, a good decade earlier than in EEA countries (where legal cases are still pending).[4]

In EEA countries, case administration was vested in the competent judicial authorities who were – despite some internationalist remarks – bound to execute *national* bankruptcy and general insolvency laws, and are doing so.[5]

No level of co-ordination among the supervisors could have helped to ease the bank's global exit. National laws in EEA countries vested jurisdiction in judicial authorities, who are more concerned with the treatment of depositors and creditors relative to each other (i.e. with problems of division of assets), than with the maximisation of the total of assets available to them all. Meanwhile, the total pie available to non-US creditors was shrinking due to multi-fora litigation, including criminal RICO proceedings against the BCCI in the United States. Clearly, the case challenged the European preferences for private systems of enforcement of bank insolvency law over more robust exit policies in the United States. The Federal Reserve Board, for example, imposed a civil money penalty (US$200 million) in connection with secret acquisition of the shares of First American Bank Shares Inc., which pro tanto reduced the pool of funds available to non-US claimants.[6]

The BCCI affair brought to the surface underlying conflicts of interest as events unfolded. No global rules or standards of the kind that would have secured a more even-handed result existed then, nor have they been created since. Nothing required the countries involved to settle their conflicts of interest to their mutual satisfaction. It is hard to say whether the national decision-making by which the process of allocation of remaining assets functioned generated any 'tit-for-tat' (that is, serious nonjustifiable differences or disputes) between the countries. Any overt conflicts of interest in sharing its assets between countries were settled simply by the course of events. All this remains subject to a possible political review to be carried out by the then leaders' successors, with the benefit of hindsight, culminating probably in discussions in the appropriate international fora.

In the field of banking, interactions between countries may give rise both to

(i) legal concerns regarding the allocation of jurisdiction between home and host countries over a cross-border bank or grouping, and its property and assets; and to

(ii) economic concerns regarding the allocation of assets between them.

One way or another, one country's exit policies, based on its national interests as expressed in policies, laws, and regulations, may not respect the policy objectives of the other. (Analogously, of course, regulators and supervisors, acting within the confines of their own country, can pursue their own government's objectives only within the typically very narrow margins established by law.) Outside the prescribed parameters for discretionary action, regulators and supervisors are bound by a body of law (the public law of banking and general laws), which serves as a comprehensive expression of national interest. Hence, in the performance of its functions, the home country supervisor will be focused on the economic consequences in the home country not on the host country involved, whose concerns will appear to be of secondary or no importance at all. Laws seldom provide otherwise.

More generally, since the size of the EU countries varies substantially, this in itself can lead to a conflict of interest. It would not be difficult to envisage circumstances where the systemic impact in the home (large) country is much smaller than the systemic impact in the host (small) country, even though the primary operation of the bank concerned was in the home country. For example, a home country's GDP might well be, say, 20 times larger than the host country's GDP. Even if 80 per cent of the foreign bank's operations were in the home country and 20 per cent in the host country and the problem was evenly spread, the consequences would be five times as important for the host country as they were for the home country. That order of magnitude of difference is quite sufficient for the home country to be willing to allow a failure while the host would prefer to see a resolution in order to limit the systemic consequences.[7] The BCCI was the reverse of this case in that the home country was small,[8] and many of the 70 other countries were very large, including the United States and the United Kingdom.

The first call if a bank is in difficulty will be on its owners (head office, even subsidiaries and affiliates, and on its shareholders). Failing that, the presumption is that the responsibility would be on the home country as lender of last resort (Schoenmaker, 1995). It is assumed here that this would be collateralised lending, as the bank is not actually insolvent. However, much of the problem occurs because drawing the line between illiquidity and insolvency is a matter of difficult valuation of assets and liabilities, and illiquidity (e.g. failure to settle at the end of the day at the central bank) is often a sign not of transitional liquidity problems but of deeper solvency problems. In any case making this distinction requires a lot of information (a valuation) and the time available to the authorities for making a decision may preclude reaching any accurate judgement on valuation. A country facing a greater systemic risk or deposit insurance risk may take a different view from that of other administrations involved.[9] The position is complicated if the government is the owner or the part owner of the bank and its guarantee of reserves is implicit rather than explicit.[10]

Clearly a host country will have some reluctance in lending to the local branch of a foreign-based bank in difficulty, because it would be unsure whether the proceeds would accrue to the benefit of those at risk in its own jurisdiction. If it is accurate in assessing the extent of the problem it might conclude that it was in fact making advances for the benefit of foreign shareholders and hence that it was doing the job of the home country as investor of last resort. As funds are fungible, the host country cannot readily limit its support to its own jurisdiction unless it petitions the competent court to open reorganisation or liquidation proceedings in respect of the local branch, divesting the foreign bank of property and assets attributable to the branch for the benefit of local depositors and other creditors of that branch.

The problem for the host under home country control bites most strongly when foreign establishment has taken the form of branches or cross-border supply. Foreign banks operating through subsidiaries have separate prudential buffers in the host state, and it is quite possible for a subsidiary to continue to keep open and operating although the parent (100 per cent shareholder) fails. This was the case in the Swedish Gota-bank failure in the early 1990s. However this is taking us into the next topic of a lack of power on the part of host supervisors that we will return to in a moment. At this stage we consider what the implications are for EEA co-ordination.

In the case of information deficiencies, we argued that the problems caused by home country control could be reduced substantially by public disclosure of much of the relevant information. We concluded that the remaining deficiencies could be addressed either by improved operation of memoranda of understanding or by some light EEA level co-ordinating body. When it comes to a conflict of interest, however, it is much less likely that bilateral give-and-take mechanisms will work. It is the home regulator that is the lead regulator and while they would no doubt take other's concerns into account, they can be expected to put their own concerns first. In the case of crises there will be little opportunity for consultation, let alone for any give and take by negotiation among supervisors.

As the law stands, national regulators and supervisors can either bailout an insolvent bank or surrender control over it to the judicial authorities. Without appropriate treaty provisions it would not be possible to adjudicate any international concerns before any impartial and independent hierarchically superior instance. However, nothing prevents a country from appointing an expert third party (hereinafter referred to as the 'body'), to represent its interests vis-à-vis others, to be available right from the outset as a designated co-ordinator of exit policies regarding a cross-border bank or grouping. It would be able to soften the impact of negative or positive conflicts of national interest. Ideally, an impartial and independent administrative agency would have financial autonomy and other attributes of a legal entity, albeit no power to borrow in order to assist in deals.

By extension, the body could perform some of the information gathering and technical functions of an organisation that might have come into being for the implementation of a multilateral treaty or had there been agreement, say, on the various proposed EU winding up and reorganisation directives. These would have facilitated the mutual recognition of home country jurisdiction in respect of reorganisation measures taken by home countries over cross-border banks, as well as in respect of the opening by home countries of bank liquidation proceedings.

The body would have no law to apply other than what would apply in its absence. There is no new law to apply regarding the mutual recognition of winding-up proceedings and reorganisation measures, or regarding the mutual recognition and enforcement of the results of such proceedings, such as nationally confirmed reorganisation and liquidation plans. However, the fact that there is no law to apply does not prevent collaboration on the settlement of resulting differences between countries through other means, as and when countries assert authority and jurisdiction over cross-border banks or groupings in a conflicting, contradictory or otherwise mutually inconsistent manner. Here it would suffice if the body made its best efforts to settle differences arising out of such situations, including cases where the home or host regulator or supervisor refrains from appropriate action. It would also facilitate any collateral processes of collaboration and consultation between countries involved in bank insovency.

By furnishing information, expertise, and other technical services (e.g. the monitoring of particular markets of situations), or the administration of financial services (by opening and maintaining accounts, holding resources under pooling arrangements), the body would have a useful role to play. Financial and technical services could include the audit, settlement of accounts and disbursement of funds including settlements with depositors and other creditors subject to review by national courts or tribunals where desired. At a country's request, it could manage the liquidation of assets and liabilities of such banks or groupings. National banking laws would have to be reviewed to see whether such a body could be appointed by competent courts in countries to perform these functions.

Acting in a representative capacity on the account of those requesting services, the body's authority would be the agreement and general law, national and international. It would arrive at decisions by instruction of the authorities of the countries that appointed it. However, in adversarial cases in which two or more countries sought the body's services in case administration, it would have to investigate and act on its own account. In effect it would avoid conflicts of interest by internalising them.[11] Indeed, this power to investigate and report would hedge against situations where the differences between countries are of the order that precludes the joint appointment of the body to perform services for both. Its acceptance of the request of one country, might well create sufficient incentives for the adverse party to seek a solution to the mutual satisfaction of both.[12] All this would of course be achieved immediately if all cross-border banks and groupings were either supervised by a robust common institution situated at the EEA level or had their national supervision co-ordinated by an EEA-level body.

Situations where overt conflicts of interest surfaced and were taken up by either party for settlement by the designated body, should hopefully be relatively rare. Hence, there would not be a need for setting up a specialised agency to function as a permanent fully-staffed institution. So no elaborate organisation would be required to have an EEA level presence. Indeed, members of its staff could normally be employed in other productive activities, as is the case with liquidators and statutory managers that rise to the occasion only by appointment on a case-by-case basis by the competent court. Thus, the panel of available staff could well include experts from central banks, independent insolvency practitioners or officials of the European institutions according to the case.

Since the approach in the absence of a winding up or reorganisation directive of the kind that has been under discussion so long, would be administrative rather than legislative or judicial, this would imply that there would be no directive to apply and that therefore the European Court of Justice would not be directly involved. If the role of the ECB in this regard were to be enhanced, then it could be for the ECB to appoint the body to serve as an independent and impartial body charged with the monitoring of cross-border bank or grouping insolvencies in order to establish this size of the problem for each country, and to provide other technical and financial services. Involving the ECB in this instance might make rather more sense than in issues of information or more general supervision as the conflict of interest occurs when one party thinks there is a systemic problem and the other does not. Since the ECB has responsibility for overall stability in the euro area it will also want to form a judgement about whether a problem has systemic implications and where. Clearly it would be concerned if a national authority did not act when the consequences of such forbearance might destabilise the system. Nevertheless since there is the prospect of the use of taxpayer funds, the ECB may not prove to be the vehicle chosen by the national governments.

A further issue that we have thus far avoided is the question of whether the actions taken by the national authorities need in any sense to be co-ordinated. Thus far the position is somewhat unclear, which makes it difficult to arrive at a comprehensive list of potential conflicts of interests arising under redistributive schemes. For some such conflicts there is already a mechanism for the settlement of differences by an institutional decision at EEA level. Where governments or other public authorities of a country 'subsidise' banks by making public equity available when private sources judge that the returns are too low/risks too high, competitor banks whether from the same or other member states will be disadvantaged, particularly if the costs are recouped from elsewhere in the system, as is the case with some deposit guarantee schemes. In dealing with the rescue package for Credit Lyonnais in 1995 the European Commission (OJ L 308, 21.12.95) applied straight treaty rules on state aids. In effect it is only systemic concerns that provide an acceptable line of argument in support of states serving as investors of last resort.

Clearly, the above arguments arise if the public authorities in any country intervene in this way. It has particular importance in the EEA case simply because of
the Treaty's rules of competition apply to them. In Credit Lyonnais and other
cases, the European Commission acted as an external arbiter to determine
whether the national authorities had made a valid case on systemic grounds for
state aid. Or whether, in practice, they were providing assistance for other reasons
to a particular bank, when other banks could have taken over the business without
undue delay. The Commission's competence is, however, limited to this issue of
competition. Were there to be disagreement of view between the Commission and
the ECB, and the above body, regarding the terms and conditions of approval
(which have become elaborate schemes of bank regulation as such), it would be
appropriate for the view to be expressed. At present it is not clear how any such
disagreement would be resolved if the Commission asserted its prerogatives in a
sweeping manner. However, as Lannoo (1999a) points out there is a far greater
co-ordination problem stemming from the lack of similarity in the rules for
takeovers and mergers among the EEA countries. These in themselves could lead
to different requirements for the public sector to intervene in the first place.

10.4   LACK OF POWER

In addition to the general limitations on the power of action by the authorities
within the EEA, a host authority has limited powers to deal with the local
branches of a foreign problem bank, and with the branch's assets, and the assets
of the bank as a whole. This is not so much a concern that foreigners will be
unfairly treated, but ideally, that there should not be significant worries that the
'good' assets of the failing bank would not be used equally in favour of the uninsured depositors and other creditors in different countries.[13] However, this condition can only be met if all creditors of the bank can prove their claims in a single
liquidation proceeding subject to the laws of a single jurisdiction (for example,
where the home country liquidates the bank, including its foreign branches, as a
single entity in a single proceeding subject to its own laws).[14]

There has been, however, little success in resolving the formal and substantive
inconsistencies between various kinds of separate and single-entity approaches
to the exit, reorganisation and resolution of branches of foreign banks. Indeed,
most EEA countries (it would appear with the notable exception of France) seem
to follow on paper a single entity approach to liquidating, both as host country
for the local branches of a foreign bank, and as home country for their own
banks and their foreign branches.

In New Zealand a branch of a foreign bank (and a formerly licensed institution that was a branch) is subject to the Reserve Bank Act. If a difference in
interest arose between New Zealand, as host country of the branch and another

country as home country, it would be possible for the Reserve Bank to appoint a statutory manager, with wider powers than a liquidator, who could not merely take over the running of the New Zealand branch of the bank in difficulty but also create a new locally incorporated entity to take over the assets. It would then be possible to recapitalise the New Zealand branch and continue trading, if that were the outcome thought appropriate for systemic stability and the protection of the New Zealand taxpayer. In seeking its own solution, the home country would not be keen to choose a form of resolution that was more advantageous to its taxpayers and indeed creditors and insured depositors than was the case for taxpayers, creditors and insured depositors in the host country (New Zealand) as New Zealand would then not commit any funds.

If a difference arose between a host-country of a branch of the foreign bank, and another country as home-country of that branch, in a non-EEA country where a branch is subject to takeover, reorganisation and liquidation by administrative authorities, it would be possible for the government to succeed to the branch's assets and to a good portion of its liabilities. This appears to be the case in the United States, where Federal or insured branches of foreign banks are exempt from the operation of the US Bankruptcy Code, and subject to section 11 of the FDI Act. Acting for its own account as successor to the bank, to its owners' interests and creditors' rights in respect of the bank and its assets, the government would not merely take over the running of the insolvent branch of the bank in difficulty, but possibly could also create a new locally incorporated entity to take over the assets attributable to the branch, and to assume that portion of the branch's liabilities which is not under water.

If a difference arose between an EEA country where the bank did not have a branch or other establishment but where a portion of its assets and liabilities were located and the EEA home or host country, it would appear to be possible for the competent court in that third country to reorganise or liquidate the local assets under general insolvency laws. In such a situation, creditors might agree by the prescribed majority, to a reorganisation plan that prescribed the transformation of the estate into a locally incorporated entity as successor to the assets and to those of the liabilities that are not under water. The competent court may well proceed with the reorganisation or the liquidation of the assets of the foreign bank without recognising it as a bank in the first place.[15]

Where bankruptcy and general insolvency laws provide for the opening of insolvency proceedings in respect of a local branch of a foreign bank and do not restrict the ability of individual depositors and other creditors to petition the competent court to open insolvency proceedings, the authority and jurisdiction over the branch shifts to the competent court and regulators and supervisors cannot help it.

All in all, where the EEA countries seem to differ in their single entity approaches is whether their courts would liquidate as host-country the assets of the foreign branch together with the local assets of the foreign bank not attributable to the branch. Moreover, since individual depositors and other creditors of a foreign bank may lodge individual petitions, where their ability to proceed is not restricted by general bankruptcy or insolvency laws, they may of course proceed even though the home-country may have already opened insolvency proceedings with respect to the foreign bank, including against its foreign assets in a host country where the supervisors take the single-entity approach. Obviously, efficient co-ordination and co-operation are difficult to achieve here in these two situations if interests differ. The problem is then one of over-reaching powers, on one side, and lack of power, on the other.

Nevertheless, we can see that those EEA countries where the judicial authorities have a power to open insolvency proceedings in respect of a local branch of a foreign bank debtor, retain the power to reorganise or liquidate branches in default or failure. But the problem may be even greater when the difficulty falls short of legal insolvency. However, it would clearly challenge the principle of home country control if the host country could over-ride its wishes in these circumstances. For example, a statutory manager can be appointed in New Zealand while a bank is still solvent but undercapitalised. While such a manager clearly should not follow a course for owners that would be worse than they could expect under liquidation (or withdrawal of the banking licence for failure to meet the minimum prudential standards laid down), as they could successfully sue, the options available to the manager might be more advantageous for the rest of the stakeholders in the bank, including the taxpayer.

The EEA therefore faces a clear problem of allocation of authority over exit, reorganisation and liquidation of cross-border banks and groupings. The ambiguity does not only pertain to the question of who can move first, the home or host country, but also extends to the question of setting financial benchmarks as triggers for action.

Here we have identified an institutional constraint on the effective treatment of difficulties – namely, that remedies and sanctions (warnings, civil penalties, measures of provisional administration, restrictions on specified activities) should come into play at the first stages of a problem. Regulatory and supervisory actions should become progressively more severe as and when subject banks fail to respond adequately to such conduct-related remedies. Then the authorities would move rapidly to the point where they take them over for restructuring or liquidation.

If the rules of such a progressive system of first conduct-related and then structural actions are known in advance, this not only enables the authorities to act early while the problem is manageable and banks respond to it as they have an incentive to take corrective action, but it discourages banks from allowing the crisis to get worse in the hope that a little more time will allow the situation to right itself later. Beyond a certain point, banks are indifferent to financial penalties, and in these circumstances might only worsen the problem by lowering capital still further. As pointed out in Mayes (1997), the announcement of a series of actions of an ascending order of severity to be taken as a bank's problem does not correct itself, means that the authorities have tied their own hands and cannot exercise forbearance in the event and thereby allow the potential for a crisis to increase.

In the main the literature focuses on only part of the substance of the matter, which is the progressivity of remedies and sanctions imposed on the subject banks as their capital ratios fall below the required levels. However, the point can apply generally both to excessive exposures to risk and to inadequate risk management systems subject to appropriately formulated benchmarks. In any solutions to the implementation of the scheme, time is likely to be of the essence in a crisis. Thus, any prescribed financial benchmarks are likely to work only if specified in terms of precise or objective elements that are stated or defined in such a way that departure from them will be obvious to the subject bank and the authorities.

The prescribed legal consequences arising from the non-observance of the prescribed financial benchmarks relating to regulatory capital and economic solvency requirements would attach quasi-automatically, without the need for the exercise of judgement. In the meantime, each subject bank would have maximum assurance that it would not be taken by surprise. Thus, while there may be time for a few phone calls and rapid consultations, decisions must be taken on the spot in the face of the evidence available if difficulty is not to be converted into failure simply by inaction. In these cases any process that involves too complicated bureaucratic procedures and assessments will not work. As for drastic structural actions that are irreversible, such as compulsory takeovers, reorganisations and liquidations, there is a need for the exercise by government of judgement on the question whether the public interest warrants such actions or sanctions. This is only natural for the reason that, if things go badly wrong, for an erroneous hypothetical liquidation valuation of assets and liabilities of subject bank, government is bound to offer compensation to private parties divested of valuable assets.

At the national level, one solution to the co-ordination problem would be to assign the powers of conduct-related actions and remedies to one competent body, say, an administrative agency, which would have the ability to act under general banking law, reserving the power to impose structural actions in the government that would act on a delegated legislative authority for purposes that are within the public interest. At the same time, this division of responsibilities may be expected to improve co-ordination between home and host countries in a crisis. There is not really any scope for sub-delegation by government to any EEA level body of the legislative powers of takeover and restructuring of insolvent banks, which can be carried out only on the account of government. Also any possible use of public funds for bailouts would remain the responsibility of the Member States. Here, a European level body could not drive the system, but only serve as an executing agency.

Also the potential conflict of interests of home and host countries would support pushing the co-ordination responsibility, but only for conduct-related actions and remedies, 'upwards' to a EEA-level body, which would need to lay down the procedures it will follow in advance so that it is predictable. However, the 'hands-on' information on individual banks' liquidity and solvency must rest at the national level. Thus, the requirement of adequate and timely information would not be easily met. Such a body could assist in the implementation of structural actions as has been proposed above. For example, at the request of two or more governments the body could perform technical functions. It could serve as reorganiser or liquidator or help pool the assets of insolvent cross-border banks or groupings.

The very size of the home/host country problem, as banks increase their size and extend across borders, may become difficult even for a home country to handle, where cross-border banks' or groupings' assets and significant private rights and interests in respect of them happen to lie outside its effective authority and jurisdiction, for example, in third countries, or in host countries, due to their reluctance to collaborate in exit policies. Since the introduction of the euro makes a single banking market in Europe a more real prospect, cross-border banks and groupings are likely to be encouraged. As it is, the largest European banks are already large compared to the GDP of the smallest member states. As they increase in size still further the problem is exacerbated. This is a much more difficult requirement for co-ordination than those we have discussed thus far, where action does not require the use of public funds or at least only central bank funds, where the expectation is that they are adequately collateralised.

Bailing banks out because the costs are less than those expected from facing the systemic risks is very much a last resort, especially because the EC Commission has not developed criteria conditioning its approval of state aid on stipulated cost criteria. It might consider requiring that the proposed beneficiary of State aid be subject to an asset, debt (reorganisation haircut), and equity restructuring, or to outright termination through a liquidation of its assets and liabilities. In some cases, limiting the use of State aid to softening the 'systemic impact' of default or failure on other institutions, may make more sense than approving State aid for continuing a subject bank in legal personality and entity.

Even in respect of banks and groupings which have no cross-border dimension, and belong to the domestic jurisdiction of a single country, the exercise of choice between appropriate courses of action usually involves patching together an *ad hoc* discussion between the central bank, the supervisory authorities and the ministry of finance, including relevant ministers. While those involved 'know the telephone numbers to call' and may have agreed procedures and general rules of action, even a limited crisis is expected to be a very complex and unusual event, and one where a lot of the thinking will have be done on the spot. In some Nordic countries they actually conduct simulations with the parties involved to see how they react in hypothetical crises. In those and some other countries they have had painful practical experience.

However, any preparations and simulations for cross-border financial accidents are less common. This tends to be something reserved for natural disasters, and civil defence, and military or security issues. Technical systems that run across borders, such as payments and clearing systems, do of course go through regular disaster testing, at the design phase, through construction, and while in operation as the bugs are being worked out. In so far as problems are uncovered, the authorities are not likely to be particularly forthcoming about what has to be done. This might cause a loss of confidence that would be costly to rebuild. It might also be a source of embarrassment to the authorities who were responsible for agreeing the design or its implementation. They will naturally offer assurances to participating institutions that 'all that needs to be done was done'. Discussion of such issues falls into the area of proverbial counterproductive actions such as a pilot's announcement to the passengers 'There is no cause for alarm but ...':

- In conclusion, exit policy powers of the administrative authorities (regulators and supervisors) to resolve critically undercapitalised and economically insolvent banks need to be enhanced in the manner developed in Chapters 8 and 9. At the national level, therefore, countries needs to have a permanent, institutional means of taking over, reorganising and liquidating cross-border banks (head offices and their branches abroad), and cross-border groupings (bank holding companies, bank subsidiaries, and affiliates).

Where the exit policies of home and host countries of geographically dispersed banks and branches may deadlock, including in the carrying out of appropriate financial policies as deposit insurers and lenders of last resort, the specific conclusions are as follows:

- The exit policies of home country and host country may conflict, either negatively in the sense that one of them refrains from regulatory or supervisory responsibilities, or positively in the sense that two or several countries deadlock in asserting authority or jurisdiction pertaining to the same decision. For this reason, as there is no law to apply for time being, it would be appropriate to create an EEA level body to assist in voluntary collaboration between countries in forestalling and containing cross-border bank insolvencies involving either cross-border banks or groupings. The body could not impose obligations on governments without their consent.

- Individual home and host countries would have access, solely at their own initiative, to an expert EEA level body. Its purposes would include the promotion of voluntary collaboration between countries on the formulation and implementation of appropriate exit policies, the performance of functions of lender of last resort in a manner that does not distort the operation of financial markets, and the extension of facilities for disbursement abroad under home countries deposit insurance systems.

- In case of joint requests by two or several governments, the body, acting as an impartial and independent third party, would stand ready to perform requested technical and financial functions on its own account, according to the terms and conditions of the request and subject reimbursement by the parties of its expenses. If so requested by government, it could perform functions of an administratively or judicially appointed independent trustee, reorganiser or liquidator of a cross-border bank or grouping.

- In case of requests for representation and technical or financial services by a government alone, the body would stand ready to represent the government vis-à-vis third countries, and to perform requested technical and financial services for the account of the government, according to the terms and conditions agreed on the occasion of each request, subject to reimbursement by goverment of its expenses.

10.5   LIQUIDITY PROBLEMS AND THE LENDER OF LAST RESORT

Here we dismiss one problem attributed to the Eurosystem in particular, namely that there is a lack of ability to deal with liquidity problems. It is argued (CEPR, 1998; Lannoo, 1999b, for example) that because of its fragmented structure that the Eurosystem lacks the ability to respond to liquidity difficulties in the manner of other central banks.

The requirements for action in Europe are no different from those in other jurisdictions. If the problems are ones of short-run liquidity or confidence because of the problems of contagion then part of the smooth running of the system entails that adequate liquidity against high quality collateral will be provided. Such liquidity will either be provided for the system as a whole, such as in the anticipation of a rush into cash round the beginning of 2000, as people feared computer failures might lose them their savings or at least lose them access to funds. Or it will be provided to individual institutions with specific difficulties through the lender of last resort function performed by member central banks.

The ECB has been as reticent as other central banks in discussing the lender of last resort function.[16] It has been argued (Kaufman, 1996) that merely having an LOLR increases the risk that it will need to be drawn upon. Hence central banks tend to hedge, wanting on the one hand to give everybody confidence that the system will continue to function well in a crisis, while on the other trying to make risk-taking, that could contribute to such a crisis, seem as unattractive as possible. Where such a function is interpreted rather literally in terms of Bagehot's (1873) definition[17] the ECB has already sorted out very closely what collateral will be eligible for such lending and published the result (ECB, 1998). The list of collateral varies from country to country and reflects the different national central banks' views as to what should be acceptable (and indeed the different roles of those banks in their respective financial systems). Similarly the ECB calculates liquidity requirements for the system by aggregating across the national markets and the liquidity is reinjected through the national central banks. Thus the Eurosystem, reflecting its structure, permits a degree of flexibility in treatment, which is perhaps unusual in the context of established federal countries. In the event of difficulty the national central banks will provide the liquidity as before according to these rules. Should the difficulty run across borders then the ECB will help co-ordinate (Padoa-Schioppa, 1999). However, it is the reserves of the whole system, the ESCB, rather than the ECB alone that can be drawn on in these circumstances. So the chance of the system being unable to cope even with major problems (as Lannoo, 1999b, suggests), whether caused by the largest institutions or a wider shock, is less than in most other countries (given the strength of ESCB balance sheets).

Thus there is little in the way of loss of effective power over what can be done compared with the preceding regime. However, as a result of having the single currency, capital markets are much deeper than before and hence problems from lack of liquidity in some parts of the system – parts that used to represent entire markets when there were separate currencies – are rather less likely to occur. The system is thus if anything strengthened rather than weakened compared to its predecessors. Size of the economy in itself tends to reduce both the chance of systemic shocks and the importance of their impact by diversifying the risk.

The picture changes, however, if 'lender of last resort' is to be interpreted rather more generously as 'investor of last resort', where the solvency of the bank in question is open to doubt. Here the ECB structure does not offer the opportunity for bailouts. In the light of the foregoing discussion, we also regard this as a positive outcome, because it improves the incentives on the banks to manage risks well and avoid approaching insolvency, as the 'safety net', if it can be described as such, is weak. However, proscribing a role for the ECB in participating in bailouts leaves open two questions. On the one hand it does not provide an answer to the question of how bailouts of cross-border banks and groupings might be arranged where they are not clearly dominated by the interests of a single country. On the other it does not rule out a role for the ECB as an orchestrator of action by others.

There is a tendency to concentrate on the bailing out of individual banks when they have a problem that others do not share. Many crises occur however when macroeconomic conditions weaken or there is a generalised shock to the economy – vide Chapter 2. In this case it will be the banks at the margin that get into difficulties but all may be under some pressure. The authorities may therefore feel that they ought to bail out banks even though they are small because they are worried about the knock on effects to confidence. There are two sorts of contagion here. One is that similar banks will also tend to come under pressure. The other is that the system as a whole comes under pressure, as people have difficulty in deciding whether other banks are similar or not (Docking *et al.*, 1997). This has very difficult incentive effects because it implies that there will be a bail out if banks take the same unwise actions. A bank that avoids the mistake will not benefit from public capital and indeed may find itself contributing to the insurance of the less wary. The drawback therefore is that the market as a whole will tend to move into the latest opportunities even if the risks are not clear because missing out on an opportunity will harm their relative position while making the same mistake as the others will have relatively little downside if all are bailed out.

10.6   TAKING THE PROPOSALS TOGETHER

We have concluded that effective and efficient international co-ordination in the face of banking distress face three main problems: lack of information; conflicts of interest and a lack of power to act. We have suggested that:

Lack of information
- The regime of public disclosure by banks that we advocate for national administrations will be of considerable help. As providing that information allows both markets and regulators to make their own judgements as to possible emerging problems, without having to rely so much on private information from supervisors in other countries (although that will still be provided under the Memoranda of Understanding).
- Although there are arguments in favour of an EEA-level body that might monitor or co-ordinate monitoring activities, the case for such a complication is not likely to be agreed in present circumstances. More likely is an increasing role for 'lead regulators' and co-operation among authorities with substantial interrelation among their banks.

Conflicts of interest
- There is, however, a strong need for a new 'body' that can help resolve conflicts of interest in a hurry when cross-border banks (groupings) get into difficulty. This would need to be, at the request of a country (or countries) involved, an administrator who can investigate and act rapidly in the same way that statutory administrators can within single jurisdictions. While it would be helpful to develop agreed rules in advance, the failure to do so cannot prevent orderly collaboration (in the sense of give and take), as and when necessary, permitting the authorities to arrive at a wider range of outcomes than just bailing out.
- In general, however, we see the principle of home country control being able to cope with the large majority of problems, particularly given home country responsibility for deposit insurance.

Lack of power
- Even so the problems of lack of power for acting in a crisis that appear in national administrations in Europe apply at the multi-country level. It is therefore necessary for home countries to have in place a set of procedures for handling problems involving cross-border banks (or groupings) where they have responsibility. This will include understandings of how to concert any international injection of capital.
- As procedures are likely to be different across countries over when and how to intervene before insolvency is reached, there should be some executive body at EEA level to help countries co-ordinate their response.
- The body would facilitate the working of the cross-border dimension of the enhanced bank exit and resolution process we have described on behalf of the governments concerned.
- We do not see any particular problems for cross-border lenders of last resort in the euro area but some for *investors* of last resort where problems of undercapitalisation appear.
- The evolving cross-border system of supervision like the national ones needs to encourage early action and make it difficult to exercise forebearance.

11 The Way Forward

It has been our purpose in this book to explore whether, in the light of lessons from financial crises over the last decade or so and the way in which financial markets appear likely to develop in coming years, there are significant areas in which the framework of banking supervision could be improved – particularly in the European Economic Area. We have highlighted two main areas where considerable progress can be made

- The implementation of considerably more market discipline;
- The improvement of the powers to resolve difficulties in individual banks.

While the second of these may appear to lie beyond the scope of supervision as such, it is an essential component of the framework of incentives needed to encourage prudent behaviour in banks. The message from many recent crises is that banks will be bailed out, particularly if they are large. This reduces the incentive to prudence and creates a 'moral hazard' that needs to be countered.

We have concluded that an excess burden tends to be placed on supervisors in the present framework, as they cannot hope to get sufficient timely information to remain ahead of developments in today's world. They face rapid change in products and markets, increasing size and complexity of financial institutions and internationalisation of activity across national and supervisory boundaries. This last is particularly important in the EEA, where the principle of home country control introduces a major problem of co-ordination among supervisors in the home and host jurisdictions.

The people who do have the necessary information are the directors and managers of banks themselves. They need to be given the incentives to operate their banks in a prudent manner. Some of the strongest incentives come from the market, through banks' share prices, costs of borrowing, the threat of takeover, remuneration and jobs. However, market participants cannot exercise effective discipline unless they are properly informed. This therefore entails:

- Extensive timely public disclosure by banks of their financial state, their risks and the methods they use for managing those risks.

In turn, both the usefulness of the information disclosed and effectiveness of the incentives on the management of banks depend upon

- Having a good and effective regime of corporate governance.

Good corporate governance entails both clear structures and responsibilities and clear and verifiable reporting standards.

This pattern therefore entails that action is required on the following fronts if the sort of regime we are describing is to be introduced:

1. Corporate structures and governance.
2. Financial reporting, accounting and auditing standards and practice.
3. Regulations for public disclosure.
4. Enhanced co-ordination among supervisors for complex firms and financial system oversight.[1]
5. Effective market structures (such as exposure of at least some of the capital base to continuous market pressure; deep markets; strong analysts and rating agencies).
6. Enhanced powers for co-operation among authorities and early problem resolution.

Of course, not all countries would require action on all fronts.

11.1 THE RELATIONSHIP WITH OTHER RECENT PROPOSALS

11.1.1 The New Basel Committee Proposals

The list of areas for action can be reasonably limited as we take as given that a version of the revised Basel Accords will be agreed and then implemented in the reasonably near future. We have therefore not attempted to make any suggestions about the other two pillars of capital adequacy or supervisory review of institutions.

Even within the pillar of market discipline, our proposals, set out in Chapter 7, based on what is implemented in New Zealand are not strikingly different from those in the Basel Proposals (shown in full in the Appendix to this chapter). The principal differences are that:

- we explicitly suggest quarterly disclosure, as less frequent information could permit very substantial undisclosed changes to occur;
- we ask for disclosure of peak exposures, as it is these that reveal the full extent of the risks that have been run;
- we require disclosure of corporate structures and governance, to enable a better understanding of the structure of the business;
- we suggest that all directors, including the non-executives, should be liable for the disclosures, to provide a strong incentive for ensuring accuracy of what is disclosed.

In relative terms these differences are matters of detail. However, we are concerned about comparability within markets and therefore suggest that there needs to be firm agreement within each jurisdiction about what is to be disclosed and the financial reporting rules that are to be applied. Obviously the more international comparability the better. In general, what we are trying to do is to run ahead of the existing wind of change rather than against it. The one facet where we do expect some disagreement is that we are not suggesting a belt-and-braces arrangement where supervisors continue or even enhance their present intrusive regime of detailed private reporting. We are suggesting that what is disclosed is what supervisors and anyone else in the market wanting to make major informed judgements wants to know. One of the big advantages of market discipline is that banks that do not disclose enough to convince markets will be penalised. The authorities merely need to lay down common minimum standards.

11.1.2 Principles of Good Banking Regulation

We see our recommendations fitting very much into the framework of legislative principles that has been developed recently by Goodhart *et al.* (1998) and Llewellyn (1999). As Llewellyn's 25 principles are a refinement of Goodhart *et al.*'s 27 policy conclusions, we concentrate on the latter, shown in Table 11.1. Indeed there is only one of these principles that we have not discussed (6. Capital regulation should create incentives for the correct pricing of absolute and relative risk – because it lies outside our area of focus.) We would not delete any of these entries, although the list could be shortened and simplified through amalgamation.

However, our proposals go somewhat further in a number of respects, first of all because of our concern for the relationship between authorities, particularly in the smaller member states of the EEA. Secondly, our emphasis on aspects of corporate governance and the development of comparable reporting, accounting and auditing standards is probably rather broader. That said these 25 principles provide a very good basis for the framework in which our proposals can be implemented. We resist the temptation to produce over 100 explicit new recommendations of our own, like the Wallis Committee (1997). We turn instead to consider remaining problems of implementation.

11.2 THE PROCESS OF IMPLEMENTATION

The concern on the issue of implementation up to this point has been to establish whether there are any facets of the structure of the financial system in the EEA

Table 11.1 Llewellyn's (1999) 25 principles of good banking regulation

1 The objectives of regulation need to be clearly defined and circumscribed.
2 The rationale for regulation and supervision should be limited.
3 Regulation should be seen in terms of a set of contracts.
4 The form and intensity of regulatory and supervisory requirements should differentiate between regulated institutions according to their relative portfolio risk and efficiency of internal control mechanisms.
5 In some areas the regulator could offer a menu of contracts to regulated firms requiring them to self-select into the appropriate category.
6 Capital regulation should create incentives for the correct pricing of absolute and relative risk.
7 There should be appropriate incentives for bank owners.
8 There should be appropriate internal incentives for management.
9 Official agencies need to have sufficient powers and independence to conduct effective monitoring and supervision.
10 Less emphasis should be placed on detailed and prescriptive rules and more on internal risk analysis, management and control systems.
11 The design and application of safety-net arrangements should create incentives for stakeholders to exercise oversight and to act prudently so as to reduce the probability of recourse being made to public funds.
12 The extent and coverage of deposit insurance schemes should be strictly limited.
13 There needs to be a well-defined strategy for responding to the possible insolvency of financial institutions.
14 There should be a clear bias against forbearance when a bank is in difficulty.
15 Time-inconsistency and credibility problems should be addressed through precommitments and graduated responses with the possibility of overrides.
16 Intervention authorities need to ensure that parties that have benefited from risk-taking bear a large proportion of the cost of restructuring the banking system.
17 Prompt action should be taken to prevent problem institutions from extending credit to high-risk borrowers or capitalising unpaid interest on delinquent loans into new credit.
18 Society must create the political will to make restructuring a priority in allocating public funds while avoiding sharp increases in inflation. Use of public funds should be kept to a minimum and whenever used should be subject to strict conditionality.
19 Barriers to market recapitalisation should be minimised.
20 Regulators should be publicly accountable through credible mechanisms.
21 Regulation should not impede competition but should enhance it and by addressing information asymmetries make it more effective in the marketplace.
22 Regulation should reinforce not replace market discipline and the regulatory regime should be structured so as to provide greater incentives than exist at present for markets to monitor banks.
23 Regulators should whenever possible utilise market data in their supervisory procedures.
24 There should be a significant role for rating agencies in the supervisory process.
25 Corporate governance arrangements should provide for effective monitoring and supervision of the risk-taking profile of banks.

or EU law that make a more market-based banking supervision regime either impossible or unsuitable. We have noted that some of the incentives may be rather more blunted than in New Zealand, where such a scheme already operates, due to the structure of the banking system, aspects of corporate governance, the existence of deposit insurance and the history of having had to bail out the banking system during the last decade. The overall cost in the case of Finland has been variously estimated as between 8 and 17 per cent of GDP, during the last decade (Halme, 1997). We have also noted that there is a somewhat bigger step to be taken in getting the information to be released onto a generally accepted and clearly comparable basis. Auditing and accounting conventions will require some modifications.

The one area of real difficulty lies in the question of powers in the case of wishing to act quickly and early to help resolve the problems of a bank in difficulty, i.e. a bank that has become undercapitalised rather than probably insolvent. As discussed in Chapters 8 and 9 it is likely that a review of EU law is desirable in this regard. Such a review is bound to require an extended period of negotiation so we turn our attention to what can be implemented under national laws within the existing EU framework. We ask whether there are any obvious lessons that should be borne in mind when implementing the regime, if a decision is taken to move ahead. This raises two subsidiary questions:

- Are there any requirements for the ordering of change?
- What are the minimum requirements for a more-market based system to operate effectively?

11.3　THE PROCESS OF CHANGE

There is always the temptation to push steadily in the direction of change rather than take large steps and implement a new system as a whole rather than in parts.

The disadvantage of proceeding piecemeal is that a new regime may not prove effective until most of it has been implemented. In the meantime, existing controls may be weakened or the burdens on the banks and the costs on the system in general increased. Indeed both could occur, giving increased costs and decreased effectiveness. With progressive change the participants have to change on a number of occasions. There is a cost associated with making any change and hence by separating the process into separate steps the total cost may be increased. Banks might have to change their internal systems more than once for example. Secondly, the will to change may alter during the process, leaving the system between regimes.

However, this does not mean that trying to achieve more rapid and complete change is without drawbacks either. Because of the extent of the change, the number of items to be agreed on any one occasion is higher. The chance of finding at least some individual aspect with which any party to the discussions is uncomfortable is increased. If one party can hold up the whole process then the period before which any change occurs is lengthened. The costs of the change are likely to be more concentrated than if they were separated into a series of steps. That single lump may prove more difficult to accommodate in purely cashflow terms than the greater but more spread out cost of gradual change.

Implementing any change takes time. If we take New Zealand as an example, about five years was required between starting the discussions in late 1991 and full implementation in 1996. New Zealand had one important advantage in that legislative change was not required. The Reserve Bank Act of 1989 was sufficiently encompassing in its terms that the Reserve Bank had the power to introduce the new regime through regulation alone. The power of the authorities to intervene and take undercapitalised banks into statutory management was explicitly embodied in the Reserve Bank Act. However, the Reserve Bank had to ensure that what it was suggesting for the banking sector was compatible with legislation covering the corporate sector in general. Most of the time was taken up with discussions between the Reserve Bank, the commercial banks (both individually, but mainly through the New Zealand Bankers Association) and the accounting profession to ensure that the proposals would be practical, not unduly costly and would actually achieve the objectives of the change.

If New Zealand had had a previous pattern to follow progress could no doubt have been swifter as both the Reserve Bank and the commercial banks would have had other experience to turn to. Now the New Zealand example exists, other countries can implement a similar (but improved) regime rather more swiftly. However, as we have noted, there are some aspects of the system in European countries that may make change a little more cumbersome. In the first case European law tends to be rather more prescriptive in detail and hence changes to reporting requirements and incentives may require legislative change (see Halme, 1997, for the case of Finland). Indeed these requirements may extend somewhat further into aspects of corporate governance. Secondly, there may be some changes in the structure of the system necessary to ensure that the system of crisis resolution enables the authorities to reconstitute a bank rapidly without bailing out the existing shareholders and to avoid ready access to public funds, so that shareholders, management, creditors and uninsured depositors do recognise that their own funds (or jobs) may be at risk. EU legislation is in the main concerned with the imposition of minimum standards and in the case of accounting standards seeks to permit both Anglo-Saxon and continental approaches. Thus while it does not compel a disclosure regime, nor indeed does it seem likely to do so at present, it does not forbid one. However, quite recently, the European Commission has taken a stand in favour of IASC (International Accounting Standards Committee) rules as guidelines for financial sector accounting rules. Nevertheless, it seems difficult to disagree with the dictum that one should 'do as much as possible as soon as possible'. Europe has a window of opportunity, as it is important to introduce banking system regime changes when the economy is not fragile. The economy is growing rapidly, without the inflationary pressure in property prices of the scale of a decade ago. The advent of Stage 3 of EMU and the increasing integration of financial markets both enlarge the window and pose a threat.

On the one hand they make it more likely that the current economic upturn will be prolonged beyond what would have been possible had the members continued to have independently determined prices and monetary policy. Without the threat of competition from a more integrated EU economy, inflation might well have been higher, necessitating a reaction from monetary policy and a downturn to the profitability of the banking sector. Average interest rates would also have been higher, as interest rates in the historically more inflation prone countries have fallen to near the levels of the best performers.

On the other, the introduction of the euro and the increasing integration of financial markets may mean that financial innovation or entry into new markets results in the sorts of increase in risk that have accompanied other bursts of financial deregulation (Llewellyn, 1995). There is hence a threat that when the next downturn does come it will contain an increased risk of financial difficulty. The ECB has an extremely difficult job in estimating how a new currency area may work and might, for example, underestimate the degree to which there is an increase in the velocity of circulation of money. The resulting crackdown to restrict the inflationary consequences may put pressure on the banking system. Of course, at the same time, increasing integration may result in arrangements among banks that increase their capital base.

It therefore seems that rapid progress would be desirable, even if some of the changes in structure come later. The accounting and auditing requirements are already incorporated into international standards so there is a blueprint to follow that could be transposed into regulation by the FSA. However, while improved international collaboration is in principle relatively easy to achieve, as it does not in our view require much in the way of institution building, obtaining international agreement on the principles for intervention in cross-border banks that become undercapitalised is a much harder prospect. Even if a protracted discussion of the fundamental legal principles involved can be avoided some new EU directives or regulations seem inevitable. Regrettably the time this takes may mean that the main incentive to action will come from the first such bank that gets into difficulty or has to be bailed out.

11.4 CONSULTATION

It is worth recalling finally that one of the key features of the successful introduction of what was then a radical change in New Zealand was extensive consultation between the parties: the various authorities, banks and the accounting
bodies. While the Reserve Bank produced an initial draft, it was the consultation
that ensured that the proposals did not put undue pressure on banks. These discussions were held not in the framework of trying to decide whether the changes
should be made but how the principles should be implemented. Ultimately it was
still up to the Reserve Bank to decide. However, to illustrate what such discussions can achieve, two main changes, inter alia, can be observed from the initial
proposals as result of consultation: a reduction in the detail of disclosure; the
introduction of a 'standard model' for assessing market risk. (As we have seen,
the second of these was necessary to get the proposals implemented rapidly
although better compromises now seem possible as suggested in Chapter 7.)

Since the more market-based regime is intended to produce benefits for the
banks themselves as well as for society at large as customers, creditors and taxpayers, it is only appropriate to try to ensure that the nature of those potential
benefits is properly understood by the authorities when drawing up the regime.

11.5 THE NEXT STEPS

There are two key areas – ongoing supervision and crisis management. In the
case of ongoing supervision the path over the coming years is more straight
forward, albeit arduous. While it is open for the financial supervision authorities
to produce a Discussion Paper explaining outline plans, a timetable and the consultation process for the introduction of public disclosure and the change in its
focus towards systemic issues, some parallel steps would help ease the change. It
would be helpful to explore whether the appropriate incentives are likely to be
sufficient, not just in terms of penalties and legal liabilities, but also in terms of
market institutions – rating agencies, independent analysis, etc. Secondly, it
would be useful to investigate whether the system of corporate governance was
likely to produce adequate transparency and effective procedures within banks to
encourage greater prudential risk management: through audit committees and
independent directors, for example. The small co-operative and savings banks
present problems under both headings and indeed it may be more appropriate to
offer to continue with current arrangements if they wish it. Although international standards for financial reporting are now adequate for a successful disclosure regime, implementing the appropriate valuation, accounting and auditing
arrangements is likely to provide the most time-consuming part of the process.

Crisis management provides a greater problem, as it requires both the development of co-operation with supervisors in other countries and the attempt to convince markets and shareholders, in particular, that there will be no bailouts – without wishing to have even a small crisis that gives an opportunity to demonstrate that resolve. The development of greater powers to help resolve crises and permit the authorities to organise the management of insolvent or undercapitalised banks without bailing out the existing owners would help make that message more credible.

Given the benefits anticipated for all those involved: customers, creditors and counterparties, as they see information on the risks they face improve; shareholders, customers and managers, as they see the costs of compliance and the restraints on well-managed business fall; supervisors, as they can concentrate on systemic issues and all parties, including the taxpayer, as they see the risks of distress or failure recede – the earlier the process starts the better. While there are difficulties and the process of implementation is unlikely to be either as straightforward or as comprehensive as it was in New Zealand, where such a regime was implemented in 1996, these do not appear insurmountable. Furthermore, it has been possible to learn from experience and design a scheme more suited to the specific conditions in Europe. As economic conditions are now favourable and integration and innovation in financial markets are likely to increase the pressure on existing methods of supervision, the changes proposed would be timely.

APPENDIX 11.1 BASEL COMMITTEE DRAFT RECOMMENDATIONS FOR DISCLOSURE

CAPITAL STRUCTURE

Recommendation 1

A bank should, at least annually and more frequently where possible and appropriate, publicly disclose summary information about:

(a) Its capital structure and components of capital
A bank should disclose the amounts of its components and structure of capital based on the definitions contained within the Basel Capital Accord:

- the amount of tier one capital, with separate disclosure of:
    - (i) paid-up share capital/common stock;
    - (ii) perpetual non-cumulative preference shares;
    - (iii) minority interests in the equity of subsidiaries;

(iv) innovative or complex capital instruments (e.g., minority interests that take the form of SPVs and tier one instruments with moderate step-ups), including the percentage of total tier one capital accounted for by such instruments;
- the amount of tier two capital (split between Upper and Lower tier two), with separate disclosure of material components;
- deductions from tier one and tier two capital;
- the amount of tier three capital;
- the total capital base.

(b)   The terms and conditions of the main features of capital instruments
A bank should disclose summary information about the terms and conditions of the main features of all capital instruments, especially in the case of innovative, complex or hybrid capital instruments.
Information disclosed should provide a clear picture of the loss-absorbing capacity of capital instruments and include any conditions that may affect the analysis of a bank's capital adequacy. This would include information on:

- maturity (including call features);
- level of seniority;
- step-up provisions;
- interest or dividend deferrals and any cumulative characteristics;
- use of Special Purpose Vehicles (SPVs);
- discussion of key 'trigger' events (i.e. events which may cause the activation of significant clauses or penalties which may affect the nature or cost of capital instruments);
- fair value and terms of derivatives embedded in hybrid capital instruments.

Recommendation 2

A bank should disclose information on its accounting policies for the valuation of assets and liabilities, provisioning and income recognition.
This information is important in an assessment of the quality and comparability of capital reserves that have been either generated through the income statement or recognised directly in equity. This disclosure could augment that envisaged in the Committee's paper *Sound Practices for Loan Accounting and Disclosure* and the Committee will consider where additional disclosure in this area might be appropriate.

RISK EXPOSURES

Recommendation 3

A bank should publicly disclose qualitative and quantitative information about its risk exposures, including its strategies for managing risk.
In discussing each risk area, an institution should present sufficient qualitative (e.g., management strategies) and quantitative information (e.g., stress testing) to enable users to understand the nature and magnitude of these risk exposures. Further, comparative information of previous years' data should be provided to give the financial statement user a perspective on trends in the underlying exposures.

Credit Risk

Credit risk disclosures should enable the user to understand the extent and nature of an institution's credit exposure, both on an overall basis and in terms of significant components. These disclosures should also be sufficient to allow users to develop an understanding of how an institution manages credit risk and to what extent its strategies have been effective. The recommendations contained in the committee's papers, *Recommendations for Public Disclosure of Trading and Derivatives Activities of Banks and Securities Firms* (which discusses quantitative and qualitative disclosures in the areas of market risk, credit risk, liquidity risk and other risks and quantitative disclosures in the area of earnings and qualitative disclosures in the area of accounting and valuation methods) and *Best Practices for Credit Risk Disclosure* (which discusses disclosures in the areas of accounting policies and practices, credit risk management, credit exposures, credit quality and earnings), set out the types of disclosures that banking institutions should seek to make with respect to risk exposures in this area.

Market Risk

As with credit risk, an institution should provide both quantitative and qualitative information regarding its market risk exposure. Recommendations on disclosures that are considered to be necessary in this area by the Basel Committee are discussed in *Recommendations for Public Disclosure of Trading and Derivatives Activities of Banks and Securities Firms*.

Operational, Legal and Other Risks

Risk exposures such as operational, legal and strategic risk can be difficult to quantify. However, they can be highly significant and relevant disclosures in these areas should be made. More detailed requirements for disclosures of operational risk factors may be required once the Basel Committee has published its proposed regulatory treatment of operational risk. In addition, banks should provide quantitative and qualitative disclosures on interest rate risk in the banking book.

Operational risk disclosures should include information about the main types of such risk and should identify and discuss any specific issues considered to be significant. Legal risk disclosures include legal contingencies (including pending legal actions) and a discussion of probable liabilities. Qualitative information about how the bank identifies, measures and manages these risks should be provided (i.e. methodologies used and organisational procedures), including the use of risk Mitigation techniques.

CAPITAL ADEQUACY MEASURES

Recommendation 4

(a)   A bank should, at least annually, publicly disclose its capital ratio and other relevant information on its capital adequacy on a consolidated basis

To help market participants assess a bank's capital adequacy, it should at least annually disclose its risk-based capital ratio calculated in accordance with the methodology prescribed in the Basel Capital Accord as implemented by its home country supervisor, along with any other relevant information. Other relevant information might include future capital targets, although confidential supervisory requirements would not be disclosed. This should also include information on the scope of consolidation for supervisory purposes.

(b) A bank should disclose measures of risk exposures calculated in accordance with the methodology set out in the Basel Capital Accord, as illustrated below

(i)   Calculation of Basel Accord capital requirements for credit risk
Balance sheet assets (specifying book value and risk-weighted amount for each risk bucket); Off-balance-sheet instruments (specifying nominal amount, credit equivalent amount and risk-weighted amount for each risk bucket);

(ii) Calculation of Basel Accord capital requirements for market risk.

a)   Standardised approach (if appropriate)

Banks should disclose all information relevant to understanding how their Basel Accord capital requirement for market risk under the standardised approach has been calculated, including disclosure of capital charges for component risk elements, as appropriate.

b)   Internal models approach (if appropriate);

Banks should provide all information relevant to understanding how their Basel Accord capital requirement for market risk under the internal models approach has been calculated. Disclosure of individual capital charges should be provided, as discussed in the disclosure guidance section on risk exposures. Information provided should be sufficient to allow understanding of the models used and should as a minimum include:

• Broad value-at-risk data;
• Parameters;
• Stress-testing information; and
• Back-testing information.

Recommendation 5

A bank should provide an analysis of factors impacting on its capital adequacy position. This would include:

(a)   changes in capital structure and the impact on key ratios[2] and overall capital position;
(b)   its contingency planning, should it need to access the capital markets in times of stress;
(c)   its capital management strategy and consideration of future capital plans (where appropriate);
(d)   the impact of any non-deduction of participations in banks and other financial institutions, where applicable.

Recommendation 6

A bank is encouraged to disclose its structure and process of allocating economic capital to its business activities.

Pillar two of the consultative paper *A New Capital Adequacy Framework* discusses the supervisory review and assessment of capital adequacy. It proposes that supervisors review a bank's capital position and strategy to ensure that it is consistent with its overall risk profile in order to enable early supervisory intervention if the capital strategy does not provide a sufficient buffer against the risk. The Basel Committee recommends that all banks have an internal process for assessing their capital adequacy and for setting appropriate levels of capital. This process should be objective and overseen by senior management and all banks should be able to demonstrate that the results of their internal processes are credible and reliable.

One method used by some banks is capital allocation. Capital allocation, the process of assigning economic capital to an institution's business activities, has become a useful tool for some banks in determining the adequacy of their capital and ensuring the efficient use of that capital. Specifically, capital allocation allows banks to compare the risk-adjusted profitability of diverse products and evaluate whether capital is sufficient on an individual business line basis as well as for the institution on an aggregate basis. They should also consider disclosing the amount of capital allocated to different transactions, products, customers, business lines, or organisational units (depending on the bank's methodology) so that information users may gain a better understanding of the risks and rewards inherent in the bank's activities. All banks should have a process to judge the adequacy of their own capital relative to their risks.

Notes

1 INTRODUCTION

1. If controversial.
2. The Accord itself came rather too late to head off the Nordic crises. That in Norway was already underway and those in Finland and Sweden too close for new rules to have their impact in time. However, the Accord was a long time in the making and its general flavour could have been implemented earlier.
3. Ahtiala (2000) estimates this at 17–20% compared to trend.
4. Structural distortions may have been more important in restricting growth over extended periods of time but without such a concentrated impact.
5. For example, the *Economic Journal* has had two recent features on the subject: 'The Changing Role of the World's International Financial Institutions' (November 1999) and 'The Origins and Management of Financial Crises' (January 2000).
6. Fines and related penalties will make failure more likely and could only be levied at the expense of other potential claimants on the bank rather than on those responsible.

2 THE FINANCIAL CRISIS OF THE EARLY 1990s AND ITS LESSONS

1. Final figures may well show that the Mexican and Korean crises in the 1990s were 'larger' and some countries suffered larger crises prior to joining the OECD.
2. See Ahtiala (2000), Berg (1993), Bordes *et al.* (1993), Drees and Pazarbasioglu (1998), Halme (1999b), Honkapohja and Koskela (1999), Jonung *et al.* (1996), Kiander and Vartia (1996), Kukkonen (1993), Møller and Nielsen (1995), Munthe *et al.* (1992) and Tarkka (1994), for example.
3. This is not the case for Denmark, where banking restrictions were already much lower by the beginning of the 1980s (see Munthe *et al.*, 1992), which helps explain the smoother and earlier profile of Danish difficulties
4. Deregulation can provide a complex threat. The Finnish savings banks, for example, on the one hand feared that their competitive position might be lost as the barriers came down and on the other knew that in future they would have to increase their capital ratios. There was therefore an incentive to try to establish a good position in the short run so that they would find it easier to build up capital thereafter. Contracting to build up capital might have appeared a defeatist strategy and an encouragement to takeover. The incentive was thus to follow the approach which gives more risks to the system as a whole.
5. The rationalisation by banks may have been rather less related to the longer macroeconomic outlook and more to the shorter-run atmosphere of current success.
6. If long-run growth prospects have improved then an increase in the real rate of interest is also to be expected.

7. The same discussion in Dewatripont and Tirole (1993) also provides a good survey of how a lack of competition in the banking sector leads to inefficiencies and a willingness to take excess risks, so the problem is by no means one-sided.
8. Although the phenomenal growth of Nokia and other technology stocks at the end of the 1990s has altered the picture for Finland.
9. The scope for easing the problem is greater when the output can be stored, as, for example, in the case of wool.
10. In a sense therefore he views the 'cure' as being worse than the disease, although the disease itself could have been avoided had financial liberalisation been better managed.
11. 'The Bank of Finland attempted to keep domestic interest rates as high as possible within the constraints imposed by the fluctuation range of the currency index' (p. 3).
12. In an attempt to guard against these risks in early 2000 the Finnish Supervisory Authority published a general warning to banks about these risks (Notification T/33/2000/LLO, Credit Institutions Department, 7 January 2000).
13. Kilponen *et al.* (2000) show that prior to EMU membership Finland tended to absorb adverse foreign shocks through unemployment. The exchange rate appeared to adjust to offset real increases that were unsupported by productivity growth. While the authors show that change is to be expected in response to the change in the monetary policy regime, the evidence has yet to be statistically observable.
14. As Markku Malkamäki pointed out, it also proved to be rather undiversified in the face of the shock. Hence reflecting the eighth (parenthetic) point as well.
15. By historical standards that reflected controlled interest rates, households borrowing on house mortgages in particular had not been used to changes in interest rates of the order of 4–6 percentage points in a short period of time.
16. In January 1993 the guarantee fund was increased to 50bn FIM and the declaration on guaranteeing stability of the system was explicitly incorporated into law.
17. Pohjoisaho-Aarti (2000) provides a clear description and explanation.
18. The problem is not symmetric in that a period of excess pessimism, as many ascribe to the euro economy in its first year or more, does not lead to a financial crisis. However, insofar as it leads to a much greater policy reaction than would otherwise have been required it could lead to a sharper upward cycle in the future. The Japanese case of the second half of the 1990s reflects an inability to resolve a traditional upside problem through overvaluation of assets than a new downside problem.

3   CHALLENGES TO FINANCIAL SUPERVISION IN COMING YEARS

1. Of course, the earlier period includes the response to the banking crises, which helps account for its large size.
2. Ultimately NatWest was taken over.
3. The concentration also applies in other financial sectors as well. According to Koskenkylä (2000), the banks in the Nordic countries control 70–80 per cent of mutual funds business and 30–50 per cent of life insurance (the 50 per cent is Finland).
4. Of course, no book written in Finland could fail to mention the rise of access through mobile phones to the Internet, increasing the ability of customers to access funds from any location, whether or not across borders.

4 PRINCIPLES OF GOOD FINANCIAL SUPERVISION

1. One example of preparation for the transition, which we are aware of, occurred in New Zealand in the mid-1980s when the bulk of barriers segmenting financial markets were removed and exchange controls abolished. The Treasury, which was responsible for the regulatory change, commissioned a group of projects to look into the unfortunate experiences that had occurred in earlier bouts of deregulation in other countries. Hunn *et al.* (1989), for example, considered the case of the South American countries and looked in particular at the interaction between financial deregulation and macroeconomic policy. Unfortunately, it is not possible to tell whether the publication and distribution of these reports round the financial sector and government had any salutary effect on behaviour. Even at that stage the New Zealand authorities were keen to try to place the burden for following prudent behaviour on the financial institutions themselves rather than merely on the supervisor. Some other administrations would no doubt have wanted to follow a different approach to trying to limit the dangers from the process of change.
2. Llewellyn (1999) has quite a neat way of summarising the picture by suggesting that there are six components to the regulatory regime: regulation, monitoring and supervision, incentive structures, intervention and sanctions, market discipline and corporate governance. Our book covers all of these with specific Chapters, 5, 6 and 8 on corporate governance, market discipline and intervention and sanctions.
3. The authorities face a difficult problem of balance in regulating banks. The extra regulation of banks over other commercial companies stems from the potential costs to society from bank failures and from more general crises of confidence in the banking system. Because much of these costs apply to those not directly involved in the transactions there is a role for the public sector in trying to reduce the chance of such failures and possibly in compensating those who are adversely affected but not at fault. However, in practice the protection often goes further and protects the ordinary depositors on the grounds that they are unlikely to be sufficiently informed of the risks they are running or able to cope with the costs of incurring them. It is difficult even for the informed to work out the state and prospects of banks (Poon *et al.*, 1999; Jordan *et al.*, 2000). However, if others are protected from the consequences, the risks may not be viewed as being so important and hence people will run them more readily. Both depositors and banks themselves may feel they can run greater risks and hence increase the chances of the very events that society is trying to protect itself against. The difficult task for the authorities is to try to arrange a system which discourages banks from running these risks yet protects society if something goes wrong. Our aim is to try to suggest ways of sharpening the incentives to banks while accepting the need to protect those at risk.
4. The term 'natural law' has many other meanings outside the legal context in which we use it. The current context is defined in Boucher and Kelly (1994) passim, for example.
5. A principal engages an agent to act on his/her behalf. Due to asymmetric information, however, the principal is unable to observe the actions of the agent entirely, and there is scope for the agent to deviate from the principal's wishes. There are various agent–principal relations in the field of banking regulation and supervision. Legislators can act as principals and supervisors as agents, depositors as principals and banks as agents, supervisors as principals and banks as agents, shareholders as principals and bank managements as agents, non-executive boards as principals and management as agents. We deal with all of them.

6. See Kornhauser (1989).
7. See *Journal of Financial Regulation*, June 1999.
8. See e.g. Goodhart *et al.* (1998), who conclude:

> One of the key questions that arises is the extent to which behaviour is to be altered by externally imposed rules, or through creating incentives for firms to behave in a particular way. Regulation can be endogenous to financial firm (i.e. self-control) as well as exogenous. A major issue, therefore, is whether regulation should proceed through externally imposed, prescriptive and detailed rules, or by the regulator creating incentives for appropriate behaviour.

   See also Llewellyn (1999).
9. We are concerned here with what Hyytinen and Takalo (2000) label ex ante transparency – judging what the performance of the bank is likely to be, rather than conducting a post-mortem of what went wrong after the event. (Not that the latter is unimportant.)
10. That is, information not available to everybody.
11. Especially since depositors often behave as if there were no risk involved.
12. One reason for highlighting financial crime is simply that there are international obligations to fight money laundering and tax evasion and including it in the objectives makes it clear that those obligations will be honoured.
13. This approach is usually labelled 'free banking'. Free because it is free from constraint, not that it is free to the customer.
14. These recommendations have since been implemented with only limited modification.
15. Vives (1999) emphasises the importance of separating the authority responsible for supervision from those responsible for deciding upon a bailout or having access to taxpayer funds to effect it. In that way the supervisor can operate according to rules that compel it to commence action is banks become undercapitalised without regard to whether the consequence will be failure, reorganisation or a bailout. Furthermore banks can be more convinced that they will not get the benefit of forebearance if the supervisor does not face a conflict of interest.
16. Currently the Treaty of Amsterdam.
17. It is implicit that systemic stability of banking deserves special public attention in contrast to other sectors of the economy. The main justifications in the academic literature are: (1) Occasionally public action may be required when a solvent bank encounters a liquidity problem (even without any question over asset quality) due to the illiquidity of its assets (Diamond and Dybvig, 1983) and private information embedded in the asset values. (2) Bank failures can lead to systemic crises through the breakdown of the payment systems or possible contagion of problems to other institutions. Even a small probability can imply a large expected loss to the economy (Greenbaum, 1995). (3) Safety nets (deposit insurance, lender-of-last resort, payment system guarantees) can help avoid banking panics due to liquidity problems, but the existence of the safety net can itself create the moral hazard of excessive risk-taking. In some respects it is this last risk, that consumer protection itself may lead to excessive risk-taking, which provides the basic motive for prudential regulation and supervision (Baltensberger and Dermine, 1987; Greenbaum, 1995). The other two motives entail that the authorities need prior information on the banks that may be at risk so that they can act swiftly and effectively. They may also feel that they wish to set minimum standards so as to reduce the risk. There are contrasting

views. Benston and Kaufman (1995) argue that that there is little theoretical or empirical evidence that banking is inherently unstable.

18. One strand of the literature concentrates on the discipline that what is described as the 'charter value' of banks places on their management (Acharya, 1996; Bhattacharya *et al.*, 1998; Demsetz *et al.*, 1996). The charter value in this sense is the value of being allowed to run the bank, which is in effect the discounted stream of future profits. Less profitable banks or banks in poor shape have less to lose so they are inclined to take more risks. Some of this charter value will stem from accumulated private knowledge about the quality of borrowers.

19. Mishkin (1998) argues that the most convincing way of giving a credible signal that individual banks will not be bailed out with taxpayers' money is to commit to a strong presumption that the first bank to encounter difficulties will be allowed to fail and the costs of the failure would be borne by uninsured depositors and creditors. The authorities would be ready to extend a safety net to the rest of the banking system, though still maintaining 'constructive ambiguity' of that extension, if there were a danger that otherwise the stability of the banking system would be threatened. Application of this method would naturally be complicated in banking systems that are clearly perceived to contain institutions that are 'too large to fail'.

20. One of the key premises set out in the 'Core Principles for Effective Banking supervision' of the Basel Committee on Banking Supervision (1997) is that supervision should not try to support the perception that banks do not fail and support the integrity of all institutions. Section I of the 'Principles' states that 'the key objective of supervision is to maintain stability', and that 'supervision cannot, and should not provide assurance that banks will not fail'.

21. Forbearance is one of the core problems of supervision due to the embedded time inconsistency problem (Goodhart, 1995). Even if authorities announce in advance that they will deal severely with banks that breach supervisory standards, they may fail to behave in this manner when the time comes. When the event happens, a strong response may be judged inappropriate due to the fear of weakening the condition of the institution in question further. The supervised institutions would anticipate this forbearance and factor it into their own decisions. For this reason, precommitment and strict rules for the supervisors are recommended. When there are problems across all institutions Goodhart argues that discretionary supervisory behaviour could be justified to reduce the threat of a systemic crisis.

22. There is clear evidence of difficulty in assessing asset quality from the limited information that is diclosed by banks publicly at present. See Poon *et al.*, 1999; Jordan *et al.*, 2000; Beatty *et al.*, 1995 and Genay, 1998, for example.

23. For example, the G30 has suggested, inter alia, improving market discipline through disclosure as a response to weakened possibilities for supervisory agency control of complex internationalised organisations. Moreover, the 'Principles' of the Basle Committee on Banking Supervision (1997) state in the introductory Section I that 'Supervisors should encourage and pursue market discipline by encouraging good corporate governance ... and enhancing market transparency and surveillance'.

24. There is clear evidence that the proportion of uninsured depositors is lower in lower quality banks (see Billet *et al.* 1998; Goldberg and Hudgins, 1999; Martinez Peria and Schmukler, 1998; Park, 1995; Park and Peristiani, 1998).

25. See Carletti (1999) for example.

26. By having these reputational penalties and encouraging a regime which makes early identification of problems more likely it is hoped to provide at least some

safeguard against 'go for broke' strategies (Kupiec and O'Brien, 1995). The worry is that managers, having breached the criteria for prudence have no greater downside penalty from following increasingly risky strategies. In the New Zealand system that has taken the market discipline 'doctrine' quite a long way (Mayes, 1997) the penalties for trying to cover up and get through a difficulty are intended to be greater than those from disclosing an impending problem in the first place.

27. The incentives would be weakened by any implicit or explicit government guarantees to banks.

28. The home country principle is stated in Article 13 of the Second Banking Co-ordination Directive, and the rules of consolidated supervision are stated in the Directives on the Supervision of Credit Institutions on a Consolidated Basis and on the Capital Adequacy of Investment Firms and Credit Institutions. The so-called BCCI-Directive, Article 3, stipulates that authorities shall require the bank (credit institution) registered in that country also to have its head office in the same country. The supervision of liquidity is an exception, since it is subject to host supervision.

29. This general principle is stated explicitly in the Basle Concordat, and the Core Principle 25 requires that '[host] supervisors must require the local operations of the foreign banks to be conducted by the same high standards as are required of domestic institutions'.

30. Unless, of course, one opted for a single mega-regulator at the European level covering the whole financial sector, which would itself raise organisational concerns. However, this does not appear on the political agenda at present so we do not pursue it further.

31. The 'Minimum Standards for the Supervision of International Banking Groups and their Cross-Border Establishments' issued by the Basel Committee (1992) states that 'if the host country authority determines that any of the standards (for efficient home country consolidated supervision) is not being met, it could impose restrictive measures or prohibit the establishment of banking offices'

32. Specific macroeconomic indicators that would be suited to the monitoring macroeconomic developments that could affect the financial system are detailed in Lindgren *et al.* (1996) inter alia. They suggest credit market conditions, asset price and interest rate sustainability and volatility, corporate and household debt burden and credit servicing capabilities, government finances and external balance as typical areas to be followed with the help of specific indicators.

33. The Bank of Finland has developed an extensive model of the banking sector that takes the macroeconomic conditions from the Bank's forecast (which is published in the Bank of Finland *Bulletin*) and computes the likely implications for the health of the banking sector. The results of this assessment are also published six-monthly in the *Bulletin* (Koskenkylä, 1999).

34. Lannoo (1999b) contains a useful list of the multilateral arrangements in place between supervisors in the EEA.

35. In New Zealand's supervision regime, where the home country principle does not apply, foreign banks have to disclose the operation of their branches in New Zealand so that the host country can make the necessary comparisons and market assessments.

36. The Core Principles state that 'banking supervisors must have the authority to establish criteria for reviewing major acquisitions or investments by a bank and ensuring that corporate affiliations or structures do not expose the bank to undue risks or hinder effective supervision' (Principle 5). Moreover, the Minimum Standards require that 'all international banks should be supervised by a home country authority ... that

has [a] right to prohibit company structures which impede supervision', and that 'the creation of a cross-border banking establishment should receive the prior consent of both the host country and the home country establishment'.

37. In the case of the Netherlands there is a principle of 'structural supervision' defined in the legislation concerning the supervision of credit institutions and insurance companies. According to this principle mergers and acquisitions of credit institutions or insurance companies, or acquisitions of ownership stakes between credit institutions and insurance companies, require a prior consent (a declaration of no objection) from the ministry of finance.

38. Goodhart (1996) discusses the general problems of assuring proper accountability and incentives for supervisors.

39. The Second Banking Directive and the BCCI Directive provide for the exchange of confidential information among supervisors. However, this legislation is permissive, in the sense of removing obstacles. It does not enforce co-operation.

5   CORPORATE GOVERNANCE AND FINANCIAL STABILITY

1. The main features of *managerial capitalism* and leadership culture can be charac- terised as: ownership is strategic and a company strives to increase its market share and turnover. Shareholders are not well informed, and their role is confined mainly to safeguarding the existence of adequate capital. There is also inefficiency and lax- ness in board functioning. Management compensation schemes are based on the size of the company as well as net accounting profit.

   Whereas the main features of *shareholder capitalism* and leadership culture are: ownership is seen as an investment in a profit enhancing company, and the company seeks to maximise the value of the company and dividends. Shareholders are well informed and the role of the company is to pass on most of its value added to the shareholders. The board is strong and capable of directing management's prudential risk-taking and supporting shareholders' interests. See Veranen (1996).

2. There is no common understanding about the concepts 'internal' and 'external'. Some refer to internal governance when talking about how a company's board can control management. External governance again refers to external control mecha- nisms exercised by shareholders and markets.

   Some refer to internal governance when talking about company management functions. In this connection internal governance is more or less the same as man- agement. They see a corporation as a set of incentive systems with associated deci- sion making, monitoring, and information structures. External governance in this context represents the accountability mechanisms that operate when internal gover- nance fails. It also provides the means by which outsiders intervene to discipline the management when internal governance fails. Note that in this definition set a company's board can intermediate between internal and external governance mechanisms. See, for example, Gilson (1998).

3. Lannoo (1999a) writes about problems concerning the definition of the term.

4. See, for example, Sheikh and Rees (1995), Yla-Anttila and Ali-Yrkko (1999), Kaplan (1998), Shleifer and Vishny (1997)

5. See Prowse (1997). The paper gives a good survey of research work on corporate governance of banks.

6. The legal and regulatory framework of banks differs substantially from that of ordinary companies owing to the fact that banks are assumed to have a special role in the economy. However, regulatory differences cannot be fully explained by banks' uniqueness and the existence of externalities. There is likely to be an increase in legal harmonisation across different types of companies, be they financial companies or non-financial companies. Note, however, that a new draft on the revised Basel Accord is a contrary example, at least in the short or medium term.
7. See, for example, Alworth and Bhattacharaya (1998).
8. See, for example, Dowd (1996).
9. In many countries the most common response of regulators to problems and crises in the financial sector has been to increase the amount of regulation. It is mostly since the crises of the 1980s and 1990s that the response has received special attention, by seriously considering what are the realistic chances of avoiding crises by intensified regulation. The idea of focusing on incentives created by regulation and supervision was originally emphasised by economists, and the view is today shared by regulators and supervisors.
10. See Shleifer and Vishny (1997). Differences between the corporate governance systems of these four countries are not as great as usually stated. They point out that all four countries are among the countries with the most efficient corporate governance framework.
11. See Gilson (1998), Mayes and Hart (1994).
12. See, for example, the Cadbury (1992), Greenbury (1995) and Hampel (1998) Reports in the United Kingdom, London Stock Exchange Recommendations, the Viennot Report in France (1995), the recommendation of 'Naringslivets Borskommittee' in Sweden (1994), the Recommendation of the Corporate Governance Working Group in Finland (1996), the Recommendations of the Helsinki Stock Exchange on Corporate Governance (1997).
13. See, for example, Lannoo (1999a). The Paris Stock Exchange has however announced that they are aiming at supporting the recommendations by taking them into their rules. However, the practical consequences are not yet apparent.
14. See *OECD Principles of Corporate Governance,* OECD (1999a). See also A Report to the OECD by the Business Sector Advisory Group on Corporate Governance: Corporate Governance; Improving Competitiveness and Access to Capital in Global Markets.
15. See Lannoo (1999a).
16. See CEPS Working Party Report on Corporate Governance in Europe (1995). See also Lannoo (1999a).
17. See Shleifer and Vishny (1997).
18. See Veranen (1996) and Hirvonen et al. (1997).
19. See, for example, Veranen (1996) who takes a very critical view in this respect.
20. The UK committees into the issue advocate having a majority of non-executive members.
21. Until 1991 the level of capital adequacy was measured as equity capital in relation to commitments (on-balance sheet) including part of off-balance sheet guarantees. The Basel Accord was largely incorporated in Finnish legislation in 1991 but with some major exceptions. As an example, revaluation reserves of fixed assets were treated as tier one capital, loans guaranteed by local banks' mutual insurance companies were treated as interbank lending and loan loss reserves were included in tier two capital without limit. The outcome was at least partially a result of a consensus-driven

policy favoured by regulators and supervisors combined with the fact that those subject to regulation (banks) had a remarkable influence not only in the interpretation of current legal rules (law-taking) but also in the contents of legislative drafting (lawmaking). This approach is well-known, in public choice theory, for example.

22. Finnish banking legislation allowed savings and co-operative banks to operate with lower capital adequacy levels than commercial banks until 1991. To counterbalance this, the scope of business of local banks was more strictly defined than that of commercial banks. However, regulators and to some extent even the courts diverged from this basic counterbalancing presumption.

23. See Norwegian Report (1997–98).

24. Similar findings have also been made in the United States, where it has been concluded that various solvency ratios (total risk-based capital ratio, tier 1 risk-based ratio and leverage ratio) do not in reality react quickly enough to the problems faced by credit institutions. The studies support the fact that corrective actions by authorities should be made earlier than just after the minimum solvency ratios are breached. Studies also show that ratings other than solvency ratios, such as CAMEL-rating, reveal the problems clearly before there is any erosion in capital ratios. To mitigate this problem, the FDICIA was amended so that the authorities can intervene in the activities of a credit institution even though the institution is solvent according to capital ratios. The only necessary precondition is that the financial condition of the credit institution is unsafe or unsound or the institution is engaging in an unsafe or unsound practice.

25. The City of Glasgow Bank failure revealed a number of unpleasant qualities. Not only had shares been sold on to people with less wealth but shares taken as collateral were shown to be a liability on the collateral holders in the case of default. Trustees also found themselves personally liable, when trusts had inadequate funds to pay out.

26. As an example on supervisors' historical inclination to a detailed, licence-based supervision is the behaviour of the Finnish FSA when they granted licences for banks' applications on revaluation of fixed assets. As mentioned earlier, banks were able to re-value their fixed assets to conform to the permanent (in principle higher or lower) value of the asset if it differed from, say, the value at the moment of purchase or the value in the accounts. This legal ruling was not in line with the BIS or EC Capital Adequacy Regulations until in 1994. The ruling was not, however, meant to be a day-to-day or year-to-year vehicle to adjust the values of fixed assets to changing market situations. The ruling was supposed to be exercised only in exceptional cases, where it was evident that the permanent value of, say, a certain piece of real estate was with great certainty higher than its accounting value. Neither was it the legislator's aim to end up in a situation where 80–90 per cent of the own capital of some banks, not to mention an entire banking group, consisted of asset revaluation reserves. There was thus a danger that the entire capital base could be eliminated in the event of a downward move in asset prices.

   It is interesting to note that the supervisors clearly identified the basic objective of the rule in the beginning (early 1970s). They foresaw the problems that were likely to occur if the revaluation of fixed assets became a rule rather than an exception. To overcome the potential threat of deviating from the spirit of the law, they ended up by introducing a procedure whereby every asset revaluation was subject to approval by a supervisory authority. Thus they chose a method of burdensome licence-based supervision. As long as revaluation reserves became a central instrument for increasing the capital of say, savings banks supervisors had to devote more and more resources to handling the applications. It was believed that the supervision could safeguard the reliability of the determination of asset values. And this proved to be the case to a certain extent. However, no matter how many resources were devoted to handling the applications, this kind of supervision was not able to prevent the distorted effects of asset revaluations on the actual capital base of savings banks. This is because the starting point was not in line with the objective of law, in this particular case with the objective of using the method only in exceptional cases, not as a common rule. This example shows clearly that the key issue for supervisors is to devote resources to supervision of the whole system, structural factors and systemic risk aspects.

27. US experience during the Savings and Loans crisis draws attention to situations where the authorities allowed banks to operate subject to capital adequacy regulations that were less strict than basic rules. The legal minimum levels were lowered and banks could use particular regulatory accounting rules (RAP) instead of generally accepted accounting principles (GAAP). This made it difficult, even impossible, to know what was the actual solvency of problem banks. See, for example, White (1991) and Dellas *et al.* (1996).

28. Imposing stronger capital requirements on banks is an alternative way of overcoming inefficient monitoring on the part of supervisors. Of course, this also comes at a cost. The ideal system design therefore has to balance out the costs of obtaining efficient monitoring against the costs of stronger sapital requirements (Campbell *et al.*, 1992).

29. See, for example, Quinn (1998).

30. See a short review of the requirements of the Financial Services and Markets Bill in Llewellyn (1999).

31. See Llewellyn (1999).

32. See Frydman *et al.* (1996).

33. The role of central banks in maintaining financial stability and, in particular, the division of labour between central banks and other supervisory authorities is discussed in more detail in Hawkesby (2000).

6   THE RATIONALE FOR A MARKET-BASED REGIME

1. Calomiris's scheme allows for different arrangements for small and large banks and covers the problems of banks in emerging as well as industrialised economies. The article also contains a very lucid exposition of the incentive problems facing deposit insurance, a topic we return to specifically below.

2. Shy (2000) suggests these may be considerable.

3. There can be specific difficulties in national structures that can blunt market incentives. One such example is given by the co-operative banks in Finland. They are effectively treated as a single unit as they operate their own 'central bank' and have to meet constraints such as capital adequacy jointly rather than individually. This structure is less than fully transparent and may mean that the incentives and responsibilities for individual entities are somewhat blunted. Raising market finance is an issue for the co-operative banks as a group so market signals will not tend to apply so clearly to the individual banks.

4. Since Bankers Trust was taken over by Deutsche Bank in 1999 the information has been presented somewhat differently as can be seen from the information in the

Appendixes to Chapter 7, which illustrate what actual disclosure documents look like.

5. It is interesting to note that the rating agencies were among the more vocal in support of the disclosure regime in New Zealand. Publication with liability for accuracy of statements is likely to produce information in which rating agencies can have greater confidence.

7 A DISCLOSURE REGIME

1. The web page provides not just the full handbook but a list of the registered banks with hypertext links to each of them, where one can read their latest disclosure statements and related material. It also includes the Reserve Bank's latest assessment of the state of the banking sector as a whole.
2. It is not readily possible to tell how Internet access to KISs is used.
3. There have been other public sector attempts to increase the public's perception of risk such as a campaign in 1997 to make people aware of the need to make adequate financial provision for themselves in retirement.
4. We return to this issue in Chapter 8.
5. The RBNZ 'standard model' is also compatible with the EU Capital Adequacy Directive.
6. Shifting towards public disclosure would reduce compliance costs for the banks if the range of data they have to compile solely for the supervisor's requirements is reduced. Banks can be expected to choose to publish information in a form related to their own control and monitoring mechanisms. While supervisors may decide on the minimum levels for disclosure, pressure by the market will develop it where necessary (Mayes, 1998a).

8 ROBUST EXIT POLICIES TO UNDERPIN MARKET DISCIPLINE

1. Benefits include privileges, including authorisation to take deposits from the public (unauthorised deposit taking from the public is a criminal offence), access to the central bank, and deposit insurance. Banking laws may give banks an immunity from bankruptcy petitions by individual depositors and other creditors, and limit competition between banks and nonbanks.
2. The problem of defining capital, net worth and legal insolvency has faced the drafters of laws and regulations worldwide, and the result has been a diversity of formulation. The adoption of differing concepts of insolvency has been largely in response to objectives of policy rather than the search for a single optimal definition. We have therefore opted for some simple generalisable definitions. The *regulatory capital requirements* placed on banks are typically expressed as a prescribed minimum ratio of equity acceptable for regulatory purposes (on the liability side of balance sheet) over the risk-weighted asset side of the balance sheet. This *regulatory equity* is capital (common stock, and preferred stock) that is treated as a liability by accounting convention, together with true liabilities such as certain subordinated debt (as deemed by regulators or supervisors to constitute equity).

Legal capital requirements, on the other hand, pertain to requirements expressed as nominal capital, the quantum of which is determined in the light of general corporation laws. National legislation governing publicly-held limited liability companies follows EU capital directives defining legal capital as the sum of the par or accountable value of outstanding shares. Principles governing decreases and increases of capital are uniform within EEA countries. For example, profits cannot be distributed if net assets would thereby decline below the nominal capital plus reserves. Banking directives prescribe five million euros as minimum capital for authorised banks, whether they are publicly-held companies or not.

Net worth maintenance requirements pertain to the observance of a positive ratio of assets over liabilities. Negative net worth denotes what we term *economic insolvency,* a situation that may give rise to withdrawal of authorisations.

Legal solvency requirements are triggered by a default or failure in payment (non-payment or impending nonpayment) on any undisputed debt that is due and payable by a debtor bank, without awaiting any other enforcement action, which might take years. Debts, in contradistinction from other liabilities, mean absolute and unconditional obligations of which a default or failure in payment may trigger the opening by the court or tribunal of a compulsory reorganisation, liquidation or other insolvency proceeding.

3. Financial requirements and depositor preferences do combine in operation. For example, Federal banking laws in the United States combine regulatory capital requirements with an unlimited preference for deposit liabilities (beyond the standard US$100 000 per insured depositor), including liabilities that may be owed to the FDIC as an eventual subrogee to the rights of depositors.

4. If a bank is apparently insolvent, the assets and liabilities of the debtor bank (by legal entity) must be determined by the general principles of property and contract law, the same way such law is applicable to any parties. In case of an apparently insolvent bank, the principle of valuation is that of a hypothetical liquidation valuation of assets and liabilities.

    Hypothetical liquidation valuation implies the application of rules and standards that would come into play in the liquidation of assets and liabilities, including the expenses of liquidation. Hence, the valuation of identified assets must be carried out on a break-up basis (as opposed to going concern basis), attaching market value to assets, and counting liabilities, including contingent liabilities, at net present values. Principles and methods of valuation applied in accounting are not apposite or relevant, and the authorities must proceed on estimates. For example, in order to augment assets, the court may set aside a range of transactions carried out over a prescribed period before the opening of proceedings. Future assets will be wiped out by termination of outstanding contracts by debtor bank, or by its counter parties. Counter parties may settle claims likely under water in respect of liabilities owed to them by negotiation as, in the case of reorganisation or liquidation, such liabilities could be wiped out in any event (including contingent liabilities).

5. Conservatorship may be reversible if supervisors are able to restore the bank to a sound and solvent condition.

6. The judgement of the European Court of Justice (ECJ) of March 12, 1996 in *Panagis Pafitis v. Trapetza Kentrikis Ellados, et al.* (C-441/93). In this case, the ECJ gave judgment on the reference for a preliminary ruling, holding that an increase in the capital of a bank constituted in the form of a public limited liability company by administrative measure was contrary to Article 25 of the Second Capital Directive on

companies, which guaranteed each shareholder the right to vote on the issue. It also
rejected the subject bank's new board of directors' argument that the applicants' civil
action constituted an abuse of rights, declaring: '... the uniform application and full
effect of Community law would be undermined if a shareholder relying on Article
25 § 1 of the Second [Capital] Directive were deemed to be abusing his rights
merely because he was a minority shareholder of a company subject to reorganisation measures or had benefited from the reorganisation of the company. Since Article
25 § 1 applies without distinction to all shareholders, regardless of the outcome of
any reorganisation procedure, to treat an action based on Article 25 § 1 as abusive
for such reasons would be tantamount to altering the scope of that provision.'
7. See note 6 above.
8. Finans-og tolldepartementet, Ot. prp. nr. 10 [Proposed Parliamentary Bill No. 10],
Om lov om endring i lov 24 mai 1961 nr. 2 om forretningsbanker mv Chapter 1–5
(1991–1992) (containing the 1991 amendments to articles 5, 11, and 32 of the Law
on Commercial Banks (Nor.).
9. Law on Government Support to Banks and Other Credit Institutions, SFS 1993: 765
of June 10.
10. In reorganisation cases, the parties proceed on their subjective assessment of the
value of assets and liabilities as they vote on reorganisation plans that distribute
losses and allocate entitlements. In liquidation cases, the declaration of insolvency or
appointment of receiver sets into motion the liquidation of assets and the distribution
of proceeds thereof.
11. Ibid. Additionally, an assessment of whether or not an institution's net present economic value is negative takes into account obligations undertaken by the institution
on its own account as well as any obligations incurred by related entities on their own
account for which the institution may be liable, say, by virtue of cross guarantees and
head-office guarantees (including conventional and statutory guarantees). In a grouping, assets and property held by one legal entity may be available to discharge or
meet liabilities, obligations, or losses incurred by others on their own account.

9   A NEW APPROACH TO ORDERLY BANK EXIT

1. In generalising about the regime in the EEA countries, we are in some cases ignoring the details of the particular, especially for the United Kingdom and Ireland, in
order to discuss the polar approach. (Here as elsewhere the European Economic
Area includes the current membership of the 15 EU countries plus Norway, Iceland
and Liechtenstein.)
2. The FDIC is not appointed as conservator or receiver by a court but by the US
Comptroller of Currency, or even by itself in certain cases. More appropriately,
therefore, the FDIC could be referred to as an administratively appointed receiver
(forming an administrative receivership), as opposed to a court-appointed receiver
that takes his or her instructions from the court (judicial receivership).
3. There are a number of cases on the point. See *California Housing Securities*, 959
F.2d. The Court in *California Housing Securities* held that the appointment of the
U.S. Resolution Trust Corporation as conservator and receiver of *Saratoga Savings
and Loan Association* did not violate the Fifth Amendment of the U.S. Constitution
that states that 'private property [shall not] be taken for public use without just compensation.' U.S.C.A. Const. Amend. 5; 5 U.S.C.A. § 706(2)(A).

4. These powers include taking on those of a general meeting of the existing shareholders, being able to continue the business of the bank or reforming it into a new recapitalised entity.
5. See Chapter 8 for a definition of these terms.
6. As mentioned earlier the financial benchmark that we use in most of the discussion, 'economic insolvency', is only one among several levels of undercapitalisation that could be used to trigger intervention. Its use makes the discussion a little simpler, as shareholder value is effectively zero even without withdrawal of the licence. At higher intervention levels the shareholders will be entitled to some compensation.
7. See *McNeily* v. *U.S.*, 839 F. Supp. 426, 429–430 (N.D. Tex. 1992). See also, The Federal Deposit Insurance Act ('FDI Act'), U.S.C. § 1821(c)(2)(A)(ii).
8. No similar problem exists in the judicial liquidation of the assets of a debtor firm, where an actual sale of the assets of the firm to third parties takes place. Thus the court need not carry out any valuations. The liquidation results in an exchange of the assets for cash, with the receiver starting to pay creditors (and shareholders), according to the relative ranking or priorities assigned by law to their rights and interests, until no money is left, based on the value of assets realised on the date of sale. No bargaining among stakeholders is necessary.
9. Article 6 § 1 of the European Convention on Human Rights, 3 September 1953 / 18 May 1954, provides that, in the determination of his civil rights and obligations, everyone is entitled to a fair and public hearing within a reasonable time by an independent and impartial court or tribunal established by law. Accordingly, Article 13 of the First European Banking Directive provides that member states shall ensure that decisions taken in respect of a credit institution in pursuance to laws, regulations and administrative provisions adopted in accordance with the Directive may be subject to the right to apply to the courts, and that the same shall apply where no decision is taken within six months of its submission in respect of an application for authorisation which contains all the information required under the provisions in force.
10. *Morrison-Knudsen Co.* v. *CHG Int'l Inc.*, 811 F.2d 1209 (9th Cir. 1987). The holding in *Knudsen* was reviewed in *Coit*, which confirmed that administrative agencies cannot be empowered to resolve disputes with the force of law. They can only notify the claimants of their claims and wait for a reasonable time before filing suit while the agency decided whether to pay, settle or disallow the claim. *Coit Indep. Joint Venture* v. *Federal Savings and Loan Ins. Corp.*, 489 US 561, 109 S.Ct. 1361 (1989).
11. In contrast, the FDIC's approval authority for 'open-bank' financial assistance is subject to conditions *inter alia* regarding concessions by bank shareholders and creditors. Section 13(c) of the FDI Act (12 U.S.C. § 1823(c)), governs the authority of the FDIC to provide open-bank assistance (i) to prevent the default of insured institutions, or closed bank assistance to facilitate the acquisition of insured institutions that are in danger of default by another institution or company; or (ii) if severe financial conditions exist that threaten the stability of a significant number of insured institutions or of insured institutions possessing significant financial resources, to lessen the risk to the FDIC posed by such insured institutions under such threat of instability. It provides that FDIC assistance must be provided by the least-costly resolution method and that the FDIC may not acquire voting or common stock; otherwise, Section 13(c) does not limit FDIC discretion to structure transactions. It also contains certain additional requirements for open-bank assistance added by the Federal Deposit Insurance Corporation Improvement Act of 1991 (FDICIA).

As a matter of policy, the FDIC's standards for 'open bank' assistance were revised on December 8, 1992 to accord with the statutory requirements added to Section 13(c) by FDICIA. See FDIC Statement of Policy on Assistance to Operating Insured Depository Institutions, 57 FR 60203 (December 18, 1992). Under those standards, such an assistance proposal was evaluated pursuant to a number of primarily financial criteria such as:

(1) The cost of the proposal to the FDIC must be determined to be the least-costly alternative available. In order to ensure that a proposal for open assistance is the least-costly alternative, the FDIC, in many cases, also seeks proposals for resolving the institution on a closed basis.

(2) The amount of the assistance and the new capital injected from outside must provide for a reasonable assurance of the future viability of the institution.

(3) The FDIC will consider on a case-by-case basis whether the proposal shall provide the FDIC with an equity or other financial interest in the resulting institution.

(4) Pre-existing shareholders and debtors of the assisted insured institution shall make substantial concessions. In general, any remaining ownership interest of pre-existing shareholders shall be subordinate to the FDIC's right to receive reimbursement for any assistance provided.

The above-referenced FDIC 'open-bank' policy was allowed to lapse in 1998, pending further review. A proposed revision of this policy was submitted for comments in 1996, but has not subsequently been adopted.

10   EXIT POLICY CO-ORDINATION AT EU LEVEL

1. Although also reflecting cross-border activities, wholly owned and locally incorporated subsidiaries will normally be subject to the regulation of the host country and hence will provide less of a problem in the context of our discussions.

2. The directive sets out minimum compensation arrangements but some member states offer more than this minimum.

3. The US International Lending Act restricts information about US ratings of foreign countries or companies. Many countries regulate large credits to host countries and companies through their head offices. Host countries' supervisors may therefore not know about restrictions on lending – that is, loans that will not materialise, as opposed to loans that are already on the books.

4. In New York and California the State superintendents of banking took possession of the business and property of BCCI S.A. (the Luxembourg holding company), treating its 'agencies' as a separately incorporated entities, marshalling all assets of the BCCI group to meet liabilities owed to US depositors and other creditors. At the same time Federal prosecutorial authorities seized and ordered the forfeiture of the whole BCCI group's assets located in the United States.

5. The process of liquidation and distribution of assets have been at low recovery rates.

6. The BCCI grouping and its activities were geographically dispersed, which permitted some host countries, the United States in particular, to rely on attachments by Federal government and several states of the grouping's assets held in the United States, including the takeover and resolution by regulators and supervisors of

local branches, subsidiaries, affiliates and holding companies. US bank regulatory
agencies collected a portion of remaining assets held in the United States as a result
of criminal proceedings initiated against corporate bodies involved by the US Justice
Department and State prosecutors. Civil money fines and asset forfeitures distorted
distributional outcomes, upsetting expectations of counterparties worldwide.

7. The determination of where an entity should be headquartered or registered is considered under the Basel Committee recommendations (see 'BCCI-Directive') in
terms of absolute size not size relative to the market.

8. BCCI Holdings S.A., the holding company for the group, was incorporated in
Luxembourg and its senior management was based in Abu Dhabi, together with
majority shareholders, who were the rulers and the government of that country. The
term BCCI is used generally to refer to BCCI Holdings (Luxembourg) S.A., its subsidiaries and affiliates, including related companies incorporated in the Cayman
Islands.

9. Our discussion is phrased in terms of a single host country but of course in many
cases there may be several hosts who are differentially affected.

10. Although the government may exercise its roles as lender of last resort, supervisor
and owner through different agencies (lender of last resort usually being through the
central bank) these organisations can act together readily and quite swiftly in a crisis.

11. It might also be asked by, say, the ECB to monitor particular situations.

12. The requesting countries would reimburse the body for its costs. It would adopt
appropriate 'club rules' to settle operational and housekeeping matters appropriate
for internal rule-making. On matters of governance of the body, each member would
deal with members through the same agencies. In transactions of the account of the
body, the body would deal with national administrative and judicial authorities, as
well as administrators of such banks or groupings, and those holding claims and
interests in respect of such banks or groupings.

13. Just because a bank is incorporated in one country it does not entail that its share
ownership is equally concentrated, nor that the national distribution of its owners is
similar to the national distribution of its activities.

14. The position is different for the United States, where foreign claims can be subordinated (Liuksila, 1998).

15. A foreign bank's operation in countries where it does not have a licence will not be
in banking, so it will normally be treated by the authorities, whether in the case of
failure or otherwise, like any other nonbanking company.

16. Fortunately, discussion of the lender of last resort (LOLR) function has been greatly
eased by the recent publication of a good survey (Frexias *et al.*, 1999).

17. Frexias *et al.* (1999, p. 152) define LOLR as

the discretionary provision of liquidity to a financial institution (or the market as a
whole) by the central bank in reaction to an adverse shock which causes an abnor-
mal increase in demand for liquidity which cannot be met from an alternative
source. The central bank provides liquidity (reserve money) in exchange for, or
against the security of, financial assets. Although this increases the liquidity of a
bank's balance sheet it does not change the overall value of its assets.

This summarises Bagehot's position with the exception of not mentioning that an
interest premium should be charged – in large part to ensure that this is indeed the
last resort and all possible options in the market (that is, at market rates) have been
used up.

11 THE WAY FORWARD

1. There is no common usage for the concept of financial system oversight. The ECB labels much of this function as 'macroprudential supervision' (see Koskenkylä (1999) for a description of how the Bank of Finland treats macroprudential supervision). What we are referring to is concern for the system and particular markets as a whole rather than concern for particular institutions.

2. The particular ratios which should be considered will vary depending upon the circumstances of individual institutions and the specific changes in their capital structure. However, examples of relevant ratios which should be considered might include tier 2 capital/tier 1 capital, tier 1 capital/total capital and deductions form tier 1 and tier 2 capital/total capital.

References

Acemoglu, D. and Verdier, T. (1998) 'Property Rights, Corruption and the Allocation of Talent: A General Equilibrium Approach', *Economic Journal*, vol. 108, September, pp. 1381–403.

Acharya, S. (1996) 'Charter Value, Minimum Capital Requirement and Deposit Insurance Pricing in Equilibrium', *Journal of Banking and Finance*, vol. 20, pp. 351–75.

Acharya, S and Dreyfus, J.-F. (1989) 'Optimal Bank Reorganization Policies and Pricing of Federal Deposit Insurance', *Journal of Finance*, vol. 44, pp. 1313–33.

Aglietta, M. and de Boissieu, C. (1998) 'Problèmes prudentiels', in *Co-ordination Européenne des Politiques Economiques*. Paris: Conseil d'Analyse Economique.

Ahtiala, P. (1993) 'A Strategy for Sustainable Economic Growth', *Finnish Economic Journal*, vol. 89, pp. 171–82 (in Finnish).

Ahtiala, P. (2000) 'Financial Reform in Theory and Practice: the case of Finland's depression of the 1990s', mimeo.

Alworth, J. and Bhattacharaya, S. (1998) 'The emerging framework of bank regulation and capital control', in C. Goodhart (ed.), *The Emerging Framework of Financial Regulation*, pp. 43–91.

Arestis, P., Demetriades, P. and Fattouh, B. (1999) 'Financial Policies and the Aggregate Productivity of the Capital Stock: evidence from developed and developing countries', paper presented at the Money, Macro and Finance Conference, Oxford, September.

Bäckström, U. (1997) 'What Lessons Can be Learned from Recent Financial Crises? The Swedish Experience', in Federal Reserve Bank of Kansas City, *Maintaining Financial Stability in a Global Economy*, pp. 129–40.

Bagehot, W. (1873) *Lombard Street: A Description of the Money Market*. London: H.S. King.

Baltensberger, E. and Dermine, J. (1987) 'Banking Deregulation', *Economic Policy*, (April) pp. 65–109.

Bank of England (1997) *Standards for Supervisors: the Objectives, Standards and Processes of Banking Supervision*, Bank of England, February.

Bankers Trust New Zealand (1997) *General Disclosure Statement*, December.

Bankers Trust New Zealand (1998) *General Disclosure Statement*, December.

Basel Committee on Banking Supervision (1992) *Minimum Standards for the Supervision of International Banking Groups and their Cross-Border Establishments*, Basel.

Basel Committee on Banking Supervision (1997) *Core Principles for Effective Banking Supervision*.

Basel Committee on Banking Supervision (1999a) 'Consultative Paper on a New Capital Adequacy Framework', BIS, Basel, June.

Basel Committee on Banking Supervision (1999b) 'Enhancing Corporate Governance for Banking Organisations', Basel.

Beatty, A., Chamberlain, S. and Magliolo, J. (1995) 'Managing Financial Reports of Commercial Banks: the influence of taxes, regulatory capital and earnings', *Journal of Accounting Research*, vol. 33, pp. 231–62.

Benston, G. and Kaufman, G. (1994) 'Improving the FDIC Improvement Act: What was Done and What Still Needs to be Done to Fix the Deposit Insurance Problem', in G. Kaufman (ed.), *Reforming Financial Institutions and Markets in the United States*. Dordrecht: Kluwer, Chapter 7.

Benston, G. and Kaufman, G. (1995) 'Is the Banking and Payments System Fragile?', *Journal of Financial Services Research*, vol. 9, pp. 209–40.

Berg, S.A (1993) 'The Banking Crises in the Scandinavian Countries', in *FDICIA: an Appraisal*, Federal Reserve Bank of Chicago, May, pp. 441–9.

Berger, A.N., Demsetz, R.S. and Strahan, P.E. (1998) 'The Consolidation of the Financial Services Industry: Causes, Consequences and Implications for the Future', Federal Reserve Bank of New York Staff Reports no. 55.

Berger, A. and Mester, L. (1997) 'Inside the Black-Box: what explains differences in the efficiencies of financial institutions?', *Journal of Money Credit and Banking*, vol. 27(2), pp. 404–31.

Bhattacharya, S., Boot, A.W.A. and Thakor, A.V. (1998) 'The Economics of Bank Regulation', *Journal of Money, Credit and Banking*, vol. 30(4), pp. 745–70.

Bikker, J.A. (1999) 'Efficiency in the European Banking Industry: an exploratory analysis to rank countries', DNB Staff Report no 42.

Billet, M.T., Garfinkel, J.A. and O'Neal, E.S. (1998) 'The Cost of Market versus Regulatory Discipline in Banking', *Journal of Financial Economics*, vol. 48, pp. 333–58.

Boot, A., Milbourn, T. and Thakor, A. (1998) 'Megamergers and Extended Scope: theories of bank size and activity diversity'. Paper presented in a conference 'Consolidation of the Financial Services Industry', Federal Reserve Bank of New York, March.

Bordes, C., Currie, D. and Söderström, H.T. (1993) *Three Assessments of Finland's Economic Crisis and Economic Policy*. Bank of Finland (C:9).

Boucher, D. and Kelly, P. (1994) *The Social Contract from Hobbes to Rawls*. London: Routledge.

Brash, D. (1997) 'Banking Soundness and the Role of the Market', Address to the IMF conference on Banking Soundness and Monetary Policy in a World of Global Capital Markets, Washington, 30 January.

Buchanan, J.M. and Tullock, G. (1965) *The Calculus of Consent: Logical Foundations of Constitutional Democracy*. Ann Arbor: University of Michigan Press.

Buiter, W. (1999) 'Alice in Euroland', *Journal of Common Market Studies*, vol. 37(2), pp. 181–210.

Calomiris, C. (1999) 'Building an Incentive-compatible Safety Net', *Journal of Banking and Finance*, vol. 23, pp. 1499–519.

Calomiris, C. and Karceski, J. (1998) 'Is the Bank Merger Wave of the 90s Efficient? Lessons from nine case studies'. Paper presented in a conference 'Consolidation of the Financial Services Industry', Federal Reserve Bank of New York, March. (To appear in S. Kaplan (ed.), *Mergers and Productivity*. University of Chicago Press.)

Campbell, T.S., Chan, Y.-S. and Marino, A.M. (1992) 'An Incentive-based Theory of Bank Regulation', *Journal of Financial Intermediation*, vol. 2, pp. 255–76.

Carletti, E. (1999) 'Bank Moral Hazard and Market Discipline', Bank of Finland/CEPR Workshop on the future of the Financial Services Industry and New Challenges for Supervision.

Centre for European Policy Studies (CEPS) (1995). 'Working Party Report on Corporate Governance in Europe', Brussels.

Centre for Research in Economics and Business Administration (1992) Report on 'The Banking Crisis in Norway'.

Chan, Y.-S., Greenbaum, L.S. and Thakor, A.V. (1992) 'Is Fairly Priced Deposit Insurance Possible?', *Journal of Finance*, vol. 47, pp. 227–46.

Cordella, T. and Yeyati, E.L. (1998) 'Public Disclosure and Bank Failures', CEPR Discussion Paper 1886.

Corporate Governance Working Group (1997) 'Final Report of the Corporate Governance Working Group', Helsinki.

Corsetti, G. and Roubini, N. (1996) 'Budget Deficits, Public Sector Solvency and Political Biases in Fiscal Policy: a Case Study of Finland', *Finnish Economic Papers*, vol. 9(1), pp. 18–35.

Cottarelli, C., Ferri, G. and Generale, A. (1995) 'Bank Lending Rates and the Transmission Mechanism of Monetary Policy', *IMF Staff Papers*, vol. 42 (September), pp. 670–700.

Cowling, K. and Tomlinson, P.R. (2000) 'The Japanese Crisis – A Case of Strategic Failure', *Economic Journal*, vol. 110(464), pp. F358–81.

Craine, R. (1995) 'Fairly Priced Deposit Insurance and Bank Charter Policy', *Journal of Finance*, vol. 50, pp. 1735–46.

Dale, R.S. (1993) 'Bank Regulation After BCCI', *Journal of International Banking Law*, vol. 8(1), January, pp. 8–17.

Danthine, J.-P., Giavazzi, G., Vives, X. and von Thadden, L. (1999) *The Future of European Banking*, Monitoring European Integration no. 9, London: CEPR.

Davis, E.P. (1995) 'Financial Fragility in the Early 1990s: what can be learned from international experience?', London School of Economics Financial Markets Group, Special Paper.

Deane, R. (1996) Acceptance speech, NZIER-Quantas Award, Wellington, New Zealand.

Dellas, H., Diba, B. and Garber, P. (1996) 'Resolving Failed Banks: The US S & L Experience'. Discussion Paper 96-E-22, Institute for Monetary and Economic Studies. Bank of Japan.

Demsetz, R.S., Siadenmerg, M.R. and Strahan, P.E. (1996) 'Banks with Something to Lose: the disciplinary role of franchise value', Federal Reserve Bank of New York, *Economic Policy Review* (October), pp. 1–14.

Dewatripont, M. and Becht, M. (1998) 'The European Corporate Governance Dilemma'. Conference on Corporate Governance, September, Helsinki, SITRA.

Dewatripont, M. and Tirole, J. (1993) *The Prudential Regulation of Banks*, Cambridge, MA: MIT Press.

Diamond, D.W. (1984) 'Financial Intermediation and Delegated Monitoring', *Review of Economic Studies*, vol. 51, pp. 393–414.

Diamond, D.W. (1991) 'Monitoring and Reputation: the Choice between Bank Loans and Directly Placed Debt'. *Journal of Political Economy*, vol. 99, pp. 688–721.

Diamond, D.W. and Dybvig, P.H. (1983) 'Bank Runs, Deposit Insurance and Liquidity', *Journal of Political Economy*, vol. 91, pp. 401–19.

Docking, D., Hirschty, M. and Jones, E. (1997) 'Information and Contagion Effects of Bank Loan-Loss Reserve Announcements', *Journal of Financial Economics*, vol. 49/50, pp. 219–39.

Dornbusch, R. (1976) 'Expectations and Exchange Rate Dynamics', *Journal of Political Economy*, vol. 84 (December), pp. 1161–76.

Dowd, K. (1996). 'The Case for Financial Laissez-Faire', *Economic Journal*, May, pp. 679–87.

Drees, B. and Pazarbasioglu, C. (1998) *The Nordic Banking Crises: Pitfalls in Financial Liberalisation*, Occasional Paper 161, Washington, DC: International Monetary Fund.

ECB (1998) *The Single Monetary Policy in Stage Three: General Documentation on ESCB Monetary Policy Instruments and Procedures*, Frankfurt, September.

Edison, H.J., Luangaram, P. and Miller, M. (2000) 'Asset Bubbles, Leverage and Lifeboats: elements of the East Asian crisis', *Economic Journal*, vol. 110(460), pp. 309–34.

Eichengreen, B. (1999) 'Kicking the Habit: moving from pegged rates to greater exchange rate flexibility', *Economic Journal*, vol. 109(454), pp. C1–14.

Enoch, C., Stella, P. and Khamis, M. (1997) 'Transparency and Ambiguity in Central Bank Safety Net Operations', International Monetary Fund, Working Paper WP/97/138.

Estrella, A. (1995) 'A Prolegomenon to Future Capital Requirements', *Federal Reserve Bank of New York Economic Policy Review*, July, pp. 1–11.

Evans, L. and Quigley, N. (1995) 'Shareholder Liability Regimes, Principal–agent Relationships and Banking Industry Performance', *Journal of Law and Economics*, vol. 38, pp. 497–520.

Federal Reserve Bank of San Fransisco (2000) 'Structural Change and Monetary Policy', *Economic Letter*, no 2000–13 (28 April).

Feldstein, M (ed.) (1991) *The Risk of Economic Crisis*. Chicago: University of Chicago Press.

Financial Regulation Report (1999) *European Union, Ambitious Financial Regulation Action Plan* adopted. June 1999.

Financial Services Authority (2000) *A New Regulator for the New Millennium*. London, January.

Flemming, J.S. (1987) 'Debt and Taxes in War and Peace: the case of a small open economy', in M.J. Boskin, J.S. Flemming and S. Gorini (eds), *Private Saving and Public Debt*. Oxford: Basil Blackwell.

Frexias, X., Giannini, C., Hoggarth, G. and Soussa, F. (1999), 'Lender of Last Resort: A Review of the Literature'. *Financial Stability Review*, 7, pp. 151–67, Bank of England.

Friedman, M. (1953) *Essays in Positive Economics*. Chicago: University of Chicago Press.

Friedman, M. and Schwartz, A. (1963) *A Monetary History of the United States 1870–1960*. Princeton: Princeton University Press.

Fries, S., Mella-Barral, P. and Perraudin, W. (1997) 'Optimal Bank Reorganization and the Fair Pricing of Deposit Guarantees', *Journal of Banking and Finance*, vol. 21, pp. 441–68.

Frydman, R., Gray, C. and Rapaczynski, A. (ed.) (1996) *Corporate Governance in Central Europe and Russia*, vol. 1, *Banks, Funds and Foreign Investors*, Budapest, London: Central European University Press.

Genay, H. (1998) 'Assessing the Condition of Japanese Banks: how informative are accounting earnings?', *Economic Perspectives*, vol. 22(4).

George, E. (1996) 'Some Thoughts on Financial Regulation', *Bank of England Quarterly Bulletin*, May, pp. 213–5.

Gilson, R. (1998) 'Corporate Governance – The Issues and Opportunities', Conference on Corporate Governance, Helsinki, September.

Goldberg, L.G. and Hudgins, S.C. (1999) 'Depositor Discipline and the Behaviour of Uninsured Deposits: FSLIC vs. SAIF', Annual Meeting of the European Finance Association, Helsinki.

Goodhart, C. (1995) 'Some Regulatory Concerns', LSE FMG, Special Paper, 79.

Goodhart, C. (1996) 'An Incentive Structure for Financial Regulation', LSE FMG, Special Paper, 88.

Goodhart, C., Hartmann, P., Llewellyn, D., Rojas-Suarez, L. and Weisbrod, S. (1998) *Financial Regulation: Why, How and Where Now.* London: Routledge.

Graham, G. (2000) 'An Uncertain Footing', *Financial Times*, 10 January.

Greenbaum, S. (1995) 'Comment: is the banking system fragile?', *Journal of Financial Services Research*, vol. 9, pp. 299–302.

Hadjiemmanuil, C. (1996) *Banking Regulation and the Bank of England.* London: LLP.

Halme, L. (1997) 'Banking Crisis and the Challenge for Regulation'. *Bank of Finland Working Paper*, 3/97

Halme, L. (1999a) 'On Incentive-based Regulation'. Paper presented in the CCBS Conference on Financial Stability, London, 20–25 September.

Halme, L. (1999b) *Banking Regulation and Supervision. A Legal Policy Research on the Risk Taking by Savings Banks* (in Finnish except the summary). Doctoral thesis in the Faculty of Law of the University of Helsinki, April.

Harrison, I. (1996) 'Disclosure of Registered Banks' Market Risks', *Reserve Bank Bulletin*, vol. 59, no. 2, pp. 146–54.

Haubrich, J.G. (1994) 'Risk Aversion, Performance Pay and the Principal–Agent Problem', *Journal of Political Economy*, vol. 102(2), pp. 258–76.

Hawkesby, C. (2000) 'Central Banks and Supervisors: the question of institutional structures and responsibilities', in CCBS series 'Financial Stability and Central Banks: Selected Issues for Financial Safety Nets and Market Discipline', London: Bank of England.

Hayek, F.A. (1982) *Law, Legislation and Liberty: a new statement of liberal principles of justice and political economy.* London: Routledge & Kegan Paul.

Hirvonen, A., Niskakangas, H. and Wahlroos, J. (1997) *Efficient Board* (in Finnish). Juva.

Honkapohja, S. and Koskela, E. (1999) 'The Economic Crisis of the 1990s in Finland', ETLA Discussion Paper 683.

Houston, J.F. and James, C. (1995) 'CEO Compensation and Bank Risk: is compensation in banking structured to promote risk taking?', *Journal of Monetary Economics*, vol. 36(2), pp. 405–31.

Hunn, N., Mayes, D.G., Williams, N. and Vandersyp, S. (1989) *Financial Deregulation and Disinflation in a Small Open Economy: the New Zealand experience*, Research Monograph 44, NZ Institute of Economic Research.

Hyytinen, A. and Takalo, T. (2000) 'Enhancing Bank Transparency: a re-assessment', mimeo, Bank of Finland, July.

IMF (1999) *Code of Good Practices on Transparency in Monetary and Financial Policies: Declaration of Principles*, Washington D.C., September.

Issing, O. (1999) 'The Eurosystem: Transparent and Accountable or "Willem in Euroland"', *Journal of Common Market Studies*, vol. 37(3), pp. 503–20.

Jackson, P., Maude, D.J. and Perraudin, W. (1996) 'Bank Capital and Value-at-Risk', mimeo, Birkbeck College London, August.

John, K., Saunders, A. and Senbet, L.W. (2000) 'A Theory of Bank Regulation and Management Compensation', *The Review of Financial Studies*, vol. 13(1), pp. 95–125.

Jonung, L., Söderström, H.T. and Stymne, J. (1996) 'Depression in the North – Boom and Bust in Sweden and Finland, 1985–93', *Finnish Economic Papers*, vol. 9(1), pp. 55–71.

Jordan, J.S, Peek, J. and Rosengren, E.S. (2000) 'The Market Reaction to the Disclosure of Supervisory Actions: implications for bank transparency', *Journal of Financial Intermediation*, vol. 9, pp. 298–319.

Kaminsky, G.L. and Reinhart, C.M. (1999) 'The Twin Crises: the causes of banking and balance of payment problems', *American Economic Review*, vol. 89(3), June, pp. 473–500.

Kane, E.J. (1989) *The S&L Insurance Mess: How Did It Happen?* Washington, DC: Urban Institute Press.

Kaplan, S. (1998) 'The American Model – Evolution or Revolution', Conference for Corporate Governance, Helsinki, September.

Kaufman, G.G. (1996) 'Bank Failures, Systemic Risk and Regulation', *Cato Journal*, vol. 16(1), pp. 17–45.

Kiander, J. (1993) 'Public Debt and Fiscal Expansion', in *Täyskäännös – Taloutemme valitojen edessä*, T. Allen, V. Heinonen and M. Pantzar (eds). Helsinki: Gaudeamus (in Finnish).

Kiander, J. and Vartia, P. (1996) 'The Great Depression of the 1990s in Finland', *Finnish Economic Papers*, vol. 9(1), pp. 72–88.

Kilponen, J., Mayes, D.G. and Vilmunen, J. (2000) 'Labour Market Flexibility in the Euro Area', *European Business Journal*, vol. 12(2), pp. 100–10.

King, M. (1994) 'Debt Deflation: theory and evidence', *European Economic Review*, vol. 38, pp. 419–55.

Kontulainen, J. (1991) 'The Market for Certificates of Deposit', *Bank of Finland Bulletin*, Special Issue on Financial Markets, pp. 17–22.

Kornhauser, L. (1989) 'The Economic Analysis of Law: legal rules as incentives', pp. 27–55, in N. Mercuro (ed.), *Law and Economics*. Boston: Kluwer.

Koskela, E. and Paunio, J. (1991) 'Budget Deficits Can Be Financed By Monetary Expansion', *Helsingin Sanomat*, 13 December (in Finnish).

Koskenkylä, H. (1998) 'The Nordic Banking Crises', Conference of the Federal Deposit Insurance Corporation, Washington, September.

Koskenkylä, H. (1999) 'How a Central Bank Can Prevent Financial Crisis', Bank of Finland Working Paper 3/99.

Koskenkylä, H. (2000) 'Threats and Opportunities for Today's European Banks', Institute of Economic Affairs Conference on European Retail Banking, Geneva, February.

Kukkonen, P. (1993) 'On the Macroeconomic Problems', *Finnish Economic Journal*, vol. 89, pp. 319–21.

Kupiec, P.H. and O'Brien, J.M. (1995) 'Recent Developments in Bank Capital Regulation of Market Risks', Federal Reserve Board, November.

Kupiec, P. and O'Brien, J. (1997) 'Regulatory Capital Requirements For Market Risk and the Precommitment Approach', paper presented in a conference 'Financial Regulation and Incentives', Bank of England, November.

Kupiec, P. and O'Brien, J. (1998) 'Deposit Insurance, Bank Incentives and the Design of Regulatory Policy', Federal Reserve Bank of New York, *Economic Policy Review* (October), pp. 201–11.

Lannoo, K. (1999a) 'A European Perspective on Corporate Governance', *Journal of Common Market Studies*, June.

Lannoo, K. (1999b) 'Challenges to the Structure of Financial Supervision in the EU', mimeo, CEPS.

Lawson, N. (1992) *The View from No. 11: memoirs of a Tory radical*. London: Bantam Press.

Ledingham, P. (1995) 'The Review of Bank Supervision Arrangements in New Zealand: the Main Elements in the Debate', *Reserve Bank Bulletin*, vol. 58.

Lehmussaari, O.-P. (1990) 'Recent Economic and Financial Market Developments', *Bank of Finland Bulletin*, vol. 64(8), pp. 3–4.

Lindgren, C.-J., Garcia, G. and Saal, M. (1996) *Bank Soundness and Macroeconomic Policy*. Washington, DC: International Monetary Fund.

Lindgren, C.-J., Baliño, T.J.T, Enozh, C., Gulde, A.-M., Quintyn, M. and Teo, L. (2000) 'Financial Sector Crisis and Restructuring: lessons from Asia', *IMF Occasional Paper* 188, January.

Liuksila, A. (1998) 'Bank Restructuring in EEA Countries: a comparison with US Federal banking and bankruptcy laws', mimeo, IMF.

Llewellyn, D.T. (1995) 'The Crisis and the Lessons', Public lecture. University of Helsinki, October.

Llewellyn, D. (1999) 'Alternative Approaches to Financial Regulation'. Paper presented at the 1999 Institute of Economic Affairs. Financial Regulation Lecture. October.

Mailath, G. and Mester, L. (1994), 'A Positive Analysis of Bank Closure', *Journal of Financial Intermediation*, vol. 3, pp. 272–99.

Malkamäki, M. and Solttila, H. (1991) 'Developments in Financial Markets in the 1980s', *Bank of Finland Bulletin*, Special Issue on Financial Markets, pp. 4–11.

Malkamäki, M. and Topi, J. (1999) 'Strategic Challenges for Exchanges and Securities Settlement', *Bank of Finland Discussion Paper* 21/99.

Martinez Peria, M.S. and Schmukler, S.L. (1998) 'Do Depositors Punish Banks for "Bad" Behaviour?', Policy Research Paper N 2058, World Bank.

Massey, P. (1995) *New Zealand: Market Liberalization in a Developed Economy.* Basingstoke: Macmillan – now Palgrave.

Matthews, D. and Mayes, D.G. (1993) 'The Evolution of Rules for a Single European Market in Leasing', *National Institute Discussion Paper*, 35.

Matutes, C. and Vives, X. (1996) 'Competition for Deposits, Fragility and Insurance', *Journal of Financial Intermediation*, vol. 5, pp. 184–216.

Matutes, C. and Vives, X. (2000) 'Imperfect Competition, Risk Taking and Regulation in Banking', *European Economic Review*, vol. 44, pp. 1–34.

Mayes, D.G. (1979) *The Property Boom.* Oxford: Martin Robertson.

Mayes, D.G. (1997) 'A Market Based Approach to Maintaining Systemic Stability', *Bank of Finland Discussion Paper* 18/97.

Mayes, D.G. (1998a) 'Improving Banking Supervision', *Bank of Finland Discussion Paper* 23/98.

Mayes, D.G. (1998b) 'Market-Based Methods of Banking Supervision: Implications for the Transition Economies.' South Bank University workshop on The Future of Banking and Regulation in the Transition Economies, February.

Mayes, D.G. and Hart, P.E. (1994) *The Single Market Programme as a Stimulus to Change: Comparisons between Britain and Germany.* Cambridge: Cambridge University Press.

Mayes, D.G. and Vesala, J. (1998) 'On the Problems of Home Country Control', *Bank of Finland Discussion Paper* 20/98 revised version, *Contemporary Politics and Economics of Europe*, vol. 10(1), pp. 1–26, 2000.

Mayes, D.G. and Vilmunen, J. (1999) 'Labour Market Flexibility in a Small Open Economy', *Bank of Finland Discussion Paper* 9/99.

Merton, R. (1995) 'Financial Innovation and the Management and Regulation of Financial Institutions', *Journal of Banking and Finance*, vol. 19, pp. 461–81.

Mishkin, F. (1998) 'Financial Consolidation: Dangers and Opportunities.' Paper presented at a conference on 'Consolidation of the Financial Services Industry', Federal Reserve Bank of New York, March.

Mishkin, F. (2000) 'Lessons from the Tequila crisis', *Journal of Banking and Finance*, vol. 23, pp. 1521–33.

Møller, M. and Nielsen, N.C. (1995) 'Some Observations on the Nordic Banking Crisis: A Survey', Institute of Finance, Copenhagen Business School, Working Paper 95-8.

Molyneux, P., Altunbas, Y. and Gardner, E. (1997) *Efficiency in European Banking.* Chichester: John Wiley & Sons.

Morgan, D.P. (2000) 'Rating Banks: Risk and Uncertainty in an Opaque Industry', Federal Reserve Bank of New York, April.

Mortlock, G. (1996) 'Banking Supervision: placing a new emphasis on the role of bank directors', *Reserve Bank Bulletin*, vol. 59.

Munthe, P., Andersen, B.D. and Knudsen, G. (1992) *Report by the Commission on the Banking Crisis*, Norwegian Official Reports NOR 1992: 30E (31 August). Oslo: Government Printing Service.

Nagarajan, S. and Sealey, C. (1995) 'Forbearance, Deposit Insurance Pricing, and Incentive Compatible Bank Regulation', *Journal of Banking and Finance*, vol. 19, pp. 1109–30.

Nicholl, P. (1996) 'Market Based Regulation.' Paper prepared for the World Bank conference on Preventing Banking Crises, 15–16 April.

Norwegian Report (1997–98) *til Stortinget fra kommisjonen som ble nedsatt av Stortinget for a gjennomga ulike arsaksforhold knyttet til bankkrisen*, Dokument nr. 17 (1997–98).

Nyberg, P. and Vihriälä, V. (1994) 'The Finnish Banking Crisis and its Handling', *Bank of Finland Discussion Paper*, 7/94.

OECD (1997) *Regulatory Reform in the Financial Services Industry: Where Have We Been? Where Are We Going?* Paris.

OECD (1999) Ad Hoc Task Force on Corporate Governance, *OECD Principles of Corporate Governance*, Paris.

OECD (n.d.) *Corporate Governance: Improving Competitiveness and Access to Capital in Global Markets.* A report to the OECD by the Business Sector Advisory Group on Corporate Governance.

O'Hara, M. and Shaw, W. (1990) 'Deposit Insurance and Wealth Effects', *Journal of Finance*, vol. 45, pp. 1587–600.

Orphanides, A. (2000) 'Activist Stabilization Policy and Inflation: the Taylor Rule in the 1970s', mimeo, Board of Governors of the Federal Reserve System, February.

Padoa-Schioppa, T. (1987) *Efficiency, Stability and Equity: A Strategy for the Evolution of the Economic System of the European Community.* London: Oxford, University Press.

Padoa-Schioppa, T. (1999) 'EMU and Banking Supervision', London School of Economics Financial Markets Group, 24 February.

Park, S. (1995) 'Market Discipline by Depositors: evidence from reduced form equations', *Quarterly Review of Economics and Finance*, vol. 35, pp. 497–514.

Park, S. and Peristiani, S. (1998) 'Market Discipline by Thrift Depositors', *Journal of Money, Credit and Banking*, vol. 30, pp. 347–64.

Pohjoisaho-Aarti, P. (2000) 'How to Build Supervisory Capacity to Meet Future Challenges: the experience of the Finnish Financial Supervisory Authority', MEFMI , Harare.

Poon, W.P.H, Firth, M. and Fung, H.G. (1999) 'A Multivariate Analysis of the Determinants of Moody's Bank Financial Strength Ratings' *Journal of Financial Markets, Institutions and Money*, vol. 9, pp. 267–83.

Prebble, M. (1994) *New Zealand: the Turnaround Economy.* London: Institute of Directors.

Prowse, S. (1997) 'Property, Control and Corporate Governance of Banks', *Banca Nationale del Lavoro, Quarterly Review*, Special issue, March.

Quah, D. (1997) 'Empirics for Growth and Distribution: Polarisation, Stratification and Convergence Clubs', *Journal of Economic Growth*, vol. 2(1), pp. 27–59.

Quinn, B. (1998) 'Rules v Discretion: the case of banking supervision in the light of the debate on monetary policy', in C. Goodhart (ed.), *The Emerging Framework of Financial Regulation*, pp. 119–32.

294 *References*

Reid, M. (1982) *The Secondary Banking Crisis, 1973–5.* London: Macmillan.
Reserve Bank of New Zealand (1995a) *Inflation: a Sixth-form Resource.*
Reserve Bank of New Zealand (1995b) 'Review of Banking Supervision: Reserve Bank's policy conclusions', *Reserve Bank Bulletin*, vol. 58, pp. 73–8.
Reserve Bank of New Zealand (1996) *The PIE Kit (People, Inflation and Economics 1970s–1990s).*
Reserve Bank of New Zealand (1998) *Annual Report.* Wellington.
Reserve Bank of New Zealand (1999) *Banking Supervision Handbook* (available at www.rbnz.govt.nz).
Rhoades, S.A. (1998) 'The Efficiency Effects of Bank Mergers: an overview of case studies of nine mergers', *Journal of Banking and Finance*, vol. 22, pp. 273–92.
Ruthenburg, D. (1997) 'Bank Capital, Market and Interest Rate Risks'. Workshop on Systemic Risks in Financial Markets, Bank of Finland, August.
Schoenmaker, D. (1995) 'Lender of Last Resort – the European Central Bank', *Central Banking*, vol. 3, no. VI, 1995/6, pp. 98–103.
Sheikh, S. and Rees, W. (1995) *Corporate Governance and Corporate Control.* London: Cavendish Publishing.
Shleifer, A. and Vishny, R. (1997) 'A Survey of Corporate Governance, *Journal of Finance*, vol. 52, no. 2, June, pp. 737–83.
Shy, O. (2000), 'A Quick-and-easy Method for Estimating Switching Costs', *International Journal of Industrial Organisation*, vol. 1, pp. 1–17.
Tarkka, J. (1993) 'Is Stabilisation Policy Only a Matter of Will?,' *Finnish Economic Journal*, vol. 90, pp. 5–17.
Thatcher, M. (1995) *The Downing Street Years.* London: HarperCollins.
Tirole, J. (1996) 'A Theory of Collective Reputations, with Applications to the Persistence of Corruption and to Firm Quality', *Review of Economic Studies,* vol. 63, pp. 1–22.
Tirole, J (1999) 'Corporate Governance, Industrial Organisation', Discussion Paper no. 2086, Centre for Economic Policy Research, February.
Valkonen, T. and Vartia, P. (1992) 'Current Outlook and Economic Policy', *The Finnish Economy*, no.1.
Vennet, R. (1996) 'The Effect of Mergers and Acquisitions on the Efficiency and Profitability of EC Credit Institutions', *Journal of Banking and Finance*, vol. 20, pp. 153–58.
Veranen, J. (1996) *The Shareholders in the Chase for Profitability* (in Finnish), Porvoo.
Vives, X. (1999) 'Banking Supervision in the European Union', CEPR/European Summer Institute Conference, September.
Wahlroos, B. (1997) *The Organisation of Banking and Insurance Supervision in Finland.* Report to the Ministry of Finance (in Finnish).
Wallis Committee (1997) *Financial System Inquiry: Final Report.* Canberra: Australian Government Printing Company.
Whidbee, D. A. and Wohar, M. (1999) 'Derivative Activities and Managerial Incentives in the Banking Industry', *Journal of Corporate Finance*, vol. 5(3), pp. 251–76.
White, L. (1991) *The S & L Debacle. Public Policy Lessons for Bank and Thrift Regulation.* New York: Oxford University Press.
Yla-Anttila, P. and Ali-Yrkko, J. (1999) 'Ownership Internationalises – Corporate Governance System Will Change'. Helsinki: The Research Institute of the Finnish Economy.
Zodgekar, S. (1996) 'New Proposals for Netting and Settlement Finality.' Reserve Bank of New Zealand, August.

Index